Music

of the

Baroque

Music
of the
Baroque

DAVID SCHULENBERG

Second Edition

New York • Oxford
OXFORD UNIVERSITY PRESS
2008

Oxford University Press publishes works that further Oxford University's
objective of excellence in research, scholarship, and education.

Oxford   New York
Auckland   Cape Town   Dar es Salaam   Hong Kong   Karachi
Kuala Lumpur   Madrid   Melbourne   Mexico City   Nairobi
New Delhi   Shanghai   Taipei   Toronto

With offices in
Argentina   Austria   Brazil   Chile   Czch Reublic   France   Greece
Guatemala   Hungary   Italy   Japan   Poland   Portugal   Singapore
South Korea   Switzerland   Thailand   Turkey   Ukraine   Vietnam

Copyright © 2008 by Oxford University Press, Inc.

Published by Oxford University Press, Inc.
198 Madison Avenue, New York, New York 10016
http://www.oup.com

Oxford is a registered trademark of Oxford University Press

ISBN: 978-0-19-533106-6

Printing number: 9 8 7 6 5 4 3 2 1

Printed in the United States of America
on acid-free paper

To Mary

CONTENTS

Preface   xi

1 **Introduction**   1

Music History, 1600–1750: Some Basic Ideas   1
Historical Background: Western Europe, 1600–1750   3
Music in European History, 1600–1750   7
The Place of Music and Musicians in Society   8
Performance Practices   12

2 **A Sixteenth-Century Prologue: Motet and Madrigal**   15

The Late Renaissance Motet: Palestrina and Lassus   18
The Madrigal: Gesualdo and Monteverdi   34

3 **Transitions around 1600**   41

Some General Developments   42
The Basso Continuo   45
Instruments   46
Monody   50

4 **Monteverdi and Early Baroque Musical Drama**   61

Claudio Monteverdi   61
Monteverdi's *Orfeo*   65
The *Combattimento di Tancredi e Clorinda*   76
Venetian Opera   82

5 Secular Vocal Music of the Later Seventeenth Century   90

   Barbara Strozzi   91
   Alessandro Scarlatti and the Later Cantata   95
   The Dissemination of Italian Baroque Style   106

6 Lully and French Musical Drama   112

   The French Style   113
   Lully's *Armide*   125

7 Seventeenth-Century Sacred Music   135

   Sacred Music in Venice: Giovanni Gabrieli   136
   Sacred Music in Germany: Heinrich Schütz   144
   Seventeenth-Century Oratorio   151
   Sacred Music in France: Michel-Richard de Lalande   154

8 Late Baroque Opera   158

   Handel   167
   Rameau   175

9 Late Baroque Sacred Music   185

   J. S. Bach   187
   Handel and the Eighteenth-Century Oratorio   204

10 Music for Solo Instruments I: Toccata and Suite   214

   The Lute and Its Repertory   216
   Keyboard Instruments of the Seventeenth and Eighteenth Centuries   225
   Baroque Keyboard Music in Italy   230
   Baroque Keyboard Music in France and Germany   236

11 Music for Solo Instruments II: Fugues and *Pièces*   248

   Later Baroque Keyboard Music in Germany   248
   J. S. Bach's Music for Solo Instruments   259
   Eighteenth-Century Keyboard Music in France   265
   Other Eighteenth-Century Keyboard Composers   269

12 **Music for Instrumental Ensemble I: The Sonata**   272

The Chief Ensemble Instruments of the Baroque   273
Types of Baroque Music for Instrumental Ensemble   285
The Baroque Sonata   289

13 **Music for Instrumental Ensemble II: Sinfonia and Concerto**   310

The Bolognese Trumpet Sinfonia   310
The Baroque Concerto   312

14 **A Mid-Eighteenth-Century Epilogue: The *Galant* Style**   326

The *Galant* Style   327
Telemann   330
Carl Philipp Emanuel Bach   334

Bibliography   343
Index   360

PREFACE

This is a study of European music history from the late sixteenth century through the mid-eighteenth century, the period that music historians call the Baroque. It is intended primarily as a textbook for historical surveys typically offered to upper-division music majors, and for graduate courses in music history and literature. It is accompanied by an anthology of musical scores, most of which are discussed in depth within the present text; items in the anthology (*Music of the Baroque: An Anthology of Scores*) are referred to by number ("anthology, Selection 1"). Although it has proved impossible to offer an anthology of recordings, a discography can be found on the author's website (www.wagner.edu/faculty/dschulenberg).

The Baroque is the period of such composers as Monteverdi, Schütz, Lully, Handel, and J. S. Bach. It saw the invention of opera and oratorio and the emergence of independent instrumental genres: sonata, suite, and concerto. This same period saw the first orchestras and the first public concerts in the modern sense as well as the invention of the piano and the cello and the development of other instruments to something resembling their modern forms. Performing techniques and practices also drew significantly closer to those of today while remaining distinctly different. The music discussed in this book remained largely within the sphere of the wealthy, yet, by the end of the Baroque, members of a growing middle class were becoming important both as audiences and as amateur performers of an expanding body of printed music. Moreover, during this period a musical tradition that had been confined to western Europe made its first substantial steps toward becoming a global phenomenon.

Since the first edition of this text was prepared, a great deal has been learned about Baroque music, its performance traditions, and its cultural context. Whole new repertories have become available in published scores and recordings. In addition, the advent of Internet CD sales, downloadable music, and digitized information through *Grove Music Online* and other electronic resources has changed the ways in which readers obtain information. Yet the need for hardcopy books and scores remains, and may be even greater than before, in an era when the availability of masses of unsorted online information can turn electronic search and browsing into a confusing and unproductive process.

During the ten years or so since the first edition was written, certain trends in the discipline of academic musicology have become more palpable. Interdisciplinary approaches have emphasized music history as an aspect of larger cultural histories. An increasingly internationalized consciousness among academics and students has altered perspectives on the study of music that arose within a small corner of the Eurasian continent. Meanwhile, study of European music from the seventeenth and eighteenth centuries has become a part of the education of music students throughout the world. Concerts and new CD recordings of Baroque music continue to appear, despite changes (not all of them positive) in the structure of the commercial music business.

This book balances pedagogical effectiveness with changing approaches to music history. Ideas of the "canon" evolve, yet students still need to acquire a repertory of music that excites, moves, and challenges them, whether these are works by Monteverdi and J. S. Bach, whose effectiveness in doing so has been proved by generations, or those of a more recently recognized composer such as Barbara Strozzi. Some current models of music history are characterized by postmodern diversity and decentralization, others by views of music as reflecting political and social realities. Yet love for and curiosity about sounding music continue to be the chief reasons for studying this subject; for music of the Baroque, the composer and his or her work remain the primary nexus within which we see historical societies and cultures intersecting with the individual.

This edition retains the book's original organization but substantially revises some chapters, especially those on instrumental music. Responding to reviews and readers' comments, it incorporates a broader range of music, including "new" seventeenth-century sonatas, several pieces for lute, and a Bolognese trumpet sinfonia as well as a French *grand motet*. To prevent the book from growing unwieldy, a number of works have been dropped from the anthology, but shortened discussions of most of those compositions remain in the text for those who wish to continue to teach them. The anthology replaces a number of reprinted scores with new ones, but some facsimiles remain, giving students practice in the use of older editions.

The idea of the "Baroque," whether in music or in European culture generally, is largely an invention of twentieth-century historians. But it is undeniable that Europe during the period 1550–1750 saw the emergence of distinctive musical traditions, some of which are traced in this book. Among these are the unbroken stream of dramatic and quasi-dramatic vocal music represented by opera and cantata, the equally powerful strand of sacred vocal music that includes the cantatas and oratorios of Bach and Handel, and new genres of music for solo instruments and for instrumental ensemble. In general, the book traces each of these traditions integrally, hence departing from an organization that is either strictly chronological or strictly generic. Two introductory chapters lead to a survey of seventeenth-century vocal music, including early opera and cantata (Chapters 3–7). There follows an examination of early eighteenth-century transformations of those traditions (Chapters 8–9). Next come separate "sweeps" of instrumental traditions, first for solo instruments (lute and keyboard: Chapters 10–11), then for instrumental ensemble (Chapters 12–13). A concluding chapter examines *galant* music, providing a transition to the Classical style of the later eighteenth century, now with expanded coverage of emerging sonata-allegro form.

This plan encourages students to understand the development of a concept such as musical rhetoric from its emergence in sixteenth-century vocal polyphony through the earliest examples of monody to late Baroque masterpieces such as the Bach cantatas. One disadvantage is that the music of certain composers (notably Bach and Handel) must be treated in several different chapters of the book. But no survey of the period can entirely avoid such difficulties, and much could be said for returning periodically to the most important figures, to clarify and reinforce what was truly creative and distinctive about their music. Those preferring a more strictly chronological approach might follow an alternate plan, proceeding from the introductory chapters to vocal music of the earlier Baroque (Chapters 3–5 and Chapter 7 through Schütz) and then to associated works for instrumental ensemble (Chapter 12). Study of the distinctive French Baroque vocal tradition (Chapter 6, Chapter 7 on Lalande) might then lead to related works for lute and keyboard (the main focus of Chapter 10), followed by later vocal music (Chapters 8–9) and instrumental traditions (Chapters 11 and 13).

This book does not attempt to be comprehensive. Among the criteria for including particular repertories were the availability of recordings and the relevance of a composer or a composition to one of the major traditions mentioned earlier. Although this excludes many categories of music worth studying, the book balances "must-know" works by Monteverdi, Bach, Handel, and the like with additional repertory that is of great value both musically and pedagogically.

The reader of this book is assumed to have had some experience with score reading and the rudiments of tonal analysis, such as the identification of keys and chord functions. But the book requires no special knowledge beyond this, and virtually all musical terms are defined on first use. While situating music within its broader cultural context, this book differs from others in its close examination of individual musical compositions. Many students at some point in their theoretical or practical training devote intense study to a few Baroque compositions, but these are often limited to a few inventions, fugues, or four-part chorale settings of J. S. Bach. This book offers in-depth analysis of at least one example of each of the major genres studied, giving the reader the opportunity to understand some of the distinctive features of the individual works and composers covered.

Another feature of this book is its attention to historical instruments and performance practice. The book raises issues of performance practice for most works, and the repertory selected for detailed discussion includes music that is available in recent, reasonably stylish recorded performances. Each score in the accompanying anthology is joined by a commentary that explains important points of the notation and its interpretation.

Accompanying Anthology

A companion volume, *Music of the Baroque: An Anthology of Scores,* includes works by such celebrated Baroque composers as Bach, Handel, Lully, Monteverdi, and Schutz while also featuring compositions by lesser-known composers including Barbara Strozzi and Elizabeth-Claude Jacquet de la Guerre. This second edition complements the textbook's emphasis on performance practice while adding important instrumental works for lute (Gaultier), chanmber emseble (Rossi, Castello, and Legrenzi), and trumpet with strings (Torelli), as well as excerpts from a *grand motet* (Lalande). Newly prepared scores are provided for works by C. P. E. Bach, Biber, Frescobaldi, Froberger, Lully, and other composers. Offering an unparalleled portrait of European music from 1600 through 1750, the collection is an ideal instructional package for courses in the history of Baroque music.

I have been fortunate in having had the opportunity to teach this material numerous times at various institutions. I am grateful to the students whom I have had the privilege of teaching, many of whom provided me with valuable feedback about early versions of this text and the accompanying anthology. In addition to those who assisted in the preparation of the first edition, I would like to thank Victor Coelho, Andrew Dell'Antonio, and Catherine Gordon-Seifert for helpful advice. As in the first edition, André P. Larson, director of the National Music Museum at the University of South Dakota, and members of his staff have generously made available illustrations of instruments and other material from the museum collection.

Acknowledgments

I extend my thanks to the following reviewers commissioned by Oxford University Press: Dale Bonge, Michigan State University; Andrew Dell'Antonio, University of Texas at Austin; Olga Haldey, University of Maryland, College Park; Deborah Kauffman, University of Northern Colorado; Arved M. Larsen, Illinois State University; Stephen D. Press, Illinois Wesleyan University; Louise K. Stein, University of Michigan, Ann Arbor; and Laurel Zeiss, Baylor University. I am grateful as well to John Koster, Marcellene and Walter Mayhall, and Terence Noel Towe for furnishing illustrations. Janet Beatty and her staff at Oxford University Press handled two complex manuscripts with great care, furnishing innumerable helpful suggestions. Above all, I thank my wife, Mary Oleskiewicz, for support, love, and advice based on her teaching experience and her vast practical and scholarly knowledge of Baroque music.

A Note on Dates and Pitch References

Where a precise date for a work or a composer's birth is unknown, the year may be given as "1530/2" or the like. In this case the expression means "at some point during the period 1530 to 1532."

Citations of exact pitches (as opposed to pitch classes) use the Helmholtz system, according to which middle C is designated as c′, the note below it is b, and the note above it is d′. An octave higher these notes are b′–c″–d″, an octave lower they are B–c–d, and so forth.

CHAPTER 1

INTRODUCTION

MUSIC HISTORY, 1600–1750: SOME BASIC IDEAS

This book explores the music of the Baroque, the predominant culture of western Europe from the early seventeenth century through the mid-eighteenth century. Historians of European music think of Baroque compositions as following those of the **Renaissance** and leading to those of the **Classical** period.

Musicologists of the early twentieth century borrowed the terms *Renaissance* and *Baroque* from art historians, who in turn took them from literary and cultural history. The noun *Renaissance* originally referred to the rediscovery of ancient Greek and Roman literature by fifteenth-century scholars, whereas the word *Baroque* is an adjective referring to what were thought to be the ostentatious and elaborately ornamented forms of art, architecture, and literature favored in the seventeenth and early eighteenth centuries.[1] Art historians (like most historians in general) consider the Renaissance to extend from around 1400 to the mid-sixteenth century. For them the Baroque coincides roughly with the seventeenth century. In music, however, we tend to apply both terms to slightly later periods: roughly 1450 to 1600 for the Renaissance, 1600 to 1750 for the Baroque. Music historians rarely speak of a revival of ancient Greek or Roman music during the Renaissance, for none was then known to survive. Likewise, few today regard Baroque music as unduly ostentatious or overly decorated.

Nevertheless, use of these terms is so engrained that we can hardly avoid employing them. Indeed, a word such as *Baroque* refers not only to a time period but to the musical style that was customary during that period. Yet the use of a particular musical style rarely coincides in a precise way with a particular historical era. Innovative composers such as Giovanni Gabrieli and Claudio Monteverdi were writing in what we recognize as Baroque musical styles well before the beginning of the seventeenth century. At the end of the Baroque period—that is, around 1750—composers such as Johann Sebastian Bach were still looking back to the sixteenth century and employing elements of

---

[1] Outside the study of music, the word *baroque* has the implication of gaudy or overdecorated.

Renaissance style in certain works. Yet Bach's personal style and the types of music that he composed are enormously different from those of Gabrieli and Monteverdi. Thus it would be a mistake to think of music from 1600 to 1750 as constituting a single Baroque style that is entirely distinct from that of the Renaissance; there is great diversity within both periods. For this reason it will be important to identify individual musical compositions not simply as "Baroque" but as belonging to individual countries and more specific periods— for instance, "German music of the early eighteenth century."

In considering various types of Baroque music, we will be concerned particularly with musical **style**. Style can be thought of as a set of practices that define a given musical tradition; it can also be viewed as a set of common musical patterns that help a listener make sense out of a large number of works. Style can be defined broadly or narrowly: we can speak of the style of Baroque music in general as well as the style of early seventeenth-century opera. We can, moreover, speak of the style not only of musical compositions but of musical performances. Performance techniques as well as the ways in which performers interpreted music varied enormously during the Baroque, reflecting the development of new types of instruments and changing conventions in the use of musical notation. Deveopments in performance practice are as much a part of music history as those affecting the style of compositions.

A particularly useful idea in considering musical style is **genre**. A genre is a category of musical compositions written for a particular purpose and employing a particular type of scoring, form, verbal text (if any), and performance practices. For example, the genre of the cantata in the Baroque consists of works for solo voices and instruments, usually in several sections or movements and with a poetic text. Originally the texts of cantatas were lyrical in nature and the works were performed by small ensembles, most often for the enjoyment of individual music lovers in private homes. Later Baroque cantatas may have dramatic or even sacred texts and were performed during services or public concerts in churches and other public spaces.

Our history of music will be to a considerable degree a history of genres. Thus it will be important to bear in mind the defining features of each category (genre) of music that we study: cantatas, sonatas, concertos, and so on. But composers and performers do not create "categories"; they create individual works or performances of music, each with a particular character and containing some unique or innovative feature. It will therefore be equally important to recognize the distinctive aspects of each individual work that we study. In studying a cantata by Bach, one might begin by identifying those features of the scoring, text, and form that define it as a cantata. But to appreciate what makes this one cantata special—what makes it worth studying—it is necessary to analyze the music, observing what makes the composition an individual work of genius. Analysis also helps identify any special demands the work imposes on the performer and what interpretive decisions one must make in performing it.

As we examine individual works, we shall find that general labels of style and genre do not always fit each piece equally well. For example, there are works by Monteverdi that can be described as either madrigals or cantatas; there are instrumental works by Telemann that were called both concertos and sonatas. We shall also find that certain labels apply to multiple, very different types of music; the word *concerto*, for example, originally described a type of music for voices and instruments and only later came to refer strictly to orchestral compositions.

In this book the first discussion or definition of an important term is signaled by the use of **boldface** type. A few terms, such as *concerto*, are introduced more than once, as different uses of the same word come up. A number of important concepts are discussed in depth in boxes outside the main text; other boxes contain additional useful information, such as plot summaries for operatic works and biographical information about composers. Texts and translations of most of the vocal works are included in the accompanying anthology (*Music of the Baroque: An Anthology of Scores*).

HISTORICAL BACKGROUND: WESTERN EUROPE, 1600–1750

The period we are studying saw important social, economic, and political developments throughout Europe (see map, Fig. 1.1). Nevertheless, certain things remained constant. The great western states of France, England, and Spain retained their identities as more or less unified kingdoms, as did the Austrian empire, which included not only modern Austria but a larger surrounding region, including much of northern Italy, Hungary, and southern Germany. Elsewhere, particularly in what is now Germany, western Europe remained a patchwork of large and small states, most ruled by variously titled dukes, counts, and princes; a few functioned as republics, though none were democracies in the modern sense. Many smaller states were under the dominion of larger powers; others struggled to maintain their independence.

Despite their diverse political structures, life in these states had certain things in common. The great majority of the population consisted of the lower classes, composed mainly of poor rural peasants. They grew the food and provided the labor that made everything else possible. Their lot remained hard and primitive throughout our period, and it actually got worse in parts of Germany, Spain, and Italy.

Considerably better off were the middle classes, composed especially of merchants and tradespeople in the cities. On the whole, their numbers had grown in size, wealth, and political power during the Renaissance. In Italy and Germany, a number of independent city-states such as Venice and Hamburg were governed by councils of wealthy businessmen or minor aristocrats, as opposed to kings or individual nobles. A few such states could still achieve political and cultural importance that rivaled that of the major kingdoms, extending their rule far beyond their immediate city boundaries. But the power and economic condition of the cities (and of many rural areas as well) was declining during the seventeenth century. Instead, the latter saw a centralization of power in the ruling dynasties of the great monarchies, leading to what is referred to as royal absolutism; this was true above all in France and, to a varying degree, in most other European states, large and small.

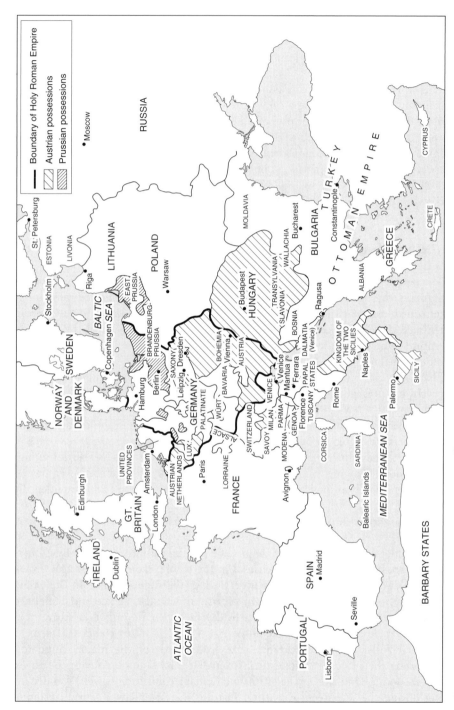

Figure 1.1 Europe in 1721 (LUX = Luxemburg; WÜRT = Württemberg).

The growth of royal absolutism coincided, particularly in Germany and Italy, with a relative decline in the fortunes of the middle classes. At the same time there was spectacular growth in the major **courts,** that is, the administrative and cultural institutions centered around the rulers of the various monarchies (the latter term can refer to the petty duchies and principalities of Germany as well as the great kingdoms). Each court was now—in some countries for the first time—permanently located in a capital city. Thus during the Baroque such municipalities as Paris, Vienna, and London became the chief centers of artistic production. Of the independent city-states that survived beyond the Renaissance, by 1700 only Venice retained some importance. Even the Roman Catholic Church, which had been the single strongest western European institution for the thousand years preceding, was eclipsed by the great kingdoms, although the pope, with his capital in Rome, remained a local monarch, the absolute ruler of a region in central Italy.

Many rulers were important patrons of the arts. But the most typical preoccupation of many rulers was warfare; hardly a year of true peace went by. Although the pretexts for warfare varied from one conflict to another, most of the fighting during the seventeenth century was due to rivalries between France, Spain, and Austria for control of Italy and parts of northern Europe (including Germany, Poland, and the Netherlands). The greatest conflagration occurred early in our period: the Thirty Years' War (1618–48), which involved most of the states of western Europe. Further conflicts of a relatively limited nature continued into the eighteenth century. Among these was a series of wars involving France, England, and the Netherlands in the second half of the seventeenth century, as well as the War of the Spanish Succession (1700–1713), which actually took place mainly in Italy, Germany, and Poland. There were also major internal conflicts, notably the civil wars in England and France in the 1640s and 1650s, respectively. Each conflict wrought devastation; in particular, the Thirty Years' War, which was fought mainly in Germany, left that region depopulated and economically deprived until well into the eighteenth century—with severe consequences for the composition and performance of music, among other things.

Conflicts such as these were, ultimately, the products of underlying social and economic forces that are still incompletely understood. One major factor was the Protestant Reformation: the long historical process by which various states and peoples, primarily in northern Europe, broke the religious, cultural, and political ties that had linked them with Roman Catholicism since the Middle Ages. Associated above all with the German theologian Martin Luther (1483–1546), the Reformation had led to the establishment of separate Protestant churches in the countries of northern Europe. After a period of intense doctrinal debate and warfare during the sixteenth century, the situation had stabilized to one in which Spain, France, Austria, southern Germany, and Italy remained predominantly Roman Catholic; northern Germany and Scandinavia were mostly Lutheran; the Netherlands and parts of Germany and Switzerland were Calvinist (Reformed); and England had its own Protestant denomination known as the Anglican (or Episcopal) church.

Figure 1.2 A Baroque cityscape: *View of Dresden with the Frauenkirche at Left*, 1747, oil on canvas by Bernardo Bellotto (Italian, 1720–80). North Carolina Museum of Art, Raleigh, Purchased with funds from the State of North Carolina (52.9.145). Dresden, capital of Saxony, is seen here from across the river Elbe. At the far left is the Lutheran Frauenkirche (Church of Our Lady), destroyed during world war II and recently rebuilt. The figures at the center foreground facing the viewer have been identified as members of the royal chapel choir, which performed in the Catholic Hofkirche (Court Church) seen at the center. Bach, Handel, and numerous other musicians visited this city, a musical center where Heinrich Schütz had worked in the seventeenth century.

These confessional politics are important, for much Baroque music originally served religious purposes. Under the terms of the Peace of Westphalia, which ended the Thirty Years' War in 1648, residents of the Empire—that is, modern Germany and Austria, together with portions of Italy, the Czech Republic, and other regions—theoretically enjoyed freedom of choice between Catholicism, Protestantism, and Calvinism. In practice, rulers throughout most of Europe continued to impose their faith on those under them. Thus the Lutheran elector or duke of Saxony ruled over Lutheran subjects, whereas the inhabitants of Austria, northern Italy, and Bohemia (now in the Czech Republic) were Roman Catholics like the emperor who reigned over them. But religious conditions could change as the result of wars and political developments. In 1697 the ruler of Saxony, Augustus II, converted to Catholicism as a prerequisite to his becoming king of Poland. Roman Catholic churches were immediately established in the Saxon capital of Dresden (Fig. 1.2), yet the vast majority of the population—including J. S. Bach and other important composers—remained Lutheran. The ruler's conversion was nevertheless important for music history, since the Saxon court, which had previously been a patron of distinctively Lutheran religious music—notably that of Heinrich Schütz—now commissioned numerous Roman Catholic works. This did not prevent Lutherans, Bach among them, from continuing to provide music for the Saxon court. In general, however, religion was a critical factor in the careers of musicians. Many musicians found it necessary or expedient to convert in order to gain employment, and non-Christians are extremely rare, although not unknown, as Baroque musicians.

MUSIC IN EUROPEAN HISTORY, 1600–1750

Music was, presumably, cultivated wherever there were people. But the music whose scores have survived for us to study—music of the type we now refer to as "art" music—was associated almost exclusively with perhaps the top 2 or 3 percent of the population: the royalty and aristocracy and the wealthiest and best-educated members of the middle classes. As in previous periods, much of this music was written for the church—not the local parish churches of the peasants and lower middle classes, but churches associated with the upper classes: the private chapels of the rulers, as well as the cathedrals and central churches of the great cities. In Roman Catholic regions, certain monasteries and convents also served as patrons and producers of music. But several developments led to a somewhat wider dissemination of art music than in earlier times and its increasing use for secular purposes.

First, during this period the church's power and wealth relative to those of the state diminished; moreover, its very identity had been and continued to be profoundly altered by the Protestant Reformation. Second, the continuing development of music printing, which had begun in 1501, meant that art music no longer had to be copied by hand by and for a narrow group of specially trained professionals (mostly churchmen). Trained amateurs could begin to participate in serious music making outside the church, and sacred music too could achieve wider distribution. Nevertheless, printed music remained expensive until the end of the Baroque; manuscripts continued to be the chief means of preservation and dissemination of music through the mid-eighteenth century.

A third factor was the centralization of wealth and power in the major courts and the largest cities. This led to the development of new genres of music that involved new types of ensembles, new instruments, and new combinations of music with poetry, dance, and other art forms. The most spectacular of these new developments was the emergence of opera around 1600, an event that is in some respects synoymous with the beginning of the Baroque. The tremendous expense of opera meant that productions could be undertaken on a regular basis only in the great musical centers, often under royal or aristocratic patronage. Many lesser rulers nevertheless followed the lead of the great monarchs by investing considerable sums of money in their musical and theatrical establishments, which might consist of small-scale but still first-rate vocal and instrumental ensembles. A number of cities—notably Venice, Hamburg, and London—saw the founding of public opera theaters that were intended, at least in principle, to be self-sustaining commercial ventures. Nevertheless, most professional musicians aspired to a position in the court of an important ruler or, at least, in one of the principal churches of a major city.

Particularly in Lutheran Germany, the Protestant Reformation had led to the development of new genres of church music. Meanwhile the Counter-Reformation, the Roman Catholic response to Protestantism that had commenced in the six-teenth century, continued to influence musical style in Italy and other Catholic countries well into the Baroque. But secular patronage became decisive for musi-cal innovation during the seventeenth and eighteenth centuries, when the presence of a sophisticated musical establishment came to be seen as a symbol of a ruler's wealth and benificence. During the late sixteenth and early seventeenth centuries, the greatest musical centers had been the aristocratically ruled cities of northern Italy. But by the end of the seventeenth century these were being overtaken by the capitals of France and other monarchies to the north: Paris, Vienna, London, and Dresden. Venice, despite its diminishing political importance, remained a musi-cal center of the first rank throughout the Baroque; so too was Rome, at least until around 1700.

The development of Baroque musical genres and the careers of individual musicians were directly influenced by the rise of these new centers. Whereas musicians and musical forms during the Middle Ages had often originated in northwestern Europe and migrated south- and eastward, by the end of the Renaissance the trend had been reversed. Throughout the seventeenth and eigh-teenth centuries, Italian artists and styles traveled north to Germany, France, and England and west to Spain, Portugal, and even America; French music and musicians became equally influential in Germany and England by the end of the seventeenth century.

THE PLACE OF MUSIC AND MUSICIANS IN SOCIETY

By and large, the musicians with whom we will be concerned were members of the middle classes, that is, not farmers or laborers and not aristocrats or rulers either, though many worked for the latter. Lully in Paris was head of the musi-cal establishment of King Louis XIV; Monteverdi was choirmaster (*maestro di capella*) at the Basilica of St. Mark's, the personal church of the ruling *doge* (duke) of Venice; Bach in Leipzig was the city's director of church music, overseeing performances for the entire population but composing new music chiefly for the two churches whose congregations included the wealthiest citizens. Just as most middle-class printers, bakers, and other artisans passed their skills and occupa-tions on to their descendents, most musicians' families continued their profes-sional activity in music from one generation to the next. Of course, the wealthy could afford to study music for its own sake, and a number of rulers and noble amateurs (such as King Frederick II of Prussia and the Marcello brothers of Venice) composed music of distinction. But the chief importance of the upper classes for music history was as patrons: buyers of music and employers of musicians.

Most music was produced on demand for a particular occasion or purpose: an aristocratic wedding celebration, a religious service, a diplomatic ceremony (Fig. 1.3). This does not mean, however, that music once composed was for-gotten; most works were written in the expectation that they would circulate, either in manuscript or in printed form, once the occasion for which they were written was over. Many works were doubtless performed in a variety of private

Figure 1.3 Banquet following the swearing of allegiance to the future emperor, Charles VI, as arch-duke of Austria, 8 November 1705, engraving from Johann Baptist Mairn von Mairsfeld, *Beschreibung was auf Ableiben weyland Ihrer Keyserl. Majestät* (Vienna, 1712). This is an example of the type of grand ceremonial occasion in which Baroque musicians played an essential role. From the balcony, an ensemble of trumpets and strings, directed by the figure holding a rolled-up sheet of paper, adds splendor to an elaborate formal dinner.

as well as public settings (see Figs 1.4–6). Nevertheless, to understand compositions of this period it is necessary to know for what or for whom they were originally written. For example, Monteverdi's opera *Orfeo* was composed for private performance in a room of a noble palace; its first audience was a society of aristocratic enthusiasts who had a special interest in the culture of ancient Greece. This helps explain the work's mythological plot, its relatively short duration and small cast of major characters, and the lack of what we would consider realistic action. When we turn to sacred music, we find that most works were still, as in the Middle Ages and Renaissance, composed for performance in church as part of a particular service on a particular day. Thus a work for Christmas employs a text and other features that distinguish it from a work for a saint's day or some other occasion.

Figure 1.4 Pieter de Hooch (Dutch, 1629–1684). *Portrait of a Family Making Music*, 1663. Oil on canvas, 98.7 × 116.7 cm. © The Cleveland Museum of Art, 2000, Gift of the Hanna Fund, 1951.355. This painting depicts members of a well-off urban family engaged in domestic music making. The seated woman at the center holds a music book in her lap and beats time with her right hand; she is probably singing, accompanied by recorder, cittern, and violin (at left, a bass viola da gamba leans against a table). Note the relaxed position in which the violin is held, resting on the chest rather than squeezed between the neck and shoulder as in present-day practice.

Many patrons were unconcerned about the particular religious faith of their musicians. Handel, a Lutheran, wrote music for the Anglican chapel of the king of England; Bach, also a Lutheran, sent an early version of his B Minor Mass to his sovereign, the Roman Catholic elector of Saxony, who was also the king of Poland.[2] This was possible because musical style was not, in general, dependent on religion. Genres that originated in Roman Catholic Italy, such as the cantata, were enthusiastically adopted by Protestant patrons and musicians. Indeed, throughout the Baroque there were few essential differences between sacred and secular music. The same music could even be used for both purposes; Monteverdi, Schütz, and Bach all followed the common practice of adopting secular music to church use, attaching new sacred words to existing compositions.

---

[2]Bach eventually received in return the honorary title of Saxon court composer.

Figure 1.5 *Concert*, drawing (pencil, ink, and washes on blue paper), French, eighteenth century, attributed to Lancret. National Music Museum, Vermillion, South Dakota, Witten-Rawlins Collection, 1984 (no. G-8). An ensemble of cello, harpsichord, violin, and transverse flute performs before an audience; such a scene might have occurred during one of the many semipublic concerts held in the homes of both the aristocracy and certain better-off musicians during the Baroque.

Throughout our period, the place of women in society, and therefore in music, was particularly restricted. A small number of aristocratic women had already achieved distinction during the later Middle Ages as rulers, writers, and composers. But only in the second half of the sixteenth century do women begin to emerge as professional musicians, notably as singers in a few northern Italian courts. During the 1600s, women musicians—as well as dancers and actors— became highly visible in Paris and a number of Italian cities; a few became composers. But in most places laws and customs continued to bar women from participation in church music and from careers as professional musicians. Some states, notably Rome, restricted the appearance of women in operas and other

Figure 1.6 A public ball during celebrations of the marriage of the Dauphin (French crown prince) to Princess María Teresa of Spain, Paris, 23 February 1745, engraving from *Fêtes publiques donnés par la ville de Paris* . . . (Paris, 1745). A large band provides music for a public dance sponsored by the city of Paris; the dancing is informal, by contrast to that of the royal court or at the opera and ballet.

theatrical performances. This was one reason for the widespread use of male voices for the higher vocal parts in both sacred and secular music, with men even taking female roles in opera and ballet.

PERFORMANCE PRACTICES

The use of men in what we would consider women's roles is one instance of a historical performance practice that today seems strange and unexpected. In every work we study, it will be useful to ask how the composer expected the music to be performed. Baroque musical notation is generally close to that of today—far closer than that of earlier periods. But many things that we expect to be indicated in a musical score were often omitted, even the names of the specific voices and instruments for which it was written as well as dynamic and tempo markings. Many performance practices were understood by convention rather than fixed in notation.

This remains true today. We do not, for example, expect an orchestral score to tell us precisely how many violins play each part or what bowings they should use, even though decisions about these matters can drastically affect the sound of a work. To some degree these matters are open to the discretion of the conductor or section leader. But beyond a certain point they are governed by convention; one would not, for example, perform a Beethoven symphony with just two or three first violins. We are so accustomed to the symphonies and other works of the modern concert repertory that we rarely think about the conventions they involve. But in earlier music the conventions are less familiar to us. Thus care is needed in interpreting Baroque scores—both the notes themselves and any verbal indications for such things as instrumentation or tempo. For example, the word *soprano* in a Bach choral work may mean not a section comprising several female singers but a single boy or an adult male falsettist. Instrumental parts also require careful consideration. For instance, the word *flute* sometimes means not the modern transverse flute, which is held to the side, but the recorder, a distinct woodwind instrument held vertically. By the eighteenth century, most of the instruments of the modern orchestra existed in some form. But all differed in important ways from their modern counterparts, with respect to playing technique as well as their physical structure and materials.

Modern concert performers are accustomed to playing or singing exactly the notes on the page. But professional musicians of the Baroque were trained in the improvisation of embellishments and variations, much as modern jazz musicians are. Most musicians understood how to interpret certain signs used as shorthand for ornaments; many could also improvise harmony or counterpoint, sometimes following written clues notated through the symbols of what is known as figured bass. Many musicians also understood conventions that involved the alteration of certain notated rhythms. Conventions varied from time to time and place to place; principles that govern the performance of ornaments such as trills in Bach's music do not necessarily apply in the earlier music of Monteverdi or Lully.

Hence, in addition to understanding the development of compositional style and the notable elements of individual works, it is important to understand distinctive aspects of the notation and performance practices of each piece. The study of performance practice includes such considerations as (1) *where* works were performed, (2) *who* performed and listened to them, and (3) *how* musical scores were interpreted. Given, say, an oratorio by Handel, we would like to know (1) the sort of hall or theater for which it was written; (2) the size and makeup of the ensemble that Handel's own performances used, including the precise number and type of voices and instruments; and (3) the conventions that governed the interpretation of Handel's score and the vocal and instrumental techniques used—for example, the bowings used by the string players, or the use or nonuse of vibrato by singers as well as instrumentalists.

Usually we know far less about such things than we would like. Scholars often differ with one another about the use of a particular historical performance practice. So-called authentic performances or recordings may adopt very different approaches to the same work. Nevertheless, specialists in early performance practices have acquired an impressive amount of knowledge and practical experience in the repertories that we will be considering. Music that several decades ago seemed dry or impossible to perform has been revealed as exciting and eminently practical. Long-familiar works, including those of Bach and Handel, have appeared in a new light. Musicians who are not in a position to acquire old types of instruments or to learn historical techniques can still gain new ideas about performance by studying historical practices. And even as specialists in early music continue to refine their ideas about historical performance, Baroque works continue to be performed by mainstream musicians as well.

CHAPTER 2

A SIXTEENTH-CENTURY PROLOGUE
Motet and Madrigal

To understand the beginnings of Baroque music, it will be helpful to examine some music of the preceding period, the Renaissance. We shall consider works belonging to two genres—motet and madrigal—from the end of the Renaissance, that is, the late sixteenth century. These works will give us a good idea of the state of European musical style as the year 1600 approached. The motet was perhaps the most important form of sacred vocal music at the end of the Renaissance; the madrigal was in many ways its secular counterpart. Both genres continued in use during the Baroque, although in considerably altered forms.

The composers discussed in this chapter took contrasting approaches to the motet and to the madrigal, respectively. Yet all four remained known and influential during the Baroque, and their works continued to be performed well into the seventeenth century. Many seventeenth-century musicians must have seen themselves as continuing in the traditions represented by the present works, unaware that later historians would regard the Baroque as a distinct period and style. Indeed, much that applies to sixteenth-century music remained important through the next century and a half.

Renaissance Composers

The chief composers of the early Renaissance—Guillaume Dufay (1397–1474), Gilles Binchois (ca. 1400–1460), and Johannes Ockeghem (ca. 1410–1497)—had been northerners: natives of the Netherlands or northern France who found employment with some of the great rulers of their time: kings of France, dukes of Burgundy, and the like. Most spent at least a portion of their careers in southern France and Italy, and as far we know they wrote exclusively vocal music. Moreover, all were singers; that, at least, is how they were usually described in contemporary documents, although some obtained titles as church or court officials as well. Josquin des Prez (ca. 1455–1521), the greatest composer of the next generation, still led such a career, but by the mid-sixteenth century things had begun to change. Palestrina and Lassus (discussed below) both worked in the choirs of important rulers, and both continued to write only vocal music.[1] But Palestrina was Italian, spending his entire career in his native country: the first of many such composers whom we will meet. Moreover, he began his career as an organist, signaling a trend that would continue through the Baroque, when the majority of important composers would be instrumentalists—particularly keyboard and string players. Nevertheless, the typical career path of a composer remained constant throughout the fifteenth and sixteenth centuries: early training as a choirboy in the church of one's native city, followed by a series of appointments as singer, organist, or choir director in increasingly prestigious ecclesiastical or court positions.

Vocal Polyphony of the Renaissance

The music of the composers mentioned above is for vocal ensembles in which each part has an independent melodic line. Such music is referred to as **vocal polyphony**; it is for three, four, or more voices, each equally important and similar to the others in rhythm and melodic content. It is probable that in most performances each part was sung by a single person, not by a section in a large chorus as is often heard today in this repertory. Instruments sometimes replaced or doubled one or more of the voices, but in principle this music remained purely vocal, the complete verbal text appearing beneath the notes in each part. Adult male voices were the rule, although boys might have sung the top lines of some works, women as well in secular music.[2] We will be particularly interested in two aspects of late Renaissance polyphony: its use of *imitative counterpoint* and its increasing emphasis on *musical rhetoric*. Both features continued to be of great importance throughout the Baroque.

Musical Rhetoric

Perhaps the most important single element in vocal music of the late Renaissance and the Baroque is the composer's approach to the setting of texts. By the end of the sixteenth century, writers on music had articulated the principle of **musical rhetoric.** By itself, the word *rhetoric* refers to the effective presentation of ideas through the spoken or written word. Rhetoric in this sense has been a fundamental element of European education since ancient times, and Renaissance and Baroque writers, emulating those of ancient Greece and Rome, used numerous special devices or *figures* of rhetoric, such as metaphors and similes, to render their arguments more compelling or their poems more beautiful.[3] When Joachim Burmeister and other late Renaissance and Baroque theorists began to apply similar ideas to vocal music, they were in effect considering a musical composition as a *reading* of its text. That is, just as a speaker

---

[1]A number of keyboard works published under Palestrina's name are probably not actually his compositions.

[2]Women probably participated in sacred polyphony in some convents and in domestic (at-home) music-making, but public performances of any kind by women were extremely limited.

[3]We still use the expression "figures of speech" to refer to metaphors, rhetorical questions, and other verbal devices that ultimately derive from ancient rhetoric.

or writer uses particular verbal techniques to articulate the form, meaning, and expressive content of a piece of writing or an oration, a composer uses musical devices to articulate the structure and content of the text that he is setting to music. This principle remained paramount in vocal compositions through the Baroque. Thus, in analyzing vocal music, one can consider how the composer "reads" the text, that is, uses musical means to reflect both the form of the text and its content.

Texture

One of the many tools employed in the service of musical rhetoric was the manipulation of musical **texture.** Musicians speak of texture in various ways; in vocal polyphony, texture is, in essence, a particular type of relationship that prevails between the individual parts of a polyphonic composition. Three fundamental textures used in vocal polyphony are *homophony, counterpoint*, and *antiphony*; counterpoint (*contrapuntal* texture) often includes imitation, a device that received particular attention from sixteenth-century composers. Each of these textures will be considered below, in the context of the individual works in which they occur.

Sacred Polyphony of the Renaissance

By the mid-sixteenth century, the motet and the cyclic mass had been for a hundred years or so the chief forms of sacred polyphony. Both terms, *motet* and *cyclic mass,* are modern expressions, each encompassing several types of music. Today the word motet can refer to almost any sacred polyphonic vocal work of the Renaissance, except for masses and a few other special categories.[4] The motets considered below were composed primarily for the liturgy of the Roman Catholic church—that is, to be heard during a worship service. These works resemble thousands of other motets from the period in their use of four to six voices to set a Latin text, which is presented phrase by phrase, generally with new music for each phrase and little or no musical repetition except where the words themselves are repeated.

Mass is the principal worship service of the Roman Catholic church; its elements include the **proper,** a set of readings and ritual actions that vary from day to day, and the **ordinary,** another set that in principle remains the same throughout the year. Since the fifteenth century, five sections of the ordinary of the mass have customarily been set to polyphonic music; these are the Kyrie, Gloria, Credo, Sanctus, and Agnus Dei, each named after its opening word or words. In an actual religious service, most of these sections are separated from one another by elements of the proper; nevertheless, composers frequently set them as a group, creating a **cyclic mass.** In most cyclic masses of the Renaissance, the five movements are unified by their common use of preexisting

---

[4]The word *motet* is also used for certain types of medieval vocal compositions, both sacred and secular, and for nineteenth-century sacred vocal music composed in imitation of the Renaissance motet.

musical material: either a popular or sacred melody (such as a Gregorian chant), or a motet or some other polyphonic work.[5]

Baroque composers continued to write motets and masses, often in styles close to those of the late sixteenth century. One of J. S. Bach's last works, the B Minor Mass, completed in about 1749, contains several movements that reflect his study of and admiration for the music of Palestrina, composed some two centuries earlier.

THE LATE RENAISSANCE MOTET: GIOVANNI PIERLUIGI DA PALESTRINA AND ORLANDE DE LASSUS

Palestrina

Giovanni Pierluigi da Palestrina (1525/6–94) was probably the most influential composer of church music during the late Renaissance. Named after his birthplace, the Roman suburb of Palestrina, he spent much of his career in the service of high church officials at Rome, including several popes. His works continued to be performed, studied, and imitated as models of vocal polyphony through the seventeenth and eighteenth centuries and into modern times. This was exceptional for a composer of his time; no doubt his fortunate position at the heart of the institutions of Roman Catholicism had something to do with it, but it also reflected the fact that contemporaries and later musicians alike responded to the combination of technical perfection and restrained yet effective use of musical rhetoric in his works. Monteverdi, Schütz, and Bach are among the Baroque composers who wrote works modeled more or less directly on those of Palestrina.

The greatest part of his extant output consists of about one hundred cyclic masses and several hundred motets and related sacred works. Particularly famous is the *Pope Marcellus* Mass, named for a pope who held the office for just three weeks in 1555. During his brief papacy, Marcellus is supposed to have encouraged his musicians, including Palestrina, to write in a style that made the words readily comprehensible to listeners. Whether true or not, the story reflects the tendency of the Counter-Reformation—the Roman Catholic response to the Protestant movement—to favor sacred music that renders the words of the text in a clear and distinct manner.

Most of the texts that Palestrina set to music are in Latin, the official language of the Roman Catholic Church throughout the period that we are studying. The language of the ancient Roman Empire, Latin was still understood and even used in everyday speech by the Roman aristocrats and churchmen for whom

---

[5]The modern terms *paraphrase* and *parody* describe different techniques by which preexisting material is incorporated into a mass or other work. A cyclic mass based on portions of a preexisting melody is a paraphrase mass; one that incorporates portions of a complete polyphonic work such as a madrigal is a parody mass. Sixteenth-century musicians described such techniques as *imitation*, a term preferred by some scholars today (imitation in this sense is distinct from the technique of imitative counterpoint).

Palestrina worked. Hence the texts that he set to music would have been familiar to his chief patrons. Indeed, educated Europeans through the Baroque would continue to understand the Latin (and Italian) texts used in vocal works that were performed throughout the continent.

Palestrina's Music

Palestrina's music is for vocal ensembles of from three to twelve voices. Four-, five-, and six-part writing predominates. Following the practice of the time, works sometimes remained in manuscript for many years prior to their publication. Because few of Palestrina's own manuscripts survive, in most cases we know only the dates of publication, not of composition. The masses were his best-known works; about half of them were based on preexisting music, including twenty-four of Palestrina's own compositions.[6] Palestrina is famous above all for his perfection of compositional devices that had been pioneered by earlier Renaissance composers. He is especially known for his mastery of imitative counterpoint, and musicians to this day study his works as examples of the polished use of this difficult compositional technique.

The Motet *Dum complerentur*

This work (anthology, Selection 1) was first published in 1569, two years after the *Pope Marcellus* Mass. Its Latin text is based on the account in the New Testament of Pentecost, originally a Jewish festival. Christians believe that at the observation of this holiday fifty days after Jesus's resurrection, the Holy Spirit was manifested to the disciples (the followers of Christ) in the form of a great wind. This the text describes in lines 3–4. Palestrina and his contemporaries probably understood this account as literally true; today, regardless of one's personal faith or convictions, it remains possible to appreciate the craft and expressive values of the composition by considering its text in relation to Palestrina's music, which most likely was meant for performance in church on Pentecost.[7]

The Text of the Motet

One way to begin considering a vocal composition of this period is by examining both the form and the content of its text. In form, this text falls into two parts, each comprising four lines (see the text and translation accompanying the musical score in the anthology). The last line of each part is the same; this is indicated by the three dots (*ellipsis*) after the opening words of line 8. In addition,

---

[6]An example of such a work is the *Missa Dum complerentur*, based on the motet *Dum complerentur*, which is discussed below.

[7]Line 6 of the motet's text is not found in the New Testament; it is instead an anti-Semitic addition to the biblical text. Its presence shows that even in a musical work one must confront the prejudices characteristic of the time and place in which it was composed.

lines 2, 3, and 4, each end with the word *alleluja*—an expression of joy—as does line 8. As a first principle of musical rhetoric, one might expect the music to reflect these formal aspects of the text in some way.

One might also expect the music to reflect the content of the text—both its meaning and its emotional implications. Today we might expect the music to reflect the joyful character of the text, which is indicated by the repeated *allelujas*. But a sixteenth-century composer did not necessarily express joy through the same musical means as a later composer, nor did listeners perceive joy in the same types of music as we do. This particular work may not even sound especially joyful to us—particularly if it is not sung with the lively tempo that the composer probably expected. But what does it mean to say that a musical composition is joyful? How does music convey an expressive idea such as joy to a listener? Questions such as these, which had been asked already by the ancient Greeks, would occupy many writers of the late Renaissance and Baroque. Many answers are possible, and no one explanation can apply to all music or all listeners.

Music historians often speak of theories of *affect* that arose during the sixteenth through eighteenth centuries; the term refers to an approach to musical expression that was common to many works of the period. Expressive concepts such as joy are associated with specific technical features of the music, such as the use of a particular tonality or individual intervals in a melodic line. Moreover, these musical features are frequently associated with specific words in the text. Thus Palestrina's motet focuses on individual words and brief phrases of the text—some of which indeed represent ideas relevant to joy—highlighting each in some distinctive way. To understand how the music reflects the words, one needs to look not only at the treatment of the text as a whole but for distinctive musical settings of individual words and phrases.

Texture in Palestrina's Motet

As in any piece of music, one's initial impression of the motet arises from what one actually hears. At the outset, three relatively high vocal parts sing together, presenting line 1 of the text (see score, mm. 1–3). The top part, or **cantus** (soprano), is joined by two lower voices, the **altus** (alto) and **tenore** (tenor), which at first sing in precisely the same rhythm. This produces the type of texture known as homophony; the term derives from Greek words meaning literally "same sound," although it is applied in various ways to music.

In measure 3 the altus and tenore begin to move independently of the cantus, and in the next two measures all three have distinctive rhythms and melodic contours. This produces a **contrapuntal** texture typical of much vocal polyphony; the three voices move in **counterpoint**, from Latin words referring to distinct musical lines that move against ("counter to") one another.

At measure 6 the cantus and altus drop out, and we now hear a group of four low voices, again presenting line 1 of the text. We can, then, speak of an alternation between two contrasting groups of voices; such alternation is an example of **antiphony** (from Greek words meaning "against" and "voice"). This is a third basic type of texture. Yet, although one can speak of measures 1–11 as being **antiphonal,** within each of the first two phrases one can also find separate homophonic and contrapuntal passages.

Thus far Palestrina has avoided the **imitative counterpoint** for which he is famous. Such a texture first occurs with the upbeat to measure 18, when the cantus and altus together introduce the word *allelujah.* One measure later, the **quintus** (second tenor) enters with the same melodic idea, overlapping with the lines of the two upper voices, which continue.[8] Gradually, the remaining voices enter in imitation, and in measure 23 the cantus does so for a second time, still with the same melodic idea. In our modern score—but not in Palestrina's original notation—this second cantus entry now begins on the second beat of the measure.[9] The first note of the cantus in measure 23 is written as a dotted quarter, but musically it is identical with the entry in measures 17–18; it is all too easy to overlook such renotated entries.

The brief melodic idea that is treated in imitation is termed a **subject.** Each entry of this subject (save for the first) joins an existing group of voices, taking part in an increasingly complex web of counterpoint. The subject itself takes various shapes. Some entries exactly imitate its first statement by the cantus (through the downbeat of m. 19). In other entries only the rhythm or the general melodic contour is recognizable. Later composers took a similarly flexible approach to imitation; only rarely was the latter expected to be exact.[10]

Text and Music in Palestrina's Motet

Palestrina's use of imitative counterpoint has long been admired as a finely developed aspect of compositional craft. But, to the composer and his listeners, it was chiefly a means toward the effective presentation of the text—that is, an element of musical rhetoric. Palestrina's music reflects not only the form of the text but its grammar and accentuation; in a few instances it clearly responds to its meaning as well. Each of these aspects of musical rhetoric is carried out through the use of specific compositional devices.

One such device is musical form. **Form** includes such elements as the division of the music into sections and the recurrence or repetition of individual passages. The form of this motet directly reflects that of its text, which falls into two sections, each ending with the same words (line 4 = line 8). The music, like that of many sixteenth-century motets, is similarly in two sections, which correspond to those of the text. The two identical lines of the text receive essentially identical musical settings (compare mm. 53–84 of part 1 with mm. 35–66

---

[8]The word *quintus* is Latin for "fifth"; this voice, together with the **sextus** or "sixth" voice (second alto), was viewed as an addition to the four basic parts of cantus, altus, tenor, and **bassus** (bass).

[9]The work was originally printed not as a score but as six separate vocal parts, without barlines (and therefore without ties). Commentaries in the Anthology explain how modern scores alter the notational appearance of late-Renaissance and early-Baroque works, often with implications for performance practice.

[10]A piece, or a section of a piece, constructed through exact imitation is called a **canon.**

of part 2). This repetition of text and music is somewhat unusual among six-teenth-century motets, most of which are **through-composed**: each section employs new music, without any substantial repetitions or restatements of pre-viously heard material.[11]

Musical form operates at various levels. In addition to considering form at the large scale, one can analyze form within each of the two sections of the motet. Even at the local level, the musical form reflects that of the text. For instance, lines 1 and 2 of the text each present complete ideas; in the original Latin, each is a self-contained clause. The music for these two lines accordingly falls into two distinct passages of different types. Line 1, as we have seen, is set antiphonally—sung once by the upper voices, once by the lower ones. Line 2 is sung by all six voices together (mm. 12–17). The beginning of line 2 is also marked by a change of texture: the antiphony of line 1 is replaced by six-part homophony. The change of texture thus articulates the beginning of a new seg-ment in the musical form. A subsequent shift to imitative texture, in m. 18, articulates the beginning of a third segment.

Another element of musical rhetoric arises through musical **declamation**: the music reflects the rhythm and accentuation of the words as they occur in spoken language. Modern English speakers think of accentuation as a matter of volume or dynamics: an accented syllable is spoken more loudly than another, and one might assume that this applies to singing as well. But this motet, like most of the music we shall study, contains no written dynamics or accent marks. Nor did performers necessarily stress the first note of each measure; indeed, the original printed parts for the piece lacked barlines, an element of notation that became common only in the course of the following century.

Musical declamation in Renaissance and Baroque music is a product of the specific rhythms and melodic contours used to set individual words. For exam-ple, most of the words in lines 1–2 receive a **syllabic** setting, a single note falling on each syllable. Syllables that would receive an accent in spoken Latin may receive longer note values, like the first syllable of *erant* ("were") in mea-sure 12.[12] Other accented syllables fall on relatively high notes or are preceded by leaps. On the accented third syllable of *complerentur* (m. 3), the cantus and altus ascend by step, while the tenor leaps down by a fifth. An accented sylla-ble can be further highlighted by a **melisma**: a series of notes sung to the same syllable. This occurs on the word *dies* ("day") in mm. 3–4 and again on *dicentes* ("saying") in mm. 15–17. Longer melismas occur later on *alleluja*.

Palestrina must have considered the text grammatically before setting it to music, observing where each verbal clause begins and ends. The musical form of the composition reflects this analysis of the text. He must also have consid-ered the accentuation and relative importance of individual words, and this is

---

[11]The repeated final line of text and music functions as a refrain, a device employed in a number of Renaissance and Baroque genres; for an example from early opera, see the anthology, Selection 6b (the lines beginning "Ahi, caso acerbo," from Monteverdi's *Orfeo*).

[12]Our edition of the music adds accent marks over the relevant vowels in the text, but only in words of three or more syllables.

reflected in the musical declamation. Until the mid-sixteenth century, form and declamation were the principal elements of musical rhetoric, and they remain so in Palestrina's music. But Palestrina was also concerned with the meaning of the words. This becomes evident when we consider the changes in texture in the first section of the motet. The words refer to a gathering of people, an idea represented by the use of antiphony—two different groups of voices—for line 1. All six voices then join in homophony at the word *omnes* ("all") in measure 13. A similar change of texture marks the beginning of line 3: the words et *subito* ("and suddenly") correspond with a sudden shift back to antiphonal homophony (m. 32). The focus on individual words is typical of much of the vocal music of the sixteenth through eighteenth centuries. But later composers went far beyond Palestrina in their attention to the meanings of specific words in the texts they set to music.

Cadences

We have seen how the two halves of the motet are subdivided by changes in scoring (number of voices), texture, and treatment of the text. Generally, each subdivision ends with a **cadence,** a form of musical punctuation that marks the end of a distinct segment. Music theorists of the eighteenth century and later described cadences as products of certain chord progressions (symbolized today as IV–V–I and the like). Renaissance musicians, on the other hand, thought of cadences in a way that reflects the linear or contrapuntal character of vocal polyphony. This view was made explicit in the writings of sixteenth-century theorists such as Gioseffo Zarlino (1517–1590). For him and his contemporaries, a cadence was the product of motion by two voices from an imperfect to a perfect consonance.[13]

Thus, at the end of example 2.1 the cantus and altus come to rest on an octave (c′/c″); this is preceded by a major sixth (d′/b′).[14] In Renaissance theory, this series of two vertical intervals between cantus and altus is sufficient to define a cadence; what the other voices are doing is, in principle, irrelevant. Yet a glance at the full score reveals that, as the cantus and altus reach their cadence in m. 26, the tenor (fourth voice) also completes a phrase, adding what we would consider the harmonic bass (V–I) of the cadence. At the same point the sextus (third voice) is in the middle of a phrase, and the quintus and bass are just entering. Hence this cadence involves only three of the six parts; the overlap between phrases in the different voices reflects the independence of parts typical

---

[13]The octave is a perfect consonance, as are fifths and fourths; thirds and sixths are imperfect consonances (all other intervals are dissonances). Fourths count as perfect consonances only when they do not involve the lowest sounding voice. Thus, on the downbeat of m. 11 the fourth between sextus and tenor (d′/g′) is a consonance, but the one between bass and quintus (g/c′) is a dissonance.

[14]The natural on the note b′ is an editorial addition to the original notation and therefore is placed above the notehead. Renaissance composers often omitted necessary accidentals, expecting performers to add them based on their knowledge of style; such altered notes are often referred to today as **musica ficta.**

of sixteenth-century polyphony. Only at the most important cadences, such as the end of the first allelujah section (m. 31), do all six voices come to rest at the same time. (For more on Renaissance cadences, see Box 2.1.)

Example 2.1 Palestrina, *Dum complerentur*, mm. 24–26 (cantus and altus only; lower four voices omitted)

Modality

Despite the differences between Renaissance music theory and that of later music, it is possible to hear this motet as being in F major. One could even analyze it as if it were a tonal composition, using Roman numerals to represent the harmonic functions of individual sonorities. But this is not true of all Renaissance polyphony. Even in the Baroque repertory, one encounters progressions, even entire compositions, whose pitch structure is best understood in another way, using the principles of **modality**. For instance, Selection 2 in the anthology ends with a progression that would be considered a half cadence in tonal music; such an ending is typical for sixteenth-century polyphonic works in certain modes. A **mode** is, fundamentally, a set of melodic principles that govern a particular tune or, in polyphony, the individual vocal parts. In sixteenth-century polyphony the mode determines the ranges of the individual voices as well as their predominant notes and melodic intervals; this affects the types of cadences and the successions of chords that arise in this music as well. As a product of the linear qualities of individual voices, modality differs substantially from the **tonality** of eighteenth- and nineteenth-century music. Tonality is primarily harmonic in nature: a system involving the qualities of chords and their relationships.

The theory of modality originated in ancient Greece. It was applied during the Middle Ages to chant, which by definition is monophonic. Only in the mid-sixteenth century did certain composers, including Palestrina, apply modality to polyphony in a consistent way. Paradoxically, they did so at a time when other composers, such as Lassus in certain works, were consciously writing music that avoids modal principles. Nevertheless, Palestrina's motet is a clear-cut example of the fifth, or Lydian, mode. This is evident from the melodic characteristics of the individual voices, especially the tenor (see Box 2.2).

Baroque theorists continued to refer to the principles of modality, even as they developed concepts that would be incorporated into theories of tonality during the nineteenth and twentieth centuries. Most Baroque compositions show modal as well as tonal characteristics, in varying proportions. One can think of

Box 2.1

Cadences in Sixteenth-Century Music

In Renaissance polyphony, cadences are understood as being formed through the motion of pairs of voices from an imperfect consonance (third or sixth) to a perfect consonance (unison, fifth, or octave). Example B2.1a shows several such cadences.

Example B2.1a Cadences (two voices)

Each simple cadence can be ornamented by introducing a **suspension**. For instance, in the second cadence in Example B2.1a, the note f′ is lengthened by a dot. This creates a **dissonance**, the major second f′/g′. The dissonance then **resolves** to an imperfect consonance, the minor third e′/g′. The latter in turn completes the cadence by moving to a unison, f′/f′. This progression constitutes the most common sort of cadence in both sixteenth-century music and the Baroque.

Any two voices in a polyphonic composition can form a cadence. Usually, the voice pair that forms a cadence is accompanied by at least one other voice. Typically this is a lower voice, such as the bass line given in Example B2.1b. Such a bass is likely to leap by a fourth or a fifth at the cadence, as shown in the first three cadences of the example. Each of these cadences would be considered a full (or perfect) cadence in tonal music.

Example B2.1b Cadences (third voice added)

Not every cadence follows these patterns. In measures 5–6 of Palestrina's motet, the cantus and altus come to rest on a major third (f′/a′); the same is true of the sextus and quintus in measure 11 (c′/e′). These major thirds are imperfect consonances; strictly speaking, then, one might not identify these resting points as cadences. But in both cases another pair of voices *does* form a perfect consonance at the end of the phrase: altus and tenor in measure 6, quintus and bass in measure 11.

Box 2.2

Modes in Sixteenth-Century Music

A mode can be thought of as a way of describing certain *melodic* characteristics of a single musical line, whether a monophonic chant or a single part (voice) in a polyphonic composition. To say that a melody is in a mode is to imply that it forms cadences to certain notes and that it emphasizes certain melodic intervals.

A key (or tonality) is a way of describing certain aspects of the *harmony* and *form* of a polyphonic composition, considered as a whole. To say that a work is in a key, or that it is tonal, is to imply that it forms cadences to certain chords and that it uses certain recurring chord progressions.

- Most Gregorian chant is modal.
- Most medieval polyphony is neither clearly modal nor clearly tonal.
- Renaissance polyphony usually shows some aspects of both tonality and modality.
- Most Baroque, Classical, and Romantic works are predominantly tonal.

THE MODES IN CHANT

Western theories of modality originated in relation to Gregorian chant, the sacred song of the medieval Roman Catholic liturgy. Chant consists of unaccompanied melodies for a solo voice or for several voices singing in unison. The mode of a chant melody is determined from (a) its last note or **final**, (b) its range, and (c) its principal melodic intervals and cadence points. Most chant melodies move within the range of an octave. If the highest note lies an octave above the final—that is, if the melody moves largely *above* the final—the mode is said to be **authentic**. If the highest note lies a fifth above the final—that is, if the melody tends to move on both sides of the final—then the mode is **plagal**.

Medieval theorists recognized eight modes: four authentic and four plagal, using the finals d, e, f, and g. It is possible to think of each mode as a diatonic scale, as shown below. Each mode can be identified by either a number or a Greek name. The final for each mode is shown in italics.

1. Dorian	*d*	e	f	g	a	b	c′	d′
2. Hypodorian	A	B	c	*d*	e	f	g	a
3. Phrygian	*e*	f	g	a	b	c′	d′	e′
4. Hypophrygian	B	c	d	*e*	f	g	a	b
5. Lydian	*f*	g	a	b	c′	d′	e′	f′
6. Hypolydian	c	d	e	*f*	g	a	b	c′
7. Mixolydian	*g*	a	b	c′	d′	e′	f′	g′
8. Hypomixolydian	d	e	f	*g*	a	b	c′	d′

The final is only one of several notes on which phrases are likely to end; other such *cadence points* may be the third or fifth above the final. In addition, a chant in a given mode will tend to repeat or outline certain melodic intervals. For example, a chant in mode 5 will frequently leap between f and c′ or trace melodic lines rising or falling between those two notes.

THE MODES IN RENAISSANCE POLYPHONY

During the sixteenth century, Palestrina and his contemporaries often wrote motets and other polyphonic works that represent specific modes. In such works, each voice follows the melodic principles outlined above for Gregorian chant and thus possesses its own mode. The mode of the composition as a whole is considered to be that of the tenor.

Thus, in the first part of Palestrina's motet *Dum complerentur*, the tenor ends on the note f and has the range f–g′. Another frequently occurring cadence point in this voice is c′ (as at the end of part 2). The tenor, and therefore the entire motet, can be assigned to mode 5, even though the tenor does not actually end on the final (f). What matters, from the perspective of modality, is that the melodic contours of the tenor emphasize both the final f and the *confinal* c′.

Today we are likely to attach significance to the fact that the bass harmonizes the final cadence of both halves of the motet with the note f. Strictly speaking, however, the bass note is irrelevant to the determination of the mode. Equally irrelevant, at least in a work whose final is f, is the use of what we would call a key signature of one flat. In other cases, however, a "key signature" in a sixteenth-century work indicates a *transposed* mode. For example, a work with a signature of one flat whose tenor ends on g might be in the Dorian mode transposed from d to g.

In Palestrina's motet, the cantus (soprano) and quintus (tenor 2) are also in mode 5. But whereas the quintus moves in the same range as the tenor, the cantus lies an octave higher. On the other hand, the altus and sextus (alto 2) are in the plagal version of this mode—that is, mode 6. These voices tend to move about a fifth above the tenor, yet they have the same final. The bassus is in the same mode as the altus and the sextus, an octave below them.

In addition to the eight modes of chant, some Renaissance theorists recognized four more modes. These correspond to the modern major and natural minor modes, but they were referred to by Greek names:

9. Aeolian	*a*	b	c′	d′	e′	f′	g′	a′
10. Hypoaeolian	e	f	g	*a*	b	c′	d′	e′
11. Ionian	*c′*	d′	e′	f′	g′	a′	b′	c″
12. Hypoionian	g	a	b	*c′*	d′	e′	f′	g′

Not every Renaissance work can be assigned to a mode. Lassus's *Timor et tremor* is not clearly modal or tonal, although portions of it might be considered to be in either a mode or a major or minor key. Baroque composers sometimes included traditional modal labels in their titles, but their music can often be described as well in terms of common-practice tonality.

modality and tonality as two different systems, each useful for understanding different aspects of a given composition. Whereas modality is helpful in describing the individual vocal parts of Palestrina's music, this book will use the more familiar language of tonality to analyze later music.

Modality is not just a theoretical concept. Zarlino and other writers, inspired by ancient Greek music theory, argued that each mode is associated with particular expressive or emotional qualities, sometimes described as modal *ethos*. Today the two modes of tonal music continue to carry general emotional associations, the major mode being associated with happy or positive feelings, the minor mode with sad or negative ones. The greater number of modes in sixteenth-century polyphony—eight, or even twelve in some systems—led some theorists to propose much more specific associations between modes and expressive qualities. Different writers proposed different relationships—one reason for questioning whether composers and listeners actually made any such associations. Yet the evidently cheerful or celebratory character of *Dum complerentur* does seem generally to have been associated with the work's Lydian mode. The principle of modal ethos was not forgotten in the Baroque. It influenced later theories that related the general expressive character, or *affect*, of a work, to specific musical features. Those features include not only the modality or tonality of a work but also its tempo, rhythm, and even use of particular melodic intervals.

Lassus

Orlande de Lassus (1530/2–94), also known as Orlando di Lasso, was, with Palestrina, one of the two most renowned and influential composers of the sixteenth century. Although almost exact contemporaries, the two led very different careers and wrote different types of music. Whereas Palestrina worked all his life in and around Rome, Lassus was born in northern France and held a series of positions in France and Italy before becoming a singer and eventually music director for the Duke of Bavaria, at Munich in southern Germany (see Figs. 2.1 and 2.2). In addition to writing sixty masses and hundreds of motets, he also wrote substantial numbers of secular works: Italian madrigals, French chansons, and German part-songs or lieder. The linguistic and stylistic diversity of his output reflects his international career, reminiscent of that of earlier northern composers such as Josquin des Prez. It must also reflect to some degree his cosmopolitan and gregarious nature, seemingly quite different from Palestrina's. We have some evidence about Lassus's personality from his surviving letters to the Bavarian dukes, from which we learn that he had a lively wit. He was not above taking roles in staged comedies, in which he must have acted as well as sung.

Lassus's Music

The great extent and diversity of Lassus's output makes generalizing about it difficult. He was capable of the most refined contrapuntal writing in the style now associated with Palestrina, whose madrigal *Io son ferito* he made the basis of one of his own cyclic masses (Palestrina never returned the favor). On the other hand, some of his secular works adopt a simple, direct style in keeping with their humorous and sometimes bawdy texts.

His contemporaries and followers noted Lassus's particular concern for musical rhetoric. Indeed, the vivid musical rhetoric of his motets had as great an impact on later musicians as did Palestrina's counterpoint. Apart from the greater variety of his output, Lassus is distinct from Palestrina in the more individual character of his melodic and rhythmic ideas, which more frequently reflect both the meaning and the rhythm of the words. Hence Lassus's music gives the impression of being more rhetorical than Palestrina's. Because homophonic textures are more effective than contrapuntal ones for declaiming a text, homophonic textures are probably more frequent in Lassus's music. But complex imitative counterpoint is by no means rare, particularly in his sacred works. Early in his career he wrote a few stylistically radical compositions (the *Sibylline Prophecies* of ca. 1555) that anticipate certain extreme music-rhetorical devices used by Gesualdo and other composers at the end of the century. There are hints of the same devices in the work considered below, but in general Lassus avoided the types of exaggerated musical expression that came into fashion toward the close of the sixteenth century.

The Motet *Timor et tremor*

This motet (anthology, Selection 2) is a famous example of Lassus's heightened concern with musical rhetoric. First published in 1564, early in Lassus's Munich period, it was presumably composed for performance in the Bavarian court chapel. Like all sixteenth-century motets, it is ostensibly for voices only, but it is likely that some of the six vocal parts were sometimes doubled or replaced by instruments. A painting in an illuminated manuscript by the Bavarian court painter Hans Mielich shows Lassus seated at a harpsichord, surrounded by players of recorders, violas da gamba, sackbuts (trombones), and other instruments. A similar picture graces the title page of a 1589 collection of Lassus's masses (Fig. 2.1).[15] Although an ensemble of this sort would not have performed in every piece, such music making must have made an impression on the Venetian composer Giovanni Gabrieli, who worked at Munich during the 1570s and later wrote an equally original setting of the text of *Timor et tremor*, also in six voices.

The text is a compilation of fragments from the Book of Psalms; like the text of Palestrina's motet, it is divided into two parts (see anthology). It constitutes a prayer for protection and comfort; the final line *non confundar* implies something like: "do not confuse [or distress] me by failing me in my hour of need." Each half of the text falls into two distinct sentences, the second of which directly addresses the deity as "Lord" (*Domine*). This grammatical structure is emphasized in Lassus's setting, which closely reflects the form and speech rhythms of

---

[15]The Mielich picture has been widely reproduced; further discussion in George Kubler, *Studies in Ancient American and European Art* (New Haven: Yale University Press, 1985), 184–88.

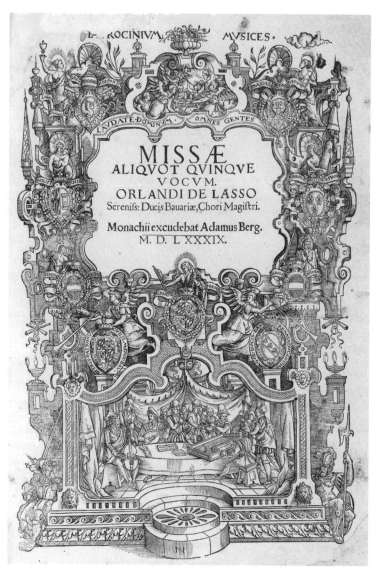

Figure 2.1 Orlande de Lassus, *Patrocinium musices: Missae aliquot quinque vocum* (Munich: Adam Berg, 1589), title page. © The British Library Board. All rights reserved. London, British Library, K. 9. 6. 8. This elaborate title page is typical of late-Renaissance printed collections of vocal polyphony. In the borders around the title are the heraldic arms of the pope, emperor, and other European rulers; those of Lassus's patron, the Duke of Bavaria, are at the center, immediately above a picture depicting the musicians of his chapel. They are performing from the part books lying open on the table. The seated player at the keyboard instrument (a virginal) is possibly intended to be Lassus; the two boys just behind the table are probably singers. Other instruments include flute, cornettos, trombones, lute, and viols. Although this image suggests that Lassus's sacred music might be performed by some such mixed vocal and instrumental ensemble, pictures on title pages and elsewhere do not always depict realistic scenes or actual practices.

the text. Both the grammatical divisions and the accentuation of individual syllables are marked musically in ways described earlier for Palestrina. Lassus also finds vivid ways of responding musically to the specific content of text phrases and individual words.

At the very beginning, the six voices repeat the three opening words in a predominantly homophonic texture. This already suggests a highly rhetorical approach to the text; the first three words do not even form a complete clause, comprising just two nouns joined by the conjunction *et* ("and"). By repeating the three words as a unit, the music suggests that they are of special significance, the main subject of the entire work. Musical highlighting of an opening textual phrase would remain an important device in the Baroque, although the exact musical means by which the emphasis is accomplished would be quite different.

Cross Relations and Chromaticism

Lassus's music not only articulates the words of the text distinctly; it also represents their meaning. A vivid example of this process occurs at the beginning of the motet, where the alto sings alone, then is joined by the other voices. Together, the six voices form a C-major chord that lasts through the first half of measure 3. At that point, however, where the five lower voices sing the word *tremor*, the sonority changes to an A-major chord. Lassus and his contemporaries would not have described the passage in such a manner; they might have pointed to the **cross relation** that occurs in measure 3: the note C in the first half of the measure (alto and bass) is followed immediately by C♯ in the second half

Figure 2.2 Octave virginal by Onofrio Guarracino, Naples, 1694. National Music Museum, Vermillion, South Dakota. Purchase funds gift of Margaret Ann and Hubert H. Everist, Sioux City, Iowa, 1997 (no. 6041). This small virginal, sounding an octave above written pitch, is an example of the type of keyboard instrument shown in Figure 2.1.

(sextus). Cross relations are a variety of **chromaticism**; another variety, encountered later in the motet, is discussed below. Both passages involve the juxtaposition of "natural" notes against notes altered by accidentals. In a cross relation, the juxtaposition involves two (or more) different voices; in extreme cases the two forms of the note may even be sounded simultaneously.[16]

Text Painting

Cross relations are unusual in sixteenth-century music; within its largely diatonic structure, cross relations sound strange and abnormal. In addition, they negate the sense of mode, for no modal scale contains both natural and sharp versions of the same note. Hence, cross relations were appropriate to words describing abnormal or negative feelings or ideas—including the word *tremor* ("trembling"). Lassus's use of a cross relation at this point is therefore an example of **text painting** or **word painting**: the use of music to represent the meaning of an individual word or phrase in the sung text. Lest there should be any doubt that Lassus intended to draw an association between the extreme emotion of the text and the cross relation in the music, the latter is repeated in m. 6. There the note B♭ on the downbeat (cantus and sextus) is juxtaposed with B♮, again on the word *tremor* (alto).

Virtually any musical device can serve the purposes of word or text painting when used in an appropriate context. In the Palestrina motet, the entrance of all the voices on the word *omnes* ("all") was another example. The present motet contains many further examples. Text painting is a part of musical rhetoric, and as such it is an important aspect of music composed throughout the late Renaissance and Baroque.

Musical Rhetoric in Lassus's Motet

The arresting opening of this motet sets the tone for the whole work; it tells us that this is to be a highly rhetorical composition paying close attention to each significant word in the text. Musical rhetoric can operate at various levels: (1) A composition can reflect the spoken accentuation of individual words, and (2) it can be divided into phrases and larger formal divisions that reflect the grammatical division of a text into sentences and paragraphs. Music can also (3) accentuate (emphasize) particular words, and it can (4) reflect the meanings of individual words or (5) the general mood or emotional character of a text as a whole. Whereas Palestrina's music is particularly concerned with the first three of these types or levels of musical rhetoric, Lassus's motet vividly reflects all of them, with particular attention to the third and fourth varieties listed. This work proceeds as a series of short phrases, each employing one or more devices of musical rhetoric to reflect specific words or expressions in the text (for a list of such devices, see Box 2.3).

---

[16]For an example of a simultaneous cross relation, see J. S. Bach, Cantata 127 (anthology, Selection 19), third movement, m. 2, where the oboe sounds a♮' against the second recorder's a♭".

Box 2.3

Devices of Musical Rhetoric

Devices that articulate form
  Cadences marking the ends of sections and subsections
  Changes of texture or scoring at the beginnings of sections
  Rests that separate words or larger units of the text

Devices for declamation of the text
  High or long notes on accented syllables
  Short notes on unaccented syllables
  Leaps before accented syllables
  Melismas on accented syllables
  Homophonic texture to emphasize words or expressions
  Repetition of words or expressions

Devices that reflect the meaning of words (text painting)
  Chromaticism
  Upward or downward motion
  Small as opposed to large note values (lively versus sustained motion)
  Melismas on such words as "sing," "fly"
  Unusual rhythms or melodic intervals

Not every detail in a composition is equally significant from the point of view of musical rhetoric. In Lassus's motet, the tenor has a rising melisma on the word *tremor* in measure. 7. But this brief melisma is the only one used for this word, and it is hidden within one of the inner voices. The melisma helps propel the music forward, toward the cadence that the tenor forms with the sextus on the following downbeat. But this melisma does not provide a rhetorically significant underlining of the word *tremor*.

On the other hand, the motet closes with a passage containing numerous repetitions in all six voices of the two words *non confundar* ("do not confound me"; see part 2 of the motet, mm. 28–43). The many repetitions of these words clearly emphasize this phrase of the text; the uniformly syllabic setting of the words is another device used to the same end. But the most vivid aspect of the musical rhetoric here is the text painting, which takes two forms. First, there are two instances of **chromaticism**: voice leading that involves the use of both natural and altered forms of a note within close proximity of one another. Thus at measure 30 the cantus moves from g' to $g\sharp'$; the sextus imitates this in the following measure, moving from d' to $d\sharp'$. Like the cross relations at the beginning of the work, this chromatic voice leading sounds strange in the context of sixteenth-century style and thus was appropriate for a word that means "confuse" or "confound." Beginning at measure 33, a different device represents the same word: for seven measures the cantus sings against the beat; almost every note is syncopated or tied over the barline. The text here is actually a prayer *against* confusion. It is typical of Renaissance and Baroque musical rhetoric, however, that the music reflects the single vivid word *confundar*, not the broader meaning of the phrase as a whole.[17]

THE MADRIGAL: CARLO GESUALDO AND CLAUDIO MONTEVERDI

Composers of Palestrina's and Lassus's generation knew many types of secular as well as sacred polyphony. The texts of most secular works used vernacular languges—Italian, French, German, and so forth—and different musical styles were associated with each of these languages. Hence Lassus, who wrote French chansons and German lieder as well as Italian madrigals, employed a somewhat different style for each. Nevertheless, as the century progressed, composers of secular music tended to adopt the rhetorical and contrapuntal artifice of sacred music. This was particularly true in the **madrigal,** a polyphonic setting of any of various types of Italian poetic text, usually short and lyrical.

Today the word *madrigal* is sometimes used indiscriminately for all sorts of Renaissance polyphony. But it is best applied only to the original Italian genre and its imitations in other countries, such as England. Madrigals were meant for a single voice on each part; as in sacred polyphony, instruments might substitute for one or more voices. The madrigal continued as an important genre well into the seventeenth century, albeit with quite different musical characteristics. What remained constant, however, was the use of poetry written at a high level of diction and craft—that is, not folk poetry (or pseudo-folk poetry) as in more popular genres such as the *villanesca*, and not a strophic song like the *canzonetta*, in which successive stanzas or verses are sung to the same music.[18] The musical settings of madrigals are accordingly elevated in style, taking particular care for musical rhetoric. For this reason madrigals are **through-composed:** music within a madrigal is rarely repeated, and the same music is almost never used for different words.

The madrigal, like other types of sixteenth-century song, originally played an important role in amateur and domestic music making. During the middle decades of the sixteenth century it was fashionable to sing polyphonic songs as a form of after-dinner entertainment, and in Italy and elsewhere educated members of the upper classes were expected to be able to sing such music at sight during social gatherings. The enjoyment of these songs lay as much in the words as in the music; as in the motet, a major attraction of the polyphonic madrigal lay in the graceful melding of music and text. Among the composers of such madrigals were Jacopo Arcadelt (?1507–1568) and Cipriano de Rore (1515/16–1565), Flemish or Franco-Flemish musicians whose popular four-part

---

[17]One might argue, on the other hand, that the unusual musical devices in this section of the motet represent unusual emotional urgency rather than a response to the single word *confundar*.
[18]For more on strophic songs, see the discussion of the early aria on p. 69.

madrigals composed in the 1530s and 1540s continued to be reprinted and performed into the early seventeenth century.

In the course of the sixteenth century, however, the musical rhetoric of the madrigal, at first relatively restrained, became increasingly intense. In addition, the vocal requirements of the music became more demanding: the ranges of the individual parts widened, and composers increasingly wrote out melodic embellishments that had previously been heard only as improvised additions to the written parts.[19] As a result, the madrigal gradually moved out of the sphere of amateur music making and into that of the professional. By the end of the sixteenth century, the most important of these works were being performed not by cultivated amateurs but by professional specialists attached to the courts of the aristocracy. Venues for performance included both court palaces and meetings of the many *accademie* (academies), gatherings of learned men interested in the arts and culture, which flourished in northern Italian cities during the late Renaissance and the Baroque. De Rore was among the pioneers of a more vivid sort of madrigal, responding to certain texts with heightened word painting, including chromaticism. Four later composers—all but one Italian, and all working in Italy—are particularly noted for further extending the style of the madrigal: Luca Marenzio (1553/4–1599), Giaches de Wert (1535–96), Gesualdo, and Monteverdi. We shall examine examples composed by the last two.

Gesualdo

Don Carlo Gesualdo, Prince of Venosa (ca. 1561–1613), was technically an amateur, that is, a music lover rather than a professional musician. Such was the only socially acceptable role for a musically accomplished Renaissance nobleman such as Gesualdo, who nevertheless composed some of the most astonishing works ever written. A wealthy landowner in southern Italy, he spent much of his time at the northern Italian court of Ferrara, a center of musical innovation and experimentation during the late sixteenth century. He gained notoriety for murdering his first wife after discovering her in bed with a lover (who was also murdered). Apart from this, his reputation rests on the last two of his six published books of five-voice madrigals, in which he extended the expressive devices of sixteenth-century music to the most extreme point ever reached. No composers directly emulated Gesualdo, but musicians used similar devices throughout the seventeenth century, though rarely if ever with the same intensity.

Gesualdo's *Beltà poi, che t'assenti*

This work (anthology, Selection 3) is from Gesualdo's Sixth Book of Five-Part Madrigals, published in 1611 but probably composed significantly earlier. Unlike earlier madrigal poems, its anonymous text is of scant literary quality

---

[19]The addition of unwritten ornaments and embellishments was an important part of Renaissance and Baroque performance practice; some examples are discussed in later chapters.

but, as in many of Gesualdo's madrigals, comprises a few brief phrases capable of conveying the extreme emotional effects that the composer sought to express in his music.

The most striking feature of this music is its chromaticism, expressed at the very beginning by a progression that we would describe as moving from a G-minor chord to an E-major chord.[20] As in Lassus's *Timor et tremor*, the chromaticism discourages hearing the passage in any particular mode or key; coming at the outset of the work, it establishes the work's sharply painful tone. Surprisingly, the chromaticism falls on the word *beltà* (beauty), which would normally receive a less disturbing diatonic setting. The use of chromaticism here suggests that this "beauty" is not what it (or she) seems; perhaps, then, this work is a contemplation of the deceptiveness of superficial beauty, even as it creates beautiful effects out of what were conventionally regarded as ugly or unnatural sounds.

Despite his radicalism, Gesualdo follows earlier madrigal composers—and Palestrina and Lassus in their motets—in setting the text in a predominantly through-composed fashion. Only the final section, presenting the last two lines of the text, is repeated, reflecting the fact that those two lines present a single thought that serves as a conclusion to the poem as a whole.[21] Notwithstanding the strangeness of the music, it employs many of the same music-rhetorical devices used by Palestrina and Lassus. For example, line 1 and the first half of line 2 (mm. 1–4) are set homophonically; the second half of line 2 (mm. 5–11) is thus set off by its use of imitation. The subject used for the latter, however, is highly chromatic, representing the word *tormenti* ("torments"). Subsequent passages continue to alternate between homophony and imitative counterpoint; the beginning of the final section is marked by the sudden outbreak of simple diatonic homophony at measure 20.

It could be argued that the contrasts in style between successive passages are so great that they reduce the work to a series of vivid moments that lack overall coherence. Yet so original and striking are Gesualdo's effects that they have captured the attention of generations of musicians—including the twentieth-century Russian composer Igor Stravinsky (1882–1971), who arranged this madrigal in his orchestral work *Monumentum pro Gesualdo* (1962).

Monteverdi

Already by the 1590s, a composer who would eventually occupy a central position in European music history was making a name for himself in the northern Italian city of Mantua. We shall meet Claudio Monteverdi (1567–1643) again when we turn to the developments that are considered to mark the beginning of the Baroque in music.

---

[20]Gesualdo and his contemporaries might have described this passage in the language of modality, speaking of a shift from the Dorian mode—transposed so that its final is G—to the Phrygian mode with raised third degree (G♯).

[21]Similar repetitions of concluding lines occur in earlier madrigals and in contemporary chansons.

Monteverdi published his first music—a collection of motets for three voices—at the age of fifteen. By 1592 he was working as a player of stringed instruments for the duke of Mantua, eventually becoming the latter's music director (*maestro di capella*). Monteverdi published nine books of madrigals in all; Books 6–9 represent the Baroque version of the genre and depart substantially from the sixteenth-century tradition. Already in Books 4 and 5 Monteverdi established himself as something of a radical, like Gesualdo, but one with a greater interest in integrating each madrigal into a fully coherent composition. Moreover, instead of using brief texts compiled from fashionable clichés, Monteverdi retained a genuine interest in and appreciation for good poetry. When an attack published in 1600 accused Monteverdi of arbitrarily abandoning the principles of proper composition, he was able to reply convincingly that he did so the better to express the content of his poetic texts.

Monteverdi's *Luci serene*

Monteverdi's Fourth Book of Madrigals was published in 1603, but by then some of the works had been in existence for a number of years. *Luci serene* (anthology, Selection 4), the eighth madrigal in the volume, might have been a response to Gesualdo's Fourth Book of Madrigals, which opens with a setting of the same text.[22] The poem is relatively short and concludes with a witty twist or conceit, like other madrigal texts set by Gesualdo and by Monteverdi in his Fourth Book. Although the words refer to elemental emotions of pain and pleasure, by this date those ideas had become clichés in madrigal poetry. Texts such as this one must have been understood ironically or appreciated as clever variations on familiar themes. Yet they served well as the basis for expressive or ingenious musical settings. Monteverdi's madrigal gives this brief text a monumentality that its poet could hardly have expected.

In some respects, much of what Monteverdi does here is familiar from earlier sixteenth-century vocal polyphony. Each poetic line or other unit of the text becomes associated with particular textures and melodic ideas, and the more vivid images of the poem receive the expected text painting. Notable examples occur on the noun *foco* ("fire") and the verb *strugge* ("melt, be consumed") in lines 8 and 9. These words are represented through a lively twisting or turning figure (tenor, m. 42) and a syncopated rhythm (tenor, m. 44), respectively. Even the first word of the text is depicted musically: on the word *luci*, here a poetic word for "eyes," each singer would have seen two semibreves (whole notes) in his or her part. The notes would have been understood as symbols for two eyes, a convention established by earlier madrigal composers.

---

[22]This is only one of many instances of a text set by multiple composers, who vied with one another to produce the most effective setting. Another madrigal text, Marini's "T'amo mia vita," was set not only by Gesualdo and Monteverdi (each in his respective fifth book of madrigals) but by Luzzaschi (discussed in Chapter 3) and the latter's pupil Vittoria Aleotti (ca. 1575–1620), one of the first women to compose and publish madrigals, as well as the Danish composer Mogens Pedersøn (1583–?1623).

Yet Monteverdi's musical rhetoric goes deeper than conventional text painting. Not only does he "paint" the first image of the poem—the eyes of the beloved, which the poet addresses in lines 1–3; he sets it off from what follows. This is accomplished through the homophonic setting of the word *luci* on long notes followed by a rest. This is the same device that Gesualdo used to mark his opening word, *beltà*, but without the latter's chromaticism. Later, instead of mechanically following the division of the poem into lines, Monteverdi follows its sense and grammatical structure. Thus the end of line 2 combines with the beginning of line 3 in a single musical phrase (mm. 13–16), creating a musical equivalent for the poetic device of **enjambment**. The phrase is sung homophonically, in chords whose lively rhythm approaches that of actual speech.[23]

Form

Monteverdi's sensitivity to the text extends beyond individual words and phrases to the poem's overall structure, for which he finds a unique musical reflection. The poem falls into three stanzas, each comprising three lines; Monteverdi accordingly divides his setting into three sections. The first two sections have much the same music, whereas the last section is repeated with alterations, producing the musical form AA′BB′. The reuse of the A music is contrary to the through-composed writing characteristic of the sixteenth-century madrigal and is very unusual in Monteverdi's output. But it reflects the fact that lines 4–6 of the poem are a variation of lines 1–3, with parallel grammar, syntax, and meaning. Virtually the same music can be employed for both, although Monteverdi transposes the repetition upward. Thus the first word of line 4, *dolci* ("sweet"), is sung to an E-major chord in measures 20–21, a whole step above the opening D-major harmony.

This transposition reflects an important discovery made by composers of the late sixteenth century: that a passage could be restated within a composition at a different pitch level. We take this procedure for granted, thanks to its common use in music of the eighteenth and nineteenth centuries. But transposed repetition is rare in works written before 1600, except in very short passages. The procedure that Monteverdi used here to reflect a particular aspect of the poem would become a fundamental compositional element by the eighteenth century.

The Artusi–Monteverdi Controversy

In 1600, the Bolognese music theorist Giovanni Maria Artusi (ca. 1540–1613) published an attack on Monteverdi's style, focusing on the as yet unpublished

---

[23]The use of declamatory homophonic passages in polyphonic madrigals anticipated the same procedure in monophony (see Chapter 3). Monteverdi's use of this device has been traced to the influence of Wert, who as *maestro di capella* at Mantua from 1565 onward was Monteverdi's superior there during the 1590s.

madrigals of the composer's Fourth and Fifth Books. This was part of an exchange of writings alternately attacking and defending Monteverdi; the most famous installment was a reply to Artusi written by Monteverdi's brother Cesare. Cesare, who was a composer himself, clearly reflected his brother's own views.[24]

Essentially, Artusi objected to certain departures that Monteverdi had made from the type of counterpoint found in the works of earlier composers. Monteverdi defended his innovations as justified by the need to express the meaning and emotional content of the text. He applied the term *prima pratica* ("first practice") to the older tradition, describing his own method as the *seconda pratica* ("second practice"), although he argued that de Rore, Marenzio, and others had already used it before him.

Neither writer's argument was entirely sound. Artusi simply refused to accept practices that lacked the stamp of tradition. Monteverdi claimed that his music was merely a "servant" of the text, as if his departures from tradition were dictated to him by the poetry. But this failed to explain the musical rationale for his innovations. For if Monteverdi was justified in using irregular dissonances to express, say, "pain" mentioned in a poetic text, why did he use one particular dissonance and not another? In fact, neither side in the controversy was able or willing to see that all musical expression is governed by conventions, and that the conventions were undergoing a transition at just this time.

Dissonance Treatment in the "Second Practice"

Even in *Luci serene*, most of the dissonance treatment is conventional; that is, most dissonances are prepared and resolved by the same voice moving by step. Thus, in the cadence in measures 9–10, the quinto (second soprano) has a suspension: a prepared dissonance against the canto (first soprano) that is resolved by the motion of the note f' downward to e' (Ex. 2.2). (To review sixteenth-century cadential practice, see Box 2.1.)

Elsewhere in the same passage, however, Monteverdi repeatedly contradicts the *prima pratica*. On the downbeat of measure 9 the canto is holding the note c", which forms a seventh with the quinto (d') and a ninth with the bass (B♭). These dissonances are properly prepared—no cause for objection on that account. But instead of resolving these dissonances conventionally, the canto drops by a fifth to f'; we never hear the expected b♭' in the upper voice. Similarly, on the downbeat of measure 11 the canto's d", which forms a dissonance against the bass's e, resolves upward instead of falling downward. Monteverdi presumably would have justified both procedures as part of the impassioned statement of the word *voi* ("you!").

Even worse, from Artusi's point of view, is the situation in measure 53 (Ex. 2.3). The canto, whose e" forms dissonances with the quinto and tenore,

Example 2.2 Monteverdi, *Luci serene*, mm. 8–10

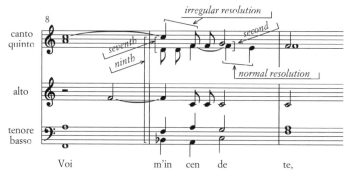

resolves the dissonances improperly by leaping downward to b′. But the latter note is still dissonant, forming a tritone (augmented fourth) with the quinto's f′ and a ninth with the alto's a. We might imagine Monteverdi's defending this passage as expressive of the canto's word *more* ("dies").

Monteverdi was right in his claim that he had not invented such things. They also occur in the music of Gesualdo and other contemporaries. Many irregular dissonances must also have arisen when performers improvised embellishments. But in Monteverdi's *seconda pratica* the non-traditional dissonances and other departures from convention are notated on the page for all to see. Despite Artusi, Baroque composers continued to commit flagrant violations of the rules of sixteenth-century counterpoint, particularly to express violent emotions or abnormal states of mind. Nevertheless, the rules of counterpoint followed by Palestrina and Lassus remained the basis of Baroque composition.

Example 2.3 Monteverdi, *Luci serene*, mm. 52–55

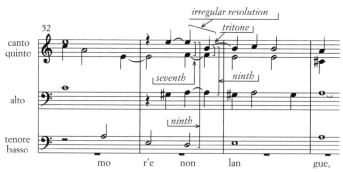

Even Monteverdi wrote a number of old-fashioned pieces in the *prima pratica*. In the course of the seventeenth century, although dissonances were treated more freely than in sixteenth-century music, the ostentatiously of irregular dissonance treatment characteristic of Monteverdi's "second practice" became a rarity; composers had more significant innovations to think about.

CHAPTER 3

TRANSITIONS AROUND 1600

Since the early twentieth century, it has been customary for music historians to see significant changes in European musical style as having taken place around 1600. Generally these changes are described as the transition from Renaissance to Baroque style. All history is transition, yet certain periods see more rapid and more widespread types of change, and the decades on either side of the year 1600 were such a period. That many composers were aware that aspects of musical style and technique were changing around 1600 is shown by several instances of self-proclaimed "new musics," notably Caccini's publication of that title (discussed below). Moreover, that work and others reveal that the practices of performers as well as composers were changing in significant ways. By the 1630s the genres, styles, performing practices, and even the social place of music in western European culture were substantially different from those of fifty or sixty years earlier.

To be sure, it is all too easy to focus on a single round-number year, such as 1600, and suppose that it marked a turning point in music history. The madrigal had been undergoing crucial developments during the previous decades, and it continued to develop for another forty years; thus the years right around 1600 may not have been especially crucial for the madrigal when viewed within the complete history of the genre. The same is probably true of other genres, such as the motet. Moreover, musicians in many places continued to write and perform after 1600 just as they had done previously. If, for example, a musical revolution ever took place in musically conservative England, it did not occur until the 1660s or later, when the restoration of the monarchy (following the civil wars of midcentury) led to the influx of large numbers of more up-to-date musicians from France and Italy.

In fact the transition from Renaissance to Baroque began within a limited area. It initially involved a relatively small number of experimental or avant-garde musicians in a few northern Italian cities whose rulers or upper classes were unusually open to new types of musical composition and performance. Thus, as we begin our consideration of musical developments in the seventeenth century, we shall be particularly concerned with the manner in which musical practices associated with one city or region spread elsewhere. Certain unusual or experimental practices of Ferrara, Mantua, and Florence were carried only gradually to Venice and Rome, and from there to France, Germany, and eventually England. On the way, moreover, these musical practices changed, so that what was characteristic of early Baroque music in one location might not be so in another.

Some General Developments

Although generalities can be misleading, a number of basic distinctions between Renaissance and Baroque music hold true for many genres and repertories.

Distinct National Styles

First, whereas music of the sixteenth century was, at least in certain genres, relatively homogeneous from one western European country to the next, in the seventeenth century we find striking national differences, particularly between France and Italy.

New Genres of Composition

Although the sixteenth century had certainly known many types of music, the number of distinct vocal and instrumental genres seems to expand considerably after 1600. In Italy, alongside the old genres of polyphonic motet and madrigal, there emerged new types of secular song for solo voice and instrumental accompaniment, each involving new styles of composition and performance; among these were the distinct varieties of recitative and of aria that became basic elements in the new vocal genres of cantata and opera. New types of sacred vocal work, such as the oratorio, employed the new types of solo vocal writing. At the same time, new categories of instrumental music, such as the sonata and the concerto, emerged as well. Such older genres as did survive, such as the motet and the cyclic mass as well as dances and other types of instrumental music, were transformed, employing new compositional and performing techniques.

Changes in the Underlying Structure of Music

Most serious sixteenth-century music was conceived for four, five, or six parts, all, in principle, equal to but independent of one another. After 1600, a greater number of compositions involve just two or three parts, or—to be more precise— the polyphonic conception of music grows less pronounced and many genres reveal a freer, less strictly contrapuntal texture. Most compositions, even old-fashioned multivoice motets, show a sharpened distinction between the bass and the upper parts, with the bass typically moving more slowly than the others and proceeding more frequently by leaps; in modern terms, the lowest part is now clearly the basis of the harmony. The new way of thinking about musical texture and the relationship of the parts to the whole is evident above all in the rapid adoption of the *basso continuo* (discussed below) as an element of both performance and practice and composition. It also made possible the freer use of dissonance that Monteverdi had described as the "second practice," in which musical coherence depended more on harmonic progressions, in the modern sense, than on intervalic relationships between pairs of voices in a contrapuntal texture.

Tonality

The new bass-oriented approach to harmony was related to an even more fundamental shift in musical structure, described today as the gradual replacement of modality by tonality. Both systems remain evident in seventeenth-century music, as they are in that of the sixteenth. But by 1700 such tonal practices as modulation and the establishment of contrasting key areas, which we take for granted in later music, had become firmly established, while the modes had for practical purposes been reduced to two, the major and the minor.

Ornamentation and Improvisation

In addition, composers increasingly wrote out various types of melodic decoration that previously had been left for performers to improvise. Baroque melodies thus incorporate melodic figures that had originated as improvised additions to existing music. These figures might be specified either as regular notes or through special symbols that were developed especially in France over the course of the Baroque. Improvisation nevertheless remained important, perhaps even more so than previously. It was, for example, an essential element in the realization of the basso continuo—and the presence of the basso continuo in most Baroque ensemble works is another important distinction between sixteenth-century music and later.

Use of Instruments

Another fundamental shift involved the way in which composers and performers thought about scoring, that is, the assignment of individual parts of a composition to particular voices or instruments. Most sixteenth-century vocal polyphony was composed in principle for unaccompanied voices. In instrumental music, parts were usually for unspecified instruments, each part being playable on any instrument with an appropriate range.[1] In the seventeenth century, however, composers increasingly wrote specifically designated instrumental parts, and even vocal works usually contain a substantial instrumental component. Whereas previously only the small number of composers writing for solo keyboards or plucked strings needed to understand the idioms characteristic of these instruments, now composers in general needed to know how to write idiomatically for instruments, especially for members of the violin family.

---

[1] An exception exists in the case of music for solo keyboard and plucked string instruments (such as the lute).

New Performing Practices

The development of new genres and new compositional techniques went hand in hand with the emergence of new performance practices for both singers and instrumentalists. New practices were conditioned by various factors, including new performance venues and new social contexts for music (both of which are exemplified by the opera houses that emerged during the seventeenth century). Particularly critical to performance practice was the increasing emphasis on solo virtuosity. The range (or compass) of pitches used in both vocal and instrumental music grew wider, and many special techniques that had formerly been confined to improvised use by virtuosos became standard practice. For the first time, dynamics were indicated notationally as well, leading to greater cultivation of such effects as sudden contrasts of *forte* and *piano* or gradual crescendos and diminuendos.

It was once assumed that the evolution of performance was a matter of gradual improvement, leading from simple or primitive techniques to the now-familiar practices of nineteenth- and twentieth-century musicians, which were taken to be superior to earlier ones. During the twentieth century, however, as specialists recreated historical practices and instruments, it became clear that musicians of every period develop practices to meet artistic demands and aspirations which themselves change over time. Baroque instruments are quieter than modern ones, indicating that musicians and audiences were less concerned with the production of high volumes of sound than is now the case. This is because only a limited number of performance locales, such as the largest of the public opera houses of Venice, approached the size of modern concert halls. The majority of works were composed for relatively small ensembles performing in fairly close quarters. Under such conditions, the continuous, unbroken legato favored today was less prized than the clear, controlled articulation of rapid embellishments and ornamentation.

To be sure, performance traditions varied depending on time, place, and the particular genre of music being performed. Today one can find books devoted to supposed "rules" of Baroque performance, but in fact it is impossible to devise universal solutions to the questions of interpretation that arise in the many different types of music practiced during the seventeenth and eighteenth centuries. In particular, the French style of composition that emerged in the course of the seventeenth century was accompanied by performing practices very different from earlier ones in Italy. Even in Italy, early Baroque practice differed substantially from that of one hundred years later.

Retention of Older Styles

Although most musicians (and their patrons) accepted the innovations described above, many continued to compose and perform works whose conservative style was based on that of the late sixteenth century. The selection of which style to use—older or newer—was only partly a matter of personal choice. Particular genres, especially sacred choral music and certain types of contrapuntal keyboard piece, tended to be associated with older compositional styles. The latter came to be known as the *stile antico* ("former style") as opposed to the *stile moderno* ("current style"). Most works in the *stile antico* are not, however, in a pure "Renaissance" style. They include such "Baroque" elements as a basso continuo part, and in performance they would have included current types of scoring and ornamentation. Even had there been interest in older, historically authentic performance practices, little was known about them.

The Basso Continuo

The basso continuo, already mentioned several times, was an important element of both theory and practice throughout the Baroque. Indeed, some older histories of music refer to the Baroque as the "thoroughbass" period, using a term equivalent to the expression *basso continuo*. The latter is Italian, reflecting the origin of this device in Italy around 1600. The term literally means "continuous bass," refering to the origin of the basso continuo during the sixteenth century as a form of instrumental accompaniment for vocal polyphony. At first, organists and other accompanists seem to have aimed at doubling all of the voices, and to this end they would copy the separately printed parts into a score. But this was tedious, and by 1600 musicians had found that an acceptable accompaniment could be produced by writing only the bass line and improvising appropriate upper parts.

Players found it helpful to add numbers and other symbols, known as figures, above or below the bass line to eliminate some of the ambiguities that inevitably arose as to the intended harmony. The resulting form of notation is known as **figured bass** (examples can be seen in the anthology, beginning with Selection 5). The symbols of figured bass represent upper voices that a player improvises above the bass line. The improvisatory addition of those upper voices is the **realization** of the figured bass.

The first printed works to include figured bass parts appeared in 1600, but the device must have evolved during the preceding decades. It was rapidly adopted by many musicians and by the mid-seventeenth century had become an element of most Baroque ensemble music. To be sure, a significant number of ensemble works continued to be composed without continuo parts, and even where such parts are present composers did not always provide complete figures for their bass lines; often accompanists still had to guess at the proper harmony, using their musical intuition and sense of style.

Instruments used for playing the basso continuo included organ and harpsichord as well as various types of plucked string instruments such as the lute. Composers rarely specified which instrument was intended for a given work; several continuo players might have played in a composition for many voices or instruments. Hence the continuo part, notated as a single figured bass, might actually have been realized by a group of instruments. In addition, by the eighteenth century it had became customary for one or more melodic bass instruments (such as cello or bassoon) to double the bass line itself in many types of music. In earlier music, if the composer desired to have the bass line doubled by a melodic instrument, a separate part was generally provided for it.

The use of a basso continuo part simplified the composer's task by freeing him or her from the necessity of writing out the complete polyphonic texture of a composition. It also allowed accompanists to follow the soloist closely without being concerned with the niceties of counterpoint in a fixed number of voices. A harpsichordist could, for example, strike a many-voiced chord under a particularly emphatic note in a solo vocal part and then reduce the accompaniment to just a note or two when the voice grew soft. Each instrument, moreover, could employ its own idiomatic means of varying or embellishing the underlying harmony. Thus players of lute and harpsichord could break, or **arpeggiate,** certain chords, playing the notes one at a time instead of striking them all at once. A swift arpeggiation might produce the effect of an accent, a slower one that of a gentle crescendo—the choice of effect being determined by the intensity of the musical expression at any given moment.

The disadvantage of this practice was, of course, that the performer had to understand the symbols used in notating the figured bass and the conventions for realizing them. These, however, are explained in a number of treatises from the seventeenth and eighteenth centuries.[2] Modern players have used these treatises, together with knowledge of the instruments, to reconstruct Baroque traditions of continuo playing. By the eighteenth century, not only keyboard and lute players but all serious musicians were expected to understand figured bass realization, which had become the basis of the teaching of harmony. Indeed, well into the nineteenth century composers such as Beethoven and Brahms learned figured bass and occasionally used it in their compositional sketches. Figured basses continued to be used in certain types of score, especially recitative and sacred choral music, into the 1820s.

Modern editions often include written-out realizations of the figured bass. But these are the work of the editor and thus reflect the editor's understanding of Baroque practice; many realizations, especially those found in older editions, depart from the original conventions. Today a practiced continuo player can improvise a realization idiomatic to the instrument on which the part is being realized—harpsichord, organ, lute, harp, guitar, or occasionally even a bowed string instrument capable of playing multiple stops, such as the viola da gamba. Such an improvisation is likely to include rapidly arpeggiated chords and other devices that cannot be easily notated—which is why composers left the realization of such parts to the performer in the first place.

INSTRUMENTS

Instruments today are heavily standardized; an orchestra in Germany or Japan employs instruments virtually identical to those found in an American orchestra and perhaps produced by the same manufacturer, and players use essentially the same techniques. Things were very different in the Baroque, when most instruments were built by hand by individual craftsmen who followed specific local customs. Consequently, although most Baroque instruments correspond roughly to those of today, there are important differences not only between Baroque instruments and modern ones but also between, say, a French violin and bow of about

---

[2]See especially the works by Arnold, North, and Williams in the bibliography, which summarize much matter from the historical treatises.

1675 and Italian ones of the same period. Only by reconstructing the instruments of a particular time and place and learning to play them in period style can musicians begin to have a good idea of how a particular piece sounded. Specialists in the discipline known as **historical performance practice** have reconstructed early instruments and their performance techniques; they have also rediscovered early vocal techniques. Thanks to careful work in performance practice by musicians and scholars, much is now known about the sound and, therefore, the expressive qualities of Baroque music, although much also remains uncertain.

Baroque instruments include winds, strings, and keyboards. This discussion focuses on strings and keyboards, for these were the chief instrumental components of vocal music throughout the period (more detailed information about these and other instruments can be found in Chapters 10 and 12). Strings include both bowed and plucked instruments, and Baroque bowed strings are divided into two groups: the viol and the violin families. The Baroque viol, more precisely referred to as the **viola da gamba** (often shortened to "gamba"), has six or seven strings, and its fingerboard is fretted like that of a guitar (Fig. 3.1). It was built in several

Figure 3.1 Tenor viol by Gregor Karp, Königsberg, East Prussia (now Kaliningrad, Russia), 1693. Ex-coll.: Canon Francis W. Galpin, Harlow, England. National Music Museum, Vermillion, South Dakota, Arne B. and Jeanne F. Larson Fund, 1989 (no. 4573). Various forms of viol (or viola da gamba), a bowed stringed instrument held on the knees or legs, were used throughout the Renaissance and Baroque. Note the six strings, rounded shoulders, C-holes, frets, and fanciful scroll on this beautifully decorated example, probably made for a music-loving aristocrat (possibly Christian Ludwig, Margrave of Brandenburg-Schwedt, to whom Bach dedicated his Brandenburg Concertos).

sizes corresponding in range to soprano, alto or tenor, and bass voices. All sizes, even the soprano—known as the treble viol—are held vertically on or between the knees; the expression *da gamba* means "on the leg." The instrument's rich but gentle tone made it particularly suited to domestic music making, and during the sixteenth century it was popular among wealthy amateurs, especially when played as part of a **consort** of three to six instruments of different sizes. In the course of the Baroque, consort use of the viol diminished, but the bass viol remained important both as a solo instrument and in accompanying others.

The Baroque **violin** family includes instruments corresponding to the modern violin, viola, and cello (although the last did not emerge until the 1660s or so, its place previously being taken by various sorts of bass violin). Already in widespread use by 1600, these were sometimes distinguished from the gamba family by the name *viola da braccio*, referring to the fact that the higher members of the family were played on the arm (*braccio*). The Baroque instruments differ from their modern equivalents in the use of gut strings and shorter bows, and the neck is set at a smaller angle from the body of the instrument (see Fig. 12.1). These differences result in a somewhat lower level of physical tension and a somewhat quieter sound than with the modern instrument; on the other hand, they encourage a highly articulate type of playing, and the sound is still brighter and more piercing than that of the viols. These characteristics had led to the frequent use of violin consorts for dance music during the sixteenth century; the modern orchestra developed from such groups over the course of the seventeenth and eighteenth centuries.

Plucked strings include the guitar and harp, both of which were much used during the later Renaissance and Baroque, albeit in forms considerably different from the modern instruments. More widespread than either was the **lute**, which resembles the guitar in basic form but has a more rounded body; its strings are of gut and are normally plucked with the fingertips. By the mid-sixteenth century the lute had become the instrument most favored by amateur musicians, with a large and varied repertory. During the Baroque it became more the domain of professionals and, like the gamba, came to be restricted to special soloistic and accompanying roles. The Baroque knew various sizes and types of lutes and lutelike instruments going by several different names. Particularly important for the accompaniment of solo song during the early Baroque was the **theorbo**, also known as the **chitarrone**, one of several large varieties of lute with extra bass strings (Fig. 3.2). The bass strings were in addition to the six basic **courses**—usually, pairs of strings tuned to the same pitch—found on all Baroque lutes.

Unlike bowed strings, which are primarily melodic instruments used in ensembles, the lute and other plucked strings are chordal, capable of producing full harmony. Hence the lute possesses a substantial repertory of solo music. Most types of lute are quiet, making them suitable for the sensitive accompaniment of the solo voice; they were also employed in ensembles alongside bowed strings and keyboards.

The chief keyboard instruments of the Renaissance and early Baroque were the **organ, harpsichord,** and **clavichord.** All share the use of a keyboard connected mechanically to some type of sound-producing device; the differences lie

RAILICH-SELLAS
1639
NMM 3383

Figure 3.2 Archlute by Pieter Railich for Matteo Sellas, Venice, 1630. Ex coll.: Lord Astor. National Music Museum, Vermillion, South Dakota, Witten-Rawlins Collection, 1984 (no. 3383). The archlute is a type of lute related to the theorbo or chitarrone; note the extended neck and the second set of tuning pegs, used for extra-long bass strings that made this instrument appropriate for playing basso continuo parts as well as solo pieces. Adjustable gut frets are tied across the fingerboard, as on the guitar, lute, and viola da gamba.

in how the sound is produced. On the organ, **pipes** act, in effect, as an ensemble of wind instruments; the various types of pipe include flutes and reeds producing distinct types of sonority, which the player can select through the use of **stops**, usually knobs or levers at the side of the keyboard. Organs of the period range from elaborate church instruments to small, movable chamber organs used in private homes; the larger the instrument, the greater its potential volume and number of distinct sounds or stops.

The harpsichord is a stringed keyboard instrument; each key moves a **plectrum** that plucks a metal string, making this a sort of mechanical lute. On the clavichord, the strings are activated by small metal rods, called **tangents**, which are attached to the keys. Renaissance and Baroque harpsichords exist in various sizes and shapes, but all share a relatively bright, lively sound, as compared to the clavichord, which is extremely quiet. Thus the harpsichord was used in both solo and ensemble playing, whereas the clavichord was limited mainly to private practicing.

Keyboards, like plucked strings, are chordal instruments, and like the lute they not only possess a large solo repertory but were used widely in ensembles (see Fig. 2.1). Despite the great differences between the various keyboard instruments, composers generally avoided specifying the instrument for which keyboard music was written, assuming that it would be played on whichever one was available. Most Baroque keyboard parts can therefore be played on either harpsichord or organ. Today we tend to associate the organ with sacred music, but this was not necessarily the case during the Baroque, and both harpsichord and organ were used in sacred as well as secular music.

MONODY

The Baroque interest in music for solo voice produced some of the most important innovations of the period around 1600. The sixteenth century had already seen various types of song for solo voice with instrumental accompaniment, but the latter usually is conceived polyphonically, differing little in style from the lower parts of a work for multiple voices. Nevertheless, polyphonic madrigals and other works must have been performed frequently by a single voice, instruments substituting for the other parts. In such cases a professional singer is likely to have added various types of unwritten embellishments, converting what had been composed as a polyphonic texture into a virtuoso solo with accompaniment.[3] By the 1590s some composers were experimenting with music written from the outset as a solo vocal line with a relatively simple instrumental accompaniment. Such music is often described today as **monody**, from Greek words meaning "one song." Although any work for soloist with accompaniment might be considered monody, the term is especially appropriate for to the new forms of solo vocal music introduced around 1600.

The Greek term is apt, for many musicians around 1600 believed that in turning to monody they were recreating musical forms that had been employed in the staged tragedies of ancient Athens: such works as Euripides' *Alcestis*, first performed in 438 B.C.E. It was believed that these works were sung in their entirety and that their music contributed significantly to the extraordinary emotional effect that these dramas were reported to have had on their original audiences. Unfortunately, only tiny fragments of the actual music of ancient

---

[3]It was also possible for an instrumentalist to take the role of soloist, as in Diego Ortiz's arrangements of polyphonic madrigals for viola da gamba accompanied by harpsichord or other chordal instrument, published in his *Tratado de glosas* (Rome, 1553).

Greek drama survive, including that for small portions of two of Euripides' plays. These fragments were unknown to sixteenth-century writers, although a few works by Mesomedes, Greek poet-musician for the Roman emperor Hadrian, had become available by the late sixteenth century.

Writings from ancient Greece about music nevertheless survived, and these were an inspiration particularly to a group known as the Florentine Camerata. The Camerata, unlike other learned societies or academies of the day, was never organized as a formal body and had only a brief existence. But several of its members went on to play influential roles in the musical innovations of the next few decades. Meeting during the 1570s and 1580s at the home of Count Giovanni Bardi in Florence, the Camerata included the composers Giulio Caccini and (probably) Jacopo Peri (1561–1633); by 1598 the latter had composed a short dramatic work, *Dafne*, which is arguably the first example of what we now call opera. The central figure in the Camerata's discussions appears to have been Vincenzo Galilei (d. 1591), a lutenist and composer whose *Dialogo della musica antiqua, et della moderna* (Dialogue on the music of antiquity and of today, 1581) expressed many of the group's theoretical ideas about music.[4]

Members of the Camerata enthusiastically embraced monody as a form of musical antiquarianism and, no doubt, because it made possible a particularly clear presentation of the sung poetic text. It was, besides, a natural extension of existing musical practices, and it proved to be of great use in opera, which, not surprisingly, frequently drew its subject matter from ancient history and mythology, especially as recounted by such ancient Roman authors as Virgil and Ovid. The new monodic music actually had nothing to do with the ancient Greeks. But such figures as the mythological musician Orpheus and the god Apollo— the divine patron of the arts and leader of the Muses—would appear frequently in the texts and plots of vocal works of the seventeenth and eighteenth centuries.

Luzzaschi

The earliest monodic works clearly show their continuity with the tradition of vocal polyphony. At Ferrara, where many of Gesualdo's madrigals were probably heard for the first time, the court organist Luzzasco Luzzaschi (ca. 1545–1607) wrote madrigals for one, two, and three sopranos with instrumental accompaniment. The last, in the form of simple polyphonic parts, was evidently intended for performance at the keyboard. Although not published until 1601, these madrigals are thought to have been composed during the preceding decades for the so-called Three Ladies of Ferrara, who had been engaged by the duke of Ferrara for the specific purpose of singing virtuoso madrigals of this type in his palace.[5] Among the earliest known professional female musicians,

---

[4]Galilei was the father of the astronomer Galileo Galilei.

[5]Duke Alfonso (or more precisely, his wife, Duchess Margherita) employed various women singers at different times. At its height in the 1580s the group, known in Italian as the *concerto delle donne* (consort of ladies), included Laura Peverara (ca. 1550–1601), the most prominent, as well as Livia d'Arco (d. 1611) and Anna Guarini (d. 1598), daughter of the poet Giambattista Guarini. A fourth, very accomplished, singer in the duchess's entourage, Tarquinia Molza (1542–1617), evidently coached or advised the others.

through their skill and fame they helped inspire a fashion for similar music elsewhere. By the seventeenth century the virtuoso female soprano voice had become central to the European tradition; for the first time, too, a number of women singers achieved prominence as composers. Women composers of the late sixteenth century include Maddalena Casulana (ca. 1544–after 1583) and Vittoria Aleotti (fl. ca. 1593), who both published books of polyphonic madrigals, and Raffaella Aleotti (fl. ca. 1593–1640 or later), who published a book of motets.[6] Among the many women composers of the Baroque were Francesca Caccini, Barbara Strozzi, and Elizabeth Jacquet de La Guerre (see Chapters 5 and 10).

Despite his use of monody in a few works, Luzzaschi was in other respects a relatively conservative composer. Example 3.1 shows the opening of his madrigal *O Primavera* for soprano and instrumental accompaniment. It is a setting of a passage from Giambattista Guarini's famous and widely performed play *Il pastor fido* (The faithful shepherd, completed 1585), which became the basis of a number of operas during the Baroque. Luzzaschi's madrigal characteristically avoids the chromaticism of Gesualdo and other younger contemporaries; rather, it achieves most of its effect through sensitive declamation and the judicious use of written-out embellishment. For example, at the very outset the poem's opening address to spring—"O Primavera"—is repeated, the second time at a higher pitch. Both times a long note falls on "O" and the highest note is reserved for the accented syllable of *primavera*. Written-out embellishment begins in measure 4, where the note $c\sharp''$ is decorated by a **trill**: a rapid alternation between $c\sharp''$ and the next higher note. The trill concludes with a **turn**: a downward motion to b' that results in a circling or turning motion around $c\sharp''$. The trill with closing turn, which here decorates the cadence to the note d'' on the following downbeat, was one of several formulas used to ornament cadences throughout the late Renaissance and Baroque.

More extensive embellishment occurs in measure 7, where the voice sings a rapid scale that ascends through more than an octave, then decorates a cadence to g'' with the same trill with turn heard in measure 4. It is no accident that measures 4–5 and 7–8 both mark the ends of lines of the poem; moreover, the embellishments occur on accented syllables of important words. Luzzaschi's use of embellishment is therefore not arbitrary or capricious, but rather a form of musical rhetoric, reinforcing the structure of the poem. Similar rhetorical use of written-out embellishment occurs in monodic works by Luzzaschi's younger contemporaries as well. But unlike many of their works, Luzzaschi's madrigals retain the fundamentally polyphonic texture of the older polyphonic madrigal. This texture is evident in the four-part accompaniment of the present work; the vocal part is an embellished version of the top line of the instrumental accompaniment, which could be performed by four singers with only minimal alterations of a few notes. It is possible that the unembellished part writing of the accompaniment reflects Luzzaschi's first draft of

---

[6]It is uncertain whether the names Vittoria and Raffaella Aleotti refer to sisters or were different names for the same person.

Example 3.1 Luzzaschi, *O Primavera*, mm. 1–8

1 O Primavera, gioventù dell'anno, O Spring, season of youth,
2 Bella madre de fiori, Beautiful mother of flowers,
3 D'erbe novelle e di novelli amori, Of fresh plants, and of new loves,

the work, which might have been a conventional polyphonic setting for four voices in a style reminiscent of the early madrigals of Luzzaschi's teacher Cipriano de Rore.

The Florentine *Intermedi* of 1589

Luzzaschi's transformation of a simple polyphonic texture through soloistic embellishment probably reflected a way of performing madrigals that was growing increasingly common in late-Renaissance Italy. The same approach is documented in portions of a famous work of 1589, the *intermedi* for Girolamo Baragagli's play *La pellegrina* (The pilgrim). The latter, a comedy, was performed as part of the festivities celebrating a marriage that united the powerful ruler

Figure 3.3 The sixth and final *intermedio* from *La pellegrina*, engraving by Epifano d'Alfano after Bernardo Buontalenti, from Raffaello Gualtarotti, *Descrizione del regale apparato* (Florence, 1589). This is an idealized depiction of the work's actual performance as part of the Medici wedding festivities of 1589. In this scene, musicians representing Jupiter's gift of harmony and rhythm to earthly mortals descended from the clouds, a spectacular effect achieved through ingenious stage machinery.

of Florence with one of the great French noble families.[7] An important political event, the wedding was attended by hundreds of invited guests; following custom, it was accompanied by lavish musical and dramatic productions, including *La pellegrina*. The play itself was less substantial than the six musical interludes or ***intermedi*** that took place between its acts. Independent of the plot of the play, each *intermedio* consisted of a staged scene based on ancient mythology, with dances, solo songs, and choruses in up to thirty parts. Many of the leading composers of the day, including Caccini and Peri, took part, as did famous performers such as the soprano Vittoria Archilei (fl. 1582–1620).

Among the numerous musical numbers was one, described as a madrigal, that was sung as a monody to the accompaniment of a theorbo. *Godi turba mortal* occurs in the sixth and last *intermedio* (Ex. 3.2). Here, earthly mortals rejoice in the harmony that Jupiter, king of the gods, has established among them (Fig. 3.3). As in many Renaissance and Baroque stage works, the scene could be readily interpreted symbolically as praise for the local ruler (the duke of

---

[7]Grand Duke Ferdinando de' Medici of Tuscany married Christine of Lorraine.

Example 3.2 Cavalieri, *Godi turba mortal* (complete), from Intermedio VI for *La pellegrina*. Text by Ottavio Rinuccini.

1 Godi, turba mortal felice e lieta,

2 Godi di tanto dono,
3 E col canto e col suon
4 I faticosi tuoi travagli acqueta.

Rejoice, fortunate and happy
  mortal gathering,
Rejoice in this gift,
And with singing and playing
Break off your difficult labors.

Florence). The short poem was by Ottavio Rinuccini (1562–1621); the music is by Emilio de' Cavalieri (ca. 1550–1602). Rinuccini had been associated with count Bardi of the Florentine Camerata; in 1600 Cavalieri would write a work that is sometimes considered the earliest oratorio.[8]

Like Luzzaschi's *O Primavera*, the present composition consists of an embellished vocal part accompanied by four unspecified instrumental parts, the highest of which again comprises a simple unembellished version of the vocal line. In the 1589 performance it was sung by Onofrio Gualfreducci, a castrato singer (see Chapter 8). The accompaniment must have been adapted for performance on theorbo, possibly by Antonio Naldi, whom the composer Cavalieri credited with inventing the instrument; its use in the Florentine *intermedi* is the first known. More than in Luzzaschi's music, the embellishment includes a number of figures whose rhythmic diversity reflects Baroque than Renaissance ideals of melodic decoration. For example, the rising dotted figure at the opening (g″–a″–b♭″) is an upward slide of the type that Caccini called an *intonazione* (see below). In measures 2 and 6, the eighth-note motion is sharpened by dotted rhythms in both long-short and short-long patterns. Perhaps most surprising of all is the eighth rest in measure 13, which cuts off what seems to be the beginning of a written-out trill (e♭″–f″). The interruption of such a standard ornament is highly unusual. A dramatic gesture, it may be a bit of text painting on the word *acqueta* (cease)—although the same word is immediately repeated and sung to a climactic melisma (mm. 15–17).

Caccini

A more decisive break with the past can be seen in the music of Giulio Caccini. Together with Peri (1561–1633), Caccini is usually credited with composing

---

[8]*Rappresentatione di anima et di corpo* (The drama of the soul and the body), published in Rome 1600. On Baroque oratorio, see Chapters 7 and 9.

the first operas; each published a setting of Rinuccini's *Euridice*, Caccini in December 1600, Peri two months later. Both musicians had previously participated in the Florentine *intermedi* of 1589, each serving not only as composer but as singer. But despite their common interest in reviving what they understood to be the musical style of Greek antiquity, they became rivals, disputing the "invention" of recitative and of opera. Peri had clearly preceded Caccini in the composition of musical drama, for his short pastoral *Dafne* had been performed at Florence in 1598 and 1599.[9] Later, when Caccini was engaged to perform in Peri's *Euridice*, he insisted on substituting his own music for portions of the work, which evidently became the core of his complete setting.

In many respects the operas of Caccini and Peri, composed for princely gatherings at Florence, had more in common with the old *intermedio* than with later opera. By the same token, the monodic songs that Caccini and others began to publish during the early years of the seventeenth century clearly drew on the same traditions as the works by Luzzaschi and Cavalieri discussed above. Yet when Caccini published his own first collection of vocal compositions, in 1602, he gave it the ostentatious title *Le nuove musiche*: literally, The New Musics. Some of its contents had been in circulation for a number of years, and a few songs might have been initially composed as polyphonic madrigals, not unlike those of Luzzaschi. Nevertheless, as published the work consists entirely of monodies for voice and instrumental accompaniment, the latter taking the form of a basso continuo part, notated as a figured bass. Caccini might originally have accompanied himself, realizing the continuo part on a theorbo or on the harp or the *lira da braccio*, both of which he is also known to have played.[10] In any case, the musical style of the songs is significantly different from that seen in the examples above.

Le nuove musiche

Caccini's collection is distinguished by its introduction to the reader, in which the composer sets forth his claim of having invented a new style that has been taken up by "the most famous singers in Italy, both male and female." More importantly, he offers a theoretical justification for the new style and explains certain aspects of his manner of singing.[11] Referring to the ancient Greek philosopher Plato, Caccini claims that monody is uniquely suited to meeting

---

[9]Peri composed *Dafne* in collaboration with the Florentine composer and fellow Camerata member Jacopo Corsi (1561–1602); the music is mostly lost, but Rinuccini's text survives.

[10]The *lira da braccio* was a bowed string instrument used in the Renaissance and early Baroque especially to accompany monodic singing. Distinct from both the viol and the violin, it also existed in a larger form known as the *lirone*. The latter, especially, can be heard in recent recordings of early Baroque vocal music.

[11]Translations of Caccini's introduction can be found in Oliver Strunk, *Source Readings in Music History*, ed. Leo Treitler (New York: Norton, 1998), 608–617 (selections, trans. Margaret Murata) and in H. Wiley Hitchcock's modern edition of *Le nuove musiche* (Madison, Wis.: A-R Editions, 1970).

the requirement that vocal music should set forth its text in a clear and effective manner; this had been a doctrine enunciated within the Florentine Camerata. Caccini criticizes other singers' use of improvised embellishments, which sometimes obscure the text. Yet he also describes various types of ornament that he uses in his own singing to intensify the effects of certain words.

Some of these ornaments are written out in Caccini's music. Others are to be added by the singer at appropriate moments. A number of Caccini's written-out decorations are identical to ones used by Luzzaschi and Cavalieri. Among these are the trill with closing turn and the upward slide (seen in Examples 3.1 and 3.2); Caccini's names for these were *groppo* and *intonazione*, respectively, terms that continued to be used throughout the seventeenth century. Unwritten devices mentioned by Caccini include various types of dynamic swell (*esclamazione*), used for expressive purposes on sustained notes, and the *trillo*, which despite its name is not a trill but a rapidly repeated note or perhaps an intense type of vibrato, sung most often on the penultimate note of a cadence. Although rarely indicated in notation, these devices must have been in wide use among singers by 1600.

Caccini's preface was only the first of many important Baroque writings on vocal performance practice.[12] Any such treatise applies to a particular style and repertory; there never was any one type of "Baroque" vocal technique or method of interpretation. Caccini's preface is especially relevant to Italian secular music of around 1600, including early opera, and to seventeenth-century German music written in imitation of it. But his advice is of little relevance to contemporary French music or to eighteenth-century vocal works.

Sfogava con le stelle

Caccini's *Le nuove musiche*, like the early musical dramas by Peri, Cavalieri, and himself, already contains two distinct types of monody that we recognize as recitative and aria, respectively. Caccini himself describes them as arias and madrigals. The arias are **strophic**: songs in which essentially the same music is repeated for several stanzas, or strophes, of poetry. Polyphonic settings of such poems, known as *canzonette*, were common in the late Renaissance. In principle, both the poetry and the music of Caccini's arias are simpler and more regular than those of his madrigals, which are through-composed. But in practice, Caccini usually varies the subsequent stanzas of the arias, sometimes in very elaborate ways. Both types of aria played an important role in early opera (see Chapter 4) and, although used with diminishing frequency in later Baroque opera, continued to be composed as independent songs.

---

[12]Later examples include the *Remarques curieuses sur l'art de bien chanter* (Paris, 1668) by Bénigne de Bacilly, a French musician of the mid-seventeenth century, and Pier Francesco Tosi's *Opinioni de'cantori antichi, e moderni* (Bologna, 1723), an influential work that was translated into English and German. Both works are available in modern editions; see the bibliography. Particularly useful is Julianne Baird's translation of the German version of Tosi's treatise by Johann Friedrich Agricola, a pupil of Bach.

The madrigals are through-composed settings of free poetry. In this they resemble earlier polyphonic madrigals, but as monodies they naturally differ in many other respects. One of the madrigals, *Sfogava con le stelle* (anthology, Selection 5), is to a text by Rinuccini.[13] The music is printed on just two staves: the upper staff is notated in treble clef but might have been composed originally for Caccini's own performance (he was a virtuoso bass singer); the lower staff is a figured bass. Caccini avoids both the imitative counterpoint and the exaggerated chromaticism found in many polyphonic madrigals of the period. The vocal part is predominantly syllabic, with an irregular melodic line and declamatory rhythm meant to reflect the speaking voice. High or long notes are used to accentuate important syllables—notably the exclamation "o" (m. 6), just as in Luzzaschi's *O Primavera*. Generally, however, Caccini aims at a more "speaking" approach to declamation, setting whole series of syllables to simple repeated notes. Such writing would be extremely important throughout the Baroque.

Such passages (mm. 1, 12, etc.) can be described as **recitative**: an imitation of speech for solo voice and accompaniment, characterized by declamatory rhythm, a relatively simple melodic line, and largely syllabic treatment of the text. Recitative is sometimes of limited musical interest, but its purpose is to permit a vivid recitation of the words, and it makes all the more dramatic those moments in which the voice breaks into more florid or expressive singing. This happens twice in the present work, in two long melismas that mark the ends of the first and second halves, respectively (mm. 15 and 26–27). Dramatic contrasts in singing style would be an important resource for Monteverdi, who took up the monodic style a few years later.

The harmony of *Sfogava* is deceptively simple. Cadences are limited to what we would call four full (or perfect) cadences on the tonic G (measures 5, 16, 21, and 28) and several half cadences on the dominant D (measures 8, 12). Moreover, the first two segments of the work (mm. 1–5a and 5b–16) share the same basic shape, the vocal line ascending from g' to d'' and then returning to g'. Yet what might have been bland is made striking and expressive by variations in harmony, rhythm, and pacing. The second segment of the work (mm. 5b–16, corresponding to lines 3–12 of the text) is far longer than the first, and it concludes with the first of the two long melismas (on *ardori*, "flames"—an instance of word painting as well as word emphasis). Each ascent to d'' up to this point is harmonized by what we would call the relative major: chords of B♭ major in measures 3, 6, and 13. But the final section *begins* with the note d'' in the vocal part, which then ascends further, by a poignant half step to $e♭''$ (the highest note yet) on the significant word *pietosa* ("merciful," m. 19).

Like Gesualdo, Caccini repeats the last two lines of the text as a refrain, but the repetition is not literal. The final words are repeated yet again in the second melismatic phrase, which echoes the one on *ardori*. But whereas the latter is harmonized by chords of G minor, the madrigal ends largely with major

---

[13]A polyphonic setting of a slightly different version of the poem appears in Monteverdi's Fourth Book of Madrigals, published two years later. Another, by Salamone Rossi (see Chapter 12), published in the same year as Caccini's setting, appears to quote from the latter.

harmonies, the voice rising to e♮'' in measure 26. Perhaps the unexpected brightness of these major chords is a symbol of hopefulness felt by the "lovesick man" of the poetry, whose words are being recited here.

During the following decades many publications comparable to *Le nuove musiche* appeared. Among the composers to take up the style was Caccini's daughter Francesca (1587–after 1640), who published her own collection of solo songs in 1618. Another was the Sicilian composer Sigismondo d'India (ca. 1582–by 1629), active in northern Italy, who published five collections of monodies and duets with continuo. During the same period, composers in France and England were publishing songs for voice and lute that resemble Caccini's in their monophonic texture and, sometimes, their use of styles that resemble recitiative. Yet in most of these works, such as the songs of the English lutenist John Dowland (?1563–1626), the instrumental part is still fully written out; when Dowland's son Robert included two of Caccini's madrigals in an English anthology (*A Musicall Banquet*, 1610), he included a realized lute accompaniment, since the Italian convention of basso continuo had not yet reached England. Even d'India published no fewer than eight books of polyphonic madrigals. But the techniques that Caccini and other Italians developed in their monodic works would prove far more useful for the new genres of opera and cantata that emerged in the early seventeetn century.

CHAPTER 4

MONTEVERDI AND EARLY BAROQUE MUSICAL DRAMA

Opera, oratorio, and ballet were the three most important types of Baroque musical drama. Each emerged around 1600; opera and ballet developed from the sixteenth-century *intermedio* and remained closely linked throughout the following two centuries. Both differed in important respects from their later counterparts; in particular, ballets generally included singing as well as dancing and thus closely resembled operas, into which they were often incorporated. The next few chapters trace the history of Baroque operatic and balletic writing, as well as the closely related form of the cantata. Oratorio, a form of unstaged sacred musical drama, will be taken up in Chapters 7 and 9.

CLAUDIO MONTEVERDI

By 1610 Claudio Monteverdi was clearly the central figure in the new musical practices that were considered in Chapter 3. Although he seems to have had few pupils as such, his works were studied and imitated throughout the seventeenth century. We have already examined one of his polyphonic madrigals in the context of the late sixteenth century (see Chapter 2); now we shall consider his output after 1600.

Born in the northern Italian city of Cremona in 1567, by 1592 Monteverdi was working at the nearby court of Mantua (see Box 4.1).[1] He remained there, with one or two interruptions, until 1612; a year later he became *maestro di cappella* (director of church music) at St. Mark's Basilica in Venice, an appointment he held until his death in 1643 (see Fig. 4.1). St. Mark's was, in essence, the official church of the government of Venice, at the time the leading cultural center of Italy and arguably of all Europe; hence, in attaining his position Monteverdi had reached the pinnacle of success as a musician.

Monteverdi's initial appointment at Mantua had been as a string player, and many of his later compositions include idiomatic instrumental interludes and

---

[1]Cremona is best known today as the home of the great violin maker Antonio Stradivari (1644–1737). Both Cremona and Mantua were early centers of violin making and playing.

Box 4.1

Claudio Monteverdi (1567–1643)

1567. Born at Cremona in central northern Italy (about one hundred miles west of Venice); studies with Marc'Antonio Ingegneri, *maestro di cappella* at Cremona cathedral and composer of madrigals.

1582–84. Publishes books of motets, sacred madrigals, and canzonettas (polyphonic strophic songs).

1587. Publishes his First Book of Madrigals.

1590–92. Publishes two more madrigal books; enters service of duke of Mantua (between Cremona and Venice). Some works influenced by Giaches de Wert, *maestro di cappella* (1535–96).

1595–99. Travels in Austria, Hungary, and Flanders (Spanish Netherlands) with the duke. Marriage (1599) to court singer Claudia Caffaneo.

1601–5. Becomes *maestro di cappella* at Mantua (1601). Publishes Fourth and Fifth Books of Madrigals, both criticized by Artusi; Book 5 contains his first reply.

1607. First version of *Orfeo* performed at Mantua in February (lost); revised version published in 1609. *Scherzi musicali* published in July, containing his brother Cesare's reply to Artusi. His wife Claudia dies (September). Begins work on *Arianna*.

1608. *Arianna* performed at Mantua; lost except for Arianna's Lament (published 1623).

1610. Marian Vespers published.

1613. Becomes *maestro di cappella* at St. Mark's, Venice; numerous performances of sacred music, but continues to compose operatic works and ballets, some lost.

1630–31. Plague at Venice; reduction in musical activities followed by a large-scale Mass of Thanksgiving. Monteverdi enters the priesthood.

1632, 1638, 1640. *Scherzi musicali* (second volume), Book Eight of Madrigals, and *Selve morale* published.

1639–40. Begins providing operas for Venetian public theaters: a revival of *Arianna* as well as *Il ritorno d'Ulisse* and *Le nozze d'Enea in Lavinia* (lost).

1642–43. First performance of *L'incoronazione di Poppea*; Monteverdi's death in Venice.

1649, 1651. *Messa et psalmi* (sacred works) and Ninth Book of Madrigals published.

---

dances that reflect his string-playing experience. Yet not a single purely instrumental composition by Monteverdi survives. Like most of his sixteenth-century predecessors, he apparently directed his energies solely to the production of vocal music, albeit vocal music of a constantly changing nature. As with Haydn, Stravinsky, and other composers active during transitional periods in music history, Monteverdi's works cover an enormous variety of genres and styles. Thus

Figure 4.1 Claudio Monteverdi, engraved portrait on the title page of Giovanni Battista Marinoni, *Fiori poetici* (Venice, 1644), a memorial collection of poetry issued shortly after the composer's death. The depiction of numerous instruments, some real, some fanciful, is symbolic of Monteverdi's occupation as a musician and is not intended to represent an actual performing ensemble.

it is difficult to find common stylistic elements among all his many compositions. Almost invariably, however, his works show sensitivity to both the form and the content of their texts. Not only did Monteverdi use all of the traditional means of musical rhetoric, but he was also constantly inventing new devices to render each composition an imaginative and dramatic presentation of its words.

Monteverdi's Works

Monteverdi's surviving compositions from Mantua include his first five books of polyphonic madrigals, published from 1587 to 1605. These madrigals, with the exception of several in Book 5, use the traditional all-vocal scoring.[2] Already in Books 4 and 5, however, Monteverdi was employing those innovations of the *seconda pratica* that had aroused the ire of Artusi. Moreover, the last six madrigals of Book 5 include basso continuo parts, and one contains two interludes for strings, signaling Monteverdi's expansion of the madrigal to a mixed

---

[2]In later editions of Books 4 and 5, Monteverdi added optional continuo parts for all the madrigals.

vocal-instrumental genre. By 1607 Monteverdi had also adopted the monodic style of Peri and Caccini, employing it through much of his opera *Orfeo*, which is recognized as the first great example of such a work.

At Mantua Monteverdi also composed sacred music. Some of it is in the conservative polyphonic idiom that Monteverdi called the first practice, essentially equivalent to what was later termed the *stile antico*. At the same time, however, he was writing motets for solo voice and continuo in the new monodic style. His best-known sacred works from this period are those published in 1610 as part of a large-scale collection of music for vespers (the evening office service) dedicated to the Virgin Mary.[3]

Monteverdi arrived in Venice as *maestro di cappella* shortly after the death of Giovanni Gabrieli (see Chapter 7). Although the latter had held a different position (organist), Monteverdi effectively succeeded him as the principal musician in the leading European musical center. As music director at the city's most important church, Monteverdi was involved in a busy schedule of sacred performances, to which he contributed his own music. The latter included both small monodic works and large polychoral works resembling those of Gabrieli. But probably his most important creative activity remained in the area of secular music, particularly music for the theater.

Monteverdi's theatrical works included ballets and operas, some written for commissions from aristocratic patrons outside Venice (including Mantua). Unfortunately, much of this output is lost, although a number of ballets and related works were published in his later books of madrigals, and two of the three operas that Monteverdi composed near the end of his career survive: *Il ritorno d'Ulisse in patria* (Ulysses' homecoming) and *L'incoronazione di Poppea* (The coronation of Poppea).[4] Unlike his first operas, commissioned for princely celebrations, these were written for the public opera houses that had begun to open in Venice in the late 1630s. The public nature of Monteverdi's late operas helps explain their considerable differences in style and scoring from the earlier *Orfeo*. An additional factor must also be the evolution of Monteverdi's style, which unfortunately cannot be traced in detail because of the loss of much of his previous output for the theater and the difficulty of dating that which does remain.

During his late years Monteverdi also published several large collections containing mainly earlier works. It is primarily through these publications that we can follow the development of his dramatic style. Among these collections is the Eighth Book of Madrigals (1638), which was actually an anthology of diverse compositions, including several short stage works. Another is the *Selva morale* (literally, "Spiritual forest") of 1640, a collection of sacred works, some

---

[3]Often described today as the "Vespers of 1610," this monumental work actually includes a mass in addition to settings of many of the traditional psalms and other texts for vespers; it has been published in several modern editions and numerous recordings.

[4]It appears that the aging Monteverdi either failed to complete *Poppea* or intentionally left portions of its score, especially the final scene (with its famous concluding duet), to one or two other composers whose identity remains controversial.

of them parodies of earlier secular compositions.[5] Two more large anthologies followed after his death.

CLAUDIO MONTEVERDI'S *ORFEO*

Monteverdi's opera *Orfeo* (Orpheus; anthology, Selection 6) is rightly regarded as one of the pivotal works in music history. In it the leading composer of the time turned to what was then regarded as the most exciting recent innovation in European music. First performed at Mantua in 1607, during the composer's lifetime it was actually overshadowed in fame by his opera of the following year, *Arianna*. Of the latter, unfortunately, only one portion, the famous Lament of Arianna, survives.[6] Both the subject matter and the music of *Orfeo* reveal the exalted intentions of the composer and the poet Alessandro Striggio.[7] In ancient Greek mythology, Orpheus was the greatest of musicians, challenging the gods with his ability to sing and play. For Renaissance and Baroque artists he was a symbol of the power of music, and he continued to be a favorite subject of opera throughout the Baroque and beyond.[8] Box 4.2 contains an outline of the work, including a synopsis of the action and a list of the major roles.

Early Opera

Opera is characterized by two basic features: (1) the entire text or **libretto** is sung, and (2) the plot is acted onstage by the singers, who represent specific characters. In addition, *Orfeo* has the following features typical of most Baroque operatic works: (a) the music includes a variety of types and genres; (b) the text and plot are drawn from Classical antiquity or ancient history, involve noble and divine figures, and ostensibly point a moral lesson; and (c) the action incorporates a variety of special scenic effects, including the appearance of supernatural beings who descend from heaven or otherwise come into view of the audience by means of elaborate mechanical devices—for instance, airborne chariots suspended from the ceiling by complex systems of ropes and pulleys (see Fig. 3.3). These mechanical contrivances sometimes required designs by the leading engineers of the day. Thanks to such special effects, some Baroque operas were as much visual spectacles as musical events. In addition, they employed virtuoso singers who became the most highly paid musicians of the period.

---

[5]"Parody" in this case refers to the substitution of new sacred words for those of an existing secular composition, a common practice throughout the Baroque.

[6]Arianna's lament, a monody in recitative style for soprano and continuo, was so famous that Monteverdi eventually published it as a separate work (Venice, 1623); by then he had also published his own arrangement of it for five voices and continuo in his Sixth Book of Madrigals (Venice, 1614).

[7]Striggio, son of a sixteenth-century madrigal composer, was a friend and frequent correspondent of Monteverdi's, and a member of the Accademia degli Invaghiti that saw the first performance of *Orfeo*.

[8]Later musical settings of the Orpheus myth were written by the seventeenth-century composers Luigi Rossi and Marc-Antoine Charpentier and, in the eighteenth century, by Christoph Willibald Gluck and Haydn.

Box 4.2

Monteverdi: *Orfeo*

Full title: *L'Orfeo: Favola in musica* (Orpheus: A tale in music).
Libretto by Alessandro Striggio, after various models, notably *Euridice*
by Ottavio Rinuccini and ultimately the *Metamorphoses* of the ancient
Roman poet Ovid.
First performed in Mantua, 1607, commissioned by Prince Francesco
Gonzaga for the Accademia degli Invaghiti. The music for this first
version is lost; what survives is the revised version (with happy
ending) published in 1609 and reprinted in a new edition
in 1615.
The work consists of a prologue and five acts performed without a break.
The anthology's Selection 6 comprises portions of Act 2.

Characters

Orfeo (tenor), the mythical singer and symbol of musicians—by far the
most prominent part

Euridice (soprano), a wood nymph (dryad) whom Orfeo is to marry

Sylvia, referred to in the score as Messenger (soprano), one of Euridice's
companions, who witnesses her death and narrates it to Orfeo

Music (soprano), a personification of music who sings the prologue

Hope (soprano), another personification who leads Orfeo to the entrance
to the underworld

Charon (bass), a supernatural being who ferries dead souls across the River
Styx to the underworld

Pluto (bass), god and ruler of the underworld

Proserpine (soprano), queen of the underworld

Apollo (tenor), god of the arts, medicine, and prophecy, who appears at
the end of the opera to take Orfeo up into heaven

A chorus of nymphs and shepherds, several of whom sing substantial solos

SYNOPSIS

Following a brief instrumental introduction, a prologue sung by Music sets the
scene: the fields of Thrace in what is now northern Greece. Thracian nymphs and
shepherds celebrate Orfeo's impending marriage to Euridice in Act 1. In Act 2
Orfeo, having briefly departed, rejoins the celebration, initiating a series of arias.
These are interrupted by the news that Euridice has died of a snakebite. After a
moment of shock and indecision, Orfeo vows to bring her back from the dead,
and the chorus laments her death.

In Act 3 Orfeo enters the underworld (home of the dead) after charming Charon with his music and passing over the river Styx. Pluto's wife, Proserpine, persuades him to grant Orfeo's wish in Act 4—if Orfeo can pass a test of self-resolve. But Orfeo fails; as he leads Euridice away from the dead, he cannot help looking at her and thereby loses her. In the original Act 5, Orfeo then returned to Thrace and was killed by worshipers of the god Bacchus, as in the ancient myth. In the surviving version of the opera, Apollo consoles Orfeo by taking him up into heaven.

Baroque operas also tended to require lavish sums for costumes, lighting, and the machinery required to transport figures on- and offstage.

The earliest operas were commissioned and produced for specific occasions, such as royal weddings, just as were the *intermedi*. This was true of Monteverdi's *Orfeo*, and it remained so through much of the Baroque in many places. For example, at Rome during the 1620s a number of popes and members of their families became regular patrons of court opera, as it is known; not surprisingly, the operas performed there employed sacred as well as secular subjects. Thus, in 1632 Cardinal Francesco Barberini, nephew of Pope Urban VIII, oversaw the production of the opera *Il Sant'Alessio* (Saint Alexis) by the Roman composer Stefano Landi (1587–1639).

The first commercial opera theater opened in Venice in 1637, and within a few years several different opera theaters were competing there with one another. The leading composers included Monteverdi and his presumed student Francesco Cavalli, who continued to write operas for Venetian performance into the 1670s. Yet the expense of opera was such that elsewhere it remained for a long time confined largely to specially commissioned performances at wealthy courts; commercial theaters like those of Venice opened at Hamburg, London, and other cities only in the later seventeenth and eighteenth centuries. Nevertheless, by midcentury opera had been brought to other countries by means of royal commissions for special works by Italian composers: Cavalli and Luigi Rossi (1598–1653) in Paris, Marc' Antonio Cesti (1623–69) in Vienna. Italian opera—that is, opera with Italian-language text—predominated even outside Italy. But certain cities, notably Paris and Hamburg, saw the establishment of their own distinctive traditions of opera in the local languages.

In many respects, *Orfeo* differs from later operas in its proximity to the tradition of Renaissance theatrical works such as the *intermedio*. It was not composed for public performance but was specially commissioned for the Accademia degli Invaghiti, a learned assembly of Mantuan aristocrats. Its first performance was not in a public theater but simply in a room specially prepared for the occasion. The room, to be sure, was presumably a large one in a noble palace. The production of *Orfeo* at Mantua was a unique event, using court musicians plus outside soloists specially engaged for the performance, rather than a dedicated opera troupe. With the rise of permanent commercial opera companies during the 1630s and 1640s, the nature of Italian opera was considerably altered. The expensive choruses—which included dancers as well as singers—were dispensed with, as was the large group of accompanying instruments employed in *Orfeo*. Outside Venice, the tradition of aristocratically sponsored opera continued, notably at Paris. There the operas of Lully (discussed in Chapter 6) constituted in some respects a more direct continuation of the tradition begun by *Orfeo* than did later Italian opera.

Orfeo

Orfeo's publication in score in 1609 was a rarity, a mark of both its commissioned nature and the importance attached to it. Although full scores of a few other early operas also appeared in print, until the nineteenth century only portions of most operas were published, if they appeared in print at all.[9] Consequently, most surviving Baroque operas remain in manuscript to this day, and they present particularly difficult problems of performance practice. Modern productions, once rare, have become more frequent, although performances using genuinely historical staging and performance techniques remain few and far between, especially in America. Fortunately, the printed score of *Orfeo* specifies details about the original production that were not usually included in musical manuscripts or prints of the time. It calls for what was then an unusually large instrumental ensemble, with varied scoring for different sections. Such information has been invaluable in modern reconstructions of early Baroque opera, even if *Orfeo* was an atypical example.

Although comprising five acts, the work is shorter than later operas—it contains less than two hours of music—and it was presumably performed without a break. As in later Baroque operas, the curtain, if any, would have risen at the beginning of the work and stayed up throughout. Thus scene changes would have taken place in full view of the audience, as at the end of Act 2, when the scene shifts from the plains of Greece to the shores of the underworld. Such transformations were accomplished through cleverly devised stage machinery; the resulting visual effects were among the great attractions of early opera. The accompanying instrumental music lent a magical aura to such devices.

The brevity of *Orfeo* meant that only a few characters—chiefly Orfeo himself—could be fully drawn. Moreover, the action had to be delineated through bold strokes of music and poetry. For example, the main event in Act 2 is the arrival of the messenger, who brings news of Euridice's death at the center of the act.[10] This event marks a turning point not only in the action but also in the music, which changes in emotional character, instrumentation, and style. The nature

---

[9]Exceptionally, full scores were issued later in the seventeenth century for operas by Lully and a number of other French composers. More typical of later opera was the publication of favorite arias and instrumental numbers, as was the case for many eighteenth-century examples by such composers as Handel (see Chapter 8). On the other hand, throughout the Baroque, complete librettos were customarily printed so that listeners could follow the text in performance or study it at their leisure, as remains true of opera today.

[10]The messenger scene, used to avoid the depiction of death onstage, was a convention borrowed from ancient Greek tragedy.

of this change becomes clear if we consider the different types of music heard in the course of the opera.

Types of Music in *Orfeo*

Four types of music can be distinguished in *Orfeo:* (1) monodic singing, (2) ensemble singing, (3) choral singing, and (4) instrumental passages. Monody includes recitative as well as aria; in *Orfeo,* both are accompanied by basso continuo alone, although later works would involve more elaborate types of scoring. Even in *Orfeo,* Monteverdi specifies different instruments to realize the continuo part for certain passages or characters; for instance, a small organ with wood pipes joins the traditional theorbo to accompany the messenger and is later used to accompany Orfeo's lament. In later operas one finds various types of recitative—simple (or *secco*), accompanied, and arioso (see Box 4.3)—but clear distinctions between these types emerged only in the course of the seventeenth century, and Monteverdi's recitative is very fluid in style. At its simplest, it involves straightforward recitation: a syllabic vocal part characterized by numerous repeated notes of short duration (mostly eighths) and a slow-moving bass. Because this type of music is meant to respond to the individual words of the text, there are no recurring melodic or rhythmic patterns; important words may be marked by abrupt changes in harmony, sharp dissonances, or sudden leaps or pauses. As in Caccini's madrigals, the style can broaden out into more lyrical singing involving longer note values and a more active bass to mark important words or phrases (as at the end of Orfeo's lament, mm. 261–64 in anthology, Selection 6b).

Arias, on the other hand, involve regular rhythmic and melodic patterns in both voice and continuo, and the latter moves at a pace much closer to that of the vocal part. Many arias in early opera are in triple meter (almost never used for Italian recitative), and in *Orfeo* they are usually strophic, like the arias of Caccini and other monodists. These arias are usually short and dancelike, unlike those of later opera, reflecting their origin in the *canzonetta* of the late Renaissance, a type of strophic song.[11] Although prominent in Act 2 of *Orfeo,* arias form a relatively minor component of the later acts, which consist primarily of recitative.

Only in the course of the seventeenth century did the aria become the main component of Italian opera, and in the process it changed drastically in nature, losing its strophic form and becoming a vehicle for virtuoso display by the chief singers. The one common element of arias throughout the Baroque is that their texts are relatively short—often just four lines to a strophe—and these follow simple but regular rhyme schemes (such as ABAB) as well as equally regular metrical schemes (e.g., lines of eight syllables). In this they contrast with the surrounding recitative, whose poetry tends to fall into

---

[11]Whether actual dancing accompanied the arias in *Orfeo* is uncertain, although the opera concludes with a purely instrumental number (called a *moresca*) that seems to call for a choreographed dance.

Box 4.3

Types of Music in Baroque Opera and Cantata

VOCAL (FOR VOICES AND INSTRUMENTS)

Recitative

Music composed in imitation of speech, used chiefly for dialogue, narration, and action. Its *text* usually lacks regular rhyme or metrical schemes; Italian recitative texts usually comprise lines alternating irregularly between seven and eleven syllables in length. Its *music* is relatively simple but irregular, avoiding recurring patterns, melismas, and sustained notes; usually syllabic in style, the music of recitative is based on speech and incorporates numerous repeated notes and other elements suggesting recitation. Words of the text are rarely repeated. The various types of recitative described below can already be identified in the earliest examples of monody from around 1600. But early monody tends to shift fluidly from one type to another (as in Monteverdi's *Orfeo* and *Combattimento*), and therefore examples illustrating these terms have been taken from later works.

Simple recitative (*recitativo semplice*). The usual type of recitative in Baroque works, scored for solo voice and basso continuo. The term is applied especially in music of the later Baroque, when the type of recitative used for dialogue and action becomes notably simpler in style than the more ornate varieties described below. Sometimes described misleadingly as *secco* (dry) recitative. Example: Handel, *Orlands*, Act 1, scene 9 (anthology, selection 18b).

Accompanied recitative (*recitativo accompagnato*). Recitative accompanied not only by basso continuo but by other instruments, most often strings; usually the musical style is somewhat more elaborate than in simple recitative. It is used for speeches of special importance. Example: J. S. Bach, Cantata 127 (selection 20), movement 4, measures 1–13.

Arioso. Literally, "in aria style"; most often used for a passage within a recitative in which the musical style broadens to approach that of an aria, for instance, through the use of melismas or sustained notes. Arioso is often used to underline individual words or longer parts of the text that are of special importance. Example: J. S. Bach, Cantata 127 (selection 20), movement 4, measures 14–20.

Aria

Song or songlike music, used in later Baroque opera especially to provide the climax of a scene, in which one character expresses an emotional reaction to the preceding events or dialogue and then (usually) exits; in early opera used more freely, in rapid alternation with recitative. An aria *text* is relatively short, with regular rhyme and metrical schemes (lines typically of four, six, or eight syllables), often two or more strophes or stanzas. Its *music* is relatively elaborate, with songlike melody often incorporating melismas and sustained notes, and rhythm often based on that of a dance. Especially after 1650 the music often calls for substantial virtuosity and may include independent instrumental parts, each line of text is likely to be repeated several times, and the aria may have a complex formal design. Baroque aria texts can be set for ensembles (duets, trios, etc.), but the great majority of settings are for soloists.

Strophic aria. An aria whose text comprises two or more stanzas having the same poetic structure, each sung to the same or similar music. (If the music of successive strophes is a variation of that of the first strophe, one speaks of strophic variation form). Strophic arias occur frequently in early opera but grow increasingly rare after 1650. Example: *Orfeo*, Act 2 (selection 6a, mm. 25–54 including ritornello; see below).

Ternary (da capo) aria. An aria whose text comprises two stanzas, often expressing contrasting ideas or emotions; the first stanza, with its music, is repeated after the second has been sung. The da capo aria became by far the most common type of aria in Italian opera of the later Baroque; ranging enormously in length, expressive effect, and degree of technical virtuosity, in opera after 1700 or so da capo arias make up the great majority of the music. Example: Alessandro Scarlatti, "Fresche brine" (Selection 11a).

Chorus

Music sung by the ensemble of four or more vocal parts that usually participated in early opera and in later French Baroque opera. The music may range from brief interjections to extended settings in madrigal style or in aria form. Choruses are relatively rare in Italian opera after 1650; when the effect of a chorus was needed, the solo singers might join together to form a choir (especially at the end of an opera). Example: *Orfeo*, Act 2 (Selection 6b, mm. 216–47).

INSTRUMENTAL

Overture

An independent instrumental composition used to open a dramatic work. The term is most appropriate for the relatively lengthy overtures of eighteenth-century Italian operas, which can be substantial works in several movements and as such were precursors of the Classical symphony. The relatively brief opening instrumental music of early opera is more often termed a *sinfonia* or, in Monteverdi's *Orfeo*, a *toccata*. The **French overture** is a special type of opening instrumental number used chiefly in French Baroque opera but also by Handel and other composers (see Chapter 8). Example: Lully, overture to *Armide* (selection 12a).

Ritornello

Originally, an instrumental passage that alternates with the vocal (texted) sections of an aria. Early examples may be musically separate from the arias' vocal passages or even optional (as in Scarlatti's "Fresche brine"), but after 1650 the ritornello is increasingly integrated with the vocal passages and may be repeated several times (in whole or in part) within the body of an aria. In the eighteenth century the term is also applied to passages in concertos and other instrumental works scored for the full ensemble and alternating with solo episodes. Example: Handel, *Orlando,* "Oh care parolette" (Selection 18a, second part), measures 1–9a, 19b–22a, 34–39a.

Sinfonia

General term for instrumental music in Italian Baroque opera, most appropriately used for transitional music played during scene changes but sometimes applied to overtures and even ritornellos. Example: *Orfeo,* opening of Act 2 (Selection 6a, mm. 1–12).

irregular combinations of seven- and eleven-syllable lines, usually without any regular rhyme scheme.

Segments of an opera involving more than one solo singer can be referred to as **ensembles.** Most of the duets and other ensembles in *Orfeo* take the form of short dancelike settings of strophic aria texts. But within a few years Monteverdi and other composers were regularly incorporating more elaborate ensembles into their operas. Duets became an especially important type, both as an operatic ensemble and as an independent form; Monteverdi would include more than a dozen such works (for two voices and continuo) in his Seventh Book of Madrigals, published in 1619, and a famous duet occurs at the end of the opera *Poppea.*[12]

The use of the **chorus** in early opera reflects that in ancient Greek drama. There the chorus always represents a specific body of characters—groups of citizens, soldiers, and so forth—that participate in and comment on the action, remaining onstage throughout. For the Greeks, the word *chorus* referred to an ensemble that danced as well as sang. In Baroque opera these functions were usually divided between different groups of performers, although all singers would have had some training in dance, which was considered essential not only to proper stage movement but to polite social behavior.

Baroque choruses, whether in opera or in other genres, did not necessarily involve multiple singers on each part; indeed, single voices would become the norm in Italian opera. Nevertheless, a chorus differs from an ensemble in that it represents a homogeneous group of people rather than individuals. In Act 2 of *Orfeo,* choral singing is used for the nymphs and shepherds gathered to celebrate Orfeo's impending marriage; they present one stanza of a strophic aria

---

[12]Monteverdi probably was not the composer of the duet in *Poppea* (see below).

and three repetitions of a lament that is first sung monodically by the messenger. The choral restatements of this lament are therefore polyphonic arrangements of recitative—odd by later standards of vocal scoring, but common at the beginning of the seventeenth century.[13] Some of Monteverdi's polyphonic madrigals of a few years earlier had likewise included declamatory passages close to recitative; conversely, in *Orfeo* the chorus's restatement of the lament (at the end of Selection 6) is extended to become, in effect, a short polyphonic madrigal.

Ritornellos and sinfonias form the bulk of the purely instrumental music in *Orfeo*. A **ritornello** is an instrumental passage that is repeated (in whole or in part) at one or more points in the course of an aria. In early opera, ritornellos usually occur before or after each stanza of a strophic aria. In *Orfeo* Monteverdi assigns different instrumental ensembles to the ritornellos for the various arias; the vocal passages themselves, however, are accompanied by continuo alone, a pattern typical of early opera.

Most of the remaining instrumental passages, including the one that precedes Orfeo's aria at the opening of Act 2, are referred to as **sinfonias**. The term is related to the later word *symphony,* but in Baroque vocal works it can refer to any purely instrumental passage. Such music served to introduce scenes or even whole works—as in the overture—and to accompany stage action or changes of scene.[14] The style and scoring of sinfonias usually reflect the character of the music and action that follow. In *Orfeo* the sinfonia for Orfeo's first aria is in the same key and uses the same dance rhythm as the aria itself. It sets the tone not only for Orfeo's aria but for the series of dancelike arias that follows. At the end of Act 2 a solemn sinfonia for seven-part brass ensemble and continuo accompanies the shift to the underworld scenes of Act 3.

The instrumentation of *Orfeo* was unusual for the time in its diversity. Despite his focus as a composer on vocal music, as a string player Monteverdi must have known strings and other instruments and their capabilities intimately. The score of *Orfeo* calls for exotic instruments such as *violini piccioli alla francese*—apparently, small violins of a type then associated with French music—and *flautini*, probably small recorders (end-blown flutes). Both are used in the ritornellos of Act 2. Also notable is Monteverdi's use of the term *viola da braccio* to specify the regular members of the violin family, which furnish the ritornellos for Orfeo's second aria in Act 2. The *viola da braccio* group included the **bass violin**, similar to today's cello but somewhat larger and tuned a step lower.

Despite the variety of instrumental colors employed in the sinfonias and ritornellos, the instrumentation of the continuo part is indicated only in a few special passages. Among these is the messenger scene, where a small organ joins the continuo accompaniment for the messenger's speeches, imparting to them a solemn or perhaps otherworldly character. The organ contrasts sharply with the harpsichord and bass violin that accompany the shepherd. Most of the

---

[13]Monteverdi published a polyphonic arrangement of the monodic lament from his next opera, *Arianna*. Some of Caccini's solo madrigals underwent similar arrangements by other composers.

recitative, however, may have been accompanied by nothing more than a single theorbo or chitarrone, the large lute that was the usual accompaniment for Italian song in the early seventeenth century.

Orfeo, Act 2

Act 2 of *Orfeo* opens with an instrumental sinfonia followed by a series of five arias, presented without a break in celebration of Orfeo's arrival on the scene and his impending marriage. The first aria, whose text consists of a single stanza, is for Orfeo himself ("Ecco pur," anthology, Selection 6a, mm. 12b–24). It is followed by an aria of two stanzas for one of the shepherds (not in the anthology). The three succeeding arias include stanzas sung by a pair of shepherds and by the entire assembly of nymphs and shepherds, singing as a chorus in five parts.

As is typical in early opera, the vocal writing of all five arias is primarily syllabic. Each falls into a few short phrases, one for each line of text. Orfeo's opening aria concludes by repeating its first line of text and music, producing a **ternary**, or **da capo**, form that can be symbolized through the letters ABA (mm. 20–24a = 12a–16a). This aria is therefore a miniature example of a type that, in expanded form, would come to dominate later opera. Although this form is of minor significance in Monteverdi's music, by the early eighteenth century the da capo aria had replaced recitative as the main element in Italian opera.[15]

Elsewhere in *Orfeo* are two strophic arias of a different type: the prologue, which consists of an aria for the personification of Music, and Orfeo's aria "Possente spirto" in Act 3. Much longer than the simple arias of Act 2, these are composed in a declamatory style that resembles recitative more than dance music. Instead of repeating exactly the same music for each strophe, successive stanzas are set as variations of the first one—hence the expression **strophic variation** applied to this form. An example of such an aria in Monteverdi's *Combattimento* is considered later in this chapter.[16]

The series of arias at the beginning of Act 2 is rounded off by a short speech, still in aria style, by one of the shepherds ("Mira, deh mira Orfeo," Selection 6b, opening). With the ensuing arrival of the messenger, who announces the death of Euridice, the entire character of the act changes. Although the text setting remains syllabic, the dancelike rhythms and strophic designs of the arias are abandoned in favor of recitative. Monteverdi's recitative displays extraordinary originality, characterizing each role by a particular type of writing. Thus the messenger sings in relatively sustained notes, reflecting her sadness, whereas the shepherd's brief responses to her (e.g., m. 27) are composed of quick, irregular rising and falling lines, suggesting his emotional distress. Orfeo's music is more

---

[14]*Orfeo* opens not with a sinfonia but with a **toccata**. The latter term, usually reserved for a type of keyboard music, is here applied to a fanfare for a five-part ensemble of trumpets doubled by the other instruments.

[15]Whereas Orfeo's entire aria comprises a single four-line poetic stanza, later ternary-form arias usually set two strophes of at least four lines each, repeating the first strophe at the end.

[16]See also the cantata by Barbara Strozzi discussed in Chapter 5.

complex, ranging from the very brief, simple phrases in which he expresses his initial shock at Euridice's death (mm. 66–71, 81–82, 86–87) to the elaborate lament that begins at measure 72.

Monteverdi's recitative makes much use of what he called the second practice. For example, the messenger's opening speech includes an **unprepared dissonance** in measure 17: the voice sings g#' against bass A, neither part having prepared the dissonance by suspending or repeating its note from the previous beat.[17] The unprepared dissonance is a response to the word *acerbo* ("bitter") sung here. The same passage contains an unresolved dissonance—the ninth d/e'' between bass line and voice—on the phrase *ciel avaro* ("cruel heaven," m. 246). Also typical of Monteverdi's recitative are the syncopated rhythms (mm. 19, 23–24), which seem to reflect the messenger's breathlessness in expressing her feelings. These syncopations create additional irregular passing dissonances.[18] Notable as well in this speech are the choppy rhythms and the unusual melodic leaps, including a downward seventh on the interjection *Ahi* ("Ah," mm. 21–22), all further indicative of the messenger's emotional trauma.

A long scene composed primarily of recitative might have seemed formless. But Monteverdi (in collaboration with his librettist Striggio) included here a **refrain:** a recurring passage of text and music, which in this case helps unify the scene. The messenger's opening speech is echoed later by the shepherd and by the chorus (mm. 216–47). The idea, suggested by the choral refrains of ancient Greek tragedy, recurs frequently in seventeenth-century opera.

To some degree, each scene is also unified by a coherent tonal structure that is articulated by what we would call *modulations* from one key to another. In Monteverdi's time one would have spoken of shifts between modes; the modern idea of major and minor tonalities is misleading if these are understood here as being exactly equivalent to the key areas of a movement from a Beethoven symphony, for example. Nevertheless, modern terminology sheds light on the organization of Act 2, whose first part opens in G minor and concludes with Orfeo's second aria ("Vi ricorda i boschi ombrosi," not in anthology) in G major. The shepherd's speech that follows ("Mira, deh mira," opening of Selection 6b) is in C major; thus it and the entry of the messenger (m. 15) in A minor create a tonal contrast to what has come before. The contrast is heightened by the first harmony of the messenger's first speech: what we would call a first-inversion chord of A major. The bass of this chord is C#—a note reached by chromatic motion from the preceding C♮. Later in the scene, when the messenger informs Orfeo of Euridice's death, the harmony passes directly from E major (m. 79) to G minor (m. 80), again with chromatic motion in the bass. Sudden chromatic progressions of this type had been made famous by Gesualdo, whose madrigals use them so frequently that they perhaps lose some of their power. Monteverdi wisely reserves them for the most extreme emotional moments in the opera.

---

[17]The type of unprepared dissonance found here, in which the voice moves by step to a consonant note, is also termed an **appoggiatura.**

[18]See, e.g., the major ninth A/b' between bass and voice in m. 19 and the fourth B/e'' at the end of m. 23. The fourth A/d'' at the beginning of m. 18 is, however, a normal dissonance prepared and resolved by the bass line.

The passages that are described above as being in G minor are notated in Monteverdi's score with a "key signature" of just one flat, not two as we would expect today. This reflects the view at the time that such music belonged to the first, or Dorian, mode, transposed from D to G. So-called "Dorian" notation, with one less flat than we would expect, remained common through the end of the Baroque; Bach still used it in an organ work now referred to, somewhat misleadingly, as the "Dorian" prelude and fugue. Yet the Bach work is fully tonal, and the same could be argued for much of *Orfeo*, despite the presence of modal elements as well. Among the latter are the E-naturals throughout the melody of the opening Sinfonia of Act 2, even as it descends toward the cadence on G in measures 8–12. The cadence itself occurs on a chord of G *major,* yet the raising of the third in a final chord was a convention of the period that does not alter the minor mode of the preceding music.[19] In short, to determine the key of a Baroque work one needs to analyze its tonal structure rather than rely on the key signature or the final sonority.

THE *COMBATTIMENTO DI TANCREDI E CLORINDA*

After *Orfeo* Monteverdi continued for at least a while to compose madrigals and even motets and mass movements in a relatively conservative style. By the time of his Eighth Book of Madrigals (1638), however, the old polyphonic madrigal, with its homogeneous all-vocal scoring, had been replaced by various types of setting for anywhere from one to a dozen or more parts. The latter invariably included a continuo part—hence the expression **continuo madrigal** sometimes used for these works. Frequently there were independent instrumental parts as well. Sometimes the latter merely furnished ritornellos for strophic arias, as in Act 2 of *Orfeo*, but increasingly they performed along with the voices, accompanying them or in some cases participating as equal partners.

In addition, some of Monteverdi's late madrigals are divided into distinct sections, and some contain dialogue and action, constituting operatic or ballet scenes. Monteverdi was not the first to write what might be called dramatic madrigals. Before the end of the sixteenth century, several composers, notably Orazio Vecchi (1550–1605), had composed **madrigal comedies**—dramatic works that employ dialogue and narration within the traditional, purely vocal scoring of sixteenth-century polyphony. The best-known such work is Vecchi's *L'Amfiparnaso* (Modena, 1594). Monteverdi's Book 8 includes two famous works that combine sung narrative with staged action; one of these, the *Lamento della ninfa* (Lament of the nymph), is a continuo madrigal in which a solo soprano sings in dialogue with three male voices, whereas the *Combattimento di Tancredi e Clorinda* (The combat of Tancredi and Clorinda) includes a string ensemble in addition to its three solo voices and continuo. Monteverdi signaled the special

---

[19]The major harmony at the end of a piece or section otherwise in the minor mode is sometimes called a *Picardy third.*

nature of both works by attaching to each a short preface that gives details of their original quasi-theatrical productions.[20]

Monteverdi explains that the *Combattimento* (anthology, Selection 7), for three voices, strings, and continuo, had been staged in 1624 in the palace of a noble Venetian patron. On that occasion the roles of the two characters—the knight Tancredi (tenor) and his opponent Clorinda (soprano)—had been not only sung but also choreographed in a sort of pantomime. In fact, their vocal parts, although essential to the drama, are minimal; most of the singing is given to a second tenor, the *testo* or narrator. Hence the work, although not exactly a ballet in the modern sense, shared with the latter the element of choreographed action accompanied by music. It is important not only as one of Monteverdi's few surviving stage works from the middle part of his Venetian years, but also for its apparently unprecedented integration of instrumental music into a vocal setting. It is, moreover, a remarkably expressive setting of a portion of one of the great poems of the period, vividly dramatizing several of the poem's most memorable scenes. The string parts are for four *viole da braccio*—probably two violins, viola, and bass violin—joined, as Monteverdi's preface explains, by a larger bass string instrument (*contrabasso da gamba,* possible implying double-bass pitch) and harpsichord as continuo instruments. Similar ensembles became routine in later Italian opera; with the addition of extra players on each part, they became the string section that is the core of the modern orchestra.

The poet, Torquato Tasso (1544–95), was one of the leading Italian writers of the late Renaissance. A number of his shorter texts had been frequently set to music as polyphonic madrigals during the late sixteenth century by such composers as Gesualdo and Monteverdi himself, who extracted the text of the *Combattimento* from Tasso's epic poem *Gerusalemme liberata* (Jerusalem liberated, 1580). This was a romanticized poetic account of the First Crusade (1095–99), during which Jerusalem and other parts of the Holy Land were seized from their Arab Muslim rulers by western Roman Catholic nobles. In the scenes set by Monteverdi, one of the western knights, Tancredi, is in pursuit of Clorinda, a Muslim warrior. Unbeknownst to Tancredi, Clorinda is a woman in disguise, and he has previously not only met her; he has fallen in love with her. At the beginning of Monteverdi's work, Tancredi is chasing her on horseback. He confronts her, thinking she is a man, and after he has dismounted from his horse—for it would be dishonorable for him to fight her while only she is on foot—they twice engage in combat. The second encounter is fatal to Clorinda, but as she dies they recognize one another. In that moment, Clorinda accepts Tancredi's love and is converted to Christianity; she asks him to baptize her, which he does with water from a nearby stream (Fig. 4.2). Although the story seems implausible (if not offensive), it was popular in Roman Catholic countries and was a frequent subject for painters of the time, thanks in part to the poem's metaphorical references to the Counter-Reformation. Other episodes from the poem, especially

---

[20]Monteverdi's preface to the *Combattimento* is translated by Stanley Appelbaum in Claudio Monteverdi, *Madrigals: Book VIII (Madrigali Guerrieri et Amorosi)*, ed. Gian Francesco Malipiero (New York: Dover, 1991), xvii.

Figure 4.2 *Tancred Baptizing Clorinda* (c. 1586–1600), oil on canvas by Domenico Robusti (1560–1635), known as Tintoretto. Museum of Fine Arts, Houston; The Samuel H. Kress Collection (no. 61.77). In this painting Tancredi baptizes the fallen Clorinda with water carried in his helmet from a nearby stream, as described by Tasso in the poem from which Monteverdi drew the text of his *Combattimento di Tancredi e Clorinda*.

those involving the Crusader hero Rinaldo and the witch Armida, would provide subjects for many later opera librettos.

The *Concitato* Style

In his foreword to Book 8, Monteverdi writes of a *concitato* or "agitated" type of composition used for the musical representation of warlike action. For this purpose Monteverdi employs such instrumental techniques as **tremolo**—on bowed string instruments, the rapid repetition of one note—and **pizzicato** (plucked as opposed to bowed notes). It was apparently unprecedented for a composer to specify the use of these devices, although one can imagine musicians introducing them extemporaneously in the accompaniments to earlier dramatic works, as Monteverdi himself might have done in his early years as a string player at Mantua.[21] As in the madrigals of Books 4 and 5, Monteverdi justified his departure from conventional writing by citing ancient authors (chiefly Plato). But more fundamental than the use of these particular instrumental effects was the fact that the instruments now depict elements of both the action and the characters' changing emotional states. This went beyond their use in *Orfeo*, where the instrumental music played a secondary role, for the most part merely introducing each strophe of the arias and setting the scene.

The Musical Setting

The structure of this lengthy work—over twenty minutes long—is based on that of the poem, which falls into stanzas of eight lines each. Monteverdi selected sixteen of the poem's nearly two thousand stanzas for musical setting. As in shorter vocal works, however, he sometimes ignored the superficial structure of the poem—its division into lines and stanzas—in order to articulate its underlying division into sentences and larger units. In other words, the music organizes and *dramatizes* the text, as shown in Table 4.1.

Most of the text consists of narration. Much of it is sung as recitative accompanied only by continuo, sometimes in a very plain style, as at the beginning. Nevertheless, this recitative often has the same expressive character seen in *Orfeo*—particularly in stanzas 12 and 13, where Clorinda's fatal wounding takes place. Here, as in *Orfeo*, Monteverdi reserves the use of second-practice devices for climactic moments. One might note the sudden shift to a B major chord at the beginning of the passage (dominant of E minor, m. 317)—the only occurrence of this harmony in the piece—and the subsequent chromatic progressions (especially in mm. 336–37).

Use of the Strings

Clorinda and Tancredi engage in dialogue in only three sections, and except for Clorinda's final speeches these are accompanied only by continuo, like most of

---

[21]The term *tremelo* does occur in earlier works for string instruments, but in reference to a slurred tremelo known as bow vibrato (see Chapter 12).

TABLE 4.1
Monteverdi: Il combattimento

Stanza	Measure Numbers	Characters Singing[a]	Instrumentation[b]	Chief Key(s)	Event(s)
1a	1–9			d	introduction
1b–2	10–72	C, T	+ str.	D → G	T finds and challenges C
3	73–132			g	invocation of Night (aria with ritornelli)
4–6	133–219		+ str.	G	first combat
7–10	220–98	C, T	+ str.	g → a → G, d → D	rest and taunts
11	299–316		+ str.	G	second combat
12–13	317–64			e → d	C falls wounded
14–16	365–445	C, T	+ str.	g → d, a → D	C asks for forgiveness and dies

[a] C = Clorinda; T = Tancredi. Narrator is always present.
[b] + str. = with strings. Continuo is always present.

the narration. Yet the strings play an indispensable role, first representing the galloping of Tancredi's horse (mm. 18–30), then in the two battle scenes that constitute the chief action of the work. In each passage the strings play motives that, if sung, would be regarded as text painting: short rhythmic figures on repeated notes to signify the horse (mm. 18–30), then swift repeated notes and other figures during the battle scenes (mm. 148–202, 299–316). The narrator sings similar figures; for example, his rapid declamation of stanza 5, much of it to repeated notes, is a vocal equivalent of the string tremolos, a defining element of Monteverdi's *concitato* style (mm. 164–81). In these scenes the strings also play recuring broken triads, as in measures 31–36 (echoed at mm. 303–5). These are imitations of trumpet calls, used at the time as signals to relay commands in actual warfare and thus constituting a realistic detail. The voice takes up similar motives when the text refers to the sound of clattering armor (*che d'armi suone*, mm. 35–38), and similar representations of military music occur throughout the Baroque.

Another notable use of the strings, although brief, occurs with Clorinda's last words. Here Monteverdi's string parts include his original dynamic markings (see m. 366 and the final chord); the final *piano* must represent Clorinda's failing breath.[22] The strings accompany her homophonically, rather than depicting concrete images. They create a sort of halo around Clorinda's words, suggesting the gravity of the situation. This is similar to the type of setting in later Baroque works that is known as **accompanied recitative.** All recitative is normally accompanied by the continuo, but in accompanied recitative strings or other additional instruments are also present.

Strophic Variation

Stanza 3 (mm. 73–132) receives special treatment. Here the poem addresses the personified figure of Night; this rhetorical device permits the poet to insert his comments about the coming battle. Monteverdi turns the stanza into a moment of reflection, thereby making all the more dramatic the outbreak of battle that follows. For this he introduces a new formal device: strophic variation. Monteverdi treats the eight lines of this stanza as if they comprised two four-line strophes, placing an instrumental ritornello before each one.[23] Thus the setting of lines 5–8 (mm. 114–33) is a variation of lines 1–4 (mm. 88–105). This is particularly easy to see if one compares the bass lines of the two passages. Apart from rhythmic differences and repetitions of a few notes, the bass lines of the two sections are essentially the same, although the vocal part diverges significantly. Strophic variation was an important technique for composers of early Baroque vocal music, probably deriving from the improvised singing of strophic poetry during the sixteenth century. *Orfeo* includes two examples, and we shall examine another in the music of Barbara Strozzi (Chapter 5).

---

[22]Performers doubtless would have employed changes in dynamic level elsewhere, but Monteverdi specified their use here to ensure proper performance of a special effect.

[23]The printed edition labels each ritornello a *passaggio*; the first of these is preceded by a short introductory sinfonia.

In his preface to the *Combattimento*, Monteverdi asked the singers to refrain from adding improvised trills and other figuration. But he made an exception for stanza 3, for which there exist two versions of the vocal part, one more embellished than the other (for the more embellished version, see the example in the anthology, p. 62). Virtuoso strophic variations would disappear by the end of the seventeenth century. By then, singers and composers had discovered other media for virtuoso display.

Venetian Opera

Monteverdi's *Poppea*

Monteverdi's last opera, *L'incoronazione di Poppea* (The coronation of Poppea), was performed in Venice in 1642–43 at the second of the city's opera theaters, known as Santi Giovanni e Paolo (Saints John and Paul), which had opened in 1639.[24] The libretto is by Gian Francesco Busenello, who would collaborate with Monteverdi's younger colleague and probable student Cavalli in later operas. *Poppea* illustrates the trend of the new commercial operas toward smaller performing ensembles: there are few if any choruses, little or no dancing, and an instrumental accompaniment limited to three- or four-part strings with continuo. Unfortunately, the work survives only in two manuscripts copied after the composer's death, probably in conjunction with a production elsewhere (in Naples). The two manuscripts give the work in significantly different forms, each incorporating some music not by Monteverdi. This reflects a common practice throughout the Baroque; when an opera was revived, music would be added or deleted to suit the new singers, and instrumental parts might be newly composed or arranged for varying ensembles. Nevertheless, *Poppea* reveals the sure hand of a veteran composer who by this date could readily draw vivid characters and organize a compelling drama, largely through recitative.

Based on ancient Roman history, the work recounts the successful effort of the ambitious Poppea to displace Octavia as wife of the emperor Nero (reigned 54–68). Nero was a student of Seneca, a philosopher and poet; he nevertheless turned out to be a murderous tyrant, and his decision to have Seneca killed is the turning point of the opera. Even more than Monteverdi's earlier operas, *Poppea* is admired for the musical characterization of the principal figures. For example, in an early scene in which Nero confronts Seneca, the old philosopher sings in calm recitative, using phrases of homogenous length, pacing, and general style (Ex. 4.1). Nero, on the other hand, sings in short, nervous phrases of changing style and meter. He seems to grow irrationally excited or enraged at the words *ma del mondo* (mm. 32–34), repeating them quickly several times, and

---

[24]The first to open had been the theater of San Cassiano (Saint Cassian) in 1637. Despite their secular purpose, Venetian theaters were named for the church in whose parish they were located. Because it is not known precisely when these works were premiered, dates for Monteverdi's late operas are those of the winter season in which they were first performed rather than a specific year.

he indulges in a sudden, sweeping scale as he refers to his own absolute power (on the word *scettro*, literally "scepter," mm. 36–37). The part of Nero is for a soprano; it is an early example of one of the *castrato* parts that would come to dominate male roles in later Italian Baroque opera (see Chapter 8). The contrast

Example 4.1 Monteverdi, *Poppea*, Act 1, scene 9 (mm. 10–38)

mon-do ter-ren lo scet - tro è mi - o, lo scet - - - tro è mi - o.

Seneca

1 Signor, nel fondo alla maggior dolcezza
2 Spesso giace nascosto il pentimento.

3 Consigler scellerato è'l sentimento
4 Ch'odia le leggi e la ragion disprezza.

Nerone

5 La legge è per chi serve, e se vogli'io
6 Posso abolir l'antica e indur le nove;

7 È partito l'impero, è'l ciel di Giove,

8 Ma del mondo terren lo scettro è mio.

Seneca

Lord, in the greatest sweetness
Often lurks cause for
     repentance.
Sentiment is an evil counselor
That hates law and does not
     value reason.

Nero

Laws are for servants, and if I wish
I can abolish old ones and create
     new ones.
The government [of the universe] is
     divided; that of heaven is Jupiter's,
But rulership of the earth is mine.

between Seneca's low bass and Nero's shrill soprano reinforces the psychological contrast between the two characters.

Like *Orfeo*, the work includes retrospective allusions to older style, but these are chiefly limited to a single scene, in which several friends or pupils of Seneca lament his iminent death in what amounts to a three-voice continuo madrigal (Ex. 4.2). More typical of later opera is the inclusion of numerous arias for the major characters, most with ritornellos. These arias, unlike those of later opera, remain closely integrated with the surrounding recitative, and the style can pass rapidly between recitative and aria in the course of a single scene. For example, in a scene in which the lovestruck Poppea is being put to sleep by the nurse Arnalta, Poppea's reprise of a flowing arialike passage (sung once before in the same scene) gradually falls into hesitant recitative (Ex. 4.3).

Seventeenth-Century Italian Opera after Monteverdi

Vocal music at Venice continued to be influenced by Monteverdi after his death in 1643, although by then Cavalli was establishing himself as the city's leading composer. Opera would play a leading role in the city's musical life to the end of the eighteenth century, but other genres of vocal music were also cultivated, including the secular cantata and various types of sacred music.

As Italian opera houses were established elsewhere in Europe, many followed the model of the Venetian theaters. Thus, in Germany, Spain, England, and elsewhere, opera librettos generally remained in Italian, and Italian musicians received high fees to compose and perform them. Even when the music itself

Example 4.2 Monteverdi, *Poppea*, Act 2, scene 3 (mm. 22–30)

Famigliari	Friends [Seneca's students]
Famigliari	**Friends [Seneca's students]**
Non morir, Seneca, non morir.	Do not die, Seneca, do not die.

was not Italian, Venetian librettos were often reused or adopted for new operas elsewhere. Older works were frequently revived, but usually in new versions, often with substantial alterations that might extend anywhere from the expansion of the instrumentation to the omission or insertion of whole scenes.

The Growth of the Aria

The single most important stylistic development in Italian opera after Monteverdi was the increase in the number of arias and their importance to the drama. In the operas of his younger contemporaries (especially Cavalli), recitative remains the usual style for the most important speeches of the principal characters, as well as for action. Most arias remain short and dancelike, many being sung

Example 4.3 Monteverdi, *Poppea*, Act 2, scene 10 (mm. 46–60)

Poppea	Poppea
1 Amor, ricorro a te.	Love, I run back to thee.
2 Guida mia speme in porto,	Bring my hopes to fruition,
3 Fammi sposa—	Make me wife [of Nero]—
4 Par che'l sonno m'aletti,	How does sleep overcome me,
5 A chiuder gl'occhi alla quiete in grembo?	Closing my eyes as I fall silent?

by minor figures in the drama. But almost every scene now contains at least one aria or arialike passage, and with time the arias grow increasingly varied, serving to reflect the changing emotional states of the major figures.

The dramatic function of these arias is still very different from that in eighteenth-century opera, where each aria tends to be a large virtuoso set piece that serves as the climax of a scene. Instead, in Venetian opera of the mid-seventeenth century each scene typically contains a fluid alternation between recitative and aria, as in *Poppea*. Sometimes single lines of poetry within a recitative may be set in aria style (that is, as arioso); a favorite device is to repeat such a line at several points within a scene as a sort of refrain, as occurs in Act 2 of *Orfeo*. The most memorable scenes in mid-seventeenth-century Italian opera often remain lengthy monologues sung in recitative by major characters. But other types of substantial solo occur as well: strophic variation arias, such as we have noted in the prologue of *Orfeo* and the invocation to Night in the *Combattimento*, as well as extended laments of the type described below.

Another trend is the growing use of obbligato instrumental parts. Although the continuo remains the sole accompaniment to the voice most of the time, short ritornellos are increasingly common, and the instruments are more and more integrated with the voices, in the type of writing seen in portions of the *Combattimento*. Unfortunately, the loss of the original scores for many works leaves uncertainties about their original instrumentation and performance practices. Performances today, even those that purport to be historically authentic, sometimes employ modern arrangements that reflect later scoring and instrumental practice.

Cavalli

The leading composer of Venetian opera during the mid-seventeenth century was Francesco Cavalli (1602–76). Born at Crema in central northern Italy, he entered the choir of St. Mark's, Venice, in 1616. There he served under Monteverdi, who had arrived three years earlier. Apart from a brief stint (1660–62) in France, he spent his entire career in Venice, where in 1639 he became—like Giovanni Gabrieli—organist at St. Mark's. Despite his employment as an organist, his surviving works are virtually all vocal and are dominated by some thirty-three operas.

Cavalli's *Giasone*

The opera *Giasone*, first performed in 1649, was Cavalli's most famous work. Based on the Greek myth of Jason and the Golden Fleece, its libretto, by the Florentine poet Giacinto Andrea Cicognini, was typical of the period in incorporating numerous secondary characters and subplots, some of them of a comic nature (see Box 4.4). In this it represents a departure from early opera, which maintained a uniformly high-minded point of view, avoiding comic scenes. By the end of the century fashion would turn again, so that Cavalli's operas came to be dismissed as inappropriately mixing the comic with the serious. This was hardly the view of his contemporaries, however.

The most famous scene in *Giasone* is one in which the witch Medea conjures up a demon (anthology, Selection 8a). Similar scenes occur in many later works, notably by the English composer Purcell and the French Rameau. Medea's music opens with a miniature strophic aria, complete with a six-measure ritornello. The remainder of the scene alternates between aria and recitative styles; the final arialike section (*Si, si, si, vincerà*) is preceded by a chorus of spirits.

The Lament

The final scene of *Giasone* includes a long monologue for Isifile (anthology, Selection 8b). Primarily a lament, it is also an impassioned expression of her anger at Giasone, and its text contains some extraordinary imagery. Yet Cavalli chooses not to dwell on some of Isifile's more horrendous outbursts, making

BOX 4.4

Cavalli: *Giasone*

Libretto by Giacinto Andrea Cicognini (1606–ca. 1650).
First performed at the Teatro San Cassiano in Venice, 1649; numerous
revised productions in Italy during the next forty years.

Chief Characters

Giasone [Jason] (alto), Greek hero, leader of the Argonauts
Isifile [Hypsipyle] (soprano), queen of Lemnos, wife of Giasone
Medea (soprano), witch, ruler of Colchis

SYNOPSIS

The work consists of a prologue and three acts. At the beginning of Act 1, Giasone has sailed across the Aegean Sea with his followers the Argonauts to capture the Golden Fleece. The latter, sheared long ago from a magical golden sheep that had been sacrificed to the gods, is now being guarded by monsters near the witch Medea's castle in the Asian city of Colchis. Previously Giasone has spent a year on the island of Lemnos, where he has married Queen Isifile, but at Colchis Medea has become his lover. In our first excerpt (scene 14), Medea conjures up a demon, who gives her a ring that will bring Giasone victory over the monsters.

In Act 2 Giasone wins the Golden Fleece, and at the beginning of Act 3 Medea and Giasone are living happily together. But when a follower of Giasone makes an attempt on Medea's life, she is saved by a former lover, whom she now sends to kill Giasone. Giasone is saved in turn by Isifile. In the final scene, Giasone declares that he still loves Medea. But after hearing Isifile's lament—our second excerpt—he realizes that he in fact loves Isifile. The opera concludes with the two happily reunited (and Medea returning to her former lover).

little musically of her list of exhortations to Giasone in measures 29–36, for example. Instead the music focuses attention on several passages that are set lyrically, in aria style. This approach differs from that of Monteverdi in Orfeo's lament, which had been nothing more than an extended recitative of an especially intense nature. The later Venetian lament is longer and typically incorporates one or more arialike sections constructed over an **ostinato** bass—that is, a continuo part consisting of a short phrase, usually four or eight measures in length, which is repeated many times, serving as the basis for a series of variations in the vocal part.

Isifile's lament includes such an ostinato passage, beginning at the words "Regina, Egeo, amici" (mm. 71–99). The four-measure ostinato, initially played alone, is based on a descending **tetrachord** (four-note scale segment) heard in many other seventeenth-century laments. This lament treats the ostinato more freely than most, interspersing it with passages built on an inversion of the initial tetrachord (mm. 75–77) and transposing it to several different keys (e.g., B♭ at m. 79).[25] Nevertheless it is typical of the seventeenth-century lament in its triple meter and minor mode, characteristics that, together with its ostinato tetrachord, can be traced to the Lament of the Nymph in Monteverdi's Eighth Book of Madrigals. They are still found in Dido's lament, from Purcell's opera *Dido and Aeneas* (1689; see Chapter 5), and there even exist instrumental imitations, such as the *Lamento* movement of Bach's *Capriccio on His Separation from a Most Beloved Brother* for keyboard instrument (ca. 1707). So common are laments over descending ostinato bass lines that the latter have been termed emblems of lamentation, although the device also occurs in contexts where it is difficult to find a specific meaning or emotional significance.[26]

After Cavalli, Venetian opera continued to evolve through the end of the Baroque, indeed to the end of the eighteenth century. When we return to Italian opera, in Chapter 8, it will be to a new type, the *opera seria*, which emerged at the end of the seventeenth century.

---

[25]Cavalli probably meant this passage to be performed by voice and continuo alone; at least one recording adds string parts, apparently composed by the conductor.

[26]For a study of the chromatic version of this device throughout European music history, see Peter Williams, *The Chromatic Fourth* (Oxford: Oxford University Press, 1998). For the view of descending ostinato basses as "emblems," see Ellen Rosand, " The Descending Tetrachord: An Emblem of Lament," *Musical Quarterly* 55 (1979): 346–59.

CHAPTER 5

SECULAR VOCAL MUSIC OF THE LATER SEVENTEENTH CENTURY

From the 1640s onward, opera may have commanded more attention from the musically literate public than any other form of Baroque vocal music. But the rise of opera was paralleled by that of the **cantata,** the most important form of secular vocal chamber music in the Baroque and the main subject of this chapter.

The names given to Baroque genres varied considerably in meaning over the course of the period, and some expressions were applied to quite different sorts of music, even at the same place and time. The term *cantata* is one such word. Literally meaning anything that is sung, in the course of the seventeenth century the word came to be applied to various types of secular vocal music for solo voice that differed from Caccini's madrigals and strophic airs above all in their greater length. Many early seventeenth-century works now described as cantatas were originally disseminated under such headings as *aria, lamento,* or even the old *madrigal.* Today the term *cantata* is used for sacred as well as secular works for one or more solo singers and instruments; most such works from the later Baroque are composed of several distinct movements, which may even include choruses. Despite the diverse names by which these works were originally known, they share certain fundamental features, especially their attention to musical rhetoric within a predominantly lyrical (as opposed to dramatic) setting. Apart from later examples involving multiple singers, most of which were not originally designated cantatas, these compositions were meant not for theaters or churches but for intimate chamber performance before a small audience (if any).

This chapter focuses on seventeenth-century works that remain close to the original meaning of the term *cantata,* although not all the music discussed here would have been understood as belonging to that category. These works illustrate several phases in the evolution of Italian-style vocal music after Monteverdi, including its exportation from Italy to as far away as London. Cantatas were among the most popular compositions of the seventeenth and eighteenth centuries, in part because they employed the poetic and musical language of opera but could be performed without the expense and elaborate production required by a large stage work. Combining eloquent poetry and music, they appear to have taken the place of the late-Renaissance madrigal as a favorite genre for performance in the learned academies dedicated to the arts and sciences that continued to meet on a regular basis in the major Italian cities.

Perhaps the leading center for the cantata was Rome, thanks to the large number of wealthy nobles who lived or visited there (whether for religious or political reasons). During the seventeenth century three composers in particular composed hundreds of cantatas for performance in Rome, although they are now best known for other types of work: Luigi Rossi (?1597/8–1653), now famous for his two operas; Giacomo Carissimi (1605–74), known for his oratorios (see Chapter 7); and Antonio [Pietro] Cesti (1623–69), famed for operas later composed for his Austrian patrons.

BARBARA STROZZI

Among the most significant composers and performers of cantatas in the mid-seventeenth century was Barbara Strozzi (1619–77). Unlike the Roman cantata composers, whose works were distributed in manuscripts copied individually for their wealthy patrons, Strozzi took advantage of the flourishing Venetian commercial trade in printed music by publishing nine volumes of arias, madrigals, motets, and cantatas between 1644 and 1664. She was almost certainly the illegitimate daughter of Giulio Strozzi, a poet whose texts were set to music by her as well by Monteverdi and Cavalli.

Although she studied with Cavalli, the leading composer of Venetian opera, she neither wrote nor performed in opera. Rather her work as a musician appears to have been in connection with a Venetian academy founded by Giulio Strozzi known as the Accademia degli Unisoni (Academy of the Unisons). Gulio appears to have organized this academy for the specific purpose of giving Barbara a forum in which to present her compositions and to engage in learned discourse with musically inclined Venetian nobles and intellectuals.

Giulio's academy was a subgroup of a larger one, the Accademia degli Incogniti (Academy of the Disguised Ones), whose members included the librettists of Monteverdi's two last operas. The participation of women in such activities, although not entirely unprecedented, was highly unusual in Italy (France was considerably more liberal in this respect). Strozzi's works—all vocal—include numerous settings of texts by Giulio and other members of the Unisoni. Reportedly a gifted writer herself, she may have set her own texts as well. Had Strozzi's parents been married, she herself probably would have married and had a more conventional career. Within seventeenth-century Venetian society, however, this was impossible. She may, like thousands of other Venetian women of the period, have made her livelihood as a courtesan; although she never married, she bore at least four children and lived as a woman of considerable means. Among the dedicatees of her printed works were the elected chief magistrate (*doge*) of Venice and the emperor and empress of Austria, indicating that her talents were valued at the highest levels of her society.

Strozzi's *Ardo in tacito foco*

Strozzi's known works include seven published collections devoted to her cantatas and other vocal music, mostly for solo soprano accompanied by basso continuo (Fig. 5.1). These range from simple strophic arias to multisectional compositions lasting a quarter hour or so; there is also a set of continuo madrigals for as many as five voices, as well as a book of sacred monodies or solo motets.

Among Strozzi's larger works are several cantatas in the form of strophic variations, like the Invocation to Night in Monteverdi's *Combattimento*. *Ardo in tacito foco* (anthology, Selection 9) is a self-contained composition in this form, published in 1654 as the opening work in Strozzi's third printed collection. Like Monteverdi, Strozzi writes each strophe as a variation of the same basic design. But Strozzi's is an altogether larger work; each stanza is subdivided into sections that range from plain recitative to aria style, and the entire work lasts close to ten minutes. A virtuoso showpiece for a solo soprano, it is reminiscent

Figure 5.1 Barbara Strozzi, opening of *Ardo in tacito foco,* from the first page of music in her *Cantate ariete à una, due, e tre voci,* op. 3 (Venice, 1654). Strozzi was one of the most prolific publishers of cantatas in the seventeenth century, and her publications reveal exceptional care in the preparation and printing of both poetry and music. As in many other examples of seventeenth-century monody, there is no indication of the intended voice or instrumentation; these aspects of the music as well as the realization of the largely unfigured bass are left to the performer. Because the page was printed from moveable type, used throughout the Baroque for most vocal music, the staff lines are broken up into numerous short segments, each printed with a separate piece of metal type. Eighth and sixteenth notes are also printed separately, without beaming.

of the tragic monologues found in Venetian opera of the period, including that of Isifile in *Giasone*. But Strozzi's setting, not tied to the demands of a stage drama, proceeds at a more leisurely pace, permitting the music to respond vividly to each line of the poem.

The Text

Scenes of lamentation were a common pretext for Baroque cantatas, and this work is no exception. The text, thought to be by Giovanni Francesco Loredano, founder of the Incogniti, is the complaint of a speaker whose lack of confidence— or, perhaps, of candor—prevents him from declaring his love for another. The poetry is typical of that written within the Strozzi circle; the language is intentionally indirect, using numerous metaphors that today seem artificial but at the time were regarded as elegant and expressive. A peculiarity shared with many of Strozzi's compositions is the presence of a lengthy descriptive title; most cantatas and other works by Baroque composers continued to be referred to by their opening words or *incipits*.

The poem must be assumed to be the lament of a male lover, even though Strozzi probably performed it herself. Her music therefore represents a dramatic reading of the poem, not an actual dramatic scene, and we are told next to nothing about the lover and his beloved as people—why he loves her, or why he cannot name her. What matters is that the poem provides vivid pictorial images, such as fire (*foco*) and wind (*vento*), as well as emotionally charged words such as *ardore* (ardor or passion), *sospiri* (sighs), and *morte* (death). Each such word gave the composer an opportunity for an imaginative display of musical rhetoric, especially of the word-painting variety. Those words that call up energetic or lively images, such as "wind," also call forth virtuoso vocal technique in the form of rapid **passagework** (scales and other such figuration). But the work as a whole is also a display of the *composer's* virtuosity, and Strozzi finds compelling, imaginative ways of representing even such dark, static ideas as "death," at the end of the poem, or the silence that is the main theme of the text. Although the rapid alternation between sharply contrasting images and emotions might have led to an incoherent, fragmented musical setting, the use of variation form gives each stanza a recurring structure that imparts to the work as a whole a readily comprehensible design.

The Music

Although the vocal part was clearly intended for a virtuoso soprano, Strozzi did not specify what instrument provides the continuo. She reportedly played the lute and might have accompanied herself on the theorbo, although harpsichord and even chamber organ are also possibilities.[1]

Strozzi's music articulates each stanza of the poem into three or four distinct sections (see Box 5.1). These are distinguished by their contrasting meter, tempo, and

---

[1]Contrary to what can be heard on at least one recent recording, it is unlikely that Strozzi's performances would have included varied or doubled continuo instruments like those used in *Orfeo*.

Box 5.1

Strozzi: *Ardo in tacito foco*

Stanza:	1				2				3		
Lines:	1–5	6–8	9–10	11	12–16	17–19	20	21–22	23–28	29–30	31–33
Measure:	1	31	58	65	87	109	136	140	178	210	227
Meter:	C	3	C	3	C	3	C	3	C	C	C
Tempo indication:	—	adagio	—	—	—	presto	—	—	—	—	—
"Key" signature:	—	♭	—	—	—	♭	—	—	—	♭	—
First and last harmonies:	d–d	F–F	d–e	C–d	d–A	d–F	d	d–d	d–d	F–F	D–d
Significant word(s):	foco	proprio	sospiri		ristoro, pianto	vento, umor, spento	duol		venti, lamenti, asconde	pietra, foco	morte

mode or tonality. The sections in common time are in recitative style, usually the ornate variety best described as arioso. On the other hand, the triple-time passages have the character of a simple aria. Similar alternations of tempo and meter characterize contemporaneous Venetian opera, including Monteverdi's *Poppea* and Cavalli's *Giasone*.[2]

Within each stanza is a section with a "key" signature of one flat, ending with an F-major chord (as in m. 44). Today we would likely describe these sections as being *in* F major, that is, the relative major of the D-minor tonality that dominates the outer sections. Yet the one-flat signature is absent in the latter passages, suggesting that they are in the Dorian mode (mode 1). Still, the soprano part goes well beyond the one-octave range of a typical chant melody or of a part in a sixteenth-century polyphonic work. In fact, as in *Orfeo*, the structure of the music—its tendency to move toward the functionally related harmonic goals of D minor, F major, and A major—is close to the common-practice tonality of the eighteenth and nineteenth centuries, despite such modal features as the use of G *major* where we would expect G minor (e.g., mm. 20, 64).

Each of the three stanzas follows the same underlying pattern, yet Strozzi crafts the music of each strophe to fit its words exactly. For example, the opening section in each stanza begins with several measures over a sustained d in the continuo (implying a D-minor chord). Line 1 in each case ends with a

---

[2]The triple-time sections in Strozzi's original publication were marked simply by the numeral "3," as shown in Box 5.1; the edition in the anthology substitutes the modern time signature $\frac{3}{2}$ and prints the notes of these sections in half their original values.

so-called **Phrygian cadence,** the bass descending by half step from B♭ to A and concluding with a major chord on A, as in measure 9. In stanza 1 the vocal part depicts the opening word *ardo* ("I burn") with brief rising melismas. Stanza 2, on the other hand, underlines the word *ristoro* ("consolation") with a descending melisma, which is imitated by the bass (m. 89). In the third stanza, dissonant suspensions represent the meaning of the word *aspro* ("bitter," mm. 178–81); no melismas occur here at all. Nevertheless, the underlying similarities in the structure and musical phrasing for all three lines remain evident.

Strozzi similarly adjusts each stanza as a whole to suit its text. Thus the first triple-time section of the first stanza is marked *adagio* (m. 31), whereas the corresponding section of the second stanza is marked *presto* (m. 109). The *adagio* marking must reflect the unhappiness stressed in lines 6–8 of the first stanza; the unhappy lover has "imprisoned" himself.[3] The *presto* of the second stanza, on the other hand, may be a response to the liveliness of the wind and the tears mentioned in lines 18–19.[4] Yet line 19 ends in measure 133 with a sudden pause in the vocal part—a dramatic silence elicited by the word *spento* (literally, "exhausted"). Strozzi repeats the idea for emphasis (m. 135). Significantly, triple time is entirely absent from the final stanza, although there is still a passage that begins and ends on F-major chords, in which the "key" signature changes to one flat (mm. 210–26). The absence of arialike triple-time music from the final stanza prefigures the closing setting of the word *morte* (death), with its chromatic descents in both soprano and continuo (mm. 231–42). The voice's final cadence borrows a device from Monteverdi's *seconda pratica*: the note d′ forms a dissonance that would normally resolve to c♯′, but the dissonance remains unresolved.[5]

ALESSANDRO SCARLATTI AND THE LATER CANTATA

Opera and cantata continued to be the main genres of Italian secular vocal music through the eighteenth century. But the cantata of around 1700 was a different type of work from that of the early seventeenth century. Like opera and other Italian vocal genres, it came to be dominated by the aria, which replaced recitative as the main element. In addition, the rapid alternation between recitative and aria styles that characterized earlier works grew less common. Instead, most cantatas came to consist of distinct movements, and by the eighteenth century a cantata typically consisted of a pair of arias each preceded by a recitative.

Many cantatas continued to be composed for voice and continuo alone, but increasing numbers of large cantata-like works were also written that incorporated

---

[3]Strozzi places a melisma on the word *proprio* ("own") in mm. 50–55—not on *il* ("the") as shown in another modern edition—emphasizing that the lover's heart is its *own* "prisoner."

[4]The word *umor*, translated here as "the latter," that is, the "tears," is actually an old word referring to any vital fluid, an idea reflected in the long, winding melisma on which the word is sung.

[5]Compare the final cadence of the *Combattimento*. Strozzi does not necessarily allude here to Monteverdi's well-known work; similar cadences also occur in the music of Luigi Rossi and other contemporaries.

obbligato instrumental parts and multiple soloists. Such a work might be described as a *serenata* (serenade) or a *dramma per musica* (musical drama); the latter term was also used for operas, and some of the works in question approach the dimensions of operas. All were tending to share the same musical style, falling into the same types of recitative and aria. By the first decade of the eighteenth century composers in Germany, England, and even France were extending the style of the Italian cantata to settings of texts in their own languages. Some were on sacred subjects, as in two sets of cantatas published in 1708 and 1711 by the French composer Elizabeth Jacquet de La Guerre (see Chapter 11). In Lutheran Germany a type of sacred work resembling the Italian cantata or serenata became the most common form of church music, written by the hundred by such composers as Georg Philipp Telemann and J. S. Bach (see Chapter 9).

In Italy thousands of such works must have been composed during the second half of the seventeenth century alone, some for amateur musicians, others for professional performance in academies and other gatherings held in the homes and palaces of wealthy patrons. Among the most significant composers were Alessandro Stradella (1644–82), Agostino Steffani (1654–1728), and Alessandro Scarlatti (discussed below), all of whom were opera composers as well. The tradition continued into the eighteenth century; the young Handel produced over one hundred cantatas and similar works during an extended visit to Italy (1707–9).

Probably the majority of such works are on texts whose conventional poetry is concerned with love—often unrequited—between Greek nymphs and shepherds. The arias are the main element, and by 1700 the *da capo* (ABA) aria was the most common, indeed practically the only, type of aria in use. In general, the arias of these works, whatever their form, are much longer than those of earlier Italian vocal music, and they possess increasingly complex formal designs. An increasing number if these arias employ one or more obbligato instruments, especially solo violin or recorder, although Handel and other eighteenth-century composers continued to write many cantatas for voice and continuo alone. The recitatives in these works, on the other hand, are usually simpler than in earlier cantatas, containing fewer arioso passages and greater quantities of straightforward recitation.

Most of this enormous output of music was never published and remains in manuscript to this day. Even the cantatas of a composer as important as Alessandro Scarlatti have been published only very selectively. The enormous productivity of these composers was made possible by changes in style that by the late seventeenth century permitted a gifted composer, upon being handed a poetic text, to set it to music in an appropriate form and style almost instantly, as if improvising. Compositional procedures had become routine, musical forms such as the da capo aria standardized, and the poetry used for these works was so conventional that it rarely required much thought or planning on the composer's part to produce an adequate musical setting. Many cantatas must have been commissioned, the poetry dashed off, and the music composed, rehearsed, and performed within the space of a few days.

One might suppose that such a situation would lead to texts and music consisting mainly of clichés, and indeed this is true of the works of many lesser composers. Yet, in the hands of such prodigiously talented musicians as Scarlatti and Handel, this highly conventionalized approach to composition produced numerous masterworks full of attractive melodies and original, compelling harmonic surprises and dramatic effects. It is probably no accident that these composers were also talented improvisers; the prevailing approach to composition favored those who could play or write on their feet, as it were.

Alessandro Scarlatti

So many distinguished composers emerged in Italy during the later seventeenth and early eighteenth centuries that it is almost arbitrary to select one to represent the entire period. Certainly one of the most important, however, was Alessandro Scarlatti (1660–1725), whose enormous output includes over six hundred cantatas. Scarlatti was born in Palermo, Sicily, into a large family that included several musicians; his son Domenico would carry on the tradition. In 1672 Scarlatti was sent to Rome, where he must have received musical training and heard considerable amounts of music, both sacred and secular. Scarlatti would divide his career between Rome and Naples, and today he is often associated with a group of opera composers active in the latter city, although he produced operas and other works in both places.

Besides cantatas, Scarlatti's music included perhaps one hundred operas (about seventy survive), as well as some thirty-three smaller quasi-dramatic works (serenatas) and about thirty-eight oratorios and other large sacred works. He also wrote masses, over one hundred motets, and keyboard music. A virtuoso harpsichordist, he nevertheless excelled in writing readily singable yet effective arias for the high soprano voices—both male and female—that dominated the Italian opera of his day. Like his cantatas, his operas consist almost entirely of numerous arias joined by recitative; the arias in a single opera may number over sixty. The arias in his earlier operas are usually accompanied solely by continuo, but in later works they grow somewhat larger and the number of instrumental parts increases. Despite his unparalleled facility as a composer of melodious arias, Scarlatti was also skilled in the old-fashioned contrapuntal style—the *stile antico*, derived from the vocal polyphony of the Renaissance. Although the latter was now confined largely to church music, Scarlatti often incorporated a contrapuntal element into his secular works, as in the following cantata. Because of its length, we shall be concerned chiefly with two of its arias, although comments are also directed below to its opening instrumental movement and its recitatives.

Scarlatti's *Correa nel seno amato*

This cantata (anthology, Selection 10) dates perhaps from the early 1690s. Consisting of ten movements (see Box 5.2), it is longer than the typical Italian cantata of the later Baroque, which often consists of just two arias alternating with as many recitatives. In addition, its inclusion of two violin parts marks it as a more ambitious work than most contemporaneous Italian cantatas, the majority of which were still composed for solo voice and continuo; it even includes an instrumental introduction or *sinfonia*. Its anonymous text is the familiar

Box 5.2

Alessandro Scarlatti: *Correa nel sen amato*

1. Sinfonia. 2 vlns., b.c. Key: B♭

   (a) [Grave]: slow opening section
   [Allegro]: quick imitative section
   Largo: concluding phrase
   (b) *Balletto:* dance in binary form

2. Recitative, "Correa nel seno amato." Sop., b.c.

   (a) arioso, "Correa nel seno amato" (see Ex. 5.1)
   (b) simple recitative, "Rosseggiante nel viso" (see Ex. 5.2)
   (c) arioso (triple time), "Tergea tutto pietà" (see Ex. 5.3)
   (d) simple recitative, "Stanche al fine"
   (e) arioso (Largo, imitative texture), "Così con l'aure" (see Ex. 5.4)

3. Aria, "Ombre opache." Sop., 2 vlns., b.c. Key: B♭

4. Recitative, "Curilla, anima mia, gioia." Sop., b.c.

5. Aria, "Fresche brine." Sop., 2 vlns. (in rit. only), b.c. Key: C minor. Score in anthology (selection 10a). *See summary of form below.*

6. Recitative, "Piante insensate." Sop., b.c.

7. Aria, "Idolo amato." Sop., 2 vlns., b.c. Key: D minor

8. Recitative, "Ma voi, occhi dolenti." Sop., b.c.

   (a) simple recitative, "Ma voi, occhi dolenti"
   (b) arioso (imitative texture), "Ch'arda in fiamme di duolo e pianga"

9. Aria, "Onde belle." Sop., 2 vlns., b.c. Key: G minor. Score in anthology (selection 10b). *See summary of form below.*

10. Recitative, "Curilla, anima mia, deh vieni." Sop., 2 vlns. (in final section only), b.c.

    (a) simple recitative, "Curilla, anima mia"
    (b) accompanied recitative, "Volea più dir Daliso" (see Ex. 5.5)

Aria: "Fresche brine"

Da capo form framed by ritornellos.

   mm. 1–20: ritornello. C minor
   mm. 21–48: A section (lines 1–3, with motto opening). C minor
   mm. 49–98: B section (lines 4–6, twice). F minor → E♭ major
   mm. 29–48: A repeated. C minor
   mm. 1–20: ritornello repeated. C minor

Aria: "Onde belle"

Through-composed, with opening and closing ritornellos whose musical material is integrated with the vocal sections.

  mm. 1–8: ritornello. G minor
  mm. 9–17: lines 1–2. G minor → B♭ major
  mm. 18–29: lines 3–4. G minor
  mm. 30–47: line 5.* G minor

*This line of poetry = line 5 of aria no. 3, "Ombre opache."

---

shepherd's lament; here Daliso weeps over the nymph Corilla. The text focuses on a series of nature images, such as the early-morning frost on the grass, which grows within earshot of the murmuring waves of a conveniently nearby stream. As conventional as such images may have been, they served the composer well by inspiring imaginative use of the conventions of word painting.

The Opening Sinfonia

By Scarlatti's day the term *sinfonia* was most often attached to an opening instrumental movement—what we would call an overture. In the operas of Monteuerdi and Cavalli, the introductory sinfonia might consist of no more than a few short phrases. The present sinfonia, however, constitutes a short but self-contained **trio sonata** for two violins and continuo, in two brief movements.

The first movement alone corresponds to the entirety of many earlier sinfonias, being subdivided into slow and quick sections (the latter broadens out in its final phrase). The second movement is a dance in binary form: a *balletto*, equivalent to what was called in France an *allemande* (see Chapters 11 and 12). As in other vocal works of the period, the sinfonia has nothing to do with the rest of the work it introduces, apart from sharing its key (B♭) with the opening and closing vocal movements.

The term *trio sonata* is used today for what were actually several distinct types of Italian Baroque instrumental chamber work (see Chapter 12). By the late seventeenth century the most common scoring was the one used here—two violins and continuo—which served as the instrumental portion of many seventeenth-century vocal works as well. In this work, the sinfonia and the five arias all use the same instrumentation, as does the concluding accompanied recitative. Scarlatti, strangely enough, appears not to have composed any trio sonatas as such, but this sinfonia might well have been performed as a separate work.

Text

The nine vocal movements of the cantata alternate regularly between recitative and aria—an alternation determined by the poet, not the composer. As far back as *Orfeo*, aria texts had generally been short, their individual lines also tending toward brevity, typically of six or eight syllables. Recitative texts, on the other hand, usually alternate irregularly between lines of seven and eleven syllables. Earlier composers, such as Monteverdi and Strozzi, had frequently ignored the poet's division of the text, setting recitative verse in aria style and vice versa. This became less frequent in the later Baroque, as the formal designs of both poetry and music grew more conventionalized.

Recitative

The recitative movements in this cantata constitute a narrator's description of Daliso's unhappy situation; they set the scene for the arias, which express his own emotional outpourings. Thus, although composed for a single singer, without dialogue, the cantata reflects the structure of contemporary Italian opera, which likewise consisted of alternating recitative and aria.

The recitatives here are nevertheless somewhat longer and more varied in style than in the operas of Scarlatti and later composers. As Box 5.2 shows, several of these recitative movements actually fall into distinct sections of contrasting types. The first recitative movement alternates between arioso and simple recitative, and the final movement begins as simple recitative before concluding as an *accompagnato* (accompanied recitative), the two violins accompanying the voice with sustained notes and simple counterpoint.[6] Each change of style corresponds to a new idea or a new point of view introduced in the text.

The first section of the opening recitative is largely in arioso style, with melismas on a number of words, such as the initial word *correa* ("hastened"; Ex. 5.1). The melisma provides both text painting and rhetorical emphasis. This melismatic arioso describes the brilliance of the setting sun, but the style changes to simple recitative as the subject of the text shifts to Venus, the goddess of love, who is symbolized in the text by the rising of the planet that bears her name (Ex. 5.2). Still later, the poem speaks of Love's wiping away Daliso's tears; this line alone is set in aria style in triple meter (Ex. 5.3). The effect is ironic, since Love here is described as pitiless, yet the musical style is one often associated in older Italian vocal music with more pleasant aspects of love (compare Ex. 4.3). The movement concludes with another arioso section, marked *largo*, in which the soprano and continuo parts move in imitation (Ex. 5.4).[7] The imitative counterpoint, unusual in Italian recitative,

---

[6]See Box 4.3 to review the different types of recitative. Today the expression *secco* (dry) is sometimes used for simple recitative (*recitativo semplice*), but it is better reserved for the even drier recitative of late-eighteenth-century opera.

[7]The tempo indication *largo* is one of the few such markings in Scarlatti's score (the same term occurs at the end of the first part of the sinfonia). The word, which literally means "broad" in Italian, probably did not signify as slow a tempo as it does today. Scarlatti, like his contemporaries, usually left the determination of tempo to the performer; the *largo* indication here points out the presence of a contrapuntal texture and therefore the need to shift to a steady tempo, following the free rhythm of the preceding passage in simple recitative.

Example 5.1 Alessandro Scarlatti, *Correa nel seno amato*, no. 2, recitative "Correa nel seno amato," mm. 1–6

Correa nel seno amato
Ver l'occidente fretoloso il sole . . .

As the sun hurried
Toward his favored western shore . . .

Example 5.2 Alessandro Scarlatti, *Correa nel seno amato*, no. 2, recitative, "Correa nel seno amato," mm. 21–24

Rosseggiante nel viso,
Sorgea tutta ridente
Dal leto pastoral la bianca Dea . . .

Blushing red,
There rose smiling
From her soft bed the white goddess . . .

Example 5.3 Alessandro Scarlatti, *Correa nel seno amato*, no. 2, recitative, "Correa nel seno amato," mm. 56–66

Tergea tutto pietà spietato Amore.

[His tears] were wiped away in pity by pitiless Love.

Example 5.4 Alessandro Scarlatti, *Correa nel seno amato*, no. 2, recitative, "Correa nel seno amato," mm. 72–79

Così con l'aure e'l vento   In this manner, to the air and wind
Sfogava singhiozzando il suo tormento.   He gave vent, sobbing, to his torment.

Example 5.5 Alessandro Scarlatti, *Correa nel seno amato*, concluding accompanied recitative, mm. 1–6

Volea più dir Daliso,   Daliso wished to say more,
Ma punto d'improvviso   But at the point of doing so,
Dall'immenso dolore cadde svenuto.   Out of great sadness he fell mute.

distinguishes this line of text from the remainder of the movement, emphasizing that it forms a separate thought and a distinct grammatical unit.
Scarlatti uses the same effect at the end of the eighth movement.[8] In the final
movement he sets off the closing words in a different manner, through the
use of accompanied recitative (Ex. 5.5).

Performance Conventions in Recitative

Italian Baroque musicians developed a number of performance conventions
for recitative that today seem counterintuitive. One convention comes into
play when a line of poetry ends in a weak (unaccented) syllable; such lines
are often set with what are notated as two repeated notes (see Ex. 5.2, mm.
1, 2, 4). In fact, at some point it became customary to sing the first of these
notes on a pitch different from the one notated, as shown in Example 5.6.
This turns the first note into a dissonant **appoggiatura:** an unprepared
dissonance (a♭′) that resolves on the following note (g′). Appoggiaturas of
various sorts were common ornaments in later seventeenth- and eighteenth-
century performance practice, and this convention must have arisen as a form

Example 5.6 Conventional alterations of pitches in Alessandro Scarlatti, *Correa nel seno amato*, no. 2, recitative, "Correa nel seno amato," m. 3

of ornamentation. But whether it would have been employed consistently in
this work, composed by 1694, is uncertain.

A second convention concerns the notation of the continuo part, which by
this date may often have been played by harpsichord and cello together in a
work of this sort. Although notated in long values, the bass notes of recitative were, by the eighteenth century, frequently performed as short notes—
that is, not held out for their full written values. This made for a more lively
and more audible presentation, as the singer could present the rapidly
declaimed text without having to be heard over the sustained bass line. In
Example 5.1 this means that the note B♭ in the figured bass, together with
the B♭-major triad implied as its realization, was actually heard only at the
beginning of measure 1. Possibly the note (and chord) would have been

---

[8]Movement 8 is also unusual in that it ends with a passage for the continuo alone. Here Scarlatti has
written out the realization, using an imitative texture whose subject has just been sung to the words
ch'arda in fiamme ("that burns in flames"). Elsewhere the harpsichordist is expected to improvise the
realization in the usual fashion.

repeated on the downbeat of measure 3 or 4. Again, however, it is uncertain when this convention arose. Certainly, however, Scarlatti would have held out the bass notes as written in the concluding accompanied recitative, where the violins have similar notation (see Ex. 5.5).[9]

Arias

Unlike most cantatas composed during the late seventeenth and eighteenth centuries, this one is not yet dominated by arias in da capo form; three of the work's four arias are through-composed. The one da capo aria, "Fresche brine" (anthology, Selection 10a), also happens to be the shortest and simplest aria in the cantata. As such it is close to the type of aria for which Scarlatti's operas are best known: a relatively brief, lyrical expression of feeling with a singable melody and an uncomplicated instrumental component, the latter often limited to basso continuo.

By contrast to the very simple example in Monteverdi's *Orfeo*, "Fresche brine" is typical of later da capo arias in that its text falls into two stanzas, which we can designate A and B. Each stanza is set in a distinct musical section, and both the music and the text of section A are repeated after section B. The text of each stanza usually consists of two to six lines of poetry, forming a single sentence in each case; thus a da capo aria presents two concise, distinct textual ideas, each having distinctive music. The fully developed da capo aria emerged during Scarlatti's lifetime, its popularity due in part to the hundreds of attractive examples in his operas and cantatas.

"Fresche brine" is also typical of later da capo arias in that it includes an instrumental component (in addition to the basso continuo). But in this case the two violins provide only a short ritornello heard at the beginning and end of the aria, a vestige of the type of ritornello used by Monteverdi and Cavalli. By the eighteenth century, most arias would integrate the ritornello more completely with the vocal passages. This aria differs from many later da capo arias in another way as well: it includes only a partial restatement of the opening section, indicated in our score by the words *dal segno* rather than *da capo*. This was by no means uncommon, and the aria can still be regarded as a genuine if shortened example of da capo form.

The two stanzas of the text in "Fresche brine"are of equal length. The first three lines (stanza A) address the drops of frozen dew on the flowers surrounding Daliso; the last three lines (stanza B) compare the frozen dewdrops to his tears. One way of analyzing such an aria is to examine how its text is laid out relative to the music. Here the A section begins with the ritornello and concludes with a cadence in the tonic (C minor, m. 48). Shortly afterward the voice enters with the B text in a new key, F minor (m. 53). The B section contains two complete statements of its text, concluding with a cadence in another new

---

[9]Another performance convention in recitative has to do with the rhythmic and harmonic coordination of voice and continuo in final cadences; see "Performance Issues" in the section of the anthology devoted to Handel's opera *Orlando* (Selection 18).

key, E♭ (m. 96). The vocal portion of the A section is then repeated in abbreviated form, followed by the ritornello.

With its modulating tonal structure and relatively lengthy musical setting, this is a more extended and far more elaborate design than the brief ABA forms found in *Orfeo*. There the A section was a single phrase of music and poetry—more a simple refrain than a complete section. Here the A section is almost a self-contained composition in itself, yet it is only the first part of the aria. Musicians and listeners of the late Baroque evidently valued the symmetry and predictable form of the da capo aria. Nevertheless it became customary for singers to add improvised embellishments when they repeated the A section, allowing audiences to hear the same music decorated in different ways each time a virtuoso sang it. This may, however, have been more true in opera than in the present work, where the simple tunefulness of the one da capo aria would be ruined by virtuoso embellishment.

In addition to its da capo form, this aria employs another device very common in later Baroque arias. The voice, after presenting the first line of the text, rests for two measures, then repeats line 1 (with its music) and continues with the remainder of the A section. The initial vocal entrance (mm. 11–12) is called a **motto,** and an aria of this type is therefore a **motto aria.**[10] The motto is a form of musical rhetoric: by separating the first line—sometimes just the first word or two—the composer emphasizes it. Typically, line 1 contains a noun that represents the topic of the aria—in this case, *brine* ("frost")—and the motto entrance helps establish this image as the subject of the movement as a whole.

Instrumental Participation in Arias

The cantata's last aria, "Onde belle" (anthology, Selection 10b), is another motto aria: the voice enters in measure 9 and then repeats its entrance two measures later. Unlike "Fresche brine," it is not in da capo form, and in this respect it is somewhat old-fashioned. But its treatment of the violins represents a trend that would continue in the following century.

The aria opens with a ritornello, which, unlike that of "Fresche brine," is thoroughly integrated with the vocal portion of the movement. After the ritornello (mm. 1–8) the violins continue to play, accompanying the voice in a four-part contrapuntal texture and rounding off the end of the aria with a short instrumental passage. Brief instrumental passages also punctuate the body of the aria at several points. The longer of these passages—those at measures 17, 22, and 45—can also be described as ritornellos, even though none literally repeats the opening instrumental passage. All nevertheless restate and develop musical material first presented in that initial ritornello.

Particularly important is the theme stated by the second violin in measure 1. This theme can be described as a **ritornello theme,** since it opens the ritornello and is repeated, at least in part, in subsequent ritornellos. In this case, the

---

[10]Often the German equivalents of these words are used: *Devise* (motto) and *Devisenarie* (motto aria).

ritornello theme is also a subject, since it is imitated by the first violin (m. 2) and the continuo (m. 3) as each enters.[11]

The voice's entry with the same theme in measure 9 reveals that the ritornello theme is more than an abstract musical idea; its first five notes constitute word painting on *onde* ("waves"), whose first syllable is sung to a short melisma that circles or turns through the interval g'–bb'. This turning motive, as one can call it, not only dominates the ritornellos but continues to be heard in the violin parts after the voice has gone on to other textual ideas. For example, in measures 18–21, as the voice sings the single word *ascoltate* ("hear me!"), the two violins enter in imitation with a version of the ritornello theme (mm. 18–19). The violins then continue with passagework in sixteenth notes that includes several additional statements of the turning motive (mm. 20, 21). Thus a musical depiction of waves accompanies Daliso's anguished prayer that the waves listen to his complaint. Indeed, the "wave" motive permeates the texture of the entire aria, which thus becomes a sort of musical symbol for waves. Countless arias from later cantatas and other Baroque vocal compositions use instrumental parts in like manner to represent images in the text.

THE DISSEMINATION OF ITALIAN BAROQUE STYLE

Over the course of the seventeenth century, the political and economic significance of the great Italian cities declined. Yet Rome and Venice remained important destinations for aristocratic travelers, whether on diplomatic missions or for recreation and education; by the end of the Baroque it was almost expected that northern Europeans would travel to Italy to complete their acquisition of socially approved manners and culture. Many visitors gained a taste for the latest Italian music, and those who could afford to do so brought back music, musical instruments, even actual musicians. Hence knowledge of Italian composition and performance styles spread, especially in German-speaking Europe, where native composers adopted current Italian practices, spurred in part by an influx of Italian emigré musicians at major courts, such as those of the Austrian emperor in Vienna and the duke (elector) of Saxony in Dresden. Only in France was there strong resistance to Italian musical influence, in part for political reasons. Even there, however, musicians blended local traditions with those of Italy. A particularly distinctive cross-pollination of musical cultures occurred in England, where composers merged the new, fashionable types of Italian song—as well as instrumental music—with idiosyncratic native ones.[12]

---

[11]The imitative entries of the three instrumental parts follow the same pattern that would be expected in a fugue (see Chapter 10).

[12]French influence on English music was also strong, as was true as well in Germany; French music is taken up in the following chapter.

English Vocal Music in the Later Seventeenth Century

At the middle of the seventeenth century, civil war and a brief period as a republic (1649–60) had left England temporarily without a royal court and chapel. Those institutions had been important centers for music under the previous monarchs—Elizabeth I (reigned 1558–1603), James I (r. 1603–25), and Charles I (r. 1625–49)—all of whom had been strong patrons of the arts. Music had flourished particularly under Elizabeth and during the first decade of James's reign, when the leading musician in England was William Byrd (1543–1623). One of the supreme figures of Renaissance music, Byrd wrote not only sacred and secular vocal polyphony but also—unlike Palestrina, Lassus, and other contemporaries on the Continent—music for solo keyboard and for instrumental consort. His output also includes numerous songs for voice and instruments. Byrd avoided the madrigal, but his younger contemporaries are known for their **English madrigals**—settings of English texts composed in imitation of the polyphonic Italian madrigal of the late sixteenth century. They also wrote strophic songs (called airs) with lute accompaniment. The most famous composer of the latter was John Dowland (1563–1626), a lutenist who also composed many solo works for his own instrument.

War, together with the banning of elaborate sacred and theatrical music by the republican or Commonwealth government, had virtually extinguished this rich musical tradition by midcentury. With the restoration of the monarchy in 1660, however, royal and cathedral musical institutions were reestablished and commercial theaters in London were allowed to reopen. Under King Charles II, who had spent much of the preceding period in exile in France, musicians and musical genres were imported from both France and Italy. These mingled with the remnants of the native English tradition, which had been preserved by survivors from pre-Commonwealth days, such as the song composer Henry Lawes (1596–1662; his more prolific composer brother William had died in the Civil War in 1645).

Although no English theater possessed the resources needed to mount full-fledged operas, spoken plays during the Restoration period (1660–88) commonly included musical interludes. These ranged from single songs to operatic scenes with dancing and choral singing, somewhat as in the pre-Commonwealth English court **masque**.[13] In addition, in the Chapel Royal and the cathedrals the distinctively English form of church music called the **anthem** was again cultivated. The anthem had originated as the Anglican (English Protestant) equivalent of the late-sixteenth-century motet. It retained a conservative contrapuntal style through the earlier seventeenth century, although the voices were generally joined by organ and, in some works, a consort of viols (viola da gambas). After the Restoration, instrumental participation was expanded, particularly in music written for the monarch's Chapel Royal. Violins replaced viols, and composers adopted up-to-date elements of

---

[13]During the first decades of the seventeenth century, the masque had been the English equivalent of the French court ballet (see Chapter 6), combining dance and singing in a manner reminiscent of the old *intermedio*.

both the French and the Italian styles, including the use of overture-like preludes and virtuoso solo vocal writing.

Henry Purcell

The great English composer of the period was Henry Purcell (1659–95), whose lifespan corresponded roughly with the Restoration period—that is, the reigns of Kings Charles II (1660–85) and James II (1685–88)—together with that of Queen Mary II (1689–94), who in theory ruled jointly with her husband, William III (1689–1702). All except William were important patrons of musicians. Born probably at Westminster (now part of London), Purcell led a career outwardly similar to that of earlier English composers, such as Byrd. As a boy he sang in the newly reconstituted Chapel Royal, and by 1677 he was composing for King Charles II. In 1679 he became organist at Westminster Abbey, the great London church where royal coronations are still held; in that position he succeeded his teacher John Blow (1649–1708), the most talented of his English contemporaries. Purcell continued to enjoy royal patronage for the remainder of his life, composing anthems for the Chapel Royal as well as court odes and royal welcome songs—multimovement vocal works combining instrumental, solo vocal, and choral writing somewhat like the Continental serenata. He also wrote a small but very fine repertory of keyboard music and several sets of extraordinary chamber works for strings (both viol and violin ensembles).

Many of Purcell's works reveal a continuing respect for complex imitative counterpoint such as Purcell would have found in the music of Byrd and other late-Renaissance predecessors. It was in keeping with a certain idiosyncratic conservatism, evident in English music throughout the sixteenth and seventeenth centuries, that this older music was still studied and emulated in Purcell's day. Similarly, Blow, Purcell, and their English contemporaries continued to employ irregular dissonances and other elements of what Monteverdi called the *seconda pratica*, long after the ostentatious use of such things had ceased to be fashionable elsewhere. This is particularly true of the fantasias that Purcell composed for consorts of three, four, five, and six viola da gambas—a variety of scoring that had been more popular eighty years earlier.[14] The nine four-part fantasias were written during the summer of 1680; their audacious approach to dissonant harmony has echoes in the string writing for the more modern violin ensemble in Purcell's later *Dido and Aeneas* (see Ex. 5.7).

Some of Purcell's most important writing lies in his many songs, most of which were composed for musical scenes in Restoration plays. Many of these songs, such as "Music for a While" and "Hark, the Echoing Air," were published after his death in a two-volume collection entitled *Orpheus Britannicus*

---

[14]A **fantasia** in the early seventeenth century was a polyphonic work for keyboard or for a small group of instruments, usually without continuo; the style was originally modeled on that of the sixteenth-century motet, but Baroque examples often incorporate considerable chromaticism, and they may maintain the same subject throughout, developing it through various contrapuntal devices, such as inversion and augmentation.

Example 5.7 Purcell, *Dido and Aeneas*, Act 3, scene 2, Dido: "When I am laid in earth," mm. 1–14

(The British Orpheus). They have remained popular, thanks to their often jaunty melodies and rhythms (sometimes derived from those of French dances of the period) but also because of their compelling, expressive harmony. Many of these compositions, although described even today simply as "songs," originally served as dramatic musical scenes in the plays from which they are taken and incorporate distinct sections in contrasting recitative and aria styles. Hence they are effectively English cantatas. Purcell's one short opera, *Dido and Aeneas*, is similar in style to his other stage music, although only here do the main characters participate musically; its best-known music is the lament of Queen Dido, sung to her attendants as she prepares to die.[15] This famous number follows the

---

[15]The date of this work—sometimes described as a masque rather than an opera—has aroused controversy. It is known to have been performed in 1689 at a girls' boarding school in Chelsea (now part of London), but dates of composition as early as 1683, possibly for the royal court, have been proposed.

Venetian lament tradition in its use of a bass ostinato (Ex. 5.7). But characteristic of Purcell, and of English seventeenth-century music in general, are some quirky but highly expressive touches: the asymmetry of the ostinato, which is five measures in length rather than the more common four; and the combination of chromaticism with descending appoggiaturas, as on the words "laid" and "trouble."

A sort of chamber opera, written for a private performance, *Dido and Aeneas* is in some respects less significant than Purcell's four **semi-operas**—plays incorporating substantial musical scenes and produced in London's commercial theaters. Among these works is *King Arthur*, performed in 1691, with a text by the leading English poet of the day, John Dryden. Its musical portions are operatic in length and style; modeled after the *divertissements* of Lullian opera (see chapter 6), they combine recitative, solo airs, choral numbers, and dances. Here, as in his other vocal music, Purcell imaginatively adapted elements of both the French and Italian styles of his day for the purpose of setting texts written in English.

From Rosy Bowers

Among the last works of Purcell's short career were a number of musical scenes for Thomas D'Urfey's three-part theatrical adaptation of *Don Quixote*, the famous novel by the Spanish writer Miguel de Cervantes (1547–1616). Purcell's music for one of these scenes, *From Rosy Bowers* (anthology, Selection 11), was published posthumously as "the last song the author set." Like a number of Purcell's other "songs," it is an English cantata, comprising the same alternating recitatives and arias customary in Italian cantatas of the time. Yet it also reflects the stylistic blending that was possible for an English composer. One of the arias is actually a French-style **air** (the term is the French equivalent of *aria*), and the recitatives are longer and closer to arioso than was customary in the *recitativo semplice* of contemporary Italian cantatas.

Although scored only for soprano and basso continuo, this is one of Purcell's most effective stage scenes. It is sung by the female character Altesidora, who has been trying to woo the old knight Don Quixote. To gain his sympathy she sings for him this series of poignant recitatives and arias, each of a distinct type and expressing a different emotion. She ends with a so-called mad song, a common type in the Restoration theater. But Altesidora's madness is all an act; instead of being genuinely troubled or desperate, she is plotting and intriguing. Thus the concluding passage has a triumphant character that seems to look forward to Altesidora's successful accomplishment of her plan.

The opening recitative, in which Altesidora calls on the "god of love" (Cupid), contains many examples of Purcell's vivid musical rhetoric, including frequent chromaticism and sudden outbursts of melismatic arioso. The text of the following air, "Or if more influencing," refers to the arts of Venus and the three Graces, which Altesidora wishes to employ in order to win over Strephon. The poem's image of Greek goddesses dancing on a mountaintop explains why Purcell set it as a *bourrée*, one of the French dances of the period. Like his French contemporaries, Purcell frequently used dance types as the basis of vocal numbers (compare Exx. 6.3 and 6.6). The bourrée, like other French dances, is characterized by its distinctive meter, rhythm, and form: its duple time signature, melodic motion in even quarter notes (beginning with a quarter-note upbeat), and binary form are features common to most bourres.[16]

When Altesidora's dance fails to have its desired effect, she resolves in the second recitative ("Ah! 'tis in vain") to go mad. This recitative is even more vivid than the first; one instance of word painting was so extreme that an early editor apparently eliminated it from the music. On the word *death* (m. 4), Purcell asked the singer to leap up to the note e♭″ following an e♮′. This produces the rare and, in this context, expressive melodic interval of a diminished octave. The early eighteenth-century edition reproduced in the anthology omits the e♭″.

The work continues with a short air in da capo form, "Or say, ye powers," which Altesidora apparently addresses to the gods of a stream or river into which she threatens to throw herself. The air opens with a short ritornello, played by the basso continuo (mm. 1–8). But this ritornello is not heard again, except for the imitation of the opening motive by the voice (compare mm. 1, 8, and 9). The concluding recitative, "No, I'll straight run mad," begins with what might be a purposely overblown imitation of madness—compare Nero's outburst in Example 4.1—followed by a somewhat more regular arioso (starting in m. 5). The last four lines of the poem (mm. 10–20) employ frequent imitation between the two parts—a device that makes more emphatic the word painting on "fly" and "thousand" while bringing the scene to a musically effective ending. It shows, too, that for Purcell, as for Scarlatti, counterpoint was by no means foreign to the cantata, which to the end of the Baroque continued the tradition of expressive monody invented at the end of the sixteenth century.

---

[16]The two halves of the air were poabably meant to be repeated, as in the dance.

CHAPTER 6

LULLY AND FRENCH MUSICAL DRAMA

France in the first half of the seventeenth century was torn by conflict, both between the dominant Roman Catholics and the minority Protestants (known as Huguenots), and also between rival noble factions, some supporting an alliance with Italy and the Austrian empire, others opposing it. Although the level of violence did not reach that of the Wars of Religion in the sixteenth century, it did impede the flourishing of the arts until the absolute rule of King Louis XIV was firmly established, in 1661.

Musical developments reflected political ones. The royal court had dominated French musical life since the sixteenth century, and under Louis XIII's queen Anne of Austria (1601–66) and their Italian first minister Cardinal Mazarin (1602–61), Italian music was heavily patronized. Italian operas by Luigi Rossi (*Orfeo*, 1647) and Cavalli (*Serse*, 1660; *Ercole amante*, 1662) were performed in Paris, and Italian-born musicians such as Jean-Baptiste Lully, discussed below, entered the court. But Italian political influence, and the political instability associated with it, ended when Louis XIV came to power. The entire French aristocracy was required to pay homage to him on a regular basis at his palace of Versailles, which became a center for all manner of artistic activity under royal patronage. The royal musical establishment, like the country at large, was placed under a rigorously centralized administration; the latter controlled many aspects of musical production and hence had a substantial impact on the nature of French music during the late seventeenth and early eighteenth centuries. Among those to benefit were French musical institutions such as the Twenty-four Violins of the King (*Vingt-quatre Violons du Roi*), which had been furnishing dance music for the court since the late sixteenth century; under Louis XIV the Twenty-Four Violins became one of Europe's most famous ensembles, imitated at the English royal court and elsewhere.[1] Another important institution was the Royal Academy of Music, founded in 1672, which for more than a century would produce French opera under the protection (if not the direct support) of the king.

---

[1]The word "violin" (*violon*) here refers to members of the entire violin family, not just the familiar treble instrument; the Twenty-Four Violins was a complete string orchestra.

The French Style

France had developed a distinctive musical culture by the end of the sixteenth century, characterized in particular by the court air (*air de cour*) and the court ballet (*ballet de cour*). Both genres continued to flourish in the seventeenth century. The ballet, like the Italian *intermedio*, often included elaborate dramatic staging and substantial vocal music and was frequently performed before a large public audience. The *air de cour*—which was hardly confined to the royal court—grew out of the older polyphonic chanson. The seventeenth-century *air de cour* usually consisted of strophic monody with lute accompaniment, although some early examples exist in polyphonic versions as well. Among the leading composers were Pierre Guédron (?after 1564–1619/20), Antoine Boësset (1586–1643), and Etienne Moulinié (ca. 1600–after 1669). Later composers, including Lully, Charpentier, and François Couperin, composed similar songs under the headings *airs sérieux* (serious songs) and *airs à boire* (literally, drinking songs, although these were not necessarily very different in style from the serious ones). Some of these songs, notably those by Michel Lambert (ca. 1610–1696), Lully's father-in-law, contain elaborate written-out vocal embellishments for the later stanzas.

A distinctive feature of many early *airs de cour* was the absence of a regular meter. This is clear in Example 6.1, an *air de cour* by Guédron that was published in a number of early seventeenth-century anthologies.[2] There is no regular time signature; instead, the meter shifts fluidly between what we would call $\frac{3}{4}$, $\frac{4}{4}$, and $\frac{3}{2}$ time. The text is set syllabically, mainly in quarter and half notes, which correspond to short and long syllables of the French text. Syllables that receive particular stress, such as the opening word *vous* ("you") and *mourez* ("will die") at the beginning of line 3, receive melismatic embellishments, but the overall length of each of these syllables remains that of a half note.

Such rhythm resembles that of recitative, yet it does not imitate actual speech. Unlike recitative, the *air de cour* reflects the principles of *vers mesuré* (literally, "measured verse"), a theory developed in the late sixteenth century on the basis of ancient Greek poetry. The latter was (and still is) believed to have been sung in alternating long and short note values, closely reflecting the lengths of the syllables of the text. Although this type of declamation reflected the ancient Greek language as actually spoken, its application to modern French was artifical. Nevertheless, the resulting style of declamation had a profound influence on both French vocal music and the spoken French of the Baroque theater. It led to the so-called *musique mesurée* ("measured music") of Claude Le Jeune (1528/30–1600): polyphonic chansons whose syllabic settings and irregular meter were direct antecedents of the monodic type of song shown in Example 6.1.[3]

---

[2]The version in Ex. 6.1 was published in Robert Dowland's *A Musical Banquet* (London, 1610).

[3]Le Jeune's most famous work was *Le printemps* (Spring), a collection of polyphonic chansons published posthumously in 1603.

Example 6.1 Guédron, *Vous que le bonheur rappelle*

1 Vous que le bonheur rappelle
2 À un servage ancien,
3 Mourez aux pieds de la belle
4 Qui vous daigne faire sien.
[six more stanzas follow]

You whom good fortune calls
To an old servitude [i.e., love]
Will die at the feet of the beauty
Who wishes to make you her own.

Although the theory of *vers mesuré* was soon abandoned, the strict approach to musical declamation typical of the *air de cour* was retained in French vocal writing through the end of the seventeenth century. While Italian composers and performers were turning the aria into a virtuoso showpiece and the main element of Italian opera, the French *air* remained restrained in style—often similar to recitative, which likewise retained its importance throughout French seventeenth-century opera. Moreover, French composers until the end of the Baroque retained a special interest in rhythmically defined musical forms. Among these was a specifically French form of recitative as well as a large number of dance genres, each characterized by particular types of tempo and rhythm.

The Role of Lully

Paradoxically, the leading role in French music under Louis XIV was taken by the Italian-born Jean-Baptiste Lully (1632–87) (see Box 6.1). He had come to Paris from Florence in 1646 in the retinue of a French duchess related to both the Florentine dukes and the French King. By 1653 he had entered the service of the young Louis XIV as a composer of music for the court ballets. By the time the king reached adulthood and began to rule in his own name in 1661, Lully had become the head of the court musicians, a position that gave him

---

BOX 6.1

Jean-Baptiste Lully (1632–1687)

1632. Born in Florence (northern Italy) as Giovanni Battista Lulli; the nature of his early training is uncertain.

1646. In France as Italian tutor, dancer, and musician for the Duchess of Montpensier (the "Grande Mademoiselle"), cousin of the future king Louis XIV; reportedly studies composition with several French musicians.

1653. Enters the service of the young Louis XIV as composer of instrumental music after dancing alongside the king in *Ballet de la nuit*; contributes increasing amounts of music to court ballets.

1661. Louis XIV begins to rule in his own right and appoints Lully superintendent of royal chamber music.

1662. Marries Madeleine Lambert, daughter of royal musician and composer Michel Lambert.

1664. Appointed director of the Grande Bande (the Twenty-Four Violins of the King).

1664–70. Collaborations with Molière (comic playwright), including *Le bourgeois gentilhomme* (1670).

1672. Acquires right to direct the Royal Academy of Music (opera company); collaborates with poet Philippe Quinault in their first opera (*Cadmus et Hermione, tragédie en musique*), performed 1673.

1677. His first son Louis born; named for the king, who served as godfather at a ceremony in which Lully's *Te Deum* was performed.

1687. Dies at Paris of gangrene developed after injuring himself while directing a performance of his *Te Deum*.

---

control of the vast budget and personnel of the royal musical establishment. Further power came with his takeover in 1672 of the Royal Academy of Music, after it ran into financial difficulties following its first opera production the previous year.[4] Through the Royal Academy, Lully produced operatic works at the rate of usually one each year from 1672 until the end of his life, exercising the same dictatorial control over staging and musical execution that he exercised in his ballets for the royal court. Most productions were staged at the Palais Royal in Paris, the former residence of the king's brother, after first being performed privately at the king's palace in versailles. The tradition of French opera under royal protection continued until the Revolution (1791), although apart from Rameau no one composer ever again dominated the field to the degree that Lully did.

---

[4]Lully also obtained a monopoly on the printing of his own music within France. Royally protected monopolies of this type were a standard feature of the seventeenth- and eighteenth-century European economy, granted to makers of weapons, ceramic wares, and other commodities as well as to writers, printers, and musical or theatrical entrepreneurs such as Lully.

By the end of his life, Lully had amassed considerable personal wealth and power—as well as enemies. No other musicians were allowed to challenge his prominence or to perform works that might rival his. Thus Lully effectively brought to an end the career of the composer Robert Cambert (ca. 1628–77), who in 1671 performed the first French opera (*Pomone*, music mostly lost). Marc-Antoine Charpentier (1643–1704), the one French contemporary whose musical genius might have challenged Lully's, had to content himself with writing mainly sacred music until Lully's death, and even then only one of his operas was performed by the Royal Academy (*Médée*, 1693).

But it was not merely personal power that made Lully so successful and influential. He clearly was a gifted and imaginative musician, and his dance and vocal music exerted an enormous influence over several generations of musicians throughout Europe. Although a distinctive French style existed before him, it was Lully who was credited with establishing *the* French style as it was known in the later seventeenth and eighteenth centuries: a style taken for granted by later French composers, such as Couperin and Rameau, and imitated by many of the leading composers elsewhere, including Purcell in England and Handel and Bach in Germany. When the German composer Georg Muffat published a set of orchestral suites (*Florilegium primum,* 1695) in the French style, his foreword referred to them as in the "Lullian" style.

Not only does this style employ forms and compositional devices distinct from those of the Italians; French Baroque musicians also developed performing practices that were very much their own. Although the French would hold to their own traditions throughout the Baroque, by the later eighteenth century the conventions of the Lullian style were falling out of use. As a result, the French Baroque style is less familiar than the Italian to most listeners and performers today. Nevertheless, just as writings by Caccini and his contemporaries have given performers insights into the performance of early Baroque Italian music, documents such as Muffat's foreword—which contains a detailed account of French performing conventions—have made possible the revival of French Baroque traditions. Although only a few dedicated organizations regularly present full-scale productions of Lully's stage works, numerous recordings of French Baroque vocal and instrumental chamber music as well as works for solo lute and keyboard instruments can provide good introductions to both the repertory and the performance style.[5]

Lully's Works

Lully's earliest significant works were probably individual dances and airs composed for court ballets, which were collaborative efforts like the Renaissance *intermedio*. Lully's participation was not limited to composing the music, for as a talented dancer and mime he took many roles, probably providing his own

---

[5] A good impression of how the distinctive types of French Baroque music, dance, and staging function together can be gained from a DVD video of Lully's opera *Persée,* in a live performance by Toronto's Opera Atelier (EuroArts 2054178, recorded 2004). For Muffat's foreword, see Bibliography under "Instruments and Instrumental Practice."

Figure 6.1 A performance at Versailles of Molière's comedy *Le malade imaginaire*, engraving from André Félibien, *Les divertissemens de Versailles . . .* (Paris, 1676). This performance, given 6 July 1674, is presumably being directed by Lully (standing, beating time with a rolled-up sheet of paper); the king is seated at the center of the audience.

choreography.[6] Among his dancing partners was the teenaged Louis XIV—for members of the royal court took part in the ballets, and the young king was an avid dancer. In this the king followed the tradition of his father, Louis XIII, who had taken an active role in the production of court ballets, even composing the music for one. Louis XIV would be similarly involved in the production of Lully's operas, selecting their subjects and approving their librettos prior to the composition of the music.

By the late 1650s Lully was the sole composer of the most important court ballets. In the 1660s this led to a series of collaborations with the most important writers of the day, notably the comic playwright Jean-Baptiste Molière (Fig. 6.1). Among their *comédies-ballets*, as their collaborations are known, was *Le bourgeois gentilhomme* (The village aristocrat, 1670), their last and most popular work. Soon thereafter, however, Lully turned his attention to the production of opera with the Royal Academy, for which, with the poet Philippe Quinault (1635–88), he invented a distinctively French version of the Italian genre. Together they created eleven operas, or, as they termed them, *tragédies en musique* (tragedies in music).[7] We shall be examining the

---

[6]No written choreographies by Lully are extant, but those of later French dancing masters survive, including a few for music by Lully (see Fig. 6.2).

[7]Lully wrote two further operas in conjunction with other poets, and was working on a third when he died.

last such work that Lully completed, *Armide;* focusing on the end of Act 2 and portions of Act 3.

Dance in French Music

Dance was of great cultural significance in seventeenth-century France, in part due to its prominence in the social and political rituals of the royal court. Numerous dance scenes play a crucial role in French Baroque opera, and dance rhythms permeate French instrumental music throughout the period. The floor patterns traced by dancers in Lully's ballets and operas follow choreographies whose geometric designs reveal the same elaborate symmetries as the classically inspired architecture of the period (Fig. 6.2). Gestures of head, hands, and arms embellished the steps in the same expressively elegant manner with which ornaments graced French Baroque melodies.

Just as French song tended to employ accentual and durational patterns derived from the formal recitation of poetry, dance music tended to follow specific rhythmic patterns that corresponded to the steps of particular dances. For each of the common dances there was a specific type of music, defined by

Gigue a deux

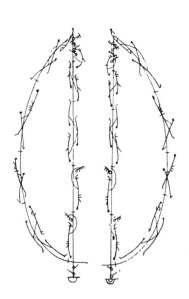

Figure 6.2 *Gigue à deux* (jig for a couple), from *Recueil de dances composées par M. Feuillet* (Paris, 1700). An example of Baroque choreography, using a system of notation invented by the author of the treatise from which the illustration is taken. Individual signs indicate the various types of steps, leaps, and other figures performed by the dancers; the geometric design of the diagram as a whole shows the path that each dancer traces across the floor or stage (note the precise symmetry, typical of French theatrical dance). Although the music is from Lully's *tragédie en musique Roland* of 1685, the choreography is not necessarily that used in the work's original staging.

tempo, meter, and certain recurring rhythmic patterns.[8] In the course of the seventeenth century, the pavane, galliard, and allemande—the chief French court dances of the late sixteenth century—gave way to the courante, sarabande, minuet, gigue, and other dances, each with its corresponding type of music. The importance of these dances extended far beyond ballets as such, for independent instrumental works, airs, and even sacred music all frequently borrowed the rhythms of particular dances. Often, the tempo and expressive character of a work could be inferred from the presence of dance elements in the music; in the absence of verbal expression markings, musicians recognized the dance type of a particular composition—and thus its proper tempo and character—from the rhythm of its opening measures.

The performance of dance music requires rhythmic precision and sureness of tempo from the instrumentalists, to avoid giving the dancer unpleasant surprises. For this reason the Twenty-Four Violins of the King cultivated a style of playing that, under Lully, became famous for its precise coordination, rhythmic sureness, and spirited articulation. Improvised ornamentation was banned, and bowings were dictated by a system that always placed downbows on accented beats. The frequent retaking or lifting of the bow required by this system led to a cleanly articulated, lively sort of melody and rhythm, much more airy than the continuous legato cultivated in nineteenth-century violin technique. Although the French string style did not encourage the solo virtuosity prized by Italian violinists, foreign listeners were amazed by the precision and unanimity of Lully's orchestra. The underlying conventions of performance were apparently unknown in Italy and elsewhere; Muffat, who had studied with Lully, published the rules as he understood them for the benefit of German string bands founded in imitation of the French one.

Conventions of Tempo and Rhythm

Another set of conventions came to govern tempo and the interpretation of rhythmic notation. Tempo in dance music was largely determined by that of the dance itself. For example, gigues tend to be quick and sarabandes slow, although there were frequent exceptions, particularly in earlier seventeenth-century works, before conventions had hardened into rules. Eventually, too, certain types of rhythm came to be performed differently from what a literal interpretation of the notation might imply.

Two important, but distinct, rhythmic conventions of the French style are known today as **overdotting** and *notes inégales* (unequal notes). Both involve departures from the rhythm as written. Overdotting has to do with the exaggeration of so-called dotted rhythms, such as a dotted quarter plus an eighth; *notes inégales* involves the imposition of dotted rhythm where none is notated. Both conventions apply only to certain note values in certain types of pieces.

Overdotting is especially associated with the dotted rhythms that permeate the overtures of Lully's operas. But free or exaggerated interpretation of dotted

---

[8]Some of the individual dance rhythms are considered in Chapter 10.

Example 6.2 Lully, *Armide*, Act 3, scene 4, *prélude* for La Haine (Hate) (three inner string parts omitted)

rhythm occurred in other genres as well. The convention might have arisen as a result of the abbreviated notation of certain sharply dotted rhythms. Thus in Example 6.2 the rhythm of measure 2 came to be notated in the simpler manner shown between the staves. Yet this later form of notation would have been executed in the same manner as the original.[9] Today the convention is sometimes described as "double dotting," since Lully's original notation in measure 2 is equivalent to a double-dotted quarter note followed by a sixteenth. The term "double dotting" is misleading, however, insofar as it implies a specific rhythmic value for the dotted note. French musicians evidently understood the dot as being variable in length, its exact meaning depending on the larger musical context. That Lully expected his dotted notation to be interpreted somewhat freely is suggested by measures 5–7, whose notation is arithmetically imprecise and cannot be played literally; what Lully may have intended is suggested beneath the staves.

The practice of *notes inégales* superficially resembles overdotting, since both involve the lengthening of the first in a series of notes. But whereas overdotting most often occurs in energetic pieces already notated in dotted rhythm, "inequality" can apply in gentler compositions that lack dotted notation. Moreover, the

---

[9]It is uncertain when this convention became established; certainly its application varied over the course of the seventeenth and eighteenth centuries.

Example 6.3 Lully, *Armide*, Act 2, scene 2, Sidonie's air "Sur des bords séparés"

1 Sur des bords séparés   On shores separated
2 Du séjour des humains,   From the ways of people,
3 Qui peut arracher de vos mains   Who can take from your hands
4 Un ennemy qui vous adore?   An enemy [Renaud] who adores you?
5 Vous enchantez Renaud,   You enchant Renaud;
6 Que craignez-vous encore?   What then do you fear?

"dotting" that results from *notes inégales* is usually less marked than in the case of overdotting. Thus in Example 6.3 notes written as eighths might actually have been performed as shown above and below the staves. The precise degree of inequality used in a given piece would, depend on the character of the music. A fairly gentle rhythm, that is, one with only a small degree of inequality, would be appropriate in Example 6.3, where the singer is consoling the unhappy Armide.

Elsewhere a more vigorous (i.e., more "unequal") rhythm may be desirable, even one that approaches the character of overdotting. The overture to *Armide* contains passages in eighth notes that many performers today convert to dotted rhythm (Ex. 6.4). Since the dotted rhythms are exaggerated in such a piece, the resulting performance uses both *notes inégales* and overdotting, but it is impossible to know whether this was Lully's intention. In general, however, overdotting is clearly distinct from inequality. Whereas overdotting, by definition, applies only to music already notated in dotted rhythm, inequality came to be

Example 6.4 Lully, *Armide*, overture (mm. 1–4; three inner string parts omitted)

a nearly universal element in French music, like the "swinging" of notes in jazz. Without inequality, much French Baroque music is lifeless—a point made by a number of French Baroque writers.[10]

Ornaments

Another important set of conventions in French Baroque music involves the use of melodic ornaments. French musicians tended to avoid the more elaborate types of melodic embellishment favored by Italian virtuosos throughout the Baroque. But French Baroque music, like Italian, also employs numerous stereotyped melodic ornaments: small figures, such as trills, that decorate single notes rather than whole phrases. Instead of being written out, these could be indicated by signs, as we do with the modern *tr* or trill sign. It is useful to refer to this standardized type of melodic decoration, which can be notated through symbols, as **ornamentation,** reserving the word **embellishment** for the more elaborate variety whose patterns can be indicated only by writing out the notes.

By the end of the seventeenth century, French players of lute, keyboard, and viola da gamba had developed numerous symbols for indicating ornaments. Although these symbols, or **ornament signs,** were never fully taken up by players of other instruments (or singers), they were imitated by lute and keyboard composers outside France, such as Bach. It was once thought that harpsichordists used these ornaments to overcome the inability of their instrument to sustain long notes. But the appoggiaturas, trills, mordents, and other ornaments of the French Baroque tradition were fundamental to the technique of all instruments— and of the voice as well, for solo and choral singing was as heavily ornamented as music for violin, gamba, and keyboards (including organ). When marked by the composer, these ornaments constitute an essential element in the shape and expressive content of a melodic line.

The original seventeenth-century printed editions of Lully's music employed only a single ornament sign—the letter *t,* set above or below the ornamented note, as in Examples 6.2–4. Lully's musicians presumably knew the conventions well enough to understand which particular ornament was required at any given point. Later composers used different signs for different

---

[10]For example, Michel de Saint-Lambert wrote in his *Principes du clavecin* (Paris, 1702): "[We play some notes unequally] because the inequality gives them more grace" (p. 25).

ornaments; there was never a standard set of ornament signs. To clarify what sign was being used for what ornament, some French composers included tables of ornaments in their publications, beginning in the late seventeenth century. Chapter 11 examines several ornament tables published in conjunction with eighteenth-century French harpsichord music, which, like other French music of that period, continued to employ many of the conventions established under Lully.

French Opera under Lully

Lullian opera was in many respects a synthesis of earlier French genres, incorporating a style of solo song derived from the *air de cour* alongside dances from the royal court ballet. But like Italian opera it also includes recitative, albeit of a distinctly French variety. As in Monteverdi's *Orfeo* and a number of other early Italian operas, the drama itself is preceded by a prologue addressed to the work's patron: in this case, the king. Most of the dialogue for the principal characters is presented in poetry of a serious character, although comic scenes do occur in Lully's *tragédies en musique*. Dialogue is set as monody: primarily in recitative, but interspersed with short airs and alternating with ballet scenes or *divertissements*—one in each act—in which dancers as well as the chorus and secondary singing characters often play prominent roles. Some *divertissements*, like the *intermedi* inserted into older comedies or the ballets that Lully had written for plays by Molière, constitute diversions from the main plot. But more often they present battles, marriage and funeral rites, and other impressive actions essential to the drama, and as such they constituted one of the main attractions of this type of opera. The fact that they mirrored actual court dance and social ritual, transferred to a mythic or legendary setting, no doubt produced a special resonance in their original aristocratic audiences.

Present throughout each such work is the chorus, which, as in *Orfeo*, was based on the chorus of ancient Greek drama, serving as both a participant in and commentator on the action. By Lully's day the chorus had disappeared from most Italian opera; thus its presence is, with the ballet, one of the defining features of French Baroque opera. Among the most typical Lullian uses of the chorus, although absent from *Armide*, is its role in scenes of lamentation where, as in *Orfeo*, it may provide a poignant refrain (as in Lully's operas *Alceste* and *Atys*).

Lullian Recitative

The charm and freshness of Lully's dance music was a major achievement and is one of the chief attractions of his works. Equally impressive was his invention of a distinctive type of recitative suitable for the French language, whose accentual patterns are very different from those of Italian. Italian recitative is invariably notated in common time, with rhythm and tempo determined to a considerable degree by the performer. Although writers of the period prescribe freedom in French recitative as well, the precision with which it was notated implies a relatively strict manner of interpretation. Lully's notation of recitative fluctuates between duple, triple, and quadruple meters; the changing time signatures are thought to determine the tempo of each section relative to the previous one, according to certain conventions. Evidently the intended result was recitative that possesses clear rhythm and a definite tempo, although the latter might vary with the sentiment of each line of poetry.[11]

Just as the Lullian air avoided the trend toward virtuosity characteristic of the Italian aria, Lullian recitative never became as "dry" or as purely speechlike as the later Italian type. Lengthy recitation on repeated notes is a rarity, and thus French Baroque recitative retains much of the melodic character of the air; indeed, the two are sometimes almost indistinguishable in style. It is sometimes said that French Baroque vocal music has a more "speaking" style than that of Italy, and indeed, Lully and other French composers explicitly modeled their vocal style on the stylized poetic declamation of the spoken French theater of their time. This in turn was modeled on that of the ancient Greeks—yet another example of the continuing influence of antiquity on Baroque artistic thinking.

Scoring

French opera never adopted the tradition of using high voices for men's roles, as became the norm in Italian Baroque opera, nor were the tenor and bass voices accordingly neglected. Tenor parts retain the prominence they had in Monteverdi's early works, and important male roles are often taken by basses. The female alto voice is unknown, however. Its place in the operatic chorus was taken by the high male voice known as the *haute-contre*, as in French Baroque choral music generally.[12]

The functional division within Lully's works between the main action, presented in recitatives and airs, and the *divertissements* or ballet scenes was reflected in a functional division of the instruments. As in early Italian opera, recitative and air are accompanied mainly by the continuo. The latter was furnished by the usual small group of instruments, which might include theorbos (large lutes), harpsichords, and bass violin and viola da gamba. Another small group of violins and woodwinds provided ritornellos and sinfonias as well as the instrumental parts that occasionally accompany the solo voices; *Armide* is unusually rich in airs and recitatives with such instrumental parts.

A larger string band essentially identical to the Twenty-Four Violins provided the music for the overture and ballet scenes. Unlike the modern string orchestra (or the Italian string ensemble of the eighteenth century), the French seventeenth-century violin band was usually scored in five parts, following a tradition inherited from sixteenth-century dance music. It was dominated by a single upper part for violin and an equally strong bass line, both of these parts

---

[11]See anthology, Selection 12b, and the accompanying discussion of performance issues. Although some questions about the conventions of French Baroque recitative remain unresolved, the very free rhythm heard in some modern performances may be contrary to historical practice.

[12]The *haute-contre* was probably not a pure falsetto voice but rather involved considerable blending of full and head voice, at least in the upper part of the range.

being doubled by numerous players. There was at first no continuo, the harmony being filled out by the three inner parts, which were played on instruments corresponding to the modern viola. Under Lully the string music may have been played from memory, perhaps reflecting another old custom. Lully himself is thought to have composed only the outer voices in most cases, leaving the inner parts to assistants. The dance music played by this ensemble was directed not by the principal violinist or from the harpsichord, as was the practice of other ensembles, but by a conductor who beat time either with a baton or a rolled-up sheet of music paper; evidently this was sometimes intentionally struck against a music desk or other object, creating an audible beat described by contemporary observers.

The prevailing string color was modified by woodwinds; the chief instruments were the **recorder,** an end-blown wooden flute, and the Baroque oboe and bassoon. Wind instruments were used chiefly for special effects. Recorders, for example, might be heard in scenes where a character sleeps or has a dream, which would be depicted by a ballet scene. Each woodwind instrument came in multiple sizes, from which an entire consort or instrumental choir could be formed, as in the sixteenth century; the bassoon served as the bass of the oboe choir. All of the woodwinds underwent modifications during Lully's lifetime; it is often claimed that the alterations were undertaken specifically to reflect the needs of his works, and if so, then the modern forms of these instruments owe something to Lully and the seventeenth-century French opera orchestra.

JEAN-BAPTISTE LULLY'S *ARMIDE*

Lully's last completed *tragédie en musique* was composed to a libretto by Quinault and first performed in 1686. Successive generations of French critics regarded it as their greatest work; revivals continued into the 1760s. The story, a popular one derived from Tasso's *Gerusalemme liberata*, was the basis for many other operas before and since, including Handel's *Rinaldo* (1711). It concerns the encounter of the medieval Christian Crusader Renaud (Rinaldo) with the sorceress Armide (Armida), whose role is central to Lully's opera. This was unusual, for Armide was not a noble heroine or historic figure but a witch, and, for Lully and his contemporaries in France, a representative of the exotic Middle East rather than the Christian West. She nevertheless becomes a sympathetic figure in Quinault and Lully's treatment.[13]

The Overture

The prologue of *Armide* is unusually short, but it opens with a type of overture that Lully had been using since his ballets of the late 1650s. So closely is this

---

[13]For synopsis of the plot, see Box 6.2. It has been suggested that the plot, with its allusions to the triumph of Catholic Christianity over its enemies, referred to the 1685 Edict of Nantes, by which Louis XIV banned Protestantism in France.

Box 6.2

Lully: *Armide*

Libretto by Philippe Quinault (1635–88).
Tragédie en musique, first performed at Paris, 1686.

Chief Characters

Armide (soprano), pagan sorceress
Phénice, Sidonie (sopranos), companions of Armide
Renaud (tenor), Crusader general

SYNOPSIS

As the opera begins, Renaud is the only Crusader general who has not been defeated by the forces of Armide and her uncle Hidraot (bass, pagan king of Damascus, Syria). Armide therefore decides to conquer Renaud through magic and deception. At the end of Act 2 Armide has captured Renaud and intends to kill him, but she stops when she realizes that she is attracted to him. She therefore has her demons carry him off to her enchanted castle.

As Act 3 opens, the theater represents the desert surrounding Armide's palace. She wanders, pondering her situation. Her companions Phénice and Sidonie arrive and remind her that Renaud is in her power, since he loves her. She replies that he loves her only because he has been enchanted, whereas she truly loves him (refrain, "my love is of a different sort"). To strengthen her resolve to kill Renaud, she calls forth the demon Hate and her followers. But after they arrive Armide changes her mind. Hate warns her of dire consequences and abandons her to Love.

As Act 5 opens, Renaud is being held prisoner by Armide in her enchanted palace. Using all her magical powers, she invites him to love in a grand *divertissement* danced and sung by a chorus of happy lovers. Immediately afterward, however, two of Renaud's companions arrive; they have obtained a magic shield that breaks Armide's spell. Renaud is freed and Armide, in despair, destroys her palace and herself—one of the few genuinely tragic endings in Baroque opera.

SELECTIONS DISCUSSED IN THIS CHAPTER

Prologue: Overture.

Act 2, scene 5: Armide standing over the enchanted Renaud: (a) *prélude* (orchestra); (b) Armide: recitative "Enfin il est en ma puissance"; (c) Armide: air "Venez seconder mes désirs"; (d) entr'acte (orchestra).

Act 3, scene 2: Armide joined by Sidonie and Phénice: (a) recitative; (b) Sidonie: air "Sur des bords"; (c) Armide: "De mes plus doux regards."

———, scene 3: Armide alone, calling on Hate: air with string accompaniment "Venez, Haine implacable!"

———, scene 4: Ballet: Hate and her followers (fellow demons). (a) *prélude*, then accompanied recitative "Je réponds à tes voeux"; (b) *prélude* and air with chorus "Plus on connait l'Amour"; (c) first instrumental air (*entrée*).

Act 5, scene 2: *Passacaille.*

type of overture associated with Lully's operas that it has come to be known as the **French overture**. It was used not only to open operas and other theatrical works but as an independent instrumental genre through the end of the Baroque. The overture to *Armide* (anthology, Selection 12a) is typical in consisting of two sections, each repeated. The first, in duple or quadruple time, is pervaded by dotted rhythms and is grand and energetic in character. The second section may be in any meter but is usually somewhat faster than the first. It often opens imitatively, in the manner of a fugue, although the counterpoint in the overture to *Armide* is not at all complex; the subject is simply a four-note motive, initially imitated by the three lowest parts (mm. 11, 12) but thereafter used largely as a melodic idea in the violin and bass parts. As in many overtures, the second half returns to duple meter and dotted rhythm (m. 26) before concluding.

Unlike the overtures of nineteenth-century works, those of Baroque operas rarely have any musical or expressive connection with what follows. Rather, the French overture was, as the French term *ouverture* (opening) implies, simply a way of starting a work. In Lully's operas, the overture is not only heard at the beginning of the prologue but is repeated at the end, where it serves as an *entr'acte* or transition to the first act. Later composers, notably Handel, sometimes employed additional overtures at other points in the opera as well. Short sinfonias and other instrumental passages within Lully's operas sometimes borrow the overture's dotted rhythm and grand style to introduce an important character or point to some significant event that is about to happen. Thus the ballet or *divertissement* in Act 3 of *Armide* opens with an orchestral *prélude* in dotted overture style (Ex. 6.2). The *premier air* (first dance) in this *divertissement* is an *entrée grave*, whose music also employs the dotted rhythm of the opening part of an overture. Modern writers have sometimes supposed that the distinctive rhythm of the French overture was associated specifically with the French king or with the idea of royalty. This type of overture was indeed recognized as a specifically French genre, but the dotted rhythm of its first section could have any number of meanings within a given work.

Other Instrumental Music

Together with the overture, the dances of the prologue and the five *divertissements* constituted most of the music assigned to the orchestral ensemble in a Lullian opera. Imaginatively choreographed, the dances were among the glories of French Baroque culture, as modern reconstructions have revealed. The basic rhythmic patterns and steps were usually those of the standard court dances. The latter were modified, however, to suit the characters and dramatic situations of each work. Thus in Act 3 of *Armide*, the *entrée* might have been entrusted to a single virtuoso male dancer; he would have represented the leader of the demons whom Armide calls onto the stage. Like the principal characters—singers as well as dancers—he would have worn a fanciful costume that indicated at a glance who he was.[14]

As in the Italian theater, the curtain went up at the outset and remained up throughout a work. Scene changes took place in full view of the audience and were one of the attractions of the opera, thanks to the beauty and ingenuity with which, for example, the "agreeable island" of Act 2 was transformed into the desert of Act 3. To accompany such changes, and also to cover up any noises made by the stage machinery, Lully generally had the orchestra repeat a dance that had been heard during the previous act. An *entr'acte* of this type often reflects the general character of the following scene, like the sinfonias in Monteverdi's *Orfeo*.

Recitative and Air

The most famous vocal music in the opera is that of Armide's monologues, particularly that which concludes Act 2 (anthology, Selection 12b). The scene is introduced by an orchestral prelude in dotted overture style (not in anthology) and concluded by an air. At its center is a lengthy recitative for the title character, who expresses her conflicting emotions as she hesitates between killing Renaud and falling in love with him. Reflecting this, her vocal line frequently rises and falls in relatively large leaps and is broken up by numerous rests (see especially mm. 34–42).

Lully's close integration of recitative and air is clear in the second scene of Act 3, where Armide's companions attempt to comfort her. Here the music shifts fluidly between recitatives and short airs; the latter resemble the *air de cour* in their relatively simple melodic lines and regular rhythm. Several employ recognizable dance rhythms. Sidonie's first air (Ex. 6.3) resembles a sarabande, a dance in triple time with a slow to moderate tempo. Armide's air "Plus Renaud m'aimera" (Ex. 6.5) employs the rhythm of the courante, a dance in compound duple time recognizable by its use of **hemiola**: an alternation between duple and triple divisions of the measure. For example, measure 1 is in $\frac{6}{4}$, as notated, with accents on the first and fourth quarter-note beats of the measure. Measure 2, however, is effectively in $\frac{3}{2}$, with accents on beats 1, 3, and 5 (as is clear from the accentuation of the last syllable of the word *serai*).

The *Divertissement* of Hate

By the end of Act 3, scene 2, Armide has decided that she wishes to hate Renaud, not love him. Her attempt to banish love from her heart is represented in an elaborate ballet or *divertissement* in which Hate itself appears onstage, personified as a

---

[14]Singing characters frequently were doubled by dancers wearing an identical costume, thus permitting the same figure to appear in both song and dance, although not simultaneously. For contemporary illustrations of such costumes, see Fig. 6.3 and the color drawings of Renaud and Armide in Philippe Beaussant, *Lully, ou Le musicien du soleil* (Paris: Gallimard, 1992), plates 14–15.

Example 6.5 Lully, *Armide*, Act 3, scene 2, Armide's air "Plus Renaud m'aimera"

Plus Renaud m'aimera, moins je serai tranquille;	The more Renaud loves me, the less I will be at peace;
J'ai résolu de le hair.	I have resolved to hate him.
Je n'ai tenté jamais rien de si difficile;	I have never attempted anything so difficult;
Je crains que pour forcer mon cœur à m'obéir	I fear that for forcing my heart to obey me
Tout mon art ne soit inutile.	All my magic will be useless.

demon and her followers (Fig. 6.3).[15] Armide calls upon Hate to "save" her from Love—also understood here through a personification—in an energetic air perhaps inspired by conjuring scenes in contemporary Italian opera, such as we saw in Cavalli's *Giasone*. Unusual here, for Lully, is the accompaniment of the solo voice by the full five-part orchestra, whose bass part has numerous statements of a lively

[15]Although Hate and her entourage are female, they are represented onstage by men, in keeping with seventeenth-century conventions of staging. Her followers are identified in the libretto as Furies—supernatural beings taken from ancient Greek mythology—and as personifications of cruelty, vengeance, rage, and "passions [emotions] dependent on Hate."

Figure 6.3 Lully, *Armide,* Act 3, opening, from *Armide: Tragedie mise en musique par Monsieur de Lully* (Paris: Ballard, 1713). The music is a reduced score omitting the three inner string parts. The image, engraved by Gérard Scotin the elder from a design by Jacques-Vigoureux Duplessis (?), is an idealized representation of the *divertissement,* showing Hate and three demons emerging from a fiery pit as Cupid (behind Armide) flees.

rhythmic motive (eighth–two sixteenths; see Ex. 6.6). The insistent use of this rhythm might have been a conscious reminiscence of what Monteverdi called the *stile concitato.* The same motive is used in slightly different form in the ballet proper, where Hate sings an air with a similar accompaniment (Ex. 6.7). Hate's followers repeat her air as a chorus of male voices.

The *Passacaille*

The most famous dance in the opera occurs in the *divertissement* in the fifth act. Here Armide, having failed in her effort to hate Renaud, conjures up a grand supernatural ballet intended to seduce him. The scene presents a lush spectacle as singers and dancers representing Armide's supernatural servants and assistants perform in groups varying from a few soloists to the entire ensemble. The music takes the form of a **passacaglia** (in French, *passacaille*); its opening is shown in Example 6.8a.

The passacaglia is usually defined today as a set of variations on a ground bass, that is, an ostinato bass line. In this it is similar to the **chaconne** (Italian

Example 6.6 Lully, *Armide*, Act 3, scene 3, Armide's air "Venez, Haine implacable," vocal entry

Venez, venez, Haine implacable,   Come, restless Hate,
Sortez du gouffre épouvantable.   Emerge from your dreadful cave.

ciacona). In fact, both genres were originally dances, not necessarily involving an ostinato bass. French Baroque chaconnes and *passacailles* are always in triple meter, with a moderately lively tempo. Phrases generally comprise four measures and frequently begin on the second beat of the measure. Hence upbeats of two quarter notes are common, as at the beginning of Example 6.8b.[16]

Although not all French Baroque chaconnes and *passacailles* employ variation form, the latter made these dances particularly suitable for grand ballet scenes, and the examples from Lully's operas are by far the longest and most elaborate of the individual numbers—vocal or instrumental—in these works. The *passacaille* in *Armide* comprises both a lengthy instrumental portion, which would

---

[16]The origins of the passacaglia and chaconne and the differences between them are not entirely clear despite long study by music historians. Passacaglias tend to be more serious and in minor keys, whereas the chaconne was originally lighter and more often in the major mode. In the later Baroque, however, the two genres often seem to be musically indistinguishable. Outside France, ostinato pieces with equivalent titles may be in duple time, as in the Spanish *pasacalles*.

Example 6.7 Lully, *Armide*, Act 3, scene 4, La Haine's air "Plus on connait l'Amour," vocal entry

Plus on connait l'Amour,   The more one knows Love (Cupid),
Et plus on le déteste,   The more one detests him;
Détruisons son pouvoir funeste.   Let us destroy his deathly power.

have been danced, and sections that follow for solo and choral voices. The ground bass employed for most of the present movement is one that was used frequently in seventeenth-century *passacailles*. It consists of a simple four-note descent, as in the first phrase of Example 6.8a. Lully occasionally substitutes other patterns, as in Example 6.8b, where the instrumental ensemble is reduced to a trio of two recorders and viola. In another trio passage the ostinato disappears entirely as the music modulates to several other keys—B♭ major, then D minor (Ex. 6.8c). The original ostinato bass line is also varied melodically, as in Example 6.8d, where chromatic intervals are interpolated.

Thanks to the magnificent effect of this type of scene, passacaglias in the Lully style became a favorite component of opera and ballet. With their hypnotically repeating ostinato basses, they could be extended almost indefinitely, making for some of the longest individual movements in the Baroque repertory. They became popular in other media as well; for example, the French composer Jean Henry d'Anglebert (1628–91), who played harpsichord for the

Example 6.8 Lully, *Armide*, Act 5, scene 2, *Passacaille*: (a) mm. 1–12; (b) mm. 24–28; (c) mm. 100–110; (d) mm. 97–101

Royal Academy under Lully, published harpsichord arrangements of several of Lully's *passacailles*, including the one from *Armide*. Among the many foreign composers attracted to the form were the Englishman Henry Purcell and the Germans Biber and Bach; Bach's Cantata 78 opens with a choral passacaglia in G minor whose initial ritornello is remarkably close to several passages in the *passacaille* from *Armide* (which Bach probably knew through harpsichord transcriptions).

Lully and Louis XIV must have hoped that the magnificence of this music would be viewed as a reflection of the political system that produced it—one that was admired in its day but was in fact a dictatorship that led France into numerous wars and near-bankruptcy, with diasastrous consequences for both the French and their neighbors. That a Protestant such as Bach could overlook those facts— which would have been common knowledge to members of his generation— suggests that musicians responded to this music for its genuine originality and expressiveness, not simply because it represented a fashionable ideal with which they (or their aristocratic patrons) could identify. Audiences would have viewed the *divertissement* of Hate or the *passacaille* in Act 5 not merely as a diverting ballet scene but as an **allegory**—an extended metaphor in which fundamental human emotions or philosophical ideas are represented symbolically. Similar scenes occur frequently in Baroque painting and in the spoken drama of the time. For Lully and other French Baroque composers, such scenes were ways of representing the evolving emotional states of the chief characters—more important, in this regard, than the brief airs.

The warlike music in a number of these scenes recalls Monteverdi's *concitato* style and its inspiration in the ancient Greek theater; he had cited Plato's approval of Greek war dances. Stylistically, Lully's music may seem almost as distant from Monteverdi's as the latter had been from that of the ancient Greeks. Yet in their integration of song, recitation, and dance, Lully's musical dramas were as success- ful as any Baroque work in realizing the recurrent dream of recreating the theater of antiquity.

CHAPTER 7

SEVENTEENTH-CENTURY SACRED MUSIC

At the beginning of the seventeenth century, while Monteverdi and other Italian composers were transforming the secular genres of the late Renaissance into those of the early Baroque, sacred music was hardly being neglected. The innovations applied to the madrigal, such as the addition of instruments and the substitution of solo voices for vocal polyphony, took place in the motet and mass as well, although more slowly and with greater deference to older traditions. Well into the Baroque, most composers of sacred music continued to write polyphonic masses and motets in *stile antico* (the "older style")—a style that remained outwardly close to that of the vocal polyphony of the mid-sixteenth century, save for the addition of a continuo part for the organ. Even Monteverdi published an old-fashioned polyphonic mass in 1610, alongside his famous Marian Vespers. As this publication showed, works in *stile antico* could stand beside up-to-date music in the *stile moderno* within the same printed volume and, presumably, within the same liturgical service.

The Sacred Concerto

Because they were intended to serve the same religious function as older works, the new types of church music continued to use traditional, mostly biblical, texts. Most can still be described as motets or mass movements, although a term frequently used to distinguish motets in the newer style is **concerto.** This word later came to be used for a type of instrumental music involving a soloist and larger ensemble. As applied to seventeenth-century music, it refers to music that includes specific instrumental parts alongside parts for one or more voices. It could be used for secular music—Monteverdi entitled his Seventh Book of Madrigals (Venice, 1619) *Concerto*—but it is more often applied to sacred works. The adjective *concertato* is also used to describe such compositions.

Sacred concertos or *concertato* works range from solo motets for a single voice and continuo—that is, sacred monody—to massive polychoral works for a dozen or more vocal and instrumental parts arranged in two or more separate group-ings or choirs. The smaller sacred concertos of Monteverdi and other early Baroque composers are close in style to their secular cantatas and continuo madri-gals. But their larger *concertato* works are composed on a scale not seen in the works considered thus far.

SACRED MUSIC IN VENICE: GIOVANNI GABRIELI

The practice of including instruments in sacred vocal music went back to the beginning of the sixteenth century or earlier, but only around 1600 did composers begin to designate instrumental parts as such in sacred vocal works. The first major composer to do so in a significant number of sacred works was the Venetian Giovanni Gabrieli (ca. 1554/7–1612; see Box 7.1). His uncle Andrea Gabrieli (ca. 1510–86) had been organist at St. Mark's, Venice, and briefly a colleague of Lassus's at Munich in Germany. Giovanni studied with his uncle Andrea and probably with Lassus as well. In 1585 he became second organist at St. Mark's, in effect succeeding his uncle as the city's chief composer of large-scale sacred music.

In addition to composing polyphonic madrigals and organ music and editing a collection of both his own and his uncle's sacred vocal works (1587), Gabrieli produced two immense collections of what he called *sacrae symphoniae*— "sacred symphonies"—which were published in 1597 and 1615. Both volumes consist primarily of polychoral vocal works; those in the second volume are in *concertato* style, that is, with designated instrumental parts alongside those for voices. The first collection also includes a separate series of purely instrumental works, and a second series of such works was published separately in 1615. Hence, Gabrieli, like his English contemporary William Byrd, was one of the few composers active before 1600 who attained supreme stature in instrumental as well as vocal composition.[1]

Because the greater part of his career fell within the sixteenth century, Gabrieli is often considered a composer more of the late Renaissance than of the Baroque. Indeed, unlike Monteverdi, whose career similarly bridged the sixteenth and seventeenth centuries, Gabrieli never took up the more obvious stylistic innovations that we associate with the new Baroque style, such as the wholesale adoption of monody or the unorthodox harmony and dissonance treatment that Monteverdi called the *seconda pratica*. Yet Gabrieli's works proved to be as influential as Monteverdi's on many younger composers, and unlike Monteverdi he was, like his uncle Andrea, a renowned teacher. In fact, Gabrieli trained many of the leading composers of the early Baroque, among them a number of important German musicians who made the difficult trip southward specifically to study with him.

Gabrieli's influence was great enough that even Monteverdi adopted elements of Gabrieli's style, in a number of sacred works written after Monteverdi came to Venice in 1613. Of those who actually studied with Gabrieli, the greatest was the German Heinrich Schütz, who closely imitated him in many works (see below). Gabrieli today is famous for the massive sonorities of his large-scale vocal and instrumental works. But his students must also have prized the expressive power of his music, including works composed on a smaller scale, such as his Italian madrigals. Gabrieli's vocal works avoid not only the contrapuntal liberties of the second practice but also the vivid word painting and other virtuoso features of late Renaissance and early Baroque vocal music.

---

[1]A very short keyboard piece by Gabrieli is given as Ex. 10.2.

Box 7.1

Giovanni Gabrieli (ca. 1554/7–1612)

---

ca. 1554–57. Born at Venice. Studies with his uncle Andrea Gabrieli.

1575–79. Musician for the duke of Bavaria, working under Lassus in Munich.

1584. Organist at St. Mark's, Venice (wins competition for permanent appointment in 1585).

1585. Andrea dies; Giovanni publishes *Concerti* (polyphonic madrigals and motets by both composers) in 1587.

1597. Publishes his *Sacrae symphoniae*, Book 1 (polychoral motets, canzoni, and sonatas).

1612. Dies at Venice. His *Sacrae symphoniae*, Book 2, and *Canzoni et sonate* are published posthumously in 1615.

But they pay careful attention to the declamation of the text, and they frequently employ massive homophonic sonorities to achieve expressive or rhetorical effects. Both characteristics occur in the music of Lassus (see Chapter 2), which remained equally influential on early Baroque composers in Germany; indeed, Gabrieli and his German students can be seen as inheriting Lassus's tradition of expressive yet relatively restrained musical rhetoric.

Polychoral Works

The ambitious scoring of Gabrieli's works reflected the opulence of the Venetian churches for which they were written. Many of these works are **polychoral**: the ensemble is divided into two or more distinct groups, each of which constitutes a separate choir or chorus.[2] Thus the eight-voice *Ego sum qui sum* (published in 1597) is for two four-part groups, each comprising soprano, alto, tenor, and bass (Ex. 7.1). Each phrase of the text is introduced by one of the choirs, then echoed by the other; the two choirs join together to emphasize important words (e.g., *consilium* in mm. 5–6) or to mark the ends of sections. The choral antiphony does more than create an effect of splendor; it is also an element of musical rhetoric, used to articulate the structure of the text.

The choirs of a polychoral work do not always comprise equal numbers or types of voices. A composition might pit a group of high voices against lower ones or a six-part choir against two four-part choirs (as in the example by Schütz discussed below). Moreover, the choirs might be physically separated, to enhance the "stereo" effect that results from hearing two or more groups performing in different locations within a church or other large structure. It was once thought that the balconies and other elevated locations within many larger churches

---

[2]The word *choir* or *chorus* can refer to a body of either voices or instruments. Another term for the use of multiple ensembles within a single work is *cori spezzati* ("separated" choruses).

Example 7.1 G. Gabrieli, *Ego sum qui sum*, mm. 1–6

Ego sum qui sum, et consilium
meum non est cum impiis.

I am who I am, and my counsel is
not with the impious.

might have been used for this purpose, for example, by placing groups of performers in choir or organ lofts on opposite sides of the central aisle. But this does not seem to have been the practice at St. Mark's, where it would have led to problems of balance and coordination. Hence the unique architecture of St. Mark's cannot have been particularly influential on the evolution of polychoral music, as was once believed. Gabrieli probably composed many of his polychoral compositions not for St. Mark's but for the Scuola di San Rocco, a religious confraternity which he also served as organist from 1585 onward.[3]

During the later sixteenth century the use of multiple choirs became common throughout Italy, as numerous polychoral compositions by Lassus, Palestrina, and other non-Venetian composers demonstrate. The practice remained popular through the seventeenth century in the major cities of Italy, France, and Germany. What distinguished the Venetian polychoral style was the regular participation

---

[3] A confraternity was a sort of fraternal organization; that of San Rocco (St. Roche), which still exists, carried out charitable work and conducted quasi-liturgical rituals at its grand hall, or *scuola*.

of virtuoso instrumentalists as well as a heightened concern for colorful sonority and massive triadic harmony. These features, already evident in the later works of Andrea Gabrieli, are characteristic of most of Giovanni's works and of the polychoral music of his students, notably the German Schütz.

The Scoring of Venetian Polychoral Works

Even in Gabrieli's posthumous 1615 collection of sacred polyphony with instruments, most of the parts are still in principle vocal and bear texts. Some works, however, have explicitly labeled instrumental parts, and many others were frequently performed with instruments replacing some of the voices. Thus a work such as that shown in Example 7.1 might have been performed with a soprano singing the top part of one choir and a tenor the third part of the second choir.[4] Instruments would have provided the remaining parts—perhaps violins or other strings those of the first choir, cornetto and trombones for the second, with an organ providing a basso continuo for each choir.

Such scoring practices, although they came to be widespread in the seventeenth century, reflected local traditions at Venice and particularly at St. Mark's Basilica. During the sixteenth and seventeenth centuries, the musicians of St. Mark's included not only several organists but wind and eventually string specialists. These instrumentalists appear to have been regular participants in performances of sacred music long before composers such as Gabrieli began to write parts specifically for them. Over the years, conventions governing the scoring of such works seem to have been worked out. One basic principle appears to have been that each choir should contain at least one singer, so that lines of text assigned to each choir would continue to be sung. Principles governing the instrumentation of such music were eventually published by Schütz and by Michael Praetorius (?1571–1621), a prolific German composer and author of an important early musical encyclopedia, the *Syntagma musicum* (Treatise on music, 3 vols., 1614–19).[5]

The most important instruments in this music—after the organ, which furnished the basso continuo—were the cornetto and the sackbut. The **sackbut** is the Renaissance trombone, similar to the modern instrument but somewhat mellower in tone; it was employed primarily in alto, tenor, and bass sizes. The **cornetto** (or cornett, *Zink* in German) usually furnished the soprano part or parts; alto and tenor versions were also used, as well as a higher *cornettino*. Not to be confused with the modern cornet, a brass instrument resembling the trumpet, Gabrieli's cornetto was rather a sort of woodwind. It has, however, a cup mouthpiece like that used on brass instruments, and its sound blends well with that of the sackbuts, despite its completely different construction and technique (Fig. 7.1). Although difficult to play, it has a fully chromatic range of more than two octaves, and once mastered it permits great virtuosity as well as expressive control of articulation and dynamics. For these reasons it was the leading wind instrument in early seventeenth-century Italy, often substituting for the violin in sonatas and other instrumental compositions.

---

[4] At Venice the soprano parts were probably sung by adult male castrati; see Chapter 8.

[5] For Schütz's and Praetorius's views on the instrumentation of their polychoral works, see Anthony F. Carver, *Cori spezzati* (Cambridge: Cambridge University Press, 1988), 1:233–34 and 216–20.

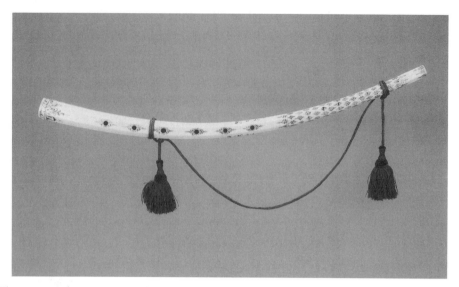

Figure 7.1 Zink, Imperial City of Nürnberg, ca. 1600. Ex coll.: Barons von Rothschild, Vienna. National Music Museum, Vermillion, South Dakota, Joe R. and Joella F. Utley Collection, 1999 (no. 7368). This ornate cornetto, made of ivory, lacks its brass-style mouthpiece. The German city of Nürnberg (Nuremberg) was a center for the production of cornettos and brass instruments. The cornetto was held somewhat like a recorder; the tasseled cord on this example is decorative.

Trumpets, although commonly used to replace cornettos in modern perfor-mances of Gabrieli's music, were rare participants in *concertato* vocal works, at least at Venice around 1600. Together with the timpani (kettledrums), which were usually played as parts of trumpet ensembles, the trumpet was considered a military and heraldic instrument. To a limited degree, modern trumpets and bugles retain those associations, but now they are largely ceremonial. In an age when military communication required simple visual and aural signals, however, trumpets and drums played practical military roles, conveying commands in bat-tle and regulating the marching of troops. Trumpeters thus served civic and social functions distinct from those of other musicians, and this set them apart in the rigid hierarchy of Renaissance and early Baroque society. Most of their music was apparently memorized or improvised, and written trumpet parts are rare in vocal or instrumental music composed before the second half of the seventeenth century.

Gabrieli's *In ecclesiis*

Today Gabrieli's most famous work is probably the *concertato* motet *In ecclesiis*, published posthumously in the 1615 collection of *symphoniae sacrae* (anthology, Selection 13). Many of Gabrieli's works are thought to have been written for the religious observances and civic festivals that filled Venice's annual calendar; *In ecclesiis* is thought to have been associated with the annual commemoration of the end of a plague that had struck Venice in 1575–77. A splendid example of the polychoral style, it is scored for three choirs: two vocal choirs, each con-sisting of soprano, alto, tenor, and bass, and an instrumental choir composed of three cornettos, "violino" (actually a viola), and two trombones. Separate from the three choirs is a continuo part for the organ, whose sustained sound helps bind the work's disparate elements together.[6]

The second of the two vocal choirs is designated the **capella**, a term that literally means "chapel" or "chorus" but which came to mean an additional or, in some works, optional vocal chorus. Gabrieli and his contemporaries were well aware that polychoral works were expensive to perform and that not all institutions had the resources to present them as written. Many such works thus include one or two *capella* choruses that add volume and grandeur but are not strictly necessary. The parts for the *capella* tend to be less demanding than those of the principal vocal chorus or choruses. We can think of the latter as being intended for soloists, although in most performances even the *capella* parts were probably sung by individual performers; **doubling,** in which two or more musicians sing or play the same part, was far from a universal practice and even at major establishments such as St. Mark's probably occurred only on special occasions, if ever. In the present work, the *capella* enters chiefly to reinforce the first choir, singing only in refrains and in the final section.

Although typical in many ways of polychoral motets from the early seventeenth century, *In ecclesiis* is unusual among Gabrieli's works for several reasons. First, it includes several monodic passages for solo voice and continuo; only in his latest works did Gabrieli employ this type of scoring. Second, Gabrieli rarely specified the instrumental forces as precisely as he did here. Perhaps this was because the instrumental choir plays an unusually prominent role in this work, having one section all to itself (mm. 26–34, marked *sinfonia*). Finally, in the climactic final section of the motet, Gabrieli employs chromatic voice leading (e.g., in m. 87, altus doubled by cornetto). A rare practice for him, it occurs on the word *Deus* ("God!"), where, like Lassus's chromaticism on the words *timor et tremor,* it might suggest awe or trepidation as the deity is invoked.

The text is drawn from various scriptural sources.[7] It includes five statements of the word *alleluia,* used here as a refrain, with essentially the same music each time (see Box 7.2). These refrains divide the work into five sections; each section builds to a climactic statement of the refrain, which thus unifies the composition in a particularly satisfying way.

The impression of a well-integrated composition is deepened by the gradual way in which the scoring is built up. Not until measure 87, at the beginning of the final section, do all fifteen parts sound together. Thus, despite the massive polychoral appearance of the score, most of the work actually has the quality of chamber music. Section 1 is primarily for solo soprano, section 2 for solo bass (both with continuo). The instrumental choir then enters, to be joined by the two remaining soloists (alto and tenor) for section 3. This section, incidentally, is composed in eight-voice imitative counterpoint, an impressive feat of polyphonic skill. It contains, moreover, eight successive imitative subjects that

---

[6]Modern performances sometimes add theorbo or other instruments to this part, but Gabrieli designates it simply *basso per l'organo* (bass for the organ).

[7]As in many Latin texts of the Renaissance and earlier periods, the anonymous author of this text appears to have drawn, perhaps from memory, on various biblical texts without exactly quoting any one in particular.

Box 7.2

Gabrieli: *In ecclesiis*

Published posthumously in *Sacrae symphoniae*, Book 2 (1615)

Section	Lines of Text	Scoring*	Measures
1	1	I: quintus	1–5
	2 (refrain)	+II	6–10
2	3	I: octavus	11–22a
	4 (refrain)	+II	22b–26
3	— (sinfonia)	III	26b–34
	5–6	+I: altus, tenor	35–56
	7 (refrain)	+II	57–61a
4	8–9	I: quintus, octavus	61b–82a
	10 (refrain)	+II	82b–86
5	11	I, II, III	87–107a
	12 (refrain)	I, II, III	107b–116

*Roman numerals designate choirs: I = soloists, II = *capella*, III = instruments. All sections include basso continuo, played by the organ.

increase in rhythmic motion, leading to the lively figures in sixteenth notes in measures 52–55. Section 4 is again chiefly for vocal soloists (soprano and bass, now singing together). In section 5, finally, all voices and instruments perform together in the homophonic chordal writing for which Gabrieli is best known.

Gabrieli's Works for Instrumental Ensemble

In addition to a number of organ works, Gabrieli composed an important body of **canzonas** and **sonatas** for instrumental ensemble. The performing forces required range from as few as four to as many as twenty-two players, arranged in one to five choirs. These works are sacred in the sense that they were intended primarily for performance in church: following a Renaissance tradition that continued through the Baroque in Roman Catholic countries, certain portions of the mass and office that were normally sung could be replaced by instrumental music. No doubt Gabrieli's canzonas and sonatas were played in other contexts as well.

Most of the instrumental works published in Gabrieli's 1597 collection declare their connection with sixteenth-century vocal tradition through their use of the title *canzona*. Literally meaning "song," the Italian word was used in the sixteenth century for French polyphonic chansons by such composers as Lassus. Andrea Gabrieli had transcribed a number of such works for solo organ, and during the late sixteenth and seventeenth centuries the word was applied to original instrumental compositions for keyboard or ensemble. In fact, instrumental canzonas rarely have much in common with the vocal genre, apart from their polyphonic texture and the fact that they often open with repeated-note motives similar to those heard in many polyphonic vocal chansons (Ex. 7.2).

Example 7.2 G. Gabrieli, *Canzon septimi toni* (published 1597), mm. 1–7

But Gabrieli's polychoral canzonas do employ the same antiphonal scoring that is characteristic of the *concertato* motets that were published alongside them; the individual parts even bear the same Latin names used for voice parts, rather than being designated for specific instruments.

Both the 1597 and 1615 collections include, in addition to canzonas, a number of works designated *sonata*. The term at this date meant little more than music that is played—as opposed to the cantata, which is sung. Gabrieli seems to have reserved the term for pieces that lacked the chansonlike characteristics of his canzonas. The sonatas include massive works in up to twenty-two parts. But one, entitled "Sonata with three violins," includes virtuoso writing of a type that would become typical of the Italian Baroque violin sonata (Ex. 7.3). With its dialoguelike exchanges between the three violins, restrained chromaticism, and written-out embellishment, this work constitutes an instrumental equivalent of

Example 7.3 G. Gabrieli, *Sonata con tre violini* (published 1615), mm. 19–28

the madrigals for three sopranos and continuo published a few years previously by Luzzaschi (see Chapter 3).[8]

SACRED MUSIC IN GERMANY: HEINRICH SCHÜTZ

The most significant German composer of the seventeenth century was Heinrich Schütz (1585–1672). In the course of a long career Schütz, like Monteverdi, moved from what we call the style of the late Renaissance to that of the Baroque. Despite his training as an organist, his surviving music consists mostly of sacred vocal compositions. Like Monteverdi, he also wrote a significant number of secular and stage works—including the first German opera—but most of these have been lost. Although he set texts in Italian and Latin, his great accomplishment was to adapt the primarily Italian style of the early Baroque to the rhythms and accents of the German language and to the texts of German writers, notably Luther's translation of the Bible. In the process he created a distinctive personal idiom that was of great influence on several younger generations of northern composers.

Born in Köstritz, a small town in central Germany, Schütz lived during a time when northern Europe was a patchwork of mostly small, independent

[8]The three upper parts in Gabrieli's sonata can also be played on other instruments, such as cornettos; the bass line, designated for organ (which provides a continuo realization), can also be doubled by an optional fourth string part.

Box 7.3

Heinrich Schütz (1585–1672)

1585. Born at Köstritz, near Gera in western Saxony (southeastern Germany).

1590. Family moves to Weissenfels, about twenty miles north.

1598. Visiting at the inn owned by Schütz's father, the ruling Landgrave Moritz of Hesse hears Schütz sing; a year later Schütz joins the court of Hesse at Kassel, about one hundred miles to the west.

1608. Enters the University of Marburg, fifty miles southwest of Kassel, and studies law (then a common course of study, not necessarily intended as preparation for a legal career).

1609–12. Studies at Venice with Giovanni Gabrieli; dedicates to the latter his Opus 1, a book of madrigals (1611).

1613–16. Again at Kassel as court musician, but twice called to Dresden (1614, 1615–16).

1617. Kapellmeister (music director) to Elector (Duke) Johann Georg I of Saxony at Dresden; holds that position (with interruptions) the rest of his life.

1619. Publishes *Psalmen Davids* (polychoral psalm settings; revised editions, 1628 and 1661).

1623. Publishes his *Auferstehung Christi* (The Resurrection, oratorio)

1624. Publishes *Cantiones sacrae* (polyphonic motets).

1627. His opera *Dafne* performed at the wedding of Georg II of Hesse (text by Martin Opitz after Rinuccini; music lost).

1628–29. Second visit to Venice; publishes there his *Symphoniae sacrae*, Part 1 (Latin polychoral works).

1631. Saxony enters the Thirty Years' War; economic hardship subsequently leads to diminishment of musical activities at Dresden, causing Schütz to find a series of temporary positions elsewhere.

1634–35. In Denmark; director of music (kapellmeister) to King Christian IV.

1636. Back in Dresden, publishes *Musicalische Exequien* (funeral music) and Part 1 of *Kleine geistliche Konzerte* (small sacred concertos).

1637. Obtains imperial privilege (a form of copyright) for his published works.

1639–41. Publishes Part 2 of *Kleine geistliche Konzerte* (1639); serves as kapellmeister to the duke of Calenberg at Hanover and Hildesheim (in northern Germany).

1641. Back in Dresden; the musical establishment there barely functioning.

1642–44. Second period in Denmark as kapellmeister.

1644–45. Serves the duke of Brunswick at Wolfenbüttel (northern Germany, southeast of Hanover).

1645. Returns to Dresden but begins partial retirement, dividing his time between Dresden and his family home in Weissenfels (about seventy-five miles to the west). Continues to receive commissions from various German rulers.

1647, 1650. Publishes Parts 2 and 3 of his *Symphoniae sacrae* (sacred concertos); also *Geistliche Chormusik* (motets, 1648)

1656. Death of Saxon elector Johann Georg I; Schütz begins full retirement from Dresden, though still providing music and services on occasion.

1660–61. At Wolfenbüttel (where he continued to hold title of kapellmeister); performs his *Historia der Geburth Christi* (Christmas Oratorio, published 1664).

1666. Performs his three Passions (Good Friday music, for unaccompanied voices).

1670–72. Moves to Dresden (1670), composes his *Schwanengesang* ("Swan Song": Psalms 119 and 100 and a Magnificat, in *stile antico*); dies there 1672.

principalities. Those states whose rulers were artistically inclined supported musical establishments of one sort or another. Schütz spent most of his career working for one or another of these rulers, in particular the duke (or elector) of Saxony, who ruled from Dresden, then as now the leading city in southeastern Germany.

For much of his life, however, Schütz was forced to follow an extraordinarily winding career path (Box 7.3). A German musician of Schütz's generation, particularly one born in a relatively provincial place, could obtain a first-rate musical education only by traveling. Schütz made two trips to Venice, first to study with Giovanni Gabrieli, later to hear the music of Monteverdi and others. Unfortunately, the main part of Schütz's career coincided with the Thirty Years' War (1618–48) and its aftermath. During this period the cities and courts of Germany were repeatedly ravaged by the marauding armies of France, Sweden, and various German princes. The degree of economic devastation varied widely; some places were destroyed, others untouched. But the general suffering and depredation were enormous, and Schütz, like other musicians, was forced to seek employment and commissions from a variety of sources. Hence, although from around 1618 onwards he held the position of kapellmeister—the German equivalent of *maestro di capella* or chapel master—at Dresden, he continued to travel, holding temporary positions in Denmark and elsewhere. The distances may seem small by modern standards; even the trip from Dresden to Venice covers only about five hundred miles. But at the time such travel involved considerable hardship—slow transport by horse-drawn coach or wagon over unpaved roads—and it is astonishing that Schütz (and his music) nevertheless traveled widely throughout Germany.

Schütz's Music

Like Monteverdi, Schütz composed so many different types of music over such a long period that it is difficult to characterize his music in general terms. Perhaps the best one can do is to emphasize, as one would for Monteverdi, his continual reverence for the text and his constant search for ways of representing it musically. Schütz, however, was more strongly committed to the *stile antico* than Monteverdi seems to have been. Although he was deeply influenced by Monteverdi's theatrical and second-practice works, the most profound influence throughout his life was certainly that of his teacher Gabrieli. Schütz never abandoned the Gabrieli style, by which is meant here not only the grand Venetian polychoral manner but also the older contrapuntal tradition handed down from Lassus and Andrea Gabrieli. Throughout his career Schütz repeatedly returned to this style in polyphonic motets, sometimes even omitting the continuo parts that had become the norm after 1600.

Schütz nevertheless composed the bulk of his music in more up-to-date styles. Like other northern musicians who studied with Gabrieli, he began his career by publishing a set of Italian madrigals probably written under Gabrieli's direct supervision (Venice, 1611). A volume of psalms in Gabrieli's polychoral style followed in 1619. He also wrote numerous sacred motets or concertos for one to four solo voices and continuo, particularly during the war years, when most German churches and courts lacked the resources necessary for performing larger works. Many of these compositions employ the new expressive devices of monody, including recitative-like declamation and virtuoso vocal writing. Many also include independent instrumental parts, constituting genuine vocal-instrumental chamber music.

The works for smaller ensembles furnished models for younger German composers such as Johann Rosenmüller (ca. 1619–84), Matthias Weckmann (1621–74), and Johann Theile (1646–1724), each of whom knew or studied with Schütz before going on to become a significant composer of sacred vocal music. Another student, Christoph Bernhard (1627–92), who succeeded Schütz as kapellmeister at Dresden, preserved the latter's teachings on composition and performance in a number of treatises.[9] Later German composers, including Buxtehude and Bach, if not directly acquainted with Schütz's style, experienced it indirectly through works by other composers who followed in Schütz's tradition of sensitive, frequently dramatic settings of German sacred texts.

Numbering Systems and Musical "Works"

Schütz, following a practice that had arisen in Italy during the seventeenth century, attached **opus** numbers to his major publications. The word *opus* is Latin for "work"; its plural is *opera*, not to be confused with the Italian word for a musical drama. The use of the word *opus* by musicians was a sign that they were beginning to recognize their compositions as permanent, substantial works of art comparable to architectural monuments and other concrete visual works. Today we take this for granted, but it was a new concept in the seventeenth century. It probably reflected the beginnings of interest in works and styles of the past—that is, music history. The continuing concern of many composers with the *stile antico* or *prima pratica*, which Monteverdi traced back to Johannes Ockeghem and Josquin des Prez, was one manifestation of this. So too were the posthumous, retrospective publications that were made of the works of a number of composers, including Andrea Gabrieli, Palestrina, and Lassus. Study of the works of older composers, such as Palestrina, would have suggested that

---

[9]See bibliography under "Baroque Theoretical Treatises."

music did not necessarily have to fade or disappear with time. Rather, music comprised a permanent body of works, just like the monuments of building, painting, and literature left behind by architects, artists, and writers. The efforts of living composers could result in monuments worthy of standing beside older, established ones, an idea implicit in the choice of the word *opus*.[10]

For seventeenth- and eighteenth-century composers, an *opus* was a large published collection. In most cases the term did not apply to individual compositions, and unpublished works, even major ones such as operas, were rarely given such a designation. Opus numbers were usually applied in chronological order. But because individual works within a collection might have been composed over a long period of time, opus numbers provide at best only a rough guide to the chronology of specific pieces.

For this reason, music historians have prepared numbered listings or catalogs of the individual works of many composers. When these catalogs quote the opening themes of the works listed, they are referred to as **thematic catalogs**. Some thematic catalogs are known by the name of the scholar who first drew up the list, as in the case of the Köchel numbers applied to Mozart's works. Schütz's works have been assigned SWV numbers, the letters standing for the German expression *Schütz-Werke-Verzeichnis* ("catalog of Schütz's works"). The Köchel and SWV lists are, at least in principle, chronological, placing early works first. Lists for some other composers, including Bach, are not. Therefore one cannot assume that a high number represents a late work. At the very least, however, such numbers provide an unambiguous way of referring to individual works. This is particularly useful when, as in the case of Schütz, there may be several settings of the same text all referred to by the same title.

Schütz's *Symphoniae sacrae*

Three of Schütz's published collections bear the title *Symphoniae sacrae* (Sacred symphonies), the same title borne by Giovanni Gabrieli's two great collections. These collections appeared as Opera 6, 10, and 12 in 1629, 1647, and 1650, respectively. Despite the title, many works are for relatively small ensembles, although in some cases these are expandable through the use of optional *capella* choirs. Even in the small-scale works, however, Schütz employs antiphonal textures that refer to polychoral style, and there are frequent passages in contrapuntal texture as well.

The works in the second volume had mostly been composed some years prior to its publication in 1647. The volume consists of vocal solos, duets, and trios with accompaniments for two treble instruments (e.g., violins or cornetti) and continuo. The third volume, published three years later as Opus 12, contains works for larger ensembles. Both reflect the influence of Monteverdi's late

---

[10]Some modern writings, notably Lydia Goehr, *The Imaginary Museum of Musical Works: An Essay in the Philosophy of Music* (Oxford: Clarendon Press, 1992), argue that the concept of musical "works" dates only from around 1800, but the evidence cited here shows that many Baroque musicians must already have been thinking along similar lines.

monodic works; indeed, one work in the 1647 collection (*Es steh Gott auf*) is a **parody:** a vocal work whose music is largely identical to that of an existing composition, new words being substituted for the original ones. In this case, Schütz fitted the words of Psalm 68 to music from two of Monteverdi's continuo madrigals.[11]

Herr, neige deine Himmel, SWV 361

This work (anthology, Selection 14), from the 1647 volume, is, like most of the compositions in that collection, a setting of a psalm text. It is scored for two bass voices with two violins and continuo. The latter is explicitly for organ, with the bass line doubled by "violone"—here probably meaning bass viola da gamba.

As in other works in Schütz's Opus 10, the style has much in common with the madrigals for one, two, and three voices in Monteverdi's Eighth Book (published in 1638). Thus Schütz takes almost every visual image in the text as a signal for word painting. The word *neige* ("bow down," m. 1) receives a downward melodic line that leaps back up for the following word *Himmel* ("heaven"), and *blitzen* ("lightning," m. 19) elicits the first entry of the violins. Where the text refers to a "new song" (*neues Lied*, mm. 43–44), the music reflects this by shifting to triple meter. This triple meter, incidentally was originally notated in the equivalent of what we would call $\frac{6}{1}$ time, using what look to us like very large note values (six whole notes to the measure). Through a notational convention familiar to musicians of Schütz's time, these would have been performed not slowly but in a lively fashion.[12]

In the work of a lesser composer, Schütz's incessant use of text painting might have reduced the music to a disconnected series of musical images. But here each pictorial musical idea becomes a motive that is extensively developed through sequence, imitation, and other means. In many respects this is what one finds in polyphonic madrigals of the later sixteenth century. But now each motive has a more distinct rhythmic profile; note, for example, the quick three-note motive used for *lass blitzen*. In addition, the pitch organization is now essentially tonal, defined by cadences in varying keys—that is, genuine modulations in the modern sense.

Thus we would say that the opening phrase begins in D minor but concludes with a cadence in A minor (m. 4), as does the following phrase (m. 9). Cadences in F major (m. 11) and D minor (m. 13) follow.[13] The downbeat of measure 13

---

[11]Schütz's *Es steh Gott auf*, SWV 356, draws on Monteverdi's *Armato il cor* and *Zefiro torna e di soavi accenti*. Parody had been an important technique for the composition of sixteenth-century masses; Schütz rarely used it, but it was important in the music of J. S. Bach and other eighteenth-century composers.

[12]According to sixteenth-century theory, the triple-time passage would have been performed with three whole notes occupying the same time as one whole note in the previous passage. It is uncertain how strictly this rule was still applied in Schütz's day.

[13]The simplest way to spot these and other cadences is to look for downward leaps of a fifth (or upward leaps of a fourth) in the continuo part that coincide with ends of phrases or pauses in the vocal parts.

actually has a chord of D *major*, as signified by the sharp in the figured bass (this raised third degree today is sometimes called a **Picardy third**). Throughout the seventeenth century, however, it was common for phrases to end on major chords regardless of their actual mode, and the phrase in measures 11–13 can be described as remaining in D *minor*. (Schütz and his contemporaries would have continued to describe these cadences in terms of the old church modes.)

One point of special interest is the writing for the bass voices. One of these almost always is doubled by the basso continuo line. Hence, when only one voice sings, as at the beginning of the work, the music consists of nothing but a bass line (plus the improvised continuo realization). This is characteristic of writing for bass voice throughout the early Baroque. Monteverdi and Schütz wrote several works for solo bass in which the entire vocal part is a decorated doubling of the continuo line; the continuo realization must then furnish all of the harmony, that is, the upper voices. Although such works are somewhat unusual, Baroque writing for bass voice in general differs from that for other voice types. Bass parts do not entirely lack the virtuoso coloratura commonly found in soprano and tenor parts of the period; indeed, such writing occurs on the word *fahr* (line 1) in this work. But vocal bass parts tend to contain greater numbers of leaps than other voices, particularly at cadences—a natural consequence of the tendency of bass lines to leap at cadences by a fourth or a fifth, that is, from the dominant to the tonic.

Saul, Saul, was verfolgst du mich?, SWV 415

Probably Schütz's most famous work, this polychoral *concertato* motet (anthology, Selection 15) was published in 1650 in the composer's third and last collection of *symphoniae sacrae*. In addition to a six-part choir of vocal soloists, the work calls for two violins as well as two optional *capella* choirs containing four voices each. Underlying the whole is a continuo group comprising organ and "violone," most likely a large bass viola da gamba.

Like Gabrieli's *In ecclesiis*, the work makes its greatest impact in its complete polychoral setting. Indeed, despite its brevity this is one of the most powerful compositions of the seventeenth century, justly famous for its vividly dramatic setting of its text. The latter, a single verse from the New Testament book of Acts, depicts the moment when Paul, on the road to Damascus (in Syria) to persecute the Christians there, has a vision. God speaks to him, addressing him by his Hebrew name, Saul; as a result, he is converted to Christianity, eventually becoming the author of the New Testament epistles (letters) attributed to him. The scene was a popular one for late Renaissance and Baroque painters, who frequently gave it a dramatic depiction showing Paul's horse rearing, throwing him to the ground.

Schütz's setting divides the scriptural verse into two halves, which are repeated in the pattern ABABA. The text repetitions are unusual in a seventeenth-century sacred work, and although the music is through-composed, each of the two text segments is associated with recurring motivic ideas. Surely Schütz's most original idea, however, is the extraordinary opening of the work, where Saul's name is repeated by rising pairs of voices, beginning with the lowest notes of the two basses and ascending to the two sopranos, who are echoed by the violins. The *capella* choirs then enter and the entire ensemble repeats the A text together (m. 9), producing a stunning effect.[14]

The two B segments, by contrast, are presented in more conventional style by the solo choir alone: first monodically, by tenor and alto soloists (mm. 13–18), then in imitative texture by all six soloists (mm. 22–34, joined by the violins). In the second B section, two words are singled out for Monteverdian text painting. The word *löcken* ("kick," mm. 24–25) receives an extended melisma. On the downbeat of measure 27 Schütz sets a harsh dissonance—the augmented fifth eb'/b' (tenor and first soprano)—on the word *schwer*, meaning "hard" or "difficult."

The A sections include a number of original dynamic markings: *forte* (m. 9) followed by *mezzopiano* and *pianissimo*. These produce a decrescendo, perhaps representing the dying echo of the words that Saul hears all about him. Gabrieli had been one of the first to use written dynamic indications, in the *Sonata pian'e forte* (Sonata with piano and forte) of his 1597 collection, an ensemble sonata for eight instruments. Although a common element in performance, dynamics were rarely specified before the mid-eighteenth century except to dictate special or unusual effects, as is the case here.

Modern performances often amplify the work through vocal and instrumental doublings of the two *capella* choirs. Yet even in its full original scoring, it may not have been intended for more than eighteen performers, one on each part (two on the continuo). That was already an enormous ensemble for most of the German churches in which the work would have been performed. Thanks to Schütz's remarkable powers of invention, it is all that is necessary for the work to make an overpowering impact. Similar considerations hold true in later Baroque works as well; bigger does not necessarily mean better.

SEVENTEENTH-CENTURY ORATORIO

In addition to the *concertato* motet and other liturgical forms, seventeenth-century musicians cultivated various types of dramatic and semidramatic sacred music. The Roman operas on sacred themes have already been mentioned; these, however, differed musically hardly at all from operas on the usual mythological or historical subjects. More distinctive was the genre now known as oratorio, which developed in Italy at about the same time as opera and, like opera, eventually traveled to France, Germany, and elsewhere.

An **oratorio** may be defined as a dramatic work on a sacred subject that, like an opera, is fully sung, although it is not normally staged and acted, nor is it normally a part of a church service as such. The origins of the oratorio have

---

[14]The opening is in triple meter, originally notated in the same large note values employed in the middle section of *Herr, neige deine Himmel*. When a version of this music returns at m. 16, it is rewritten in duple meter using smaller note values; the actual tempo is only slightly quicker than before, however.

been traced to certain quasi-dramatic types of Gregorian chant, such as the presentation of the Passion story on Good Friday. Here the chanting of the New Testament text was divided between one singer who presented the basic narrative and others who sang the words of Jesus and other figures in the story. This tradition, which extended back to the Middle Ages, continued in Baroque Germany and elsewhere. But the immediate source for the quasi-operatic type of music known as oratorio lay in the same innovations of around 1600 that led to opera itself.

Early Oratorio

The word *oratorio* derives from the oratory, a type of structure built in sixteenth-century Italy and later for quasi-liturgical services by various religious communities. Typically holding several hundred people, surviving oratories today are sometimes used as concert halls—not inappropriately, for one of their original functions was the public presentation of sacred music outside the context of an actual religious service. Such performances, which proliferated at Rome and other Roman Catholic cities during the seventeenth century, were among the predecessors of the modern tradition of public concerts. In Roman Catholic countries they were generally sponsored by religious institutions, and by the end of the seventeenth century comparable traditions had emerged in parts of Protestant Germany, where they involved performances of oratorios and similar works in existing churches.

Emilio de'Cavalieri is sometimes credited with writing the first oratorio, the *Rappresentatione di anima e di corpo* (Drama of the soul and the body), at Rome in 1600. He had been one of the musicians involved in the Florentine *intermedi* of 1589, and musically this work is similar to the earliest operas. An allegorical dialogue between body and soul, it consists largely of recitative, interspersed with choruses. The latter, in simple polyphonic texture, were meant to be danced—an indication of how far this work lies from what would become more typical of the Baroque oratorio.

Carissimi

More characteristic of the seventeenth-century oratorio are the eleven such works composed by Giacomo Carissimi (1605–74), mentioned in Chapter 5 as a writer of secular cantatas. Born near Rome, Carissimi spent his entire career there as choir director (*maestro di capella*) at a number of institutions, notably the German College. The latter was one of several religious communities—not colleges in the modern sense—run by the Jesuit order for members of foreign nationalities. The German College came to be noted especially for its musical performances under Carissimi, as well as for the longtime residence there of the German scholar Athanasius Kircher (1602–80). His voluminous writings include an encyclopedic treatise on music (*Musurgia universalis*, Rome, 1650) that mentions Carissimi and other contemporary musicians.

It is thanks in part to Kircher that Carissimi, whose cantatas constitute the largest part of his output, is today known chiefly for his oratorios. These works are essentially a special type of *concertato* motet; similar works by other composers bear the title *dialogus* (dialogue), pointing to the works' quasi-dramatic features, in which the speeches of individual characters are assigned to soloists and set monodically, with continuo accompaniment. Most such compositions are short by comparison with later oratorios, since each constituted only a small part of an oratory ritual that included psalm singing and a sermon as well. They range in length from ten to thirty minutes; contemporary accounts describe their performances as among the high points of musical life at Rome in the seventeenth century. The dates of most of Carissimi's oratorios are not known; among their subjects are the Last Judgment and the story of Jonah and the whale.

As in the sacred works of Gabrieli, Monteverdi, and Schütz, the text is divided into sections. Some sections are assigned to soloists, others to the body of singers as a whole. What distinguishes these works from ordinary *concertato* motets is that the Latin texts, which were adapted from the Bible, are narratives containing extensive dialogue. Carissimi's settings assign the speeches of the individual characters to specific soloists, as we might expect in a dramatic work. Yet the soloists also sang as members of the choir in nondialogue sections, and, as in most Baroque ensembles, the "choir" originally used in these works may well have sung one on a part. Most of Carissimi's oratorios are in five or six parts; each singer would have performed as both a chorus member and as a soloist singing the words of one or more characters.

Carissimi's *Jephte*

The oratorio *Jephte* (anthology, Selection 16) is Carissimi's most famous work, thanks to Kircher's enthusiastic mention of it in his *Musurgia universalis*. It was presumably first performed, like Carissimi's other oratorios, during Lent at the oratory of St. Marcello in Rome, no later than 1648. The anonymous Latin text is an expansion of a story from the Book of Judges. The ancient Israelite leader Jephtha, preparing to lead his forces into battle, vowed that if he returned victorious he would sacrifice the first being that emerged from his house to greet him. He indeed defeated the Ammonites, enemies of the Israelites, and was greeted on his return by none other than his daughter—whom he accordingly sacrificed to God!

Carissimi's setting is for six voices with continuo. Most of his other oratorios include parts for two violins, but the continuo is the sole instrumental component here. The words of Jephtha and his daughter are assigned to one of the two tenors and one of the three sopranos, respectively. The other voices assist in the narration, which, as in Monteverdi's *Combattimento*, takes up much of the work. But instead of assigning the narration to a single singer, Carissimi distributes it between the four remaining voices (two sopranos, alto, and bass), designating each as *Historicus* (narrator) when singing in this capacity. These parts sometimes sing their narration alone, sometimes in duos and trios. Several times, all six vocal parts join together to form a chorus of Israelites. As in all Roman Baroque religious music (and many operas), the soprano parts would have been sung by male voices, probably castratos.

The musical style is relatively conservative. The monodic passages for the soloists alternate between arioso and aria style and avoid the more extreme effects of the *seconda pratica*. The choruses resemble other Roman motets of the period in their alternation between homophony and simple imitative counterpoint; double-choral writing occurs in a few of the other oratorios, and in *Jephte* Carissimi alludes to polychoral style through the use of antiphonal exchanges between the three high and the three low voices, a device already used by Palestrina.[15] Modern performances sometimes double the parts in these choruses, thus allowing the solo parts to stand out more sharply as individual dramatic roles. Yet the composition was evidently conceived, as an expressive, fairly intimate reading of the text—literally, an *oration*—that lacks the fully fleshed-out characters of a true dramatic work.

The most famous music in the work is Jephtha's long lament, which impressed Kircher by its use of remote modulations to express Jephtha's emotional shock. These are already evident at the end of the excerpt given in the anthology, where Jephtha is greeted by his daughter, whom he now must sacrifice. Jephtha's speech "Heu, heu mihi!" contains a few restrained instances of Monteverdi's *seconda pratica*, notably the downward leap of a diminished fourth to a dissonance (f'–$c\sharp'$ in m. 3 of "Heu"). Jephtha's distress is further represented by changes of tonality: a cadence in G minor at the words *decepisti me* (m. 6) leads immediately to successive chords of G major and E major (m. 7). The close juxtaposition of G-minor and E-major harmonies is the same one that Monteverdi had used in the messenger scene of *Orfeo*.

At least a portion of Carissimi's work was known to Handel, who borrowed its closing chorus in his oratorio *Samson* and treated the same story in his last English oratorio (*Jephtha*, 1751).[16] Of more immediate significance was Carissimi's role as one of the leading musicians in Rome through the central decades of the century. Among those who heard his works, and who may also have studied with him, were the German keyboard player and composer Johann Jacob Froberger, whose works are considered in Chapter 10, and Charpentier, Lully's most important contemporary in France, who adapted Carissimi's approach to the setting of Latin texts for use in his own country, especially in a number of oratorios and similar works.

Sacred Music in France: Michel-Richard de Lalande

A native tradition of sacred vocal music had long flourished in France, centered in the *Chapelle Royale,* the part of the royal household responsible for sacred music. Formed in the sixteenth century, under Louis XIV it became a complex organization encompassing numerous composers and performers who provided music for services attended by the king, whether at his palace in Versailles or elsewhere. Like the Paris opera, the music of the royal chapel was meant to

---

[15]Compare the opening of *Dum complerentur* (anthology, Selection 1).

[16]The borrowed chorus, "Plorate filii Israel" ("Weep, daughters of Israel"), was printed in Kircher's *Musurgia universalis*. On Handel's borrowings, see Chapter 9.

reflect the official royal image of magnificence and power. Its most impressive manifestation was the **grand motet,** a lengthy work for voices and instruments, both usually in five or six parts. These works usually fall into distinct movements; sections or movements for the full group alternate with others for soloists or reduced ensembles. Many of these works are settings of psalms, although other texts were also used (naturally in Latin). Smaller works for two, three, or four voices and continuo, called *petits motets* (small motets), were also written.

The *grand* and *petit motets* succeeded older types of French sacred music that until the mid-seventeenth century lacked independent instrumental parts or even a continuo part, as in Renaissance polyphony. The first to compose regularly in the new genres was Henri Du Mont (ca. 1610–1684), a member of Louis XIV's chapel from 1663 onward. Lully contributed to both types as well, but the most famous *grands motets* are those by Michel-Richard de Lalande (1657–1726), who like Du Mont began his career as a Paris organist before entering royal service. He did so by emerging as one of four winners in a competition held after Du Mont's retirement in 1683. Louis XIV personally selected Lalande, who gradually added further "quarters" to his assignment, becoming sole director of the royal chapel shortly before the king's death in 1715.[17]

In addition to seventy-seven *grands motets,* Lalande wrote numerous other sacred compositions as well as music for ballets, comedies, and other stage works (but no *tragédies en musique*). The care that Lalande put into his sacred works is evident in the significant revisions he made to many of his *grands motets* long after their initial composition. These works, like Lully's operas, continued to be performed through the eighteenth century, forming the core repertory of the **Concert Spirituel** (Spiritual Concert), an organization that gave public concerts in Paris from 1725 to 1790. One of the first public concert series in Europe, it initially offered only sacred music in Latin but eventually presented secular and instrumental works as well (in the 1770s symphonies by Haydn and Mozart were performed).

Lalande's *De profundis*

Probably the best-known of Lalande's *grands motets, De profundis* is thought to have been composed in 1689 on the death of the king's niece Marie-Louise, queen of Spain. This explains the addition of the *Requiem aeternam*—the introit from the Roman Catholic Mass for the Dead—to a text that is otherwise taken from the Book of Psalms.[18] There are nine movements (including the Requiem); we shall consider the opening chorus and the fifth movement, "Sustinuit anima" (anthology, Selections 13a–b).

The first movement, like the work as a whole, is scored for five-part chorus, with the *dessus* (soprano) occasionally divided into two parts. The instruments

---

[17]Previously the directorship had been shared on a quarterly basis; Lalande originally served as *sous-maître* (assistant director) during the months of October through December.

[18]The psalms are numbered differently in the Jewish, Roman Catholic, and Protestant traditions; this is psalm 129 in the traditional Catholic numbering, 130 in that of the Hebrew and Protestant Bibles.

comprise four-part strings with continuo (solo winds are heard in two other movements), but by contrast to the modern string orchestra there are two viola parts, and the violin line is often divided, yielding a five-part string ensemble, albeit one disposed differently from that used in Lully's operas. Each of the choral parts, unlike those of works for smaller establishments, was sung by multiple voices; in 1708 the Chapelle Royale employed fewer than ninety singers, although these would rarely if ever have been heard together in one work. Just as Lully's orchestra included both a *grande bande* and a *petite bande,* the chapel chorus was sometimes reduced to a *petite chœur* (small choir), as was possibly the case in measures 53–54 of the present movement. Solo singers, accompanied either by continuo alone or by larger groups of instruments, might also be heard, as in the opening section of this movement. The latter is assigned to a member of the *basse-taille*, or baritone, section; it is designated a *récit,* a term also used for complete solo movements. This solo follows an instrumental introduction, called a *symphonie,* such as opens most movements of the work.

The text of the opening chorus comprises the first verse of the psalm as well as the beginning of the second; after the initial *symphonie,* the baritone soloist sings the entire text, which is then presented chorally. The polyphonic antecedents of the *grand motet* are evident in the imitative entries of the choral voices, starting in measure 44. But the texture is fairly simple throughout, although never truly homophonic. All parts are pervaded by the three-note triadic motive played by the violins in measures 1–2; with the entry of the solo baritone (*basse-taille*), this motive becomes associated with the opening words of the text. The descending melodic shape of this motive reflects the word *profundis* (depths), as do the expressive descending sequences during the *symphonie* and at the first choral entrance (mm. 10–14, 44–46, 49–51). These descending ideas are answered by rising lines for the second part of the text ("hear my prayer"), which is sung chromatically—perhaps a sign of urgency—in its first solo statement (mm. 33–35) and in the final repetition by the choir (mm. 89–92). Other expressive moments include the cries of the word *clamavi,* set apart by rests, in measures 53–54 and the modulation to F minor in measures 58–62, in which a sudden B♭-minor harmony is followed by a leap downward to an unprepared diminished-seventh chord. The prevailing dark coloration is tempered by cadences to the relative major at the center of both the solo and choral sections (mm. 32, 57).

The more hopeful text of the fifth movement is set in C major, for soprano and oboe soloists with continuo. Originally there was a different setting, for the *petite chœur*; the date of the present version is unknown, but it could well be from after 1700. This later setting shows the influence of Italian style on French music after Lully. Instrumental passages for oboe and continuo serve not only as introduction but as interludes between vocal passages, hence functioning very much like ritornellos. Long melismas on the words *verbo* (word) and *speravit* (hoped), although not exactly in virtuoso style, reflect the Italian approach to musical rhetoric. The initial phrase for the voice could even be described as a motto (*Devise*). Nevertheless this movement could not be mistaken for an Italian aria. The rhythm resembles that of a French courante (note the hemiolic cadential phrases in mm. 6–7, 22–23, etc.), and the shape of the melodic lines, with their carefully notated ornaments, is equally characteristic of French style.

The form of the movement is broadly similar to one used in solos in many other late-Baroque sacred works. Strictly speaking this movement is not an aria, due to its biblical text, which comprises a single psalm verse. But the latter is presented twice, creating a design that corresponds with that of the first (A) section in a contemporary Italian da capo aria. The first statement of the text concludes with a cadence in the dominant (m. 53); this is followed immediately by a restatement of the opening in the tonic.

Although such a design would become routine during the eighteenth century, its specific application in this movement shows great concern for the text. This psalm verse is typical in falling into two halves; Lalande gives each clause its own motivic content. Thus the opening verb *sustinuit* ("I awaited") receives a syllabic setting with a skipping rhythm, whereas the complementary verb of the second clause *speravit* ("I hoped") is sung to a distinctive melismatic motive. Passages on this word coincide with modulations first to A minor (mm. 30–33) and then to D minor (mm. 64–68); alternating with statements of the opening words in C major, these two minor keys create an expressive contrast appropriate for the idea of "hope." Similar subtlety in the integration of form, tonality, and motivic invention would become typical of the best eighteenth-century composers of opera, cantata, and oratorio, as will be seen in the next two chapters.

CHAPTER 8

LATE BAROQUE OPERA

In the late Baroque—which we may equate very roughly with the first half of the eighteenth century—European musical traditions continued on the paths they had taken during previous decades. French and Italian musicians maintained their distinct styles, which were imitated singly and in combination by musicians elsewhere. This was particularly true in opera, where the Lullian model remained supreme in France. Although gradually transformed by the addition of Italian elements—a controversial trend resisted by some French musicians—French opera retained its distinctive character during the period we are studying. In Italy, on the other hand, significant changes in the nature of both texts and music led to a new form, opera seria, which became the leading type of opera through most of the century. (For a table summarizing the distinctions between the two types of opera—and by extension the French and Italian styles of the later Baroque in general—see Box 8.1.)

Trends in Late Baroque Music

Developments in opera in the first half of the eighteenth century reflected broader changes that affected other genres as well. Some trends had been ongoing since the beginning of the seventeenth century, such as the differentiation of distinct national styles and the use of idiomatically conceived instrumental parts. Others began in the later decades of the seventeenth century and continue through the eighteenth, in effect constituting the transition from Baroque to Classical style. Among these is a gradual simplification of harmony and musical texture, leading to an emphasis on tuneful melody and a corresponding reduction of interest in counterpoint and contrapuntal genres. These trends, which led to the so-called *galant* style, are taken up in Chapter 14.

Two trends fundamental to later vocal and instrumental music became all-encompassing in the eighteenth century. The first was the use of distinctly articulated formal structures. In its most basic manifestation, this trend produced the increasingly clear division of works into self-contained movements. In vocal music, this meant that most works came to comprise arias or arialike movements alternating with separate recitatives. The arias, moreover, tended increasingly to follow a limited number of clearly defined, clearly audible musical forms—above all, da capo form. A second, related trend was that toward tonality in the

---

Box 8.1

Some Distinctions between Late Baroque French and Italian Opera

French
- Continued use of elaborate recitative and arioso
- Limited use of the aria
- Restrained melodic style

- Many ornaments indicated by signs; little free embellishment
- Use of chorus for both dancing and singing
- Frequent instrumental dances in *divertissements* (ballets)
- Standard dance rhythms common in airs and dances
- Main voice types: soprano, *haute-contre* (male alto), tenor, bass

Italian
- Recitative mainly limited to *recitativo semplice*
- Heavy reliance on the da capo aria
- Frequent virtuoso writing with passagework (lively figuration: rapid scales, etc.)
- Most ornaments unnotated; much free embellishment
- Chorus absent

- Few instrumental numbers; rarely any dance
- Identifiable dance rhythms less common (but by no means rare)
- Main voice types: soprano and alto (female and male castrato), bass

---

full sense of the word. Already in the sixteenth century, most polyphonic works were tonal in the limited sense that they included what we recognize as standard functional chord progressions, such as half and full cadences. Some such works could even be considered to be in major and minor keys, although most also contain distinctly modal features. But few sixteenth-century compositions contain true *modulations*—shifts to new keys that govern substantial sections of a piece, which thus can be said to incorporate several distinct key areas (or tonal areas). Only when musical forms came to be organized in terms of modulations between related key areas, moving away from the tonic in one or more distinct passages before returning to it for good in the final section, can we say that modality had been largely or entirely replaced by tonality as the basis of the musical structure.

The trend toward tonality is evident in some of the works already examined from the later seventeenth century. Sections or movements of these works may be organized according to a symmetrical scheme that includes modulation to one or more foreign keys, followed by a return to the tonic. Thus a binary form (such as the air "Or if more influencing" in Purcell's *From Rosy Bowers*) may modulate to the dominant or relative major at the end of the first half; the second half returns to the tonic. The A section of a da capo form or ABA design, when considered apart from the B section, often has a similar bipartite form. The middle or B section not only introduces new textual and motivic ideas but also modulates to further keys.

Tonality may seem a terribly abstract concept, yet composers of the later Baroque made it one of the bases of musical form—even in opera arias—and it would become the source of much of the power and drama of eighteenth-century music. This is one reason why keys are so often included in the titles of instrumental works, and for this reason, too, keys and modulations will be mentioned increasingly in analytical comments here. Tonality helped make possible the extension of eighteenth-century arias and other movements over much longer periods of time than in seventeenth-century music: compositions grew longer. The early Baroque concern with musical rhetoric was not abandoned, but it took a different form as composers learned to employ the longer time spans of arias and other movements for expressive and dramatic purposes.

Opera Seria

The movement toward a new form of Italian opera, now known as **opera seria** ("serious opera"), began in the late seventeenth century as a reaction against the half-tragic, half-comic mixture of spectacle and entertainment that Italian opera had become, particularly in Venice. Lighter forms of Italian musical drama, including *opera buffa* ("comedic opera"), also emerged as distinct genres during the eighteenth century, but for most of the century it was opera seria that received the most attention and was most influential. Like some other music-historical terms, *opera seria* is difficult to define because it was rarely used during the period in question (the preferred term was *dramma per musica*), and modern writers have applied it to a range of works. All such works, however, share a set of conventions that had crystallized by 1710 or so and continued to govern Italian opera on serious subjects through the end of the eighteenth century.

The conventions of opera seria, some of them already familiar from earlier Italian dramatic music, include:

- A serious plot derived from ancient history as opposed to myth, thus discouraging a dependence on the supernatural and focusing instead on human actions and decisions.
- Singing characters who are few in number, usually rulers or members of the nobility; neither servants and other lower-class figures nor divinities have dramatic roles
- A poetic text that alternates between long lines of (usually) unrhymed verse, used for narration and dialog and set mostly as simple recitative, and shorter rhyming lines used for arias.
- Division into three acts, without comic scenes; violence is avoided and, if necessary for the plot, occurs offstage. Tragic endings (such as the death of a principal character) are avoided in favor of a reconciliation of conflict, often by an act of generosity or selflessness on the part of the hero or heroine, who thus serves as a role model for viewers.
- No choral or dance numbers (a brief "chorus" sung by the chief characters may conclude a work); ensembles may be limited to a single strategically placed duet involving the two leading male and female characters.
- Most scenes ending with an aria, after which the character leaves the stage; the number and the type of arias sung by each character is determined

largely by their relative social rank, the most important characters receiving a mix of arias deliberately chosen to express a range of stereotyped emotions, such as rage, affection, and a few other conventional categories of feeling, sometimes called **affects.** Each affect is signaled by the presence of certain standard poetic metaphors in the text (such as a storm) and by widely recognized musical symbols (such as long melismas on words referring to winds and rain).

The earliest proponents of this type of opera included members of the learned academies that continued to flourish in the eighteenth century in Italy and elsewhere. One such writer, the Venetian Apostolo Zeno (1668–1750), eventually worked as a court poet for the Austrian emperors at Vienna. Even more influential, however, were the librettos of the Roman writer Pietro Trapassi (1698–1782), known as Metastasio, who succeeded Zeno at Vienna in 1729. Their librettos were regarded as serious literary works in themselves. They typically concerned figures from ancient history—Alexander the Great or the "good" Roman emperors—who, during a period dominated by royal absolutist states, were viewed as models for present-day rulers. These librettos were set repeatedly by composers over the course of the century. For instance, Zeno's *Alessandro Severo*, concerning the Roman emperor Alexander Severus, was first seen in Venice in 1717 in a setting by Antonio Lotti (1666–1740); among eight later versions was one produced by Handel in London in 1738. Handel also used Metastasio's libretto *Alessandro nell'Indie* (Alexander in India) as the basis of his opera *Poro*, performed in London just one year after its premiere in Rome in a setting by the Neapolitan composer Leonardo Vinci (?1696–1730). Handel's London operas, like Lully's, were performed by private companies under royal or aristocratic support; in most European capitals, however, opera houses were built and their productions staged under the direct control and sponsorship of rulers, as in Naples, Vienna, Dresden, and Berlin (see Fig. 8.1).

In this type of opera, minor comic characters and subplots (such as occur in Cavalli's *Giasone*) were eliminated and the structure of the libretto was regularized. A typical scene was constructed of many lines of recitative leading up to an aria whose text comprised just a few lines, although its music made it far longer than the preceding recitative. As in earlier opera, recitative contained dialogue and advanced the action. The purpose of the aria was to permit one character to express his or her emotional response to the events just portrayed; having done so, the character almost always left the stage, leaving those remaining to begin another such scene. In the hands of a master composer such as Handel, the aria became a means for defining the personalities and relative significance of the major figures in the drama—a form of musical characterization.

This type of opera appealed to eighteenth-century aristocrats, who increasingly saw themselves as rational beings behaving in a civil manner and obeying universally agreed-to rules of behavior. The inevitable conflicts that arose in life, whether between rival lovers or rival states, were settled onstage not through violence but by reason and compassion. Political disputes between nations were the products of personal differences between their rulers, one of whom eventually came to see the error of his or her ways. Poets, musicians,

Figure 8.1 The Royal Opera House, Naples, with a performance of Giuseppe de Maio's *serenata Il sogno d'Olimpia*, from *Narrazione delle solenni feste* (Naples, 1749). This performance, on 6 November 1747, celebrated the birth of an heir to King Carlo Borbone, who is seated at the center (compare the position of the royal patron, King Carlo's great grandfather, in Figure 6.1). The orchestra includes two harpsichords, one at each end, facing inward. Larger than earlier opera houses, the theater is still small by modern standards, but note the depth of its stage, which made possible impressive perspective effects.

actors, and stage managers catered to this worldview by staging dramas that presented the heroes and heroines of the past as idealized reflections of present-day rulers. Librettos that successfully presented this view, such as those of Zeno and Metastasio, were repeatedly set to music by different composers, although the texts might be significantly altered. Revivals of existing settings might see their music, too, substantially revised, with new arias inserted (or substituted for older ones) to suit the voices or preferences of individual singers. This last practice reflected the fact that a single poetic-musical form, the da capo aria, came to dominate opera. The symmetrical construction of the da capo aria offered a predictable geometric form that could encompass an astonishing variety of emotion and musical content when written by a master and performed by a sensitive virtuoso.

This rationalistic approach to opera reflected the nature of European upper-class society during most of the eighteenth century. The violence of the previous century was set aside, and rulers and their subordinates invariably behaved with tact and moderation (at least onstage). In the theater, unpleasant or intense emotions were expressed only in the most formal, stereotyped ways, and dramatic events, especially combat and death, were, as in Greek tragedy, represented only indirectly, by characters' narrating them. The regular alternation of recitatives and arias led to a highly predictable format that satisfied eighteenth-century demands for the ready comprehensibility of artworks. Moreover, audiences got to know the thirty or forty most commonly used librettos, which composers set to music over and over again, repeating the same familiar stories.

Such conditions might seem anathema to the dramatic spirit of opera, which for us may seem to require spontaneous, uninhibited action and expression. Moreover, the concentration on the aria focused attention on the great virtuoso singers, whose improvisatory embellishments in the arias were sometimes a greater attraction than the original music of the composer. Such arias became vehicles for the singers, who used them as much to display their impressive vocal technique as to express emotions appropriate to the drama or to advance the plot. Eighteenth-century writers, including singers and composers such as Pier Francesco Tosi and Benedetto Marcello (1686–1739), occasionally criticized these aspects of opera seria. From the perspective of the very different types of opera favored in the nineteenth and twentieth centuries, these features look like fatal flaws. Yet composers from Alessandro Scarlatti to Gioacchino Rossini (1792–1868) accepted the conventions of opera seria. In part this must have been due to its enormous popularity, which no musician seeking to earn a living could ignore. But it was also because in the hands of the most skilled poets and composers opera seria was a remarkable achievement. Its best librettos, if not great literature, provided composers with verbal phrases and images that Baroque musical rhetoric was well equipped to handle. The alternation of recitative and aria furnished a pattern whereby dramatic tension built up during a recitative could be released in the following aria. The largest, most impressive arias, in which singers displayed their greatest feats of technique and expression, were not randomly disposed. They served as climaxes to crucial series of events in the plot and thus were frequently placed at the ends of major scenes or whole acts. Occasionally, too, conventional patterns could be broken—for example, an aria apparently in da capo form might be broken off, left unfinished—to achieve a special dramatic effect.

Most recitative in opera seria is in the simple style previously observed in portions of the Scarlatti cantata (Chapter 5). Unusual harmonies, remote modulations, and melismas are reserved for the most emotionally or dramatically crucial moments in a dialogue. Accompanied recitative—recitative with fully scored orchestral accompaniment—is used occasionally for particularly impassioned or dramatic speeches, especially monologues or soliloquies by major characters that are crucial to the plot. With the important exception of Handel, the arias of most composers use a homophonic texture that focuses attention on the melodic line—an important feature of the emerging *galant* style (see Chapter 14). In addition to employing da capo form, virtually all arias can be described as being in **ritornello form,** with an orchestral introduction that is now firmly integrated into the body of the aria.

The conventions described above applied even in operas, including most of Handel's, that for one reason or another do not fully meet modern definitions of opera seria. For instance, the work examined below, *Handel's Orlando,* contains magical elements shunned in more conventional examples of the genre. Worse, the title character goes mad at one point, losing the decorum expected of an eighteenth-century aristocrat (in Orlando's famous mad scene he even sings a passage of accompanied recitative in 5/8 time, something that would be unheard of in conventional opera seria). Handel avoided librettos by Metastasio and other eighteenth-century poets, preferring to use updated seventeenth-century librettos. Nevertheless, his mature operas, including *Orlando*, follow most of the traditions outlined above.

In addition to many Italian composers, such as Vinci and Alessandro Scarlatti, a number of Germans achieved prominence during the eighteenth century as composers of Italian opera. Besides Handel these included Johann Adolph Hasse (1699–1783), whose career extended well into what we call the Classical period, during which opera seria remained an important genre. The Classical composers Haydn and Mozart were both major composers of opera seria, as was Bach's youngest son, Johann Christian Bach (1735–87).[1] Throughout the century, opera seria influenced all other genres, especially those of instrumental music. This was especially true of the instrumental concerto, which developed during the same period as opera seria and employed related types of form, scoring, and means of expression (see Chapter 13).

The Performers of Eighteenth-century Italian Opera

Opera seria differed from seventeenth-century Italian opera in the reduced number of singing characters, who might number as few as five or six. Even more than previous types of opera, it was dominated by high voices, especially sopranos. Through a convention that now seems strange, soprano and alto voices were employed for most adult male as well as female roles. Thus, throughout the eighteenth century, the heroic character of kings, princes, and warriors and other leading male figures was expressed in opera primarily by the virtuosity of soprano and, less frequently, alto voices.

Although women and male falsetto singers sometimes took such roles, the most frequent singing voice used for them—and for some female roles as well—was the **castrato**. Through a surgical procedure carried out before the onset of puberty, a boy's physical maturation could be prevented. By long tradition going back to the sixteenth century, boys from poor families who showed musical talent could thus retain their high voices into adulthood; contrary to modern belief, the operation appears to have been perfectly legal and socially acceptable, even encouraged, in the regions of Italy where it was practiced. Most castratos probably wound up as priests singing in parish churches; few achieved fame as opera stars. In addition to preventing sexual maturity, the operation appears to have had other physical effects that favored the development of unusually strong wind support. Although at first confined mainly to the performance of sacred music at Rome, Venice, and other Italian centers, by the mid-seventeenth century the castrato voice had entered opera. By the eighteenth century the most accomplished of the castrato singers had become the greatest stars of opera (Fig. 8.2).

---

[1]Mozart's most important contributions to opera, however, lie in his *opere buffe*: works such as *Don Giovanni* and *The Marriage of Figaro*, which are essentially comedies.

Figure 8.2 *Rehearsal of an Opera* (ca. 1709), oil on canvas by Marco Ricci (1676–1729), 19 × 22 in (48.5 × 58.0 cm), Yale Center for British Art, Paul Mellon Collection (B1981.25.523). In this satirical painting, the standing figure at the harpsichordist's left may be the castrato Nicolini (Nicolò Grimaldi, 1673–1732), who sang in Handel's opera *Rinaldo*.

Modern notions about gender and sexuality are apt to cloud our understanding of the castrato phenomenon. Although incapable of producing children, castrati were adults, able to understand the emotions of the characters they portrayed, women as well as men. The best ones were praised for their acting as well as their singing, and some, such as the soprano Carlo Broschi (1705–82, known as Farinelli), were widely respected and even took on important political and diplomatic duties.[2] Women occasionally substituted for castratos in male roles, a practice that continues today, especially in soprano parts.[3] Use of the castrato voice was hardly confined to the eighteenth century; castrato roles

---

[2]The exotic, unnatural character of the castrato has fascinated writers and other artists. The French novelist Honoré de Balzac (1799–1850) wrote his novella *Sarrasine* about an aging castrato at a time when such voices were still heard in opera. More recently, the film *Farinelli* (directed by Gérard Corbiau, 1995) presented an imaginative account of the singer's life; although its plot is largely fictional, it gives a relatively accurate portrayal of Baroque theaters and staging (the musical performance practices heard and depicted in the film are less strictly historical).

[3]During the twentieth century it was not uncommon to substitute a tenor for a soprano castrato, but transposing the music down an octave seriously diminishes the brilliance and transparency of many arias and can lead to errors in the harmony (as when the voice crosses beneath the bass line or creates parallel fifths in place of fourths).

remained a regular feature of Italian opera well into the nineteenth century, and castratos sang in the Cappella Sistina—the pope's personal choir at Rome—until 1902.[4]

Instrumentation

As the number of singers diminished, the orchestra grew: indeed, it *became* an orchestra in the modern sense. Eighteenth-century opera seria normally employed a relatively large string section of as many as two dozen or more players, joined regularly by winds—at least two oboes, and frequently other woodwinds and brass—as well as a continuo section that usually included two harpsichords. One of the latter was normally played by the composer, who coached the singers and directed the ensemble from the keyboard. Simple recitative was, as before, accompanied only by the continuo, but by now it was rare for an aria to have only continuo accompaniment. Many arias, especially those of particular importance within the work, are scored for the full orchestral ensemble, and special orchestral colors are given prominence in particular sorts of arias (e.g., recorders in quiet scenes or lamentation, horns or trumpets in hunting or military scenes). Accompanied recitatives are reserved for only the most important dialogue, but they too frequently employ special orchestration and effects.

Performance

The conventions of opera seria included rules of stage deportment and gesture that were generally known and agreed upon by actors as well as singers. Many of the poses and gestures used onstage can be seen in paintings of the period, which drew on the same conventions of costume, gesture, and placement of figures in depicting historical or mythological events. Movement onstage mirrored ordinary, everyday behavior in polite society, both being governed by rules and protocols; for example, one bowed when greeting a social superior, and one never turned one's back on such a person when leaving a room—or the stage. Proper manners of bowing, gesturing, or simply standing were inculcated from childhood by dancing masters, who instructed members of the middle and upper classes in not only dance but general social deportment. As educated members of society, trained singers therefore did not require stage directors as such. Each type of character and each event in an opera called for a conventional vocabulary of movements and gestures that, with variations, could be adopted to each individual role.[5]

---

[4]Early recordings of the Sistine Chapel choir include several castrato singers, notably its director and principal soloist Alessandro Moreschi (1858–1922).

[5]There is little within the realm of acting and theater studies to compare with the vast amount of scholarship and practical experience in the field of historical musical performance. For an introduction to stylized gesture and other aspects of historical acting one must still consult Dene Barnett (with the assistance of Jeanette Massy-Westropp), *The Art of Gesture: The Practices and Principles of Eighteenth-Century Acting* (Heidelberg: Winter, 1987).

On the whole, there was less movement than in modern operatic productions. As in the spoken theater of the day, lengthy speeches (that is, arias) might be delivered with only small gestures varying each character's basic pose; the audience's attention was instead directed on the singing itself. Thus, during the singing of an aria there was no need for the fussy stage business that modern directors often introduce in an effort to maintain the audience's attention. Eighteenth-century audiences were accustomed to listening carefully to details in the music, paying particular attention to the embellishments and cadenzas that a virtuoso singer was likely to introduce.[6]

The second A section, that is, the "da capo" of a da capo aria, was the most frequent locus of embellishment, but this aspect of performance has probably been exaggerated in modern discussions. Modern singers unfamiliar with historical style sometimes distort the music grotesquely by transposing final notes up an octave or rewriting the passagework of virtuoso arias, while leaving out or performing incorrectly trills and other ornaments that were considered essential in standard cadential formulas.[7] Instrumentalists are sometimes guilty of similar things as well. It is true that eighteenth-century virtuosos such as Farinelli sometimes embellished arias beyond all recognition, but they did so only in certain types of aria. Moreover, Farinelli and other great singers had substantial training in theory and composition that guided their improvisations. Only fully thought-out and cleanly executed embellishments were approved by eighteenth-century connoisseurs, who might have been more impressed by the addition of a single expressive appoggiatura at the right place than by cascades of banal passagework. Many arias, particularly among those of master composers such as Handel, require nothing more than the addition of a few standard ornaments. The best candidates for embellishment are slow arias and other movements in which an unusually simple melodic line suggests that the composer purposely created an opportunity for improvisatory embellishment. Other suggestions for improvisation are provided by pauses and fermatas, which often signal a cadenza—two different cadenzas, if the pause or fermata occurs in a repeated section. A number of singers and composers, including Farinelli and Handel, left written-out examples of embellished arias; these provide clues to the nature of singing in opera seria, as does the comprehensive singing treatise by Tosi, already mentioned in Chapter 3.[8]

GEORGE FRIDERIC HANDEL

George Frideric Handel (1685–1759) was, with J. S. Bach, one of the two late Baroque composers who achieved the greatest renown in later centuries. Handel

---

[6]Opera seria was sometimes criticized by observers who noted the conversations, card playing, and other diversions that went on in the audience, but such behavior was probably more common during poor productions of second-rate works.

[7]Composers of Italian music, unlike the French, rarely wrote ornament signs; performers were expected to know where to apply trills in cadences.

[8]See bibliography under "Baroque Vocal Technique."

was the more famous during his own lifetime, although his fame was due largely to his operas and not to what are now his better-known English oratorios. Handel's career differed considerably from the lives of the musicians hitherto examined. Born in the eastern German city of Halle, as a boy Handel seems to have studied music—chiefly keyboard playing—only as an avocation; his father was a surgeon-barber (the two occupations were commonly joined at the time) and evidently did not intend his son to pursue a musical career. Nevertheless, Handel studied with the Halle organist Friedrich Wilhelm Zachow (1663–1712), a composer of some significance, and in 1702 gained an organist position there himself. He seemed headed for the type of career that Bach, growing up under similar circumstances less than a hundred miles away, would pursue. But a year later he left Halle for Hamburg—the most important city in northern Germany—where within two years he had established himself as an opera composer (see Box 8.2).

Handel's Early Career in Hamburg and Italy

As the only city in Germany with a flourishing public opera, Hamburg would have been a natural destination for a talented musician whose ambitions lay in the theater, as Handel's evidently did. Initially he played second violin in the Hamburg opera orchestra, under Reinhard Keiser (1674–1739), then the leading German opera composer. But his talent must have been immediately apparent, for his first opera was premiered at Hamburg before his twentieth birthday. There he also made the acquaintance of Johann Mattheson (1681–1764), a singer, dancer, and composer who would also become an influential and prolific writer. Mattheson's writings on music are still consulted as important sources of information on eighteenth-century music and musicians; they include an account of a trip Mattheson and Handel made together to Lübeck, another northern port city. Both were interested in succeeding to the organist position there, occupied by the aging Dieterich Buxtehude (see Chapter 11), until learning that they would have to marry the latter's daughter.[9]

Despite its location on the northern shore of Continental Europe, the Hamburg opera was predominantly Italian in style. It included French overtures and dance scenes, but the texts of most works were either all Italian or in a mixture of Italian for the arias and German for the recitative (a compromise intended to help the audience follow the dialogue). In 1706 Handel left Hamburg, traveling to Italy at the invitation of a Florentine prince. He spent four years in Italy, writing operas for performance in Florence, Naples, and Venice as well as two Italian oratorios, a substantial amount of Latin church music, and over one hundred secular cantatas with Italian texts for private performance in Rome.

During these years Handel met many of the important composers in Italy, including the violinist Arcangelo Corelli and Alessandro Scarlatti and his son Domenico. He possessed the facility, melodic imagination, and virtuosity

---

[9]Marriage arrangements such as this were common at the time; Handel's father, at his first marriage, had taken over the business that had belonged to his new wife's recently deceased first husband.

Box 8.2

George Frideric Handel (1685–1759)

1685. Born at Halle, in eastern Germany. Early studies with Friedrich Wilhelm Zachow, organist in Halle.

1702. Appointed organist at Halle Cathedral.

1703. Leaves for Hamburg (northwest Germany); his first opera, *Almira*, performed two years later.

1706–10. Travels in Italy; probably goes first to Florence, later Rome, Naples, and Venice. Composes cantatas, two operas, two oratorios. Possibly returns to Hamburg during 1707–8 to direct two more operas.

1710. Appointed kapellmeister in Hannover (Germany); travels to Düsseldorf and London, where his opera *Rinaldo* is performed the following year.

1712. Moves permanently to England, composing four additional operas through 1715.

1716. Visits Germany (*Brockes-Passion* performed in Hamburg). Returns to England under the patronage of the duke of Chandos, for whom he writes anthems, the masque *Acis and Galatea* (1718), and the first version of the oratorio *Esther* (1718).

1719. Visits Germany to recruit singers for the Royal Academy of Music, newly founded London opera company.

1720. Handel's first Royal Academy opera, *Radamisto*; the company continues through the spring 1728 season, producing thirteen new Handel operas in all, plus works by other composers.

1729. Visits Italy and Germany recruiting singers for new company (the "Second Academy"); first season opens December 1729. The company lasts through spring 1737, producing fourteen new Handel operas.

1732. Revised version of *Esther* performed publicly: Handel's first English oratorio. *Deborah* follows the next year.

1733. Rival company, Opera of the Nobility, founded; both fold after four seasons.

1737. Suffers an undiagnosed crippling illness; vacations at Aachen (Germany) and recovers. During the seasons of 1737–38 to 1740–41 produces his five last operas as well as three oratorios.

1742. *Messiah* premiered in Dublin; fifteen more oratorios follow.

1750. Last visit to Germany.

1751. Composes *Jephtha*, his last complete work; its composition interrupted by blindness. Completely blind by 1753; subsequently composes only revisions and a few insertions to existing works, dictated to his assistant.

1759. Dies at London, a week after his final performance (*Messiah*).

necessary for writing the tuneful, gracefully expressive, easily singable type of music that had been made popular by Scarlatti. Yet he retained an interest in chromatic harmony and a mastery of counterpoint that reflected the German tradition in which he had been trained at Halle. Thus, although his own style became thoroughly Italian, his music has a complexity and richness lacking in that of his Italian contemporaries.

Handel in England

Like Schütz and other earlier Germans who had undertaken extended visits to Italy, Handel probably never intended to stay there. In 1710 he headed back north for Germany. But after a brief stay at Hanover—whose ruler was soon to become king of England—he went to London, which would be his home for the rest of his life. At the time, moves were afoot to establish a permanent pub-lic theater for Italian opera in London, and Handel's *Rinaldo*, first performed there in 1711, proved a resounding success. For the next thirty years Handel continued to write operas—thirty-five in all, not counting revivals and arrange-ments of earlier works, both his own and those of other composers. Meanwhile he produced instrumental and church music of various sorts, as well as several English oratorios—a genre that turned out to be surprisingly popular.

In 1741 the expense of Italian opera and its failure to turn a profit finally forced Handel to abandon the composition of such works. He was able to con-tinue his career in London by focusing thereafter on oratorio, although of a type very different from earlier Italian ones. Since 1732 Handel had been producing oratorios of this new type, with English text, at a rate of approximately one new work per year. He continued to do so through 1752, presenting the works in public concerts during Lent, when plays and other staged dramatic works were banned. Blindness forced him to cease active composition after 1752, but until a few weeks before his death he continued to direct his Lenten oratorio perfor-mances from the harpsichord.

By 1759, when Handel died, Haydn was already composing symphonies, and many of the Baroque traditions in which Handel had been brought up had become outmoded. He had few students as such, and only some minor English composers directly imitated his style. Yet it would be wrong to regard Handel simply as an old-fashioned "Baroque" composer, for the operatic conventions that operate in Handel's operas as well as his oratorios were as much a pre-Classical as a Baroque tradition. Handel's operatic style is close in many respects to that of his younger contemporaries Hasse and J. C. Bach—who in 1763 succeeded Handel as the reign-ing German composer of Italian opera in England. When, a year later, Mozart met J. C. Bach in London, both composers might have viewed themselves as continu-ing the tradition that Handel had represented. In later years, Mozart would cer-tainly be influenced by Handel, some of whose works he performed in his own arrangements (notably the oratorio *Messiah*).

Handel's Works

As his biography suggests, Handel's most important works fall into two large groups: the Italian cantatas and operas composed from the early years through

1741, and the English oratorios that followed. He wrote numerous other vocal works as well, including a few motets and other Latin sacred music composed in Italy, as well as sacred anthems and secular odes with English texts.[10] In addition, Handel was active throughout his life as a virtuoso keyboard player and left many harpsichord pieces and works for instrumental ensemble. These appeared in several published collections, including eight harpsichord suites (1720), two sets of concertos for organ or harpsichord, solo and trio sonatas, and a dozen concerti grossi composed during a four-week period in autumn 1739. Among his other orchestral works are the French overture, dances, and other pieces known collectively as the *Water Music*, composed in 1717 for royal boating outings on the Thames River in London, as well as the *Music for the Royal Fireworks*. The latter was intended for outdoor performance by a large wind ensemble during celebrations marking the peace treaty of Aix-la-Chapelle (1749). His most important instrumental works, however, are probably the overtures and related movements, numbering close to one hundred, in his operas, oratorios, and cantatas. (For a detailed account of the suite, concerto, and other late Baroque instrumental genres, see Chapters 10–13.)

Handel's *Orlando*

Despite the presence of comic and magical elements in many of them, musically Handel's operas are close to the opera seria type, composed of alternating recitatives and arias, with ensembles, accompanied recitatives, and other types of numbers interposed only occasionally. The best known include *Rinaldo*, his first London opera, as well as *Giulio Cesare*, *Tamerlano*, and *Rodelinda*, composed during a particularly inspired period in 1724–25, and *Orlando*, first performed in 1733. *Orlando* (anthology, Selection 18) marked a somewhat unfortunate milestone in Handel's professional life, for it was the last work of several that he wrote for a cast that included the great castrato known as Senesino (Francesco Bernardi). During the following years Senesino joined a newly established opera company, called the Opera of the Nobility, which had been founded to compete with Handel's. The financial strains produced by the competition contributed to Handel's abandonment of opera eight years later.

The plot of *Orlando* derives indirectly from the *Orlando furioso*, an enormously popular epic poem by the Italian Renaissance writer Lodovico Ariosto (see Box 8.3).[11] Like the later *Gerusalemme liberata* by Tasso, Ariosto's poem is on topics from medieval history: the wars of the Frankish king Charlemagne and the hero Roland ("Orlando" is the Italian form of Roland's name). The tone of

---

[10]Handel's anthems and odes are in the tradition of Purcell's sacred and secular vocal works for soloists, chorus, and orchestra. Like Purcell's, most of these were written for the English royal court.

[11]Handel's libretto was an anonymous reworking of a text by Carlo Sigismondo Capeci (1652–1728) that had been previously set by Domenico Scarlatti, son of Alessandro. Handel had met both in Rome, where he was said to have participated in a keyboard-playing contest with Domenico, Handel winning on organ, Scarlatti on harpsichord.

Box 8.3

Handel: *Orlando*

Anonymous libretto after *L'Orlando* by Carlo Sigismondo Capeci
(1652–1728), previously set to music by Domenico Scarlatti (Rome,
1711, music lost). The source of the story is the *Orlando furioso* of
Lodovico Ariosto (1474–1533).
First performed 27 January 1733 at the King's Theatre, London.

Chief Characters

Orlando (alto), a heroic defender of France under the medieval emperor
    Charlemagne.

Angelica (soprano), queen of Cathay (China).

Medoro (alto), an African prince, lover of Angelica.

Dorinda (soprano), a shepherdess.

Zoroastro (bass), a sorcerer.

SYNOPSIS

Orlando, wandering in a strange land, is warned at the outset of Act 1 by Zoroastro that he must choose between love and conquest. Orlando declares that like
Hercules he can succeed at both—a big mistake, of course. He is already in love
with Angelica, who is, however, in love with Medoro. Angelica, moreover, has
seen Orlando in the company of a certain princess whom he has previously res-
cued from danger. Meanwhile, the shepherdess Dorinda has also fallen in love with
Medoro. As Act 1 ends, Orlando has set off to fight his enemies in order to prove
his love for Angelica—while Angelica and Medoro try to convince Dorinda that
her love for Medoro is misplaced.

Later in the opera, Orlando goes mad after discovering that Angelica and
Medoro have been in love all along. He tries to kill them, but in the end all is
set right by the magician Zoroastro, who has been watching over all of them from
the beginning.

SELECTIONS DISCUSSED IN THE TEXT

Overture.

Act 1, scenes 7–8. Dorinda and Medoro meet in the woods where she lives. Medoro
    tries to tell her diplomatically that he loves another (aria "Se il cor mai ti dirà"),
    then leaves. Dorinda, alone, complains about the untrustworthiness of people:
    aria "Oh care parolette."

———, scene 9. Zoroastro informs Angelica that he is aware of her love for
    Medoro and warns her that it will anger Orlando; the latter appears, as does
    Medoro, but Zoroastro saves Medoro by concealing him magically. Angelica

tells Orlando that she cannot love *him* without his proving his faithfulness: aria "Se fedel vuoi."

————, scene 10. Orlando, alone, complains that Angelica has misunderstood his affair with the princess; he vows to fight monsters: aria "Fammi combattere."

Ariosto's poem is less serious than Tasso's, and it includes a greater variety of minor characters and subplots. Two centuries later, this feature proved convenient for opera librettists, who frequently adapted Ariosto's stories, particularly those with a magical element. Magic is especially important in *Orlando*, in which the small size of the cast—just five singing characters—would have been compensated for by elaborate stage effects. The latter included the magical disappearance of Medoro during the recitative in Act 1, scene 9 (see anthology, Selection 18b), as well as the visions of the underworld that Orlando sees in the opera's climax, his famous mad scene at the end of Act 2.

Orlando opens, as do most of Handel's operas, with a French overture. Like other Handel overtures, it is a significant orchestral work in itself, extraordinary for its key (F♯ minor) and for having an imitative opening (dotted) section in addition to the customary fugal section after the double bar. The French overture proper ends with a so-called Phrygian cadence on the dominant, which leads into a very Italianate gigue in 12/8 time; many of Handel's overtures conclude with a dance movement in this manner, recalling the sinfonia of Scarlatti's cantata *Correa*, which had a similar design (see Chapter 5).[12]

The gigue is thoroughly Italian in style, as is the remainder of the opera. Most of the arias of the major characters fall into certain more or less standard types that had been established by the previous generation of Italian composers, such as Alessandro Scarlatti. Orlando's aria "Fammi combattere" (anthology, selection 18c) is an expression of heroic might, full of virtuoso passagework for the singer and imitations of trumpet calls in the orchestra. Such arias sung at moments of anger or pathos are referred to as "rage" arias. On the other hand, the aria of Angelica (anthology, Selection 18b), a somewhat ambivalent expression of love, is relatively short, lightly scored, and sweetly restrained in emotional profile. This might have been considered an *aria d'affetto* (affective or expressive aria).

Key, instrumentation, and melodic material all help define an aria's expressive character. For example, horns appear only once in the opera, to lend extra grandeur to Orlando's aria "Non fu già men forte Alcide" in Act 1, scene 3, in which he compares himself to Hercules.[13] This aria is preceded by an

---

[12]A version of the overture for solo keyboard, possibly by Handel himself, appears together with nineteen other such arrangements in George Frideric Handel, *Twenty Overtures in Authentic Keyboard Arrangements*, 3 vols., edited by Terence Best (London: Novello, 1985), 3:31–36.

[13]Horns had been introduced to the opera orchestra during the first two decades of the century and at the time of *Orlando* were still something of a novelty in London, employed chiefly as a special effect associated with hunting scenes, the horn still being in use as a signaling instrument during hunts.

accompanied recitative whose string accompaniment and opening key—F minor, rarely used at this date—underline the prophetic visions that the magician Zoroastro has shown to Orlando.

Brass instruments are absent from Orlando's equally martial aria in scene 10, "Fammi combattere" (anthology, Selection 18c). But they are represented symbolically by the fanfare motives, reminiscent of trumpet calls, that are developed imitatively in the opening ritornello (mm. 4–5). Oboes, which double the first violins in the ritornellos of this aria, were also used as military instruments at the time and thus reinforce the martial effect. The vocal part includes lengthy melismas on two words: *combattere* ("to do battle," mm. 14–18) and *valor* ("strength," mm. 31–35). The latter word is accompanied by the fanfare motive in the first violins, thus emphasizing the two ideas most important in the text of the aria and most representative of Orlando's personality—or, at least, of his aspirations.

On the other hand, Angelica's aria (anthology, Selection 18b) is distinguished by its simple (but very beautiful) vocal line. The latter is almost entirely syllabic, but for this very reason its brief melismas—the two longest, significantly, on the word *fedeltà* ("faithfulness," mm. 10 and 12)—bear considerable rhetorical weight. Apart from two brief ritornellos, this aria is scored solely for voice and continuo, a throwback to seventeenth-century texture that creates an effect here of intimacy and sincerity, in keeping with Angelica's unhappiness and uncertainty as she pleads with Orlando to prove his faithfulness to her.

Dorinda's aria "Oh care parolette" (anthology, Selection 18a) is particularly interesting as an example of musical characterization. Although its text appears to be pessimistic—a complaint about the untrustworthiness of lovers' promises—the music is a lightly scored Italian jig, with the quick triple rhythms characteristic of that dance (as in the overture). Moreover, both the ritornello and the vocal part open with somewhat comic repetitions of a perky three-note motive. The juxtaposition of such light music with an ostensibly solemn text characterizes Dorinda as a figure who either has no profound feelings or does not take what she says seriously. The effect is one of irony—an example of the sort of sophistication that was possible within the seemingly rigid conventions of eighteenth-century opera.

Da Capo Aria Form

Despite their varying character, most of Handel's arias, and indeed most Italian arias from the first half of the eighteenth century, share essentially the same design, illustrated in Table 8.1, which analyzes Dorinda's aria.[14] In addition to their da capo form, most of these arias also employ **ritornello form**: a design in which all or part of the instrumental introduction, or ritornello, is repeated

---

[14]Dorinda's aria differs from a literal da capo aria in its abbreviated restatement of the initial ritornello after the B section (mm. 46–47a). Underscoring the aria's light, fleeting character, which would be contradicted by the formality of a complete restatement, this abbreviation does not affect the fundamental da capo character of the aria.

TABLE 8.1

Handel: *Orlando*, Dorinda's aria, "Oh care parolette"

Section A						B		A	
R	1–3	r	1–3	R		4–6		r	1–3
Key B♭	B♭ → F	F → B♭	B♭	B♭		B♭ → g		B♭ (dal segno)	
Measure 1	9	19b	22b	34		39b	45b	46	9b

R = ritornello
r = abbreviated ritornello
numerals = lines of text
→ = modulation followed by cadence to the indicated key

several times within the body of the aria. The ritornello thus becomes an integral part of the aria, not merely an external introduction or frame as in earlier arias with ritornellos.

Typically, the opening ritornello is followed by the soloist's presentation of the entire A text, which leads to a cadence in the dominant (or another closely related key). A shortened ritornello—sometimes just a restatement of the opening measure or two—may occur at this point. In the second half of the A section, its text is repeated, leading to a cadence in the tonic and another complete or partial statement of the ritornello. The B section is usually shorter—often much shorter—than the A section, and may lack instrumental participation except for the continuo. Such is the case in Angelica's aria, "Se fedel vuoi ch'io ti creda," where the strings are silent in the B section. On the other hand, the B section, although short, may contain several modulations to relatively remote keys; this is true in both Dorinda's and Angelica's arias. The cadence that marks the end of the B section is followed immediately by a repetition of the A section. In the repetition of the A section, Handel sometimes omits all or part of the opening ritornello, as in Dorinda's and Orlando's arias.[15]

Jean-Philippe Rameau

During the latter part of Handel's career in London, the leading figure on the other side of the English Channel was Jean-Philippe Rameau (1683–1764), the most important and influential French composer since Lully. Rameau's career was slow in getting started; his first opera was not performed until he was fifty (see Box 8.4). But by then he had established himself in Paris as a virtuoso harpsichordist and composer. He had also published a massive book on music theory whose principles have informed the study of harmony to the present day.

---

[15]In twentieth-century performances of Handel's works, sometimes the entire da capo was omitted, or the A section alone was performed just once. Needless to say, such practices distort the music, and Handel rarely resorted to them.

BOX 8.4

Jean-Philippe Rameau (1683–1764)

1683. Born at Dijon (about 150 miles southeast of Paris) into a musical family; presumably studies with his father, an organist, and at the local Jesuit college. Briefly in Italy (exact date unknown), afterward possibly violinist with the Lyons opera.

1702. Appointed organist at Clermont cathedral (some 200 miles south of Paris); retains title until 1708 despite moving to Paris in 1706.

1706–8. In Paris with positions as organist at two religious institutions; publishes his first book of harpsichord pieces (a single suite, 1706).

1709. Succeeds to his father's organ position in Dijon.

1713. Moves by this date to Lyon (250 miles southeast of Paris) as organist there; probably composes motets, possibly other works.

1715–22. Again organist at Clermont. He is believed to have composed secular cantatas *L'impatience, Orphée,* and others during this period, as well as writing his *Traité de l'harmonie.*

1722. Moves to Paris; publishes *Traité de l'harmonie* and two years later *Pièces de clavecin* (harpsichord pieces; a second volume of *pièces* and a volume of cantatas follows in 1729 or 1730).

1726. Marries Marie-Louise Mangot, singer and harpsichordist, daughter of a royal musician.

1733–44. His first opera, *Hippolyte et Aricie,* performed by the Paris Opera (1733); it is successful but controversial owing to its departures from Lullian tradition. Four theatrical works follow; also publishes a collection of chamber works with keyboard (*Pièces de clavecin en concerts,* 1741) and two more major theoretical works as well.

1745. Composes a ballet for the dauphin (crown prince); numerous theatrical works, many under royal patronage, follow.

1752–54. "Querelle des Bouffons" (Debate of the Buffoons): a series of published exchanges with leading French intellectuals, notably Jean-Jacques Rousseau (1712–78), over the respective merits of French and Italian music. The latter is judged by Rameau's critics to be more "natural" because of its simpler textures and more facile melodies.

1764. Dies in Paris.

Rameau's Music

Despite his apparent inclinations toward theatrical music, the first half of Rameau's career was spent as a church organist. Although he held a number of significant positions, most were outside Paris, the one city that really counted in the French eighteenth-century musical universe. Nevertheless, prior to 1722

Rameau had been developing a distinctive style of keyboard playing and composition, and his first substantial book of harpsichord pieces, published in 1724, reveals a virtuoso approach very different from the restrained manner of earlier French keyboard composers. The surviving motets and cantatas from these years also appear to have made significant departures from the traditional French style.

Rameau's Musical Innovations

Lully had so dominated French music during the 1670s and 1680s that his theatrical vocal and instrumental music established the norms for the next two generations. Nevertheless, Italian-style vocal and instrumental music, including cantatas and sonatas, grew increasingly popular in France after Lully's death. The cultivation of Italian genres by French composers eventually led to what the French composer François Couperin described in 1724 as a "reunification" of the two national styles. Nevertheless, even in those French works that employed Couperin's *goûts réunis* ("reunited styles"), the French element remained paramount, as is evident in the pervasive use of dance rhythms, the precise notation of ornaments, and in opera and ballet, the retention of the basic conventions of Lullian style.

Rameau was probably a much greater borrower from the Italian style than Couperin ever was. Yet he remained so committed to the French operatic tradition that later in life, during the so-called Debate of the Buffoons (see Box 8.4), he defended French music against younger advocates of the Italian style. The latter, with its emphasis on solo virtuosity and simple melody, was contrary to the French tradition of carefully notated and precisely performed rhythm, ornamentation, and declamation of the text. Rameau, although adhering to these ideals, nevertheless admitted a significant degree of Italian virtuosity into his music. Thus, when he first made his mark in Paris, in the 1720s and 1730s, he was viewed by some as a destroyer of the Lully tradition, when in fact he reinvigorated it for another generation, carrying it into the 1760s.

Rameau's Theoretical Writings

With the eclipse of the French Baroque style in the late eighteenth century, Rameau's musical compositions went out of fashion. His accomplishments as a composer were largely forgotten, to be fully recognized only in the late twentieth century, when fully staged performances of his theatrical works began to be reconstructed with something resembling their original music and choreography. In the interim, however, Rameau's voluminous writings on the philosophy and theory of music were always studied, particularly those portions that formed the basis of subsequent theories of harmony.

Although he published significant books on all aspects of musical composition, theory, and practice, Rameau's core ideas are already present in his first book, the *Traité de l'harmonie* (Treatise on harmony, Paris, 1722), which has remained the most widely read. The book was a manifestation of that movement in French eighteenth-century thought known as the Enlightenment, which encouraged the rational, systematic examination of all scientific and cultural subjects. In Rameau's musical theory, Enlightenment thought took the form of an innovative way of analyzing chord progressions, which Rameau viewed as the basis of all musical composition.

Rameau's Theory of Harmony

Previously, chords had been regarded as byproducts of the voice leading of individual parts in a contrapuntal texture—the incidental results of a linear or melodic process. This view, which had emerged from the study of sixteenth-century polyphony, had grown increasingly inappropriate for explaining later music, which tended to employ homophonic textures and to rely on tonal rather than modal types of pitch organization. During the seventeenth century, keyboard and lute players had developed pragmatic ways of understanding figured bass realization that in some respects anticipated Rameau. They discovered, for example, that a relationship existed between what we would call the root of a chord and its inversions. But it was Rameau who conceptualized such intuitions about harmony as a formal theory.

In Rameau's theory, the successive vertical sonorities of a composition were viewed as constituting progressions of harmonies, which Rameau represented through a form of analytical notation which he called the **fundamental bass**. Thus in Example 8.1 Rameau analyzed his own five-voice motet *Laboravi clamans* by adding a fundamental bass on the bottom staff. The fundamental bass was notated like a basso continuo part, using figured bass, but the only dissonant interval indicated was the seventh. The fundamental bass line consists primarily of what we would call the roots of the successive chords, which might appear in any of several forms or inversions. Rameau also employed the terms *tonic*, *dominant*, and *subdominant* to describe harmonies in relation to what we would call the tonality of a composition. From these ideas later writers developed various theories of harmonic function.

Some contemporaries, especially in Germany, were reluctant to accept elements of Rameau's theory, but it eventually became the basis of later theories of tonal harmony. Nineteenth-century theorists replaced Rameau's fundamental bass with various symbols, and from these developed the modern American system of analytical chord symbols: Roman numerals to indicate the roots, and arabic numerals to indicate the inversions.[16] Other systems have been adopted elsewhere. In Germany, for example, functions are indicated by the letters *T*, *D*, and *S* (for tonic, dominant, and subdominant), with additional symbols used for other functions recognized by later theorists. Only in the twentieth century was Rameau's predominantly harmonic or "vertical" view of tonal progressions seriously challenged, notably by the Austrian theorist Heinrich Schenker (1868–1935) and his followers. Schenker derived his views from eighteenth-century German theorists such as Carl Philip Emanuel Bach, whose writings represent an older, "horizontal," view of harmony; C. P. E. Bach wrote that the principles of himself and his father (J. S. Bach) had always been "anti-Rameau."

---

[16]The arabic numerals are descended from the figures of figured bass.

Example 8.1 Rameau, motet *Laboravi clamans*, mm. 1–9 (soprano and *basse-taille* omitted); the lowest staff shows the fundamental bass as given by Rameau in his *Traité de l'harmonie*

Laboravi clamans.   I suffered, crying out.

Rameau's *Les indes galantes*

Just as Rameau's theories, although highly innovative, drew on ideas recognizable in the French seventeenth-century tradition, his music was composed within existing French conventions. By the time he reached Paris, French composers were already cautiously moving away from Lullian norms. Whereas Lully's mature theatrical works are dominated by one type (the *tragédie en musique*), Rameau wrote important examples in additional categories: *comédies lyriques* (lyric comedies), *opéras-ballets* (operatic ballets), *pastorales heroïques* (heroic pastoral dramas), and others.

The newer types of work continue the Lullian tradition of combining sensitively declaimed poetry with extensive choral and ballet elements. But their plots and characters are less uniformly serious and heroic than those in most of Lully's *tragédies en musique*. This was in keeping with a loosening of conventions that had followed Lully's death in 1687. Notable among the composers of the following generation was André Campra (1660–1744; see Fig. 10.7), who wrote, in addition to operas (*tragédies en musique*), the *opéra-ballets L'Europe galante* (literally, Gallant Europe, 1697) and *Les fêtes vénitiennes* (Venetian carnival, 1710). These works reflect the growing influence of Italian opera, particularly the da capo aria, which continued to be felt by French composers of Rameau's generation.

Les indes galantes (anthology, Selection 19) is an *opéra-ballet*, incorporating dialogue and action (set in Lullian recitative) but consisting primarily of dances and Italian-influenced arias. The title might be translated as "The gallant Indies," although the word *galant* at the time could also mean "fashionable" or "modern." *Indes*, which today properly indicates the nations of South and East Asia, here seems to refer to almost any exotic, that is, non-European, country. The work originally comprised three acts, called *entrées*, that are only loosely related to one another (see Box 8.5).[17] First produced in 1735, it was revived the following year with the addition of a fourth *entrée*. Each act or *entrée* takes place in a different exotic locale; the added one is set in what later became the Louisiana Purchase of the United States.[18] The music of the final scene incorporates a reworking of a harpsichord piece, *Les sauvages*, (The savages) from a collection that Rameau had published in 1729 or 1730; it had been inspired by a performance of ethnic dancing by two Illinois Indians in Paris in 1725.

The title *Les sauvages* was extended to the new *entrée*; the term properly refers to forest dwellers untouched by civilization but implies no moral degradation or savagery in the modern sense. On the contrary, the plot of the fourth *entrée* emphasizes the supposed "naturalness" of the Native Americans, who are viewed in the libretto as ethically superior to their more civilized French and Spanish rivals. This view reflects a romantic way of thinking common among eighteenth-century Europeans, who idealized the natives of North America as "noble savages" unafflicted by the pathologies of European civilization. Although this view today seems patronizing, the French poet Fuzelier's stereotyped impression of the Indian people parallels his stereotyping of the Europeans as well. His way of understanding national character was in keeping with Enlightenment understanding of culture and ethnography in general.

Rameau's Music Contrasted with Lully's

Rameau's work is structured much like one of Lully's, opening with a French overture and prologue. The action and dialogue of each *entrée* are presented in recitatives whose frequent changes of meter and precisely notated rhythm closely reflect the rhythms of the French text. The characters frequently break into short airs, many of which employ standard dance rhythms. Each *entrée* culminates in a large ballet scene that combines singing and dancing as in a Lullian *divertissement*.

---

[17]The word *entrée* in this sense is to be distinguished from the use of the same term for a dance in dotted rhythm (see Chapter 6).

[18]The region in question was held successively by France, Spain, and France again before being acquired by the United States in 1803.

Box 8.5

Rameau: *Les indes galantes*

Opéra-ballet, composed Paris, 1735. Revised, with addition of fourth act or
entrée (originally called the *nouvelle entrée*), 1736.

Libretto by Louis Fuzelier. Comprises overture, prologue, and four acts
or *entrées*. The *entrées* take place in four different non-European locales,
which are visited in turn by several European adventurers. Each *entrée*
constitutes a self-contained dramatic ballet, with singing and dancing.
The fourth, or new (*nouvelle*), *entrée* is entitled *Les Sauvages* (The savages).

Characters (fourth *entrée*)

Zima (soprano), Indian princess
Adario (baritone), Indian commander
Damon (tenor), French commander
Don Alvar (bass), Spanish commander

SYNOPSIS

Two Europeans, one French, one Spanish, are signing a peace treaty mediated by
Zima's father, an Indian king (called the *grand Calumet*). Both woo Zima and in
so doing reveal their supposed national traits: flirtatiousness for the French, jealousy for the Spanish. But the Indian commander Adario wins Zima by his strength
and constancy.

SELECTIONS DISCUSSED IN THE TEXT

Overture.

Fourth *entrée*, scene 4. The arrival of the European and Indian armies is signaled
by a brief orchestral *prélude*, interrupting the confrontation between Adario, on
the one hand, and Damon and Alvar on the other, who now express their hopes
for peace (recit.)

————, scene 5. Adario expresses his love for Zima (recit.). She accepts in a brief
arioso in sarabande rhythm ("De l'amour le plus tendre," mm. 10–15), then
rejects his two rivals (recit., mm. 16–25) and comments on the Indians' "natural" moral superiority in an *ariette*, "Sur nos bords l'amour vole." Adario looks
forward to their marriage in a brief recitative (mm. 32–34), and they celebrate
with a duet, "Hymen, viens nous unir."

————, scene 6. Final scene, celebrating their wedding; corresponds with the
divertissements in Lullian opera. Opens with air, "Bannissons les tristes alarmes,"
for Adario, repeated by a chorus of Indians.

Long *rondeau* follows: opening instrumental version (arranged from Rameau's harpsichord piece *Les sauvages*), followed by vocal version "Forêts paisibles," set as duet with chorus.

Two alternating minuets (instrumental dances, "for the warriors and Amazons"—presumably male and female Indians).

Zima then sings a virtuoso air in da capo form (*ariette*), "Régnez, plaisirs et jeux," introduced by a lengthy ritornello.

The work concludes with a great chaconne.

Unlike Lully, however, Rameau includes relatively lengthy airs that are really Italianate da capo arias; these were known in France as *ariettes*. Among these is the air "Sur nos bords l'amour vole," sung in scene 5 by the Indian princess Zima. Despite its Italian formal design, this air continues to employ the French style. The latter is recognizable in the ornaments notated in both the vocal and the instrumental parts and in the recurring use of rhythms characteristic of a French dance, the gavotte (see Chapter 10). Closer to the style of eighteenth-century Italian opera is Zima's virtuoso *ariette* in the sixth and final scene ("Régnez, plaisirs et jeux"), which incorporates brilliant melismas and lengthy ritornellos unheard of in the Lully style. Also remote from Lully is the flexible instrumentation of Rameau's works, which routinely call for instrumental sonorities beyond the basic string ensemble, including solos and obbligato lines for flute, bassoons, even the *musette*, a type of bagpipe. The string writing, now usually in four rather than five parts, also reveals imaginative new textures, as in Zima's aria "Sur nos bords l'amour vole." Here the two accompanying violin parts provide imaginative counterpoint that weaves about the voice in expressive triplets and so-called "sigh" motives—two-note descending slurred figures, especially in the B section (mm. 16b–30a).

Not surprisingly for a composer also known for his contributions to the theory of harmony, Rameau went beyond the relatively narrow variety of harmonic progressions and modulations employed by his predecessors. Although *Les indes galantes* is fairly conservative in this respect, Rameau's operas contain passages of considerable harmonic audacity. The most famous such example, from his first opera, *Hippolyte et Aricie* (Hippolytus and Aricia), includes a stunning enharmonic passage, sung by the three Fates in an underworld scene (Ex. 8.2). In a later theoretical work, Rameau described the passage as an example of what he called "diatonic enharmony." The idiosyncratic expression alluded to the ancient Greek enharmonic genre—a sort of scale that incorporated microtones (intervals smaller than a half step). Rameau also mentions the difficulties the passage caused the original singers, apparently forcing him to shorten it.[19] In modern

---

[19]In his *Génération harmonique* of 1737. Although not involving the microtones employed in ancient Greek music, the passage would have created intonation problems for musicians accustomed to the unequal temperaments or tuning systems employed at the time (see Chapter 11).

Example 8.2 Rameau, *Hippolyte et Aricie*, Act 2, mm. 712–22 (Second Trio of the Fates; basso continuo figures omitted)

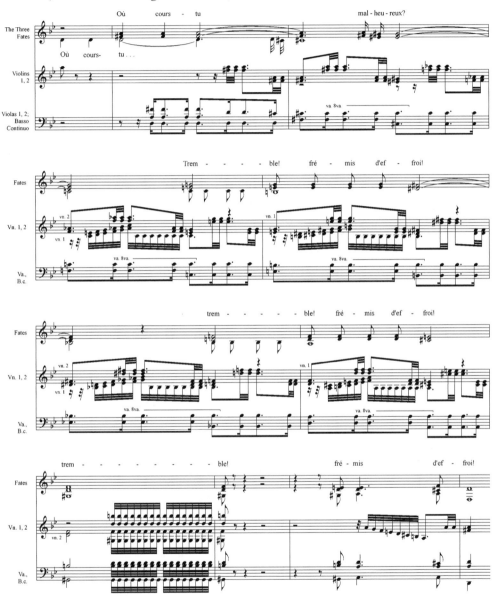

Ou cours-tu malheuereux?   Where are you running, unfortunate one?
Tremble! fremis d'effroi!   Tremble! shudder with dread!

terms, the passage incorporates enharmonic modulations, as when a chord of C♯ becomes reinterpreted as one of D♭ by the modulation from F♯ minor to F minor in measures 714–15. The passage also illustrates the virtuosity with which Rameau used orchestration to create dramatic theatrical effects, and which he demanded of the players, as evident in the fiery passages for first and second violins, both divided.

On the other hand, Rameau's recitative remains close to the Lully style, accompanied only by continuo and using changes of meter for accurate declamation of the text. Occasional lines are set in regular dance rhythms, as when Zima describes "the most tender love," using the rhythm of a sarabande (scene 5, mm. 10–15). The two lovers rejoice in an intimate duet, still accompanied only by continuo, as in similar lovers' duets in Lully's works.[20] Only then does the final scene begin, a lengthy *divertissement* celebrating their impending wedding. After a series of dances, airs, and choruses, the work concludes with a grand chaconne, distinct in sonority but using the same underlying rhythm as the great *passacailles* of Lully's operas. This chaconne lacks a regular ostinato bass, instead employing a free form related to the *rondeaux* of Rameau's keyboard pieces.[21] But it retains Lully's basic conception of presenting a magnificent succession of contrasting musical and choreographic ideas.

---

[20] An ironic example for Rinaldo and Armide occurs in Act 5 of *Armide*, just before the famous *passacaille*. The Indians in Rameau's work address their duet to Hymen, the Greek god of marriage—suggesting that the French poet identified the Native Americans with ancient Greek nymphs and shepherds.

[21] A *rondeau* alternates between a recurring theme or phrase and a series of contrasting phrases or *couplets*. Rameau's harpsichord piece *Les sauvages* is an example.

CHAPTER 9

LATE BAROQUE SACRED MUSIC

Developments in late Baroque theatrical music found close parallels in sacred vocal works. The latter is a very broad category, including not only works performed as part of actual church services but music with religious texts that was heard elsewhere, even in theaters (as was the case with Handel's oratorios). Regardless of the performance venue, however, something resembling the regular yet dramatic alternation of recitatives and arias found in opera became the norm as well in most types of eighteenth-century sacred music. Individual movements, that is, the successive recitatives and arias of a sacred work, similarly tended to fall into forms and styles close to those of secular works.

The introduction into sacred music of what had originated as secular dramatic forms may strike us as an anomaly, particularly when we consider that the opera theater of the time was dominated by castrato singers, portraying the pagan heroes of antiquity. This development represented a breaking down of a division recognized since the early seventeenth century between a conservative church style and a freer "theatrical" style. Yet, from the beginning of the Baroque, composers such as Monteverdi, Carissimi, and Schütz had been quick to employ elements of the theatrical style, such as recitative and the *concitato* style, to render the presentation of a sacred text more vivid or expressive. Moreover, the even older principles of musical rhetoric recognized no distinction between secular and sacred music. Hence, although eighteenth-century critics did occasionally complain about the presence of theatrical forms in church music, most musicians and listeners regarded theatrical musical devices as a desirable means of making sacred texts more accessible and meaningful to contemporary audiences.

The introduction of new types of sacred music did not mean that older ones were abandoned. Particularly in Roman Catholic countries, polyphonic music in the *stile antico* continued to be performed. Thus Alessandro Scarlatti and his younger contemporaries in Italy and southern Germany still produced masses and motets in contrapuntal style. These works often resemble those of Palestrina—whose music also was still performed—save for the presence of a basso continuo part. Perhaps the most influential composer of such music was the Austrian Johann Joseph Fux (1660–1741), whose book *Gradus ad Parnassum*

(Vienna, 1725) has served as a counterpoint textbook to the present day.[1] It was read carefully by the mature Bach—in a German translation by his friend Lorenz Mizler—and later by Haydn, Beethoven, and Brahms during their student years. In Lutheran Germany, *concertato* motets in the manner of Schütz continued to be composed well into the eighteenth century. Such works might still be through-composed, consisting of line-by-line settings for chorus or smaller ensembles of texts derived from the Bible or from chorales, the congregational hymns of the Lutheran church. Such was the most common type of sacred vocal work composed by Dieterich Buxtehude (ca. 1637–1707) and, until about 1708, the young J. S. Bach.

But in general the musical style and scoring of sacred works increasingly resembled those of contemporary secular music. For instance, Latin motets in the eighteenth century often took the form not of choral works but of solos for voice (usually soprano) and instruments, alternating between recitatives and arias and concluding with an "amen" or "alleluia" to constitute practically a wordless concerto for solo voice. Italian composers such as Antonio Vivaldi wrote many such works, as did Germans such as Hasse, J. C. Bach, and Mozart in a tradition that extended into the Classical period. Other sacred works, including settings of the mass (or portions of it, such as the Gloria), were composed as successions of separate movements for chorus, ensembles, and soloists, accompanied by instruments; not only Catholic composers such as Vivaldi but those in Protestant regions (including Bach) contributed to this tradition. The oratorio, which in the mid-seventeenth century had taken the form of a special type of polyphonic motet (see Chapter 7), by 1700 was in many respects indistinguishable from opera, at least as far as the music was concerned. Seen in this light, Handel's switch during the 1740s from writing Italian operas to writing English oratorios was not as huge a leap as it might seem (see below).

New Types of Sacred Music by German Composers

The English oratorio was one of several types of new sacred work that emerged in northern Europe in the eighteenth century. In Lutheran Germany shortly after the turn of the century the theologian and poet Erdmann Neumeister (1671–1756) introduced a type of sacred text modeled on that of the Italian secular cantata, serenata, and other quasi-operatic works. His first published collection of such texts, appearing in 1704, consists of librettos for works called *cantatas* that alternate between recitatives and arias; the German composer J. P. Krieger (1649–1725) set many of these for solo voice and instruments (unfortunately these settings are lost). The energence of this new type of sacred cantata coincided with the widespread influence of **pietism** in Lutheran Germany. Pietism had originated in the early seventeenth century as a movement toward individual piety and religious expression; a populist movement, opposed to the

---

[1]The title of Fux's book ("Steps to Parnassus") refers to the mountain home of Apollo and the Muses in southern Greece, a symbol of artistic perfection. The bibliography lists several modern editions under "Baroque Theoretical Treatises."

types of outward religious display especially associated with aristocratic courts, it discouraged elaborate forms of church music such as the cantata. Disputes over the appropriateness of such music adversely affected the work of many musicians, including Bach—one reason eighteenth-century musicians in Germany, as elsewhere, tended to prefer court appointments over others.

Nevertheless, the first half of the eighteenth century saw the widespread writing of German sacred poetry that reflected pietistic concern for individual religious experience yet was set to music in the current Italian theatrical style. Among the most important composers of such works were Georg Philipp Telemann (1681–1767) and J. S. Bach. Both, following the practice of Neumeister, organized their church cantatas into annual cycles: yearly series of works, one for each Sunday and holiday in the church calendar. The enormously prolific Telemann produced at least thirty-one such cycles—over two thousand individual cantatas—as well as numerous other sacred works. Bach's extant cantata cycles number only three, still a considerable quantity of music.[2] Most of these works involve multiple singers; hence in the language of the day they were not, strictly speaking, cantatas, and Bach and his contemporaries usually called them by older titles, such as *concerto* and *motetto* (or simply *Musik*). Today, however, the usual term for these works is *cantata*, which will be used here despite the fact that the closest model for many of these works was not the Italian solo cantata (as in the works by Strozzi and Scarlatti examined in Chapter 5) but somewhat larger works, such as the serenata.

The German Eighteenth-Century Sacred Cantata

Most German sacred cantatas differ from their Italian secular models in several respects. First, the language is, of course, German, whose particular pronunciation and accentuation influence the style and sound of the music, especially in the recitatives. Second, whereas the Italian cantata is essentially a genre for a solo singer, many German sacred cantatas include movements for several different solo voices as well as duets, trios, and choruses for four-part vocal ensemble. Finally, not all sacred cantata librettos in Germany are composed solely of free poetry; many also include biblical verses and stanzas from chorales. Bach's cantatas, in particular, use chorale, scripture, and free poetry to produce a composite textual and musical form.

JOHANN SEBASTIAN BACH

J. S. Bach (1685–1750) is now recognized as one of the greatest musicians in world history (see Fig. 9.1). During his lifetime, however, Bach's fame was largely confined to Germany, especially the southeastern regions of Saxony and Thuringia, where he spent most of his life. He was known primarily from his occasional

---

[2]Fragments of one or two additional cycles by Bach survive, but documentary evidence for the oft-repeated claim that he wrote five complete cycles is inconclusive.

Figure 9.1 Portrait of J. S. Bach by Elias Gottlob Haussmann (1748, copied by the artist from his painting of 1746). Courtesy of William H. Scheide, Princeton, New Jersey. Bach holds a copy of his *Canon triplex* in six parts BWV 1076; following an old tradition, the musical notation serves as an icon of the composer's skill and learning.

public appearances as an organ virtuoso; familiarity with his vocal compositions was largely confined to the cities in which he performed them, and his instrumental music was for the most part known only to other professional musicians who had performed or studied with him. Unlike his almost exact contemporary Handel, Bach never left Germany, settling for a series of positions that, with one exception, involved the composition and performance of church music. This has led to a view of Bach as primarily a composer of sacred music, and indeed the latter constitutes the majority of his surviving output. Yet like many other eighteenth-century musicians, he was active in both sacred and secular spheres, making little distinction between them insofar as musical style is concerned. Bach, moreover, was as willing as any of his German contemporaries to adopt the most up-to-date musical fashions emanating from France and Italy. He differed from most contemporary musicians in his strong interest in counterpoint and his use of sometimes highly dissonant, chromatic harmony—both carried over from the late seventeenth-century tradition in which he was brought up.

At a time when the simple *galant* style of opera seria was increasingly in vogue, this made Bach appear old-fashioned to his contemporaries, a few of whom criticized him for writing music that was, in their view, archaic and difficult to perform.[3] Although far from the whole truth, the image of Bach as a conservative writer of complicated contrapuntal forms has persisted. He indeed composed many fugues and other contrapuntal works, and to this day his contrapuntal keyboard works form part of the elementary training of many music students, as they did for Bach's own pupils. But such works constitute only a fraction of Bach's output. Indeed, perhaps the most remarkable aspect of Bach's music is its diversity, which in this respect eclipses the music of any contemporary composer, including Handel. Bach composed substantial examples in all the genres of his time; even operatic music is represented by several dramatic secular cantatas. Moreover, Bach's music successfully blends elements of both French and Italian styles with his own distinctive musical personality. The latter is evident in the elaborate formal architectures, unusual chromatic harmonic progressions and modulations, and profound contrapuntal element present in many works. Bach also combined conventional genres and styles in unconventional, highly imaginative ways, as in his incorporation of fugues into the ritornellos of his arias and concertos and his transfer of the French overture style into choral movements of his church cantatas as well as to a work for a single solo cello. His works do require greater musical insight and technical skill from the performer than those of his contemporaries. The result is music of great complexity that challenges both performers and listeners yet possesses enormous emotional depth and, frequently, immediate melodic and rhythmic appeal as well.

Bach's Life and Works

Bach's output, like that of most musicians before the nineteenth century, was largely determined by where and for whom he worked at any given time. Most of his organ music was written during his early years as a church organist, and much of his secular vocal music and music for instrumental ensemble dates from six years in the middle of his career when he directed the court musical establishment at Cöthen. The sacred vocal works were mostly written during two relatively short periods during his years at Weimar and Leipzig. The one sphere in which Bach remained steadily active throughout his life was keyboard music, especially music for stringed keyboard instruments (primarily the harpsichord).

Despite following a fairly conventional career path, Bach nevertheless exercised more self-determination than was typical of his contemporaries (Box 9.1). Although he never traveled as widely as Handel, his frequent journeys within Germany and his life-long interest in collecting music—much of it in manuscript copies that he made himself—kept him informed about the latest trends in French and Italian music, which he enthusiastically if judiciously adopted in

---

[3]See the exchange between Bach's critic Scheibe and his defender Birnbaum, reprinted in *The New Bach Reader* (see bibliography under "J. S. Bach").

BOX 9.1

Johann Sebastian Bach (1685–1750)

1685. Born at Eisenach (western Thuringia, in central Germany).

1695. Father dies; moves to nearby Ohrdruf to live and study with his older brother Johann Christoph.

1700. Enters St. Michael's School (choir school) in Lüneburg, 150 miles to the north. While there hears French dance music played by the court band of the ruling duke of Celle, possibly also opera and organ music at Hamburg, 25 miles away. Also probably studies with Lüneburg organist and composer Georg Böhm (1661–1733).

1702. Wins competition for organist at Sangerhausen (Thuringia) but is denied position.

1703. Briefly hired as "lackey" at Weimar (to serve as a musician).

1703–7. Organist at Arnstadt (east of Eisenach); composes keyboard music and possibly his earliest surviving vocal works.

1705–6. Visits Lübeck (200 miles north) for about four months to hear music by and possibly study with Buxtehude.

1707–8. Organist at Mühlhausen (north of Eisenach). Composes his first datable vocal work (Cantata 71).

1708–14. Organist at Weimar (40 miles southeast); composes organ and harpsichord music as well as vocal works.

1714. Promoted to *Concertmeister* at Weimar; begins monthly composition of church cantatas (through 1716, with interruptions).

1717. Visiting Dresden, challenges French harpsichordist Marchand to public contest; latter fails to show.

1717–23. Kapellmeister at Cöthen; composes or revises secular cantatas and instrumental works, including Sonatas and Partitas for unaccompanied violin (1720), Brandenburg Concertos (1721), *Well-Tempered Clavier*, Part 1 (1722).

1720. Visits Hamburg; his organ recital is praised by the aged organist and composer Jan Adamszoon Reinken.

1723–50. Cantor at the St. Thomas School and director of church music, Leipzig.

1723–27. Composes church cantatas on a regular basis (roughly one per week), also *St. John Passion* (1724), *St. Matthew Passion* (1727), *St. Mark Passion* (1731, lost).

1726. Publishes first partita of *Clavierübung*, Part 1 (keyboard music); the six partitas constituting Part 1 are reissued in a collected edition in 1731; Parts 2–4 follow in 1735, 1739, 1741.

1729–37, 1739–41. Directs Leipzig Collegium Musicum; regular concerts at Zimmermann's coffeehouse.

1733. *Missa* (early version of B Minor Mass) sent to the new elector of Saxony; Bach receives honorary title from him three years later.

1737. Johann Adolph Scheibe publishes famous criticism of Bach's music; Bach defended by Johann Abraham Birnbaum.

1741. Visits his patron Count Keyserlingk in Dresden; publishes Goldberg Variations, so called after Keyserlingk's harpsichordist Johann Gottlieb Goldberg, a pupil of Bach.

1747. Travels to Berlin, plays for King Frederick II, improvising fugues on a subject proposed by the latter; later that year publishes the fugues (called ricercars) and other works as parts of the *Musical Offering* dedicated to the king.

1749. B Minor Mass completed; blindness forces curtailment of composing and performing.

1750. Dies at Leipzig. *Art of Fugue* published (incomplete) one year later.

his own works. Although a prolific composer by modern standards, his output is smaller than that of Telemann and other contemporaries. In part this is because when an occasion demanded a composition from him, rather than writing a new work he often preferred to revise an existing one for the particular performance at hand. Throughout his life he would return to previously composed pieces, elaborating and correcting them to bring them to a state of perfection rarely sought by other composers. As with all eighteenth-century musicians, the outward characteristics of his works were determined by conventions of genre and style. Yet in virtually every work Bach combined diverse stylistic elements and created new formal designs, belying his popular image as a conservative composer.

In the twentieth century Bach's works were assigned "BWV" (*Bach-Werke-Verzeichnis*) numbers by the German scholar Wolfgang Schmieder (these are sometimes called "S" numbers). The numbering is nonchronological. The first two hundred works correspond to the traditional numbering (also nonchronological) of the sacred cantatas; thus Cantata no. 127, the first of Bach's compositions that we shall examine is depth, is also BWV 127. A more recent and more detailed catalog of Bach's works, the *Bach Compendium*, has its own numbering system, but this is not expected to replace the BWV numbers.

Early Years

Bach was born in 1685 in Eisenach, in central Germany, a region then noted for the unusually large number of talented musicians in its many towns and small cities. For several generations, members of the large extended Bach family had been particularly numerous among these musicians. Hence it was taken for granted that a boy such as Bach would become a musician like his father. After the latter's death in 1695, Bach studied music first with his older brother Johann Christoph and then at the choir school—a boys' school attached to a local church—in Lüneburg, 150 miles to the north. At the age of eighteen he received his first substantial position, as church organist at Arnstadt (1703–7). In this central German town he probably composed many of his earliest surviving compositions: mostly organ music, but also possibly several sacred vocal works in the old *concertato* style. During this period he also visited Lübeck, a major city on Germany's northern coast. There he probably studied with the city's Buxtehude, then the leading composer of organ and church music in northern Germany; like Mattheson and Handel, however, he appears to have had no interest in taking over Buxtehude's position.

Weimar: Organ Works and Cantatas

Two more organ positions followed, one held briefly in the small independent city of Mühlhausen (1707–8), the second at Weimar (1708–17). Weimar was the seat of a small duchy, jointly ruled by two music-loving aristocrats who had made their court a center for the performance of up-to-date vocal and instrumental music. In addition to his official duties as organist in the ducal chapel, Bach also participated in court chamber music. His promotion in 1714 to the office of *Concertmeister* (concertmaster) led to his composing church cantatas in the modern Italianate style, one each month. At Weimar, too, he probably composed most of his organ works, many harpsichord pieces, and concertos and other compositions for instrumental ensemble.

Cöthen: Instrumental Compositions and Secular Cantatas

In 1717 Bach took a position as kapellmeister at the court of Cöthen, another small princely town. It was here that he composed, or at least revised, many of his now-famous works for solo keyboard and for instrumental ensemble. He eventually gathered most of these works into collections that, although not published during his lifetime, resembled contemporary music publications in containing half-dozens of similar pieces. Such was the case with the six Brandenburg Concertos (see Chapter 13), the six suites for solo cello, and the six sonatas and partitas (suites) for solo violin. These last two collections followed a seventeenth-century German tradition of music for unaccompanied string instruments, without continuo. Bach, as usual, surpassed his models in the length and complexity of the resulting works.

Among the most important works that Bach probably composed mainly at Cöthen are the inventions, suites, and other pieces for keyboard instruments, written primarily for his students. The most famous of these Cöthen works is Part 1 of the *Well-Tempered Clavier*, an anthology of twenty-four preludes and fugues for keyboard, one in each of the twenty-four major and minor keys. The title refers to the system of keyboard (clavier) tuning or temperament that made this possible (see Chapter 11 for further discussion). Later, at Leipzig, Bach added a second volume containing another twenty-four preludes and fugues.

Bach was not required to write sacred vocal music at Cöthen. He did, however, compose an unknown number of secular cantatas for such events as princely birthdays and weddings. Bach later adapted many of these works for church use at Leipzig through the substitution of new texts and revision of the music; this process, common at the time, is known as **parody**.

Leipzig: Church Cantatas and Other Works

In 1723 Bach moved to Leipzig—after Dresden, the second most important city in Saxony (in southeastern German). Here he served both as cantor of the St. Thomas School—a choir school (Fig. 9.2)—and director of music at the

1 . *Die St Thomas Kirche*, 2. *Die Thomas Schule*
3 . *Der Steinerne Wasser = Kasten* .

Figure 9.2 The St. Thomas Church (center) and School (left), Leipzig, by Johann Gottfried Krügner, Sr. This engraving appeared as the frontispiece to *Ordnung der Schule zu S. Thomae* (Leipzig, 1723), a publication containing the rules and regulations that governed the faculty and students of the St. Thomas School. Bach and his family occupied the nearest portion of the school building, shown as Bach would have known it during his first nine years at Leipzig; renovations in 1732 added two additional stories. The building was torn down in 1908.

city's five main churches. In German schools, the position of cantor was primarily an educational one. Thus Bach was responsible not only for training the boys for participation in church music, but for teaching them Latin (a job that he assigned to a deputy). The music they were required to sing included hymns (called chorales) as well as more elaborate types of church music. During Bach's first few years at Leipzig his main creative focus lay in the composition of cantatas for performances at the two main churches, those of St. Nicholas and St. Thomas (next door to the school). At Leipzig Bach also composed and directed performances of secular cantatas for weddings and other private events, as well as for public ceremonies such as the annual installation of the city council and occasional visits by the duke (elector) of Saxony, whose domains included Leipzig.

For about four years, from 1723 to 1727, Bach produced sacred cantatas on a regular basis, writing new works or revising existing ones for performance on almost every Sunday and holiday. Bach also composed two large passions, musical accounts of the arrest and crucifixion of Jesus, based on the gospels of John (1724) and Matthew (1727).[4] Thereafter, however, Bach seems to have abandoned the regular composition of church music, turning to other projects. These included a series of publications for keyboard instruments, modestly entitled *Clavierübung* (Keyboard practice), begining in 1726. Apart from two early cantatas, these keyboard volumes were Bach's first publications; the great majority of his music remained in manuscript until the nineteenth century.

In 1729 Bach became director of the Leipzig Collegium Musicum, an organization that gave regular public concerts, some at a local coffeehouse. Among the secular cantatas presumably performed there by the Collegium is a little *dramma per musica* on the subject of coffee, a drink that had been introduced to Europe during the seventeenth century. Bach's Coffee Cantata—not the first eighteenth-century work on this subject—is a miniature *opera buffa* with two characters, a precocious girl and her impatient father. Many of Bach's works for instrumental ensemble, including concertos for violin and for harpsichord and his orchestral suites, survive in versions thought to have been also prepared for these performances, although some had been composed earlier.

Late Works

In 1741, when Bach ceased direction of the Collegium Musicum, his musical thought seems to have been turning toward encyclopedic collections that would demonstrate the arts of musical composition and performance in a comprehensive, systematic way. One product was the final installment of the *Clavierübung*, in the form of a work known as the Goldberg Variations. Published in 1741, this is a large, technically challenging set of variations for harpsichord, reportedly composed for the talented young harpsichordist and composer Johann Gottlieb Goldberg (1727–56), who had apparently studied with Bach. At about

---

[4]Bach's *St. Mark Passion* (1731) is lost; portions of it were parodies of movements in Cantata 198, from which scholars have reconstructed the passion version.

the same time Bach also wrote the *Art of Fugue*, a set of fugal compositions all on the same theme or subject, which was published posthumously in 1751. A trip to Berlin in 1747, during which Bach improvised keyboard fugues for the young king of Prussia, Frederick II (the Great), led to a volume of keyboard and chamber music dedicated to the king, the *Musical Offering*.

Perhaps the most impressive work of these years was the B Minor Mass, which Bach completed in about 1749. A major portion, the Kyrie and Gloria, had been composed by 1733, when Bach had presented it to the elector of Saxony.[5] In return, Bach had received the honorary title of electoral Saxon and royal Polish court composer.[6] Both the original portion and the remainder added in the 1740s include parodies of movements from Bach's sacred and secular cantatas, ingeniously reworked to fit the words of the mass. Bach cannot ever have performed the work in its final form. It seems instead to have served as a compilation of vocal movements intended for study, like those which Fux had included in his *Gradus ad Parnassum*. The individual movements range from choral fugues in *stile antico* to *galant*-influenced arias and duets, although even the latter are permeated by strict counterpoint and chromatic harmony.

Yet Bach during these late years was not solely preoccupied with complex contrapoint. His so-called Peasant Cantata of 1742 is a semidramatic comic work, like the Coffee Cantata; it draws on folksong as well as the popular *galant* style, and its text is partly in a low-German dialect. Even in more abstruse contrapuntal works, Bach's dissonant chromatic harmony is invariably expressive, and the use of strict counterpoint does not rule out virtuoso gestures, such as the crossed hands of the Goldberg Variations or the cadenza that ends one of the canons in the *Art of Fugue*.

The Performance of Bach's Cantatas

Since its rediscovery and publication in the nineteenth century, Bach's sacred music has been a central part of the European musical repertory. For this reason its performance practice has been investigated with particular care, and despite the loss of many essential sources and the difficulty of reaching firm conclusions about many matters, probably more is known about the historical performance of Bach's cantatas than any comparable repertory.

Bach's sacred cantatas were performed in church, during worship services; the secular works had various venues, including outdoors in Leipzig's central square. Soprano and alto parts were sung by boys or adult male falsettists, at least in the church works; women did sing in some German churches by this time, but not in any locale where Bach regularly worked. Although the exact makeup of Bach's vocal forces has been a matter of debate, the overwhelming evidence is that Bach's

---

[5] The Sanctus and other sections of the B Minor Mass also were written earlier; only a few movements were newly composed in the 1740s.

[6] The elector of Saxony was also king of Poland; Elector Friedrich August II (also known as King Augustus III) was crowned in 1733 but did not grant Bach his title until three years later.

vocal works were composed for a "chorus" comprising a single singer on each part, doubled by a single additional singer in certain special works (such as the St. John Passion). Instrumental parts, too, were rarely doubled, except for the violin and continuo lines. Thus what nineteenth- and twentieth-century listeners regarded as massive choral movements for large choir and orchestra are in fact examples of chamber music for vocal soloists and a small instrumental ensemble.

Although Bach complained several times to his Leipzig employers about the inadequacies of the student members of the ensembles he directed, it is unlikely that most performances would have been as unsuccessful as is sometimes supposed. Bach was clearly an inspiring teacher, attracting numerous talented pupils, a number of whom went on to become some of the finest musicians in Europe. Even as boys studying at the St. Thomas School, the best of them would have been well acquainted not only with Bach's own music, which they sang and played on a daily basis, but also with the performance conventions of the French and Italian styles. The same would have been true of the adult musicians who also participated, among them students from the Leipzig university and possibly visiting virtuosos. Bach, like his French contemporaries, generally notated ornaments and embellishments with great precision; thus there is rarely any need for substantial improvised additions. Bach's precision extended to specifying, more often than not, the exact choice and number of instruments; modern performances on "original" instruments have revealed the care with which he scored his ensemble works, using specific colors that can be closely matched only with eighteenth-century techniques and instruments.

The Cantata *Herr Jesu Christ, wahr' Mensch und Gott*, BWV 127

Cantata 127 (anthology, Selection 20) was composed for performance at Leipzig on 11 February 1725, the Sunday in the church year known as Quinquagesima (the last Sunday before Lent, during which few cantatas were performed). Like most of the Leipzig cantatas, it was probably written during the week immediately preceding its performance. As soon as Bach's score had been completed, he, together with his assistants, copied out individual parts for rehearsal and performance, afterward putting them away for reuse on the same Sunday in subsequent years (Figs. 9.3 and 9.4)

Cantata 127 belongs to Bach's second yearly cycle of cantatas, composed mainly at Leipzig from June 1724 to February 1725. The works of this cycle are all **chorale cantatas**: cantatas whose texts and music are derived primarily from those of a single chorale.

A **chorale** is one of the hymns of the Lutheran church. It is both a textual and a musical form: a melody joined to any number of stanzas of rhyming poetry. Many chorales stem from Martin Luther, the sixteenth-century church reformer, who created the chorale to encourage congregational participation in the service. Luther attached German poetic verses to traditional Gregorian and popular melodies; many later German poets followed his model, and musicians added many new melodies, so that by Bach's day there existed a large repertory of chorales for librettists and composers to draw on. In addition to serving as popular hymns for congregational singing, chorales formed the basis of more

Figure 9.3 The opening page of Bach's manuscript score of Cantata 9, *Es ist das Heil uns kommen her* (first half of the 1730s), Library of Congress, Washington (ML96.B186case). A chorale cantata, this work was composed in the 1730s to fill a gap in the series of chorale cantatas written in 1724–25. The six instrumental parts are (from the top down) for flute, oboe d'amore, violins 1–2, viola, and basso continuo. Like his contemporaries, Bach composed in ink, making his first draft directly into what would become his finished score; note the corrections in the oboe part, m. 10. The voices do not enter until the following page (not shown), but in the last full measure on this page Bach sketched in the entrance of the bass voice; the word "Es" at the foot of the page is the opening word of the text.

elaborate vocal and instrumental compositions, serving a function much like that of Gregorian chant in Roman Catholic church music.

Bach's chorale cantatas thus drew on a two-centuries-old tradition of Lutheran sacred music and poetry. The text of each such cantata is borrowed in whole or, more often, in part from the stanzas of a given chorale poem. In addition, the chorale's melody plays a prominent role in at least two of the work's movements. In the present work, the chorale melody is heard complete in the soprano part of the first and last movements, and is alluded to elsewhere as well (Ex. 9.1). Although many other German composers wrote chorale cantatas, few produced compositions approaching Bach's in their varied and complex contrapuntal elaborations of the chorale melody or the subtle integration of the chorale melody and text throughout the work.

Virtually all of Bach's church works include at least one chorale movement in a relatively simple style. Often coming last in the cantata, these four-part settings are the "Bach chorales" that harmony students have studied since the late eighteenth century. Bach's son Carl Philipp Emanuel helped publish a

Figure 9.4 Page 5 from the organ continuo part for Bach's Cantata 7, *Christ unser Herr zum Jordan kam*. Private collection, courtesy of Teri Noel Towe. Bach's musicians performed from manuscripts such as this one, copied by his student Christoph Gottlob Meißner and revised by Bach himself, probably for the work's first performance on 24 June 1724. Bach added the continuo figures as well as the heading "Recit[ativ]" at the top of the page and the dynamic marking *piano*, but he neglected to add a heading for the aria that begins on the third line.

Example 9.1 Some appearances of the first line of the chorale melody *Herr Jesu Christ, wahr'r Mensch und Gott* in Bach's cantata of that title: (a) movement 1, soprano, mm. 18–21; (b) movement 1, oboes, mm. 1–2; (c) movement 1, tenor, mm. 17–18; (d) movement 2, basso continuo, mm. 13–14; (e) movement 4, bass voice, mm. 13–15; (f) movement 5, soprano, mm. 1–2

collection of them in the 1780s, extracted from his father's cantatas and other works. Since the melodies in most cases are traditional, only the harmonization—the lower three parts—is actually by Bach. The *chorale* cantatas are distinguished by not only closing with a "simple" four-part chorale movement of this type but also opening with a much larger, more complex choral movement based on the same chorale melody. Usually the text of this opening movement is the first of several stanzas traditionally associated with the chorale melody; another stanza was used for the concluding movement. In between, the librettist provided a series of recitative and aria texts. These texts usually contain extracts from additional stanzas of the chorale, as well as references to or quotes from appropriate Bible verses.

The Text of Cantata 127

The chorale verses used in Cantata 127 are by Paul Eber and were first published in 1560. The melody to which Eber attached his poem had already appeared a few years earlier, in 1555. The name of the librettist who adapted Eber's chorale text for Bach's use is unknown, as is the case for all of the chorale cantatas of 1724–25.

The text of the cantata as a whole is concerned with the journey of Jesus and his disciples to Jerusalem, one of the events that eventually led to Jesus' crucifixion. Jesus' entry into Jerusalem is understood in the Christian tradition as prefiguring the coming of the Messiah as ruler of the world at the Last Judgment. Thus the cantata text includes a vivid description of the end of the world, when each individual is expected to be judged for his or her sins. It closes with a prayer that encourages the listener to remain faithful in his or her belief until death.

The Music

As in most of Bach's chorale cantatas, the full ensemble is used only in the opening and closing chorale movements. Both movements employ the traditional chorale melody as a cantus firmus (see below) in the soprano. But the first movement is a large chorale fantasia in ritornello form; only in the final movement do we hear a "simple" four-part setting of the chorale melody. The congregations of Bach's Leipzig churches would have been familiar with this and other chorales and would have recognized the tune and its poem at the outset. Today, however, it is helpful to examine first the simpler setting of the chorale in the final movement.

Movement 5: Four-Part Chorale Setting

The concluding movement is for the entire ensemble, the instruments doubling the voices as indicated.[7] The continuo, which in this work originally comprised organ, cello, and probably double bass, differs slightly from the vocal bass

---

[7] Only the trumpet is silent here, being a "natural" instrument (see below) that could not play all the notes of the soprano part in this movement.

line and therefore is set out on a separate staff. The chorale melody is sung by the soprano (Ex. 9.1f); the other parts were added by Bach and constitute his harmonization. The setting of the text is syllabic, the musical texture homophonic—but this does not mean that the music is truly simple or without a contrapuntal aspect. The bass and inner voices retain some rhythmic independence; note, for example, the moving eighth notes of the lower parts throughout the first two phrases (mm. 1–4). Moreover, Bach's harmonization reflects the words of the specific stanza of the chorale used here. For example, the second-to-last word (*einschlafen*, "to sleep") is set to a chromatic progression—text painting that serves as a reminder that "sleep" here is a metaphor for death.

A peculiarity of this chorale tune is that it opens in F but ends with a cadence on C, apparently the dominant. Tonally ambiguous structures such as this are not unusual in chorale tunes, many of which date from the sixteenth century or earlier, prior to the period of common-practice tonality. Among the modal characteristics of this type of tune is the possibility of ending on a tone other than the final, as in the present case. Such a tune presented a challenge to a later composer such as Bach who wished to use it in what we would call a tonal composition.

Movement 1: Chorale Fantasia

The first movement employs the same chorale melody in a much larger setting with obbligato instrumental parts. The movement resembles a **chorale fantasia,** a type of organ piece in which each phrase of a chorale melody is developed at length in various ways. Bach had written many such organ works at Weimar, and most of the Leipzig chorale cantatas open with comparable choral movements. In this case the chorale tune is sung in its entirety as a **cantus firmus** in long notes by the soprano, beginning at measure 18 (see Ex. 9.1a).[8]

The entrance of the soprano and the three lower voices is preceded by a ritornello (mm. 1–16), as is each of the five subsequent phrases of the chorale. In this respect Bach treats the vocal entries just like the solo sections of an aria. He makes an exception at the very end, however: before the instruments have finished stating the final ritornello (mm. 76–80), the voices reenter, repeating the final line of the chorale stanza. In this final vocal passage the soprano part is freely composed, having already presented the last phrase of the chorale cantus firmus in the previous vocal passage (mm. 68–71).

The opening ritornello is a substantial musical section in itself, combining three distinct thematic ideas in a complex contrapuntal texture. At the outset, the three thematic ideas occur as follows: (1) the oboes present a motive derived from the first eight notes of the chorale tune (Ex. 9.1b); (2) the recorders (*flauti*) present a motive in dotted rhythm; and (3) the strings present a theme in half notes. The latter is the first phrase of a second chorale melody, "Christe du Lamm Gottes" (Christ, Lamb of God). The use of two

---

[8]A **cantus firmus** (Latin, literally "fixed song") is a preexisting melody used in its entirety as a framework for a new polyphonic composition. Cantus firmus compositions based on Gregorian chant had been an important form of Western polyphony from the Middle Ages through the Renaissance.

chorale melodies in one movement is very unusual but entirely appropriate, as the text of the second chorale points to the Crucifixion. It is an example of Bach's inventive use of an unprecedented musical idea—the combination of two chorales in an elaborate contrapuntal texture—in a way that is at once expressive, technically skillful, and directly related to the work's theological subject and religious purpose.

After the initial presentation of the ritornello's three thematic ideas, Bach recombines them, using the device known as **invertible counterpoint.** When the three thematic ideas are restated at measure 9, the recorders now have the main chorale line and the violins have the dotted motive. Invertible counterpoint allows the various thematic ideas to cycle between the various instrumental parts—a technique frequently used in Bach's music and that of his contemporaries. The three thematic ideas return in subsequent ritornellos and as counterpoint to the voices after the latter have entered.

At the conclusion of the movement, the end of the ritornello is combined with newly composed choral parts. This type of counterpoint, integrating the instrumental and vocal components of a movements, is another common device in Bach's music, known by the German word *Einbau* ("insertion" or "installation").[9] An example for solo voice occurs in measures 21–26 of the third movement, where the solo soprano sings in combination with the last six measures of the ritornello. In both cases the device creates a sense of climax or heightened expressivity by increasing the complexity of the contrapuntal texture.

Elsewhere in the opening movement, the three lower voices use imitation to develop motives from the chorale melody, which the soprano is simultaneously presenting as a cantus firmus. For instance, in measure 17 the tenor enters with the eight notes of the first chorale phrase (Ex. 9.1c); the phrase is then imitated by the alto and bass voices. Such use of a preexisting melody is an instance of **paraphrase** technique, whereby the chorale (or another tune) is broken into fragments that are developed through imitation or other means. Paraphrase had been an important technique in vocal polyphony since the fifteenth century; Bach was doubtless aware of its use in chorale fantasias by Buxtehude and other older German composers.

The lower three vocal parts are often highly expressive, following the principles of musical rhetoric. For example, in measure 56 the alto has a so-called **sigh motive,** a slurred two-note descending figure. This occurs, appropriately enough, on the word *Leiden* ("suffering"), where the note ($a^{b\prime}$) acts as a dissonant appoggiatura, forming a diminished seventh with the tenor ($b\natural$). This type of accented, unprepared dissonance—a survival of Monteverdi's *seconda pratica*—is a fundamental element in Bach's harmonic style.

Movement 2: Recitative

This movement illustrates Bach's adaptation of Italian *recitativo semplice*. Even this "simple" recitative is a masterpiece of musical rhetoric, highlighting

---

[9]More specifically, *Choreinbau* refers to the addition of choral parts, *Vokaleinbau* to that of a solo voice. The same technique in a concerto or other instrumental work can be called *Soloeinbau*.

important words through high notes, striking harmonies, and changes of key. For instance, in measure 6 the word *Seufzer* ("sigh") is emphasized by being sung to a relatively high note (eb′); moreover, the word is interrupted by a rest to represent the idea of a distressed sigh or groan (a common type of Baroque text painting). In addition, the harmony at this point is a dissonance, a diminished seventh chord, as indicated by the figured bass.

Through most of the movement the basso continuo, which provides the sole accompaniment, is written in long notes. As in Italian recitative, these notes were probably not held out for their full length (see Chapter 5). But near the end of the movement (m. 13), the style shifts to arioso on the word *Ruhe* ("rest"), where the soprano momentarily "rests" on a quarter note. At the same point, the continuo has eighth notes in a motivic pattern borrowed from the opening of the chorale melody (Ex. 9.1d)—a subtle means of connecting the recitative musically to the other movements of the work. At the same time, the highlighting of this word—literally "rest," but again meaning death—points forward to the next movement.

Movement 3: Aria

The soprano aria, which falls at the center of the work, reveals Bach's attention to both tone color and certain symbolic associations between musical and extra-musical ideas that had become traditional by the late Baroque. The aria is in C minor and is set in standard da capo form. Bach's instrumentation heightens the expected contrast between A and B sections; the A section is scored for woodwinds and continuo, with violins and viola entering in the B section.

The ritornello is dominated by the oboe, whose line contains many melodic embellishments, such as the scale in thirty-seconds in measure 2. The style of these written-out embellishments is derived from the improvised embellishments of the Italian adagio (see Chapter 12). The voice takes up this embellished style in the A section, where it combines contrapuntally with the oboe. Meanwhile, the recorders and continuo provide a staccato accompaniment, the cello and double bass (if present) playing **pizzicato**, that is, plucking the strings.

Precisely what the short repeated notes of the recorders and continuo signify is revealed in the B section: bells. The word *Sterbeglocken* ("death bells," mm. 30–31) coincides with the dramatic entry of the upper strings, which up to now have remained silent; now they begin playing pizzicato, like the cello and violone, but in sixteenth notes. Bach's listeners would have recognized this texture as a representation of special funeral bells, which were distinguished by their relatively high pitch and rapid ringing. Contrary to customary Baroque word painting, the grim image of death is cast in a delightful musical setting that coincides with the modulation to a major key, Ab. Death is thus depicted as the joyous attainment of heavenly peace, in keeping with Christian belief.

Movement 4: Recitative and Aria

Bach labeled movement 4 as a recitative; in fact it opens as *accompanied* recitative, the bass voice and continuo being joined by trumpet and upper strings.

The movement then departs from conventional forms by proceeding without a break to a sort of aria composed of two alternating types of music (mm. 14–67).

The movement as a whole is a vivid representation of the Last Judgment. The trumpet, used nowhere else in the cantata, refers to the biblical sounding of the last trumpet. But it also reflects the military imagery inherent in the text's account of a battle between good and evil that will bring an end to the physical world. As in Orlando's aria "Fammi combattere" and innumerable other Baroque works, the broken-chord motives and the repeated notes of both trumpet and strings derive from actual trumpet calls used for military signaling.

The trumpet used here is a so-called **natural** brass instrument, lacking valves and thus normally confined to the natural harmonics of the instrument's fundamental tone. For instance, a trumpet in C was limited essentially to the notes shown in Example 9.2; even some of these notes were out of tune and rarely used, and only in the top octave of its range could the instrument readily produce a complete diatonic scale. Virtuoso trumpeters nevertheless had various techniques for improving the naturally out-of-tune notes. Bach calls for one of these notes, b♭′, in measures 6–7. The slightly muffled sound of that note on the natural trumpet, far from being a technical deficiency, is part of the other-worldly sound that Bach evidently desired at this point.

Following the initial accompanied recitative, the movement turns first to arioso (mm. 14–20) and then to full-fledged aria style, including a short ritornello (mm. 21–22). The arioso opens with another melodic reference to the opening of the chorale tune (sung to the words "Fürwahr, fürwahr"; see Ex. 9.1e); this is imitated by the continuo (mm. 15–16). Arioso and aria continue to alternate through the remainder of the movement—an unusual procedure, but again typical of Bach's originality in response to a vivid text. This portion of the movement falls into a modified da capo design: the first arioso and the following aria section (mm. 13b–31) together constitute the A section, which returns as a modified da capo or A′ section at the conclusion of the movement (mm. 54–67).

After this unprecedented movement, the closing four-part chorale setting serves as a moment of repose. Yet its final cadence is, as noted above, in C major, the dominant of the tonic F major. Although conditioned by the structure of the preexisting chorale tune, this ending reflects the fact that the drama narrated in the text of the present work is not yet completed, even though the cantata itself is finished. Through its "open" ending on the dominant, it looks ahead to the drama that would be reenacted a few weeks later in the passion performed on Good Friday.

Example 9.2 The harmonic series: "natural" notes on a valveless trumpet in C; notes marked * are noticeably out of tune or for other reasons difficult to use

GEORGE FRIDERIC HANDEL AND THE EIGHTEENTH-CENTURY ORATORIO

Bach's passions represent one of several distinctive varieties of oratorio written in northern Europe during the eighteenth century.[10] More properly described as **oratorio passions**, these belong to a tradition of *historiae,* elaborate musical settings of biblical narratives, that extends back to sixteenth- and seventeenth-century works by such composers as Lassus and Schütz. Seventeenth-century Lutheran oratorio passions had already incorporated strophic arias and chorales alongside biblical recitative and choruses. Eighteenth-century examples by Reinhard Keiser (1674–1739) and J. S. Bach took the logical step of including operatic recitative and aria as well. Bach wrote at least three oratorio passions as well as oratorios on other subjects, including the Christmas and Easter stories.[11]

Handel's English Oratorios

Another approach to the oratorio occurs in Handel's English works of this type, which therefore are usually referred to specifically as *English* oratorios. During his early years in Italy, Handel had composed two Italian oratorios, but these differed little in poetic or musical style from opera, resembling works by Alessandro Scarlatti and the Roman composer Bernardo Pasquini (1637–1710). Thus Handel's oratorio *La resurrezione* (The resurrection) was presented in 1708 in a Roman palace; performed on a decorated platform resembling a stage, it included virtuoso da capo arias for Mary Magdalene and even Satan. By contrast, Handel's English oratorios were commercial ventures performed in public theaters, beginning in the 1730s. Not requiring elaborate sets, costumes, lighting, or expensive imported Italian singers, English oratorio could be produced at a fraction of the cost of opera, and for larger audiences as well. Unlike Italian oratorios, which often concerned Christian saints, most of these oratorios are based on stories from the Hebrew Bible. Their English texts include recitatives and arias modeled on those of Italian opera librettos, but they also include a chorus, which, as in Lullian opera, plays an essential role as an active participant in the drama.

Handel's best-known English oratorio is *Messiah*, composed in 1741 (the year of his last opera). Yet *Messiah* is an atypical work; with its text drawn almost entirely from the Bible and lacking individual dramatic roles, it was originally termed a "sacred entertainment," not an oratorio. With one exception, Handel's other oratorios, although intended for concert performance without staging,

---

[10]The word *passion* comes from the Latin *patior* (to suffer), hence the special meaning of the word as a term for a musical genre.

[11]A distinction is made between the oratorio passion as composed by Bach, Telemann, and other (chiefly Lutheran) composers and the **passion oratorio**, that is, an oratorio about the passion whose text consists entirely of new poetry without biblical narration. An example of the latter is Handel's *Brockes-Passion,* so called from its text by the Hamburg poet Barthold Heinrich Brockes.

include named characters in dramatic roles, and their texts consist of newly written poetry. *Messiah,* as well as *Israel in Egypt,* Handel's popular English oratorio of 1739, is in effect a large-scale English anthem, the principal type of Anglican church music. Both works contain powerful music, achieving their greatest effects not through the alternation of operatic recitatives and arias but through choruses interspersed with movements for soloists.

Handel's twenty or so other English oratorios (the exact number is a matter of definition) are dramas of a more literally theatrical kind. *Jephtha* (anthology, Selection 21), Handel's last entirely new work, was begun early in 1751. But the composer's deteriorating vision forced him to interrupt work on it before completing the second part (Fig. 9.5). He was able to finish the oratorio by August, but, although he continued to perform publicly, he did little further composing. His one later English oratorio, *The Triumph of Time and Truth* (1757), is, ironically, a reworking of his very first Italian oratorio, composed half a century earlier.

Figure 9.5 Handel's manuscript composing score for *Jephtha,* Part 2, final chorus, mm. 16–24. ©The British Library Board. All Rights Reserved. London, British Library, R.M.20.e.9. Having completed this first section of the chorus, Handel wrote the date 13 February 1751 in the bottom right corner, adding in German that he had had to stop work at this point after losing sight in his left eye. Handel had just set to music the words "How dark, O Lord, are thy decrees, all hid from mortal sight"; as grimly ironic as this might have seemed, Handel might have found in these lines a ray of hope: it is impossible to know what the future will bear, for worse or for better.

Performance of Handel's English Oratorios

As concert works, Handel's English oratorios lacked the elaborate staging of his Italian operas; they differed too in the inclusion of a chorus. The latter seems to have comprised four to six boy sopranos, plus about a dozen male altos, tenors, and basses. The soloists evidently sang from the choir, stepping forward when their roles required it. It is not entirely clear where the singers stood in relation to the instruments, but it appears that Handel usually directed from the harpsichord, perhaps facing the singers and the other musicians (hence with his back to the audience).

Beginning with the first public performance of his first English oratorio, *Esther*, in 1735, Handel also performed organ concertos with the orchestra between the acts, or, as they were called, the "parts," of the oratorios. Although Italian composers had been writing concertos for solo violin and orchestra for some thirty years, concertos with a solo keyboard part were a novelty; Handel continued to play them to the end of his career.[12] Handel's solos in the organ concertos included substantial quantities of virtuoso improvisation, sometimes amounting to entire movements. As published, however, the concertos are easy to play and no doubt contributed to the popularity of the genre.

Handel's *Jephtha*

Much of *Jephtha* is unusually vehement in expression, reflecting its dark story (see Box 9.2). The libretto by Thomas Morell provides a biblically unauthorized happy ending, absent from the anonymous Latin version of the story set by Carissimi (see Chapter 7). But as Handel was completing the end of Part 2, he must have been reflecting deeply on his failing health and weakening eyesight. In place of Morell's final verse, Handel substituted a line by the English poet Alexander Pope (1688–1744): "Whatever is, is right." But the gloomy chorus that Handel composed at this point is hardly reassuring.

Jephtha, like his other English oratorios, retains many elements of Handel's *opere serie*, including the French overture at the beginning and the inclusion of a considerable number of da capo arias. But, reflecting a trend in mid-eighteenth-century opera, there are fewer of the latter than in earlier works; many arias now consist of simply an A section in bipartite form. The choral movements, which range from grand celebrations of the Israelites' military victories to the grim final chorus of Part 2, are closer in style to church music than to anything in Italian or French opera of the period. The choruses include impressive contrapuntal sections in fugal form as well as declamatory passages in homophonic texture. Unlike the arias, most are accompanied by the full orchestra, lacking only brass, which, as in most Baroque works, is reserved for a few choruses in major keys that have a particularly grand or military character.

---

[12]Among the few earlier concertos with solo keyboard parts was J. S. Bach's Fifth Brandenburg Concerto for harpsichord, flute, violin, and strings, composed by 1721; his concertos for solo harpsichord and strings date from the 1730s, as do the earliest of the many keyboard concertos by his son Carl Philipp Emanuel.

BOX 9.2

Handel: *Jephtha*

Text by Thomas Morell (after Judges 9).
First performed at Covent Garden, London, 26 February 1752; revived
in 1753, 1756, and 1758.

Characters

Jephtha (tenor), leader of the Israelites
Storgè (alto), his wife
Iphis (soprano), their daughter
Hamor (alto), in love with Iphis
Zebul (bass), Jephtha's brother

SYNOPSIS

The action takes place during the early history of the Israelites, when they are
at war with their neighbors the Ammonites. Jephtha has sworn that if he is
successful in battle against the latter he will sacrifice the first thing he sees
upon his return to the Israelite camp. Unfortunately, it is his daughter—here
named Iphis—who greets him. He reacts in horror, but despite the entreaties
of his wife, his brother, and Iphis's fiancé, Hamor, he refuses to break his vow.
Iphis cheerfully accepts her fate, but just as she is about to die an angel appears,
sparing her life.

SELECTIONS DISCUSSED IN THE TEXT

Overture.

Part 2, scene 3. Jephtha arrives and sees Iphis; after a brief recitative ("Horror!
confusion"), he sings a da capo aria violently expressing his anguish, "Open thy
marble jaws."

————, same (later in scene 3). In the quartet "O spare your daughter," in which
all four adult characters sing, Jephtha turns down the request of the three others
to revoke his vow.

————, same (later). Jephtha sings an even more agitated accompanied recitative,
"Deeper and deeper still," to which the Israelites respond with the chorus "How
dark, O Lord, are thy decrees."

Part 3, scene 1. The scene opens with Jephtha and Iphis preparing for the sacrifice,
surrounded by Israelite priests. Jephtha sings a bitter accompanied recitative,
"Hide thou thy hated beams," followed by a resigned da capo aria, "Waft her,
angels, through the skies."

The most remarkable music in the work occurs in Part 2, beginning shortly after Iphis makes her unfortunate appearance to greet her father as he returns from battle. Jephtha's initial response, after a brief recitative, is the C-minor aria "Open thy marble jaws" (anthology, Selection 21a). Its fragmented melodic line and unharmonized unison writing for voice and strings suggest his emotional trauma.[13] Although the aria employs da capo form, in its melodic harshness and barren harmony it is as far as one could imagine from fashionable *galant* style.

Equally dramatic effects occur in Jephtha's accompanied recitatives "Deeper and deeper still" and "Hide thou thy hated beams," from Parts 2 and 3, respectively. The first of these contains chromatic modulations that range widely from F♯ minor to A♭ major and F minor, ending in G minor. When the text mentions "a thousand pangs that lash me into madness," Handel writes string tremolos that bear the unusual marking *concitato* (agitated), recalling Monteverdi (Ex. 9.3).[14] Only when Jephtha, reconciled to his daughter's death, bids her farewell in the serene G-major da capo aria in Part 3, "Waft her, angels, through the skies," does his music return to something that would have been regarded as normal mid-eighteenth-century style (Ex. 9.4). Here the dotted rhythms of the first violin are slurred, suggesting not a vigorous effect as in a French overture but the gentle beating of angel wings.[15]

Ensembles—movements for more than one soloist—are rare in opera seria and oratorio. An example is the quartet "O spare your daughter" in Part 2, in which Jephtha's wife, brother, and potential son-in-law beg him to "recall the impious vow"—that is, to take back his oath and spare his daughter's life (Ex. 9.5). Handel's music clearly sets the tenor Jephtha apart from the other three figures (soprano, alto, and bass), who sing as a group in antiphony against him. Meanwhile the accompanying string parts accelerate to repeated sixteenths as Jephtha restates the words "her doom is fixed"—that is, her fate is already cast.

The most powerful writing may be in the chorus that closes Part 2 (anthology, Selection 21b). Handel's oratorio choruses generally employ the old line-by-line form of the seventeenth-century *concertato* motet, updated by the inclusion of instrumental ritornellos and other devices. Style, texture, motivic material, and instrumentation all may change radically in the course of a single movement, always in response to the text. Some choruses are unified by a common ritornello theme or recurring accompanimental motives. Others are integrated only by maintaining one expressive character or key. The latter is the case in the chorus "How dark, O Lord, are thy decrees," which falls into four sections, as shown in Table 9.1.

---

[13]The unharmonized unison texture found here occurs in many other arias by Handel from throughout his career; these are of greatly varying expressive characters, making it difficult to attach any one meaning to this type of writing.

[14]Handel was probably unaware of Monteverdi's use of the word *concitato* to describe battle music.

[15]Handel does not write out the dotted rhythm in every measure, nor the slurs, but both can be understood as applying throughout the aria—a notational abbreviation common in the Baroque and especially in Handel's music.

Example 9.3 Handel, *Jephtha*, Part 2, scene 3: recitative "Deeper, and deeper still," *concitato* passage

The first section is dominated by a figure in dotted rhythm for the string accompaniment (Handel's notation substitutes a rest for the dot). Far from signaling a French overture, this relentless accompaniment is an effect that Handel would have found in choruses by Italian contemporaries (such as Vivaldi); it lends extra energy to the voices' sustained homophonic declamation of the text. The second section switches to imitative style, and the instrumental parts now double the voices. This, too, is a type of writing familiar from earlier Italian choral music; imitation, without independent instrumental parts, was typical of the *stile antico*, invoked here to underscore the seriousness of the text.

The style grows more severe in the third section, a fugue. This section is even closer to the *stile antico*, since, unlike the preceding section, it is in the duple meter characteristic of sixteenth-century polyphony. A **fugue** is a movement in imitative texture based on a single theme; the latter, called the **subject,** is initially presented by one voice and immediately imitated by each of the others, entering in different

Example 9.4 Handel, *Jephtha*, Part 3, scene 1: aria "Waft her, angels, through the skies," mm. 9–12

keys (more precisely, at different pitch levels; see Box 11.1). Here the subject is sung in turn by the soprano, alto, tenor, and bass voice, each part being doubled instrumentally. Not all eighteenth-century fugues are as archaic in style as this one. Even here, the style is not literally that of the Renaissance, for in addition to employing specified instrumental parts (including the basso continuo), the subject contains the chromatic steps G–A♭–A–B♭, yielding a type of melodic line absent from sixteenth-century music except in radical works such as those of Gesualdo. This chromatic motive is used for the phrase *no solid peace*—an instance of word painting that, because it is present in the subject of the fugue, permeates the entire section.

The concluding section of the movement presents Pope's "maxim," added by Handel at the end of Morell's text. The first added clause ("Yet on this maxim still obey," mm. 114–20) is presented in imitative style; as in the first section of the movement, the strings accompany with a persistent rhythmic figure, here comprising repeated eighths. But the accompaniment ceases for the maxim itself, "Whatever is, is right" (mm. 121–24). This is stated in uncompromising declamatory style by the chorus, its two two-word phrases separated by rests—a particularly austere manifestation of classic Baroque musical rhetoric.

Handel's Borrowings

An oddity of Handel's compositional process in *Jephtha* and elsewhere was his borrowing of music from both himself and others. Already noted during his

Example 9.5 Handel, *Jephtha*, Part 2, scene 3: quartet "O spare your daughter," mm. 23–25

TABLE 9.1
Handel: *Jephtha*, Part 2, scene 3, final chorus

Section	Measure	Tempo	Style or Texture	Keys
1 How dark, O Lord, are thy decrees	1	Largo	homophonic	c → A♭
2 All our joys to sorrow turning	25	Larghetto	canonic	f → g
3 No certain bliss	98	A tempo ordinario	fugue	c → V
4 Yet on this maxim still obey	114	Larghetto	alternatingly contrapuntal, declamatory	c → f → E♭ → c

Example 9.6 Handel, *Lotario*, Act 2: Matilde's aria "Arma lo sguardo," mm. 4–12

Arma lo sguardo	Arm your glances
D'un dolce dardo;	With a sweet arrow;
La donna altera	Then a proud
E lusinghiera	And flattering woman
Poi nel suo core	In her heart
Del folle amore	At foolish love
Si riderà.	Will laugh.

lifetime, Handel's borrowings ranged from the reuse of individual themes or motives to the appropriation of entire sections or movements, sometimes with, sometimes without substantial alteration. Handel's borrowings went beyond conventional types of paraphrase and parody, extending to his secular as well as his sacred works, instrumental as well as vocal ones. He seems to have borrowed for his own convenience in composing, rarely implying any meaningful reference to an earlier work. Thus Handel's *Jephtha* does not borrow from Carissimi's work of the same title, although Handel knew at least its closing chorus, having quoted from it in his earlier oratorio *Samson* (1743).

Example 9.7 Franz Wenzel Habermann, Missa III from *Philomela pia* (Graslitz, 1747): Crucifixus

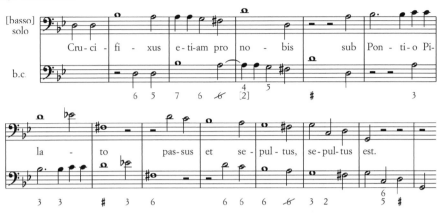

Crucifixus etiam pro nobis
sub Pontio Pilato, et sepultus est.

Also he was crucified for us
under Pontius Pilate and was buried.

Instead, Handel reused a theme from his opera *Lotario* (1729) for Jephtha's aria "Open thy marble jaws" (Ex. 9.6). Handel's borrowing reflects the flexibility of the associations that can be drawn between music and meaning or emotional expression. The two arias are very different in dramatic context and feeling; in the opera, Queen Matilda is counseling seduction! Yet the unison textures that perhaps expressed something sinister or threatening in her music are equally appropriate in Jephtha's distraught aria.

In addition, the second section of the chorus "How dark, O Lord" (mm. 25–88) borrows both its melodic material and its imitative technique from a mass published a few years earlier, in 1747, by the Bohemian composer Franz Habermann (1706–83; see Ex. 9.7). In this instance there is a clear similarity in expressive character between the texts set by the two composers. Moreover, Handel elaborated upon his model's use of two-part **canon**: the precise imitation of one voice by another. Following Habermann, Handel uses canonic pairs of voices in the "All our joys" section of the chorus. It is unknown whether Habermann knew of Handel's borrowing, but if so Habermann ought to have been flattered by Handel's interest in his music—even though Handel significantly transformed the borrowed material.

CHAPTER 10

MUSIC FOR SOLO INSTRUMENTS I
Toccata and Suite

Instruments, which played roles in both domestic and sacred music making in western Europe during the Renaissance, came to be of central importance for the first time during the Baroque. The seventeenth century saw significant innovations by instrument makers, a process that continued into the eighteenth century. Strings, woodwinds, and keyboard instruments underwent particularly extensive changes in both construction and technique, with corresponding developments in the types of music written for them. To some degree these developments reflected general trends in seventeenth- and eighteenth-century European music, when, for the first time, composition for instruments came to be equal in stature and significance to that for the voice.

Idiomatic Writing for Instruments

Many developments in Baroque instrumental writing paralleled those in vocal composition, where changes in musical texture led to new types of vocal writing in the early seventeenth century. First, the adoption of the basso continuo made possible monody, that is, music consisting of a single melodic line with instrumental accompaniment, as well as duets and other small vocal ensembles in which the improvised realization of the figured bass filled out the harmony. A corresponding development in instrumental music saw the cultivation of new genres for one, two, or three solo parts with continuo. Such scoring became predominant over older types of instrumental writing for ensembles of four or five instrumental parts, although the latter continued to be used in certain contexts, notably French opera.

Second, much of the new monodic vocal music was soloistic, employing virtuoso passagework or figuration and providing opportunities for individual expression and display by soloists. Instrumental writing developed in similar directions, sometimes imitating the types of figuration used by singers but increasingly employing writing that grew out of the unique sound and technical capabilities of each instrument. Earlier music had rarely called for specified instruments or taken advantage of the particular qualities of individual instruments, although music for solo lute and solo keyboard represents an important exception.

Music that requires the particular characteristics and performance techniques of a specific instrument is said to be **idiomatic** to that instrument. Before 1600 most European music was conceived vocally. Features idiomatic to a given instrument were added improvisatorily, as when an ensemble of viols or violins played a set of dances originally composed for unspecified instruments, each player improvising idiomatic ornamentation. In the Baroque, as composers began to specify instrumentation or write out embellishments, it became customary to write instrumental parts that are idiomatic to particular instruments. Today this seems like an obvious necessity. In 1600, however, it represented a major change: for the first time, defining the instrumental sonorities and techniques to be used in the performance of a work was part of the composer's job, not an optional detail left to the performers. Understanding the nature and capabilities of common instruments became part of the composer's training, and the seventeenth century saw the emergence of many new genres of music that exploited the idioms of specific instruments.

Instrumental music can be divided between works for single instruments and music for ensemble. The two largest repertories of Baroque music for single instruments are those for keyboard instruments, on the one hand, and for the lute and its relatives on the other. Ensemble music came to be dominated by compositions for bowed strings, especially the violin; although parts for cornetto, trombone, and other wind instruments occur in early Baroque instrumental works, not until the eighteenth century did distinctive solo repertories emerge for new (or newly transformed) woodwind instruments, such as the oboe and the flute.

Baroque Instruments

Actual instruments from the Baroque period survive in varying degrees of preservation. Some are mere broken-down fragments in museums, although even these can present a surprising amount of information to a trained **organologist**: a scholar specializing in the study of instruments. Surviving instruments from the Baroque include organs still in use in many European churches,[1] as well as numerous violins and other bowed string instruments, including those of such famous Italian makers as Antonio Stradivari (1644–1737), which can be valued in the hundreds of thousands of dollars. Functioning harpsichords, lutes, and other stringed instruments are somewhat less common, brass and woodwind instruments even less so, especially from before 1700. Virtually all surviving instruments have been altered over the centuries, often in ways that obscure their original sound and playing characteristics; this is especially true of organs and bowed strings. Nevertheless, modern instrument builders specializing in the reconstruction of historical instruments have rediscovered many of the secrets of materials and construction used by earlier makers. When based closely on originals, modern copies of antique harpsichords, violins, and other instruments

---

[1] A few Baroque organs are also preserved in the Americas, including examples in colonial churches in the United States and Latin America.

can come quite close to their historical prototypes in sound and playing capabilities—sometimes closer than actual surviving instruments that have undergone anachronistic remodeling or renovation.

Of course, playing such instruments is another matter. Seventeenth- and eighteenth-century treatises on musical performance gave increasingly specific instructions for performance, but many details remain uncertain. Moreover, there was never any one way of using a particular instrument (or of singing); one cannot produce hard and fast rules for historically authentic performance, and books that purport to do so must be read with circumspection. Still, enough is known about old instruments and their techniques to show that Baroque composers called for specific sounds and effects that can be only approximated with modern techniques and instruments.

Players of plucked instruments such as the lute shared many traditions with keyboard players, including common types of improvisation (discussed below). Some important features of Baroque keyboard music, especially in the French style, appear to have been anticipated by early Baroque lutenist-composers, whose music we shall therefore consider first.

The Lute and Its Repertory

Plucked string instruments go back to prehistoric antiquity and have had a bewildering variety of shapes, playing techniques, and even forms of notation. Held somewhat like the modern guitar but by 1600 always plucked with the fingers (rather than with a pick, or *plectrum*), the **lute** had been the principal plucked instrument in most of western Europe during the Renaissance. During the Baroque it remained fundamentally an instrument of six courses, or pairs, of strings, as it had been for most of the sixteenth century. But the range of the instrument was extended through the addition of extra bass strings, whose greater length led to the development of larger instruments, such as the theorbo (or chitarrone) and the archlute (shown in Figure 3.2).[2]

The lute had been probably the most popular amateur's instrument in the sixteenth century, but during the Baroque it gradually lost that status to stringed keyboard instruments, such as the harpsichord. By the eighteenth century players of the lute were limited largely to professionals, and their numbers were dwindling; at the end of the Baroque the instrument was being cultivated only at a few German courts, and compositions for it were rare, although the instrument had a late blossoming in the works of Bach's contemporary Silvius Leopold Weiss (1686–1750). In the early Baroque, however, the lute and its relatives were important both as solo instruments and, in Italy, as continuo instruments in monody and other new vocal and instrumental genres. Moreover, a flourishing

---

[2]The theorbo (Italian *tiorba*) differs from the archlute in that the latter retains the traditional tuning of the lute for its six main courses (a'-e'-b-g-d-A). The theorbo uses **re-entrant** tuning: the top one or two strings are tuned an octave lower. Also used on the Baroque guitar (and the modern banjo), this type of tuning would have led to the octave transposition of certain notes and corresponding irregularities in voice leading (apparently not a concern in early continuo playing).

late-Renaissance tradition of solo pieces and songs with lute accompaniment continued well into the seventeenth century; particularly famous are the fantasias, dance pieces, and four books of lute songs by the English composer John Dowland (1563–1626).

Meanwhile new genres of solo lute music were emerging in Italy and France. In Italy the most important composer was Giovanni Girolamo Kapsperger (ca. 1580–1651), of German descent but born in Venice; working chiefly in Rome, he published collections of pieces for both lute and theorbo. These contained toccatas, dances, and variation pieces, all broadly similar to those for keyboard that are discussed below (see Ex. 10.2a).

French musicians were slow to adopt Italian innovations, notably the basso continuo. But during the early seventeenth century French lutenists developed a distinctive repertory consisting largely of **stylized dances** derived from those of court ballet: instrumental pieces whose tempo, rhythm, and character were those of actual dances of court and theater—courantes, sarabandes, and the like— but that were independent compositions, not used for actual dancing. French lutenists also cultivated an improvisatory type of prelude characterized by its rhythmically free or unmeasured notation (a similar type of prelude for keyboard instruments is discussed below). During the first few decades of the century, French players also experimented with new ways of tuning the six main courses of the lute, in order to create novel sonorities and to play in previously unused keys.[3] Despite the continuing popularity of the instrument during the earlier Baroque, few French lutes survive from the seventeenth century; modern reconstructions are based on depictions in paintings and on surviving eighteenth-century German instruments, which followed the French style (Fig. 10.1).

Other plucked instruments cultivated during the Baroque include the **vihuela**, which had been especially prominent in Renaissance Spain, the **cittern** (shown in Fig. 1.4), and the **guitar**, which was common not only in Spain but in Italy and France. The Baroque guitar remained relatively small, usually comprising five courses (Fig. 10.2).[4] It was distinguished from the lute by its use of strummed as well as plucked techniques (known by the Spanish terms *rasgueado* and *punteado*, respectively). It was used especially as a continuo instrument in dance music, but Baroque composers developed a solo repertory consisting of pieces similar to those written for the lute; notable composers include the Italian Francesco Corbetta (ca. 1615–1681) and the French Robert de Visée (ca. 1655–1732/3). In addition, the Spanish Gaspar Sanz (*fl.* late seventeenth century) wrote a treatise *Instrucción de música sobre la guitarra española* (Musical instruction on the Spanish guitar, Zaragoza, 1674) that contains numerous pedagogical pieces.

---

[3]The lute has no fixed pitch and therefore, strictly speaking, does not play in specific keys in the same sense as other instruments. Nevertheless, different tunings produce distinct sorts of instrumental resonance as the intervals between the strings and the proportion of open to stopped strings used in a given piece vary.

[4]Like the theorbo, Baroque guitars usually used re-entrant tuning (typically a-d'-g-b-e'), with two strings for all but the top course; in double courses one string was sometimes tuned an octave lower. The modern tuning with six single strings (E-A-d-g-b-e') dates from the later eighteenth century.

Figure 10.1 Thirteen-course lute by Thomas Edlinger, Prague, 1728. Ex coll.: Carl Des Fours Walderode, Hrubý Rohozec Castle, Bohemia (Czech Republic). National Music Museum, Vermillion, South Dakota, NMM 10213. Purchase funds gift of Margaret Ann Everist, Sioux City, Iowa, 2002. This is one of the few lutes of this type to survive in essentially original condition, with all parts by a single maker.

Music for both lutes and guitars was usually notated not in score but through various forms of **tablature**, which used symbols to indicate the placement of the fingers of the left hand on the fingerboard rather than the actual pitches on a staff (Fig. 10.3).[5] The tablatures used for plucked instruments are inherently imprecise because they show neither the durations of notes nor the individual contrapuntal lines (that is, voice leading). Paradoxically, for this reason tablature is preferred by modern players of historical lutes and guitars, since on these instruments, unlike keyboard instruments, notes are often left ringing, undamped, until they fade away; indications of note value and voice leading in modern transcriptions are editorial and to some degree misleading. Rarely do works for plucked instruments maintain a constant number of voices, although they may

---

[5]Guitar music employing strummed (*rasgueado*) technique was notated through an alphabet system (*alfabeto*) roughly comparable to modern guitar chord symbols.

Figure 10.2 Five-course guitar by Antonio Stradivari, Cremona, 1700. National Music Museum, Vermillion, South Dakota, NMM 3976. Ex coll.: Louis Krasner, Boston. Rawlins Fund, 1985. One of only two or three guitars known to survive by the master instrument maker, better known for his violins.

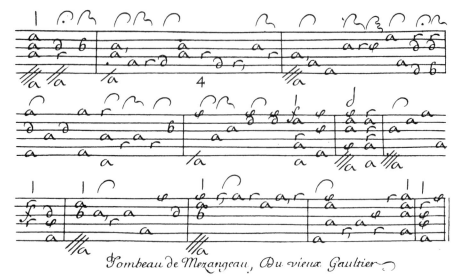

Figure 10.3 Ennemond Gaultier, *Tombeau de Mesangeau*, French lute tablature from *Livre de tablature* (Paris, 1672). The six "staff" lines represent the six main courses of strings (lowest course at the bottom); letters on these lines refer to frets ("a" is an open string). Symbols above the "staff" represent note values; those beneath refer to the unfretted bass strings.

suggest or allude to the idea of strict counterpoint. In fact the same is often true of keyboard music, for which various types of tablature notation were also developed, but, except in Germany, staff notation was preferred for these instruments.

Improvisation was particularly important for players of both plucked instruments and keyboards. Not only were they frequently called on to improvise continuo accompaniments; evidently they continued to play impromptu arrangements of vocal music, as in the Renaissance, and they also improvised variations on short ostinato bass lines. The latter represented standard harmonic patterns that could serve as the basis for endless series of inventive settings, as in the *passacaille* from Lully's *Armide* (Ex. 6.8). Example 10.1 shows pedagogical examples for guitar and archlute (the instrument depicted in Fig. 3.2); here one sees the contrast between the chordal style associated with the guitar and the more melodic style of the lute.[6] The improvisational practices documented by these examples were the basis for more refined compositions published by Kapsperger and Corbetta, among others (Ex. 10.2).[7] Improvisation over ostinato basses was not limited to lute and keyboard; instruction manuals (primarily for the viola da gamba) were published in the sixteenth

---

[6]For a facsimile and complete transcription of the archlute example, see Victor Coelho, "Authority, Autonomy, and Interpretation in Seventeenth-Century Italian Lute Music," in *Performance on Lute, Guitar, and Vihuela: Historical Practice and Modern Interpretation*, edited by Victor Anand Coelho (Cambridge, UK: Cambridge University Press, 1997), 132–3.

[7]In Example 10.2a the final measure has been added editorially; the last notes of the penultimate measure (especially the b♭) may be faulty.

Example 10.1a Anonymous variations on a *ceccona* (chaconne) for archlute, from a manuscript partly in the hand of the composer and lutenist Andrea Falconieri (1585/6–1656)

Example 10.1b *Passacalli passeggiati* (harmonic pattern for a passacaglia) for guitar, from Giovanni Ambrosio Colonna, *Intavolatura di chitarra alla spagnuola* (Milan, 1620)

Example 10.2a Kapsperger, Passacaglia in D minor for theorbo, from *Libro quarto d'intavolatura di chitar{r}one* (Rome, 1640)

Example 10.2b Francesco Corbetta, *Passachaglie* in F for guitar, from *Vari capricii* (Milan, 1643)

century by Diego Ortiz (Rome, 1553) and in the seventeenth by Christopher Simpson (London, 1659).

Baroque Lute Music in France

The two most famous lutenist-composers in seventeenth-century France were Ennemond Gaultier (1575–1651) and his cousin Denis Gaultier (ca. 1600–1672). Ennemond, known as "Old" (*Vieux*) Gaultier, held a royal court appointment early in his career, but both musicians were evidently best known through performances, teaching, and compositions that fulfilled commissions from the many noble amateurs who continued to cultivate the lute in France. Earlier French lutenist-composers, notably René Mesangeau (d. 1638), were already composing allemandes, sarabandes, and courantes, three of the dances that would dominate French instrumental music to the end of the Baroque. Specific characteristics of these dances are discussed below.

Following Mesangeau, the Gaultiers imbued these dances with a refined asymmetry of phrasing, a subtle style of melodic ornamentation, and expressively irregular rhythm; these would become fundamental features of French Baroque instrumental music. Contemporary keyboard players also took up this style, but because of the loss of nearly all French keyboard music from the first half of the century, it is uncertain to what degree keyboard music developed independent of lute composition. In any case, the nature of the lute guaranteed that its repertory would incorporate greater subtlety and allusiveness, especially in rhythm and voice leading, than in the more fully realized harmony of keyboard works.

Pieces by "Old" Gaultier

Although Denis Gaultier, like later French keyboard composers, grouped his pieces into suites, the older Ennemond apparently did not, leaving behind individual dances and other pieces. Nevertheless, performers probably played his works in groups united by a common key or tuning, perhaps preceded by a short prelude. We shall examine three of Ennemond Gaultier's dance pieces (anthology, Selections 22a–c). Although later suites would typically open with an allemande, this set follows the order in which the pieces appeared in a posthumous edition of 1680.

"L'immortelle" is the opening piece in the volume, its title (The immortal one) evidently referring to the composer, who had died more than two decades earlier but was still remembered. The piece is an example of a **courante**, which had been the most frequently composed French dance since the beginning of the century. Like the sung example in Lully's *Armide* (Ex. 6.5), courantes are invariably in triple (or compound duple) time, with a moderately quick tempo, and are normally in binary form, each half repeated. A rhythmically more straightforward version of the dance, the *corrente*, was employed in Italy (Kapsperger, among others, published numerous examples). "L'immortelle" is typical of the best French Baroque instrumental music in its apparent simplicity and restraint, which mask extraordinary subtlety and refined expression.

Example 10.3 reveals the piece's asymmetrical phrasing and its precisely notated melodic and rhythmic ornamentation. The example compares the first half of the actual piece (upper staves) with an editorial melodic reduction (lower staves). The reduction shows that certain details of the original, such as the three-note upbeat at the very beginning, are decorations of simpler lines. At a larger level, the reduction makes it easy to see that the first half of the piece falls into phrases of 3 + 4 + 5 measures, as is evident from the pauses (long

Example 10.3 Ennemond Gaultier, Courante "L'immortelle," mm. 1–12 (upper system), with editorial melodic reduction (lower system)

notes) in the melody in measures 3, 7, and 11–12. Hence the first half of the courante comprises three phrases of different lengths, with asymmetrical phrases (containing odd numbers of measures) prevailing.

Comparison of the reduction with the actual piece shows, in addition, that many notes are delayed, restruck, or displaced to another part of the measure or to another octave. For instance, in measure 3, soprano c$\sharp'$ is played after the downbeat, and bass a is repeated an octave lower on the second beat. In measure 5, the three notes of the F-major triad are struck at different times, and f is ornamented by the nonharmonic passing tone e.[8] This chord and others are, in effect, broken or arpeggiated in constantly varied ways. The result is a so-called broken style, or *style brisé*, that is fundamental to seventeenth-century French music for lute and keyboard.

"L'immortelle" is followed by an allemande also known as the *"Tombeau for Mesangeau."* The **allemande** was slower than the courante and in common time; the secondary title indicates that this allemande was a memorial (*tombeau*, plural *tombeaux*) for the older lutenist-composer Mesangeau. Memorial pieces make up an important part of the French repertory; "Young" Gaultier (Denis) would compose *tombeaux* for the lutenist known as Blancrocher and for his own wife. Writing a memorial for a fellow lutenist must have been an act of homage and respect; for players, such pieces would have served not only as recollections of the deceased but also as reminders of their own mortality. The latter was an important theme in the seventeenth-century visual arts; music, because of its ephemeral quality, was often used as a symbol of mortality in still-life paintings such as the one shown below (see Fig. 10.6). The *tombeau* for Mesangeau is remarkable for the slow rise and fall of its melodic lines, ornamented by relatively restrained application of the *style brisé* (note the breathtaking suspension of motion in m. 5).

Selection 22c is another dance, a **gigue**, or jig, known by the title "La Poste." Later gigues are lively dances in compound time $\left(\frac{6}{8}, \text{ or } \frac{12}{8}\right)$, but early French Baroque examples are often, like this one, in common or cut time, and they must proceed fairly deliberately.[9] Gigues of both types are often imitative, as in the present case. Here it is difficult to make out the entries of the subject because of the idiomatic lute ornament that is applied to it as well as variations of its rhythm and of the initial melodic interval. The opening subject is repeated at the dominant in measure 3 and subsequently imitated by the bass in measures 4 and 6. The subject disappears in the second half, which appears to be free of any recurring material. Yet despite its irregularity, the music never seems aimless, and in this it is typical of the elusive French Baroque lute repertory.

---

[8]There is also an ornament sign on the note f that calls for a *port de voix* (see Chapter 11).

[9]Some modern performers and scholars believe that duple-time gigues such as this one were actually performed in triple meter. The present gigue also exists as an allemande in slightly different rhythmic notation (discussion in anthology). For a gigue in compound time, see Ex. 10.8a.

Keyboard Instruments of the Seventeenth and Eighteenth Centuries

The keyboard instruments of the Baroque include the organ, which is actually a wind instrument, and the harpsichord and the clavichord, which are the chief stringed keyboard instruments of the period. During the Baroque, all underwent important changes, and they were joined in the eighteenth century by a third major stringed keyboard instrument, the piano. Composers rarely specified the instrument for which a given keyboard piece or part was intended. Nevertheless, it is often possible to distinguish music for one instrument or another, based on style, genre, or technical considerations. For example, works for organ often include a separate pedal part, whereas French harpsichord music can be recognized by the presence of designated dance movements. Much Baroque keyboard music can be readily appropriated to the modern piano, yet it remains helpful to understand the sounds, conventions, and techniques that the composer expected to be applied in each work.

The Clavichord

Clavichords were the simplest and least expensive keyboard instruments throughout the Baroque, and for this reason they often served as practice instruments for both professionals and amateurs.[10] Nevertheless, composers made little use of the instrument's capability for dynamic inflection by the player, perhaps because most Baroque clavichords were limited in dynamic capacity and compass (keyboard range). Only in the second half of the eighteenth century did German and Scandinavian instrument makers produce clavichords whose expanded range matched that of contemporary harpsichords and pianos. A few composers, notably Carl Philipp Emanuel Bach (1714–88), a son of J. S. Bach, wrote important works intended primarily for the clavichord, but most of these were composed after 1750 and thus lie beyond our consideration.

The Harpsichord

The chief stringed keyboard instrument of the Baroque was the harpsichord, used for both solo and continuo playing. It gradually replaced the lute as the most common domestic instrument in well-off households, and it was, together with the organ, one of the two chief keyboard continuo instruments, indispensible in both vocal music and music for instrumental ensemble. Italian players had developed an idiomatic harpsichord style by the beginning of the Baroque, apparently characterized by energetic dance music; this was refined during the early seventeenth century by player-composers such as Frescobaldi (discussed below). Less is known about early Baroque harpsichord music in France, but by the mid-seventeenth century French harpsichordists, possible influenced by

---

[10]The playing mechanisms of the clavichord and harpsichord were discussed in Chapter 3.

lutenists, had developed a distinctive performance style that became the basis of a large repertory of idiomatic harpsichord compositions. As the Lullian style of vocal music was being adopted in England and Germany during the later seventeenth and early eighteenth centuries, composers in those countries, such as Purcell and J. S. Bach, were taking up elements of the French harpsichord style in their own playing and in their compositions.

Reflecting the distinct national styles of performance and composition, harpsichords of different countries took various forms, differing, for example, in the number of keyboards and **registers** or sets of strings that they contained. Many harpsichords in the sixteenth century already had two sets of strings, sometimes tuned an octave apart. These registers could be played separately or together, permitting variation in volume and sonority. The choice of a particular sonority on such an instrument—that is, the selection of a given register or combination of registers—is referred to as **registration**.

In the course of the seventeenth century, it became common for French and Flemish harpsichord makers to include a second (upper) keyboard, playing its own set of strings, which could be combined with or played separately from those controlled by the main keyboard (Fig. 10.4). German and English makers

Figure 10.4 Harpsichord by Jacques Germain, Paris, 1785. National Music Museum Vermillion, South Dakota, Rawlins Fund, 1983 (no. 3327). This instrument, with its two manuals and five-octave keyboard range, is characteristic of French eighteenth-century harpsichords. The expensive painting and other decoration of this instrument were marks of ownership by a wealthy amateur or aristocrat.

followed course in the eighteenth century, but Italian and Spanish instruments rarely had more than a single keyboard. The sonorities, touch, and other characteristics of the various types of harpsichord varied as well. For example, Italian instruments tended toward a brilliance and clarity of attack well suited for accompanying operas and other ensemble works in public spaces. Flemish and French harpsichords, on the other hand, tended toward a relatively restrained sonority ideal for the sustained type of sound called for in many French pieces for solo harpsichord.

German harpsichord builders, maintaining traditions inherited from the Renaissance, retained individual elements found in both French and Italian types, producing instruments that proved especially suitable for projecting the contrapuntal textures of composers such as Bach and Handel. They also built exotic types of stringed keyboard instruments such as the *Lautenklavier*, a harpsichord whose undamped gut strings made it sound like a lute. Certain smaller types of harpsichord, referred to as virginals and spinets, continued to be built as well, especially in Italy and Germany. Yet the limited ranges and registrational possibilities of these instruments gradually became inadequate to the technical and expressive demands called for increasingly by French and German composers.

Harpsichordists developed techniques for playing with both expression and brilliance, and the lack of variable dynamics—an obvious limitation of the instrument—was not regarded as a significant deficiency until the mid-eighteenth century. Only then did general changes in musical style, which affected vocal and orchestral music as well, begin to render the harpsichord obsolete. Such instruments nevertheless continued to be built into the early nineteenth century, as were clavichords.

The Fortepiano

Around 1700 the Italian instrument maker Bartolomeo Cristofori (1665–1731) perfected a type of stringed keyboard instrument whose strings were struck by hammers instead of being plucked by plectra. The result was an instrument capable of variable dynamics, like the clavichord, but larger and thus more suited to playing with other instruments or for listeners other than the player himself or herself. It was referred to as a *gravicembalo col piano e forte* ("harpsichord with softness and loudness"), or *pianoforte* for short. Later this was further abbreviated, somewhat irrationally, to *piano*. Sometimes the two elements of the name were reversed, and today, by convention, early pianos are often called *fortepianos*.

Christofori's fortepiano was only one of many new types of keyboard instruments invented in the eighteenth century, and only after 1750 did it find widespread use. Apart from its action and dynamic variability, the early piano closely resembled contemporary Italian harpsichords in construction, range, and sound. Most eighteenth-century fortepianos are quite soft, like the clavichord, and are better suited for solo practice and quiet chamber music than for public performance in large halls. Fortepianos were not generally employed in public concerts until the 1760s or later, and Haydn, Mozart, and their contemporaries in the Classical period still often used the harpsichord in their keyboard concertos. They also often did so when directing operas and other ensemble works, which in many places continued to be conducted from a keyboard continuo instrument until the nineteenth century. For these reasons the fortepiano, although familiar to some late Baroque musicians, including J. S. Bach, was rarely called for explicitly. Before 1750 it is demanded specifically in only a few works by minor composers, such as the Italian Ludovico Giustini (*fl.* ca. 1732.)

The Organ

By the end of the Baroque, most significant churches and monasteries in western Europe contained an organ of some sort, and in many places the presence of large, innovative instruments become a source of civic or institutional pride. Smaller instruments were widely distributed as well, not only in churches but in private homes and aristocratic palaces. Each region developed distinctive types of organs; larger instruments, which were more typical of France, Spain, and northern Germany (as opposed to Italy, southern Germany, and England), were characterized by a considerable proliferation of sets or **ranks** of pipes, each containing all the notes of the keyboard. A rank is also often referred to as a **stop,** although the latter more properly refers to the mechanism that turns a rank of pipes on or off. Since each rank contains pipes of a distinctive size and sonority, a single organ is in effect an entire orchestra of distinct wind instruments. These can be played alone or in endless combinations; as on the harpsichord, the selection of specific sonorities is referred to as **registration.** Every organ differs in the number and type of stops available. Moreover, although many small Baroque organs continued to have but a single keyboard, larger instruments may have two, three, or even more. In addition to the **manuals**—two or three keyboards played by the hands—there may be a **pedalboard** played by the feet.

Many Renaissance organs, particularly in Germany, had already offered pedalboards and diverse possibilities for registration. By 1600 some virtuosos had developed an advanced organ technique distinguished from that of other keyboard instruments by the use of the feet to play an independent pedal part. Pedal parts, usually but not always identical to the bass line, remained rare in Baroque organ music outside Germany and France. But in northern Europe the presence of an independent pedal part became by 1700 the most distinctive feature of music for the organ. Organists there, as well as in France and Spain, invented genres of organ music that exploited the distinctive registrational possibilities of the instruments built in each national tradition. Among these genres were various types of pieces played on two or three keyboards simultaneously, each registered to produce a distinctive sonority. In some cases one manual plays a solo role and employs pipes imitating a particular orchestral instrument, such as the trumpet or cornetto, while the other keyboard or keyboards furnish a quieter accompaniment using flutelike stops. In other genres the keyboards may play equal roles in a polyphonic texture, as in Bach's trio sonatas for two manuals and pedals.

Today we associate the organ primarily with church music, although as recently as the mid-twentieth century organs were frequently found in theaters, where they accompanied plays and films. As a continuo instrument, the organ was a nearly universal component of Baroque sacred music. Much of the solo repertory of the Baroque organ is also sacred, in the sense that it was played during church services; sacred organ works include settings of Gregorian chant and Protestant hymns or chorales. But small portable organs were often used as continuo instruments in secular works, and in some cities it was customary for organists to perform public recitals. These naturally took place in churches, since that is where the larger instruments were located. The works performed often included settings of chorales and other sacred vocal music, but organ concerts must also have included the so-called free works also found in the Baroque repertory. Even explicitly sacred works employ the same styles and techniques as do secular ones—just as sacred vocal concertos and oratorios borrowed the manner of secular opera and cantata.

The Uses of Keyboard Music

At the beginning of the seventeenth century, keyboard playing and composing were confined largely to professionals. Professional keyboard players most often were employed as church organists, although some also held positions specifically as harpsichordists, particularly in the courts of France and Germany. Wealthy amateurs who could afford instruments and teachers might play the clavichord and harpsichord, and in the course of the seventeenth and eighteenth centuries their numbers increased, as did the number of works written (and published) for amateur players.

Like members of other professions in the Baroque, instrumentalists, including keyboard players, usually learned their craft and passed it on within their own family circles. Professional keyboard players differed from most other musicians, however, in that their instruments were capable of furnishing self-sufficient music on its own. Paradoxically, however, they were called upon only rarely to play such music publicly. Although it was customary in some places for organists to provide preludes or interludes during church services, most of the time keyboard players were kept busy accompanying other musicians, through improvised figured bass realizations. Hence the education of keyboard players emphasized the skills needed to accompany others and to improvise preludes, including training in counterpoint and figured bass realization. For this reason a large portion of the solo keyboard repertory of the Baroque consists of works that were intended not for public performance but for private study and practice, as models or examples of correct improvisation or counterpoint.

Keyboard music was printed only rarely, in part because early early typesetting processes were inadequate to the inherently polyphonic nature of solo keyboard music. Hence, until the 1760s, keyboard music was usually printed from specially engraved copper plates, like fine art prints. These were expensive, and professional keyboard players generally played not from printed music but from their own manuscript copies. They began their collections of manuscript music as part of their training, copying from scores that they borrowed (often for a price!) from teachers or colleagues. Most players came to own personal collections of music that constituted their own private repertories; they had little need for published music. To be sure, a number of Italian composers at the beginning of the Baroque and some French composers toward the end published significant numbers of keyboard works. But many, including J. S. Bach, left most of their keyboard music unpublished during their lifetimes. The situation changed significantly only in the mid-eighteenth century, when the growing number of amateur players finally made the widespread publication of keyboard music economical.

BAROQUE KEYBOARD MUSIC IN ITALY

As with vocal music, distinctively Baroque types of keyboard music emerged first in Italy in the early seventeenth century, especially in various improvisatory types of compositions that incorporated such new elements as a relaxed approach to voice leading and dissonance treatment. But Italian composers throughout the Baroque also continued to compose relatively strict contrapuntal pieces under such titles as *fantasia, ricercar, canzona*, and *capriccio*. These represented the keyboard version of the *stile antico*, often employing a quasi-vocal style little changed from that of the sixteenth-century motet.

The Toccata

Among the more important genres of early Baroque keyboard music is the **toccata**, an improvisatory work that may include not only virtuoso figuration but also constrasting passages consisting of either imitative counterpoint or sustained, frequently dissonant, chords. The word *toccata* comes from the Italian verb that literally means "to touch" but was used to refer to the playing of keyboard and lute-type instruments—hence the modern idea of the "touch" of a piano keyboard. Toccatas vary greatly in form, character, and length, some falling into distinct contrasting sections, others being short and homogeneous. All are normally through-composed, reflecting their improvisatory character. Toccatas were also written for lute and for harp; the latter has only a small repertory of idiomatic solo pieces, but during the Baroque it was cultivated especially in Spain and southern Italy, and players must have often adapted music composed for keyboard or other plucked instruments.[11]

The toccata had originated in the sixteenth century; among the important early composers of toccatas were Andrea and Giovanni Gabrieli, who probably performed them as preludes or interludes during church services at Saint Mark's Basilica in Venice. Example 10.4 shows in its entirety an *intonazione*, a sort of prelude or miniature toccata, by Giovanni Gabrieli. Such a work employs the same types of written-out embellishment—scale fragments, turning figures, and various types of trill—that we observed in early Baroque vocal music (see Chapter 3). These figures remained important in seventeenth-century keyboard writing, in which they were joined by additional types of idiomatic instrumental figuration. The Baroque toccata, moreover, incorporated many of the expressive

---

[11]The word *toccata* was also employed for a few special types of music for instrumental ensemble, such as the trumpet fanfare that opens Monteverdi's *Orfeo*.

Example 10.4 Giovanni Gabrieli, *Intonazione del secondo tono* (complete)

devices found in vocal music of the period, including elements of what Monteverdi called the *seconda pratica*. In the course of the seventeenth century, it became increasingly common for toccatas and related works to comprise distinct sections, which eventually, in the works of J. S. Bach and other late Baroque composers, became separate, self-contained movements.

Girolamo Frescobaldi

The most important composer of keyboard music in Italy—and indeed throughout Europe—in the first half of the seventeenth century was Girolamo Frescobaldi (1583–1643; Fig. 10.5). He was born in the northern Italian town of Ferrara, whose ruling dukes had made their court a center of the musical avant-garde, home to the so-called Three Ladies of Ferrara and visited by Gesualdo and other musicians. Frescobaldi studied with Luzzaschi, court organist and composer of madrigals for the Three Ladies. Unfortunately, the only keyboard works of Luzzaschi that survive are a number of conservative contrapuntal pieces. But it is possible that he also composed, or at least improvised, more up-to-date keyboard music that would have provided an inspiration for the works that Frescobaldi would eventually publish. Certainly this was the case with another Ferrarese organist, Ercole Pasquini (*fl.* ca. 1585–1608), whom Frescobaldi would succeed as organist at St. Peter's Cathedral at Rome.

Thus, Frescobaldi evidently grew up in an environment full of musical innovation and experimentation. Sometime after 1600 he came to Rome, where in 1608 he was appointed organist at St. Peter's. While retaining that position until the end of his life, he also worked in the households of various Italian nobles, serving from 1628 to 1634 as court musician in Florence. At Rome, in addition to playing organ during services, he performed occasional public recitals, which presumably consisted largely of his own compositions and improvisations. Like Giovanni Gabrieli at Venice, he also taught an important circle of students, among whom were some of the leading keyboard players and composers of the next two generations.

Figure 10.5 Portrait of Frescobaldi, engraving after drawing by Claude Mellan. John Koster Collection.

Frescobaldi was so overwhelming a presence in Italian keyboard music that no composer or player of equal stature emerged for over one hundred years afterward. His successors in Italy published few keyboard works of importance, apparently directing their energies toward improvisation or toward composition in other genres. Hence, his influence is most clearly documented on later music in other countries, especially France and Germany.

Frescobaldi's Music

Frescobaldi's career, like Monteverdi's, straddled what is for us the division between Renaissance and Baroque styles, and his music likewise contains elements of both. Although an innovator, like Monteverdi he also endeavored to prove his ability to write old-fashioned counterpoint, and his first keyboard publication was a set of four-part fantasias (1608). The word **fantasia** was used during the late Renaissance and Baroque for various types of composition for keyboard, lute, or instrumental ensemble. The fantasias of William Byrd and other late Renaissance English composers fall into several sections that range from austere counterpoint in the style of contemporary vocal polyphony to lively dances and virtuoso figuration. Frescobaldi's fantasias are composed entirely of music of the first type—archaic imitative counterpoint—as is his 1615 collection of **ricercars,** another name for essentially the same type of conservative imitative piece. This was followed by set of somewhat more modern but still severely contrapuntal *capricci* (capriccios, 1624). Frescobaldi also published a book of polyphonic madrigals (1608) and two books of monodies and other, more up-to-date vocal chamber music (both in 1630). An important collection of instrumental chamber works appeared in 1628, comprising thirty-five *canzoni* for one to four unspecified instruments plus continuo.

Frescobaldi's most innovative keyboard compositions are found in his two volumes of toccatas and partitas, published in 1615 and 1627. The toccatas follow in the tradition of earlier such pieces by the Gabrielis and others, but with Frescobaldi their style is clearly allied with that of Luzzaschi, Caccini, and other composers of the emerging Baroque. Published in the same volume as the toccatas were several **partitas,** Frescobaldi's term for keyboard **variations.** Most of these, like the improvisatory variations of the lutenists (Exx. 10.1 and 10.2 above), are constructed over traditional ostinato bass lines such as the Romanesca. The latter was one of several basses that served as foundations for numerous variation sets by early Baroque composers.[12] An instance of the Romanesca occurs in Example 10.5, which shows the ostinato itself and the first few measures of several variations from Frescobaldi's set of partitas on it. Keyboard and lute partitas of this sort constituted instrumental versions of the strophic-variation aria (see Chapter 4), for which Frescobaldi, Monteverdi, and other early Baroque Italian composers often used the same traditional ostinato basses.[13] Frescobaldi's keyboard variations greatly embellish the traditional Romanesca bass line; in addition, they resemble his toccatas in their use of embellished melody and expressive dissonances. Nevertheless, like Monteverdi, Schütz, and J. S. Bach, Frescobaldi never abandoned the older contrapuntal style, and his last major publication is a collection of relatively conservative organ pieces for church use, the *Fiori musicali* (Musical flowers, published 1635).

The style of Frescobaldi's published toccatas undoubtedly reflected that of his own improvisations, which in turn must have been inspired by both vocal and keyboard music he had heard at Ferrara. This type of music must still have been unfamiliar to many players when Frescobaldi published his first book of toccatas in 1615. Consequently, the volume includes a preface that, like the preface in Caccini's *Nuove musiche* (1601), explains the music's performance and notation. Particularly notable is Frescobaldi's mention that the tempo of the toccatas should vary as in "modern madrigals," which might refer as much to the monodic solo madrigals of Caccini and Monteverdi as to the older polyphonic type. Despite Frescobaldi's concern with the proper performance of these pieces, he did not discuss their instrumental medium. Although the title of the 1615 collection originally specified that it was for harpsichord, the revised

---

[12]Although some ostinati, including the Romanesca, originally were associated with melodies, the bass line was paramount. The Romanesca may originally have been a Spanish tune, with the melody shown in Ex. 10.5a. Other traditional ostinati went by the names Ruggiero, Follia, and Monica.

[13]For example, *Ohimè, dov'è il mio ben?*, from Monteverdi's Seventh Book of Madrigals (1619), is an *aria di Romanesca* for two sopranos and basso continuo, using the same ostinato bass line as Ex. 10.5.

Example 10.5 Frescobaldi, *Partite sopra l'Aria della Romanesca*: (a) the underlying melody and ostinato bass; (b) *sesta parte* (variation 6), mm. 1–3; (c) *nona parte* (variation 9), mm. 1–5. Asterisks mark the notes of the ostinato bass.

edition of 1637 changed this to "harpsichord and organ." Following a convention that continued in many Baroque genres into the eighteenth century, Frescobaldi evidently expected performance of most of the pieces in the volume on both organ and harpsichord. The same option is given in the title of Frescobaldi's second collection of toccatas and partitas, first published in 1627.

Toccata 7 from *Libro* 2

This work, from Frescobaldi's 1627 book (anthology, Selection 23), represents his late style, integrating the innovations of what Monteverdi called the *seconda pratica* with echoes of traditional counterpoint, within a formal design that comprises a series of clearly articulated contrasting sections. The solemn opening of the piece as well as the subsequent division into sections that are either free (improvisatory) or contrapuntal can be traced to older Venetian toccatas by Andrea Gabrieli and

Claudio Merulo (1533–1604). At least one work from Frescobaldi's 1615 book, Toccata 9, had been relatively close to their style, comprising just three lengthy sections whose modality or tonality remains quite stable, with flowing virtuoso passagework (similar to that of Ex. 10.4) at beginning and end.

In the present work, the individual sections are shorter, and most incorporate expressively irregular figuration of constantly changing character. There is much chromaticism, often in conjunction with the frequent modulations, although the latter term is not precisely appropriate to music that was still understood as being in a mode (despite frequent excursions to transpositions of that mode or to foreign modes). Nevertheless, Frescobaldi has transformed the toccata from a late-Renaissance to a Baroque genre, mirroring the stylistic transition undergone by the madrigal during the same period and reflecting as well the style of the new genre of the sonata (see Chapter 12).

At first glance, the piece's succession of short, highly contrasting passages seems an arbitrary patchwork:

Section	Measures	Features
1	1–9	solemn chordal introduction, establishes mode or tonality
2	10–20	short, increasingly lively motivic figures in alternating hands
3	20–31	livelier passagework against slow-moving lines and chords
4	31–40	several sustained chords followed by more passagework
5	41–55a	imitative counterpoint
6	55b–66	climactic passagework, with drive to final cadence

Yet repeated hearings in an intelligent performance reveal a logical, dramatic series of events. Despite the considerable contrasts between the sections, adjacent passages are connected in various ways. For instance, section 2 begins with an imitative development of a motive introduced in the preceding passage (in mm. 6b–9a, using dotted rather than tied notation). Section 2 ends with a new, unexpected harmony (in modern terms a G^7 chord), actually a dissonance or suspension that creates an **elision**, or overlap, between this section and the next. The pace quickens in section 3, driving to the cadence on the downbeat of m. 31, which elides into several sustained chords, again on surprising harmonies. Passagework then continues as in section 3, including a common motivic figure (compare mm. 26, upper part, and 35, lower part).

The passagework of sections 3 and 4 superficially resembles that of the older Venetian toccata in its use of running figuration in one hand accompanied by sustained notes in the other (compare Ex. 10.4). But Frescobaldi's figuration changes direction much more frequently, often making small leaps to or from dissonant notes (e.g., f″–d″ in m. 26). It also incorporates dissonant melodic intervals such as tritones and diminished fourths (mm. 27–29). The pacing of both the figuration and the underlying harmonic progressions is more varied than in earlier toccatas, and an accelerating rate of exchange between the hands produces exciting drives to the cadences at the ends of sections 3, 4, and 6. In the last of these, at the end of the piece, a syncopated ascent in the bass line (punctuated by rests, mm. 60b–64) produces additional rhythmic tension.

The work culminates in the last two sections, which not only are the longest but also present the most radical contrast between one another. Section 5 is contrapuntal, but, in contrast to the imitative sections of older Venetian toccatas, its counterpoint is very free: it is hard to identify any single subject, for the imitation rather involves several motives—one of them chromatic—that enter irregularly in the three or four voices. (Even the number of voices is rendered ambiguous by the idiomatic keyboard texture.) This section concludes with what we would call a half cadence (mm. 54–55); rushing figuration follows suddenly, dominated by written-out trills (*groppi* in contemporary terminology). The passage climaxes with a *ribatutta*, an extended trill, over a chromatic line in the tenor (m. 57).

Inconceivable in the style of Frescobaldi's late-Renaissance predecessors, this astonishing conclusion resembles the final sections of the virtuoso sonatas that were being written by his younger colleagues, such as Dario Castello in Venice (see Chapter 12). Later composers would continue to write keyboard works composed of alternating free and imitative sections, although few would match Frescobaldi's ceaseless invention, instead tending to increase the length of individual sections while employing a more limited number of motivic ideas.

BAROQUE KEYBOARD MUSIC IN FRANCE AND GERMANY

Frescobaldi's influence extended not only to fellow Italian musicians but to keyboard composers in Germany and France, who emulated both his mastery of strict counterpoint and his improvisatory freedom. Yet by 1650 or so, a distinctive French style of keyboard composition was well established, and in both France and Germany clear distinctions were emerging between music for organ and music for stringed keyboard instruments. The harpsichord was the stringed keyboard instrument of choice, and French harpsichord music came to be highly idiomatic to that instrument. German composers combined elements of the French and Italian styles, creating their own varieties of music for harpsichord (and clavichord) that often reflected a special interest in complex counterpoint. Distinct types of organ music emerged in France and Germany as well. In France, the generic term for keyboard compositions was simply *pièces*—"pieces." This could be qualified as *pièces d'orgue* ("organ pieces") or *pièces de clavecin* ("harpsichord pieces"). German composers often used similar French titles for works in the French style, although they retained Latin or Italian titles for the genres that had been cultivated by Frescobaldi.

French Harpsichord Music

At first, the repertory of French harpsichordists probably consisted largely of improvised arrangements and adaptations of dance music composed for lute or for the Twenty-Four Violins of the King and similar bands. Little of this music survives, probably because it was rarely written down. The earliest surviving French Baroque harpsichord music, from around 1650, consists, like the lute repertory, largely of stylized dances. At first these were apparently composed as individual pieces, gathered together in manuscript collections from which players would presumably make their own selections. But by 1700 or so it had become customary for composers to organize their dances into **suites**: sets of dances (and, increasingly, other types of pieces) in a specific order and in a single key. Hence the suite became the most characteristic genre of French Baroque instrumental music.

The chief exception to the dance-based character of instrumental music in the French style was the prelude, which for lute as well as keyboard players often took the form of the **unmeasured prelude** (*prélude non mesuré*). Such pieces were written largely without barlines, using what appear to be whole notes; actual note values must be determined by the player, guided by convention and an understanding of the appropriate style. Presumably an outgrowth of improvisation, similar compositions had been composed by lutenists (including Denis Gaultier) since the early seventeenth century. The most important examples for keyboard are by Louis Couperin (ca. 1626–1661), uncle of the better-known François Couperin; several of his preludes, evidently modeled on toccatas by Frescobaldi and Froberger, include central sections in imitative texture that use conventional notation. For obvious reasons, these pieces pose difficult problems of interpretation for modern players; a relatively simple example is discussed below.

The similarities between French harpsichord music and the French lute repertory seem to suggest that the French Baroque harpsichord style developed through imitation of earlier lute music. But devices of French keyboard music that resemble those of lute music, such as the *style brisé*, could have originated independently as idiomatic keyboard techniques. It may be that the lutenists only appear to have preceded keyboard players, since the latter were at first fewer in number, and their music composed before the mid-seventeenth century has been largely lost.

Among the first important French keyboard composers whose works survive is Jacques Champion de Chambonnières (ca. 1602–1672). A musician active at the royal court, in 1670 he published the first two volumes of harpsichord music printed in France. Other composers followed his example during the following decades, as in the single book of pieces published in 1689 by Jean Henry d'Anglebert (1628–91), Chambonnières's successor at court and harpsichordist at the French opera under Lully. D'Anglebert's harpsichord works include not only original pieces but idiomatic arrangements of lute pieces by Gaultier (including "L'immortelle" and "La Poste") and dances from Lully's operas and ballets. Among the latter is the arrangement of the *passacaille* shown in Example 10.6 (compare the original, illustrated in Ex. 6.8). D'Anglebert's volume followed by two years the first volume of pieces by Elizabeth Jacquet de La Guerre, whose music is discussed below. Her 1687 collection contained the first significant keyboard music by a woman to appear in print.

Froberger

In a sense, all of these French composers were preceded by the German composer Johann Jacob Froberger (1616–67). Virtually none of his music was published during his lifetime, but by 1649 he had already produced two definitive manuscript collections of his keyboard works; three more followed (two are lost).

Example 10.6 D'Anglebert, *Passacaille* from *Armide*, mm. 1–9

Although a German and a student of the Italian Frescobaldi, Froberger is of great significance to the history of French keyboard music. The keyboard suites in his 1649 manuscript are the earliest such works to survive. Moreover, through several visits to France, Froberger influenced his contemporaries there. German keyboard music as late as that of J. S. Bach also shows his influence. Like most later German composers, Froberger wrote in both the French and the Italian styles, employing each in its appropriate genres. We shall examine one of his suites, a work in the French style. He also composed toccatas as well as fantasias, ricercars, and other contrapuntal works modeled on those of Frescobaldi.

Froberger was born in Stuttgart, in western Germany. He presumably studied there with his father, a court musician, and by 1637 he was working as an organist at the court of the Austrian emperor in Vienna. By 1641 he had visited Rome, where he studied with Frescobaldi. During a second visit in the late 1640s, he made the acquaintance of Carissimi and the famous scholar Athanasius Kircher. Later travels included visits to Paris (in 1652 and 1660), England, Spain, and the Netherlands. During these trips he probably met and played for many of the local musicians and their patrons. He nevertheless retained his Viennese position until 1658, when he was dismissed. He died while serving as teacher and court harpsichordist of Duchess Sibilla of Württemberg-Montbéliard, widow of the German ruler of a small enclave in what is now eastern France.

Froberger's Music

Froberger's surviving works are almost exclusively for keyboard. A majority of them are preserved in the three manuscripts mentioned above, which the composer himself wrote out and presented to his employers, the Austrian emperors, in 1649, 1656, and 1658, respectively. These manuscripts include toccatas and other works in the Italian style and suites in the French style. The toccatas are similar to those of Froberger's teacher Frescobaldi, but, illustrating a trend that would continue with later German composers, they tend to include longer contrapuntal sections, some of which constitute self-contained fugues (see Chapter 11).

The suites must reflect Froberger's knowledge of works by Chambonnières, the Gaultiers, and other French composers, although their music was not published until after Froberger's death. His suites also incorporate elements of the Frescobaldi style, including a highly expressive type of writing marked by irregular dissonances and other elements of the *seconda pratica* as well as the use of fairly strict imitative counterpoint. The first of these elements is particularly prominent in the allemande, invariably the first dance in each of Froberger's suites. The second characteristic, imitative counterpoint, occurs in many of Froberger's examples of another dance, the gigue.

Suite 20 in D

About thirty suites attributed to Froberger are known.[14] Most consist of four dance movements: allemande, courante, sarabande, and gigue, the gigue sometimes being omitted or placed immediately after the allemande. These four dances were, and would continue to be, the most common components of Baroque suites for harpsichord and lute. Froberger was apparently the first, however, to organize them in such a regular manner. Although many later German composers (including Bach) followed him in this practice, it never became universal. Hence it would be wrong to think of the Baroque suite as having a specific form. It is likely that players picked and chose the pieces they wished to perform even from among the regularly ordered suites of Froberger and, later, Bach.[15]

The suite in D (anthology, Selection 24) was one of Froberger's later works, composed at Paris in 1660 after his dismissal from the imperial court in Vienna; it is absent from the three manuscripts there, although the composer included it in a fourth autograph manuscript that surfaced in 2006. The latter manuscript also contains *tombeaux*—memorial pieces—for Emperor Ferdinand III, Froberger's previous employer, and for the husband of Duchess Sibylla. The preoccupation with death suggested by this selection of pieces is evident as well in the opening movement of the present suite, an allemande bearing the title "Meditation on my future death." At the end of the movement Froberger wrote the traditional Latin motto "Memento mori" (Remember that you must die), addressing it to himself. Hence the piece is a musical parallel to the type of image shown in Figure 10.6, a still-life painting filled with symbols or emblems of mortality.[16]

Such concerns, which may seem unduly morbid today, were a natural response to the horrific events of the mid-seventeenth century, which saw terrible wars, famines, and other disasters across Europe, particularly in Froberger's native region. Equally typical of the period was the interest in emblems—symbols that could encapsulate fundamental principles such as life and death. An example of a conventional musical emblem is the descending bass line used as an ostinato

---

[14]Froberger's suites (he did not actually use that title, which occurs in later sources) are traditionally identified by numbers used in the early twentieth-century edition by Guido Adler. An idiosyncratic series of "FbWV" numbers, introduced in imitation of the system used for works by Bach and other German composers, has not been generally adopted.

[15]A number of Froberger's suites in which the gigue originally followed the allemande, as in Suite 20, were published after his death with the gigue moved to the end. Bach and other composers similarly altered the order and number of movements in some suites when revising them.

[16]Another version of the painting is in the collection of the Metropolitan Museum of Art in New York.

Figure 10.6 Edward Collier (Dutch, worked in England, active 1662–1707), *Still Life with a Volume of Wither's "Emblemes"* (1696), Tate Collection. © Tate, London 2007. In addition to the skull in the upper left corner, the fruit and musical instruments—including lute, violin, shawm, two recorders, cello (?), and cittern (?)—are emblems of the brevity of earthly existence. The book, opened to show the title page and frontispiece, is a guide to artistic symbolism, reflecting a seventeenth-century fascination also evident in Froberger's music.

in many Baroque laments (see Ex. 5.7). But Froberger's works incorporate more precise analogies to the visual emblems of contemporaneous art. For instance, his *tombeau* for the lutenist Blancrocher ends with a descending scale that represents the musician's death in a fall down the stairs (this was the same Blancrocher who was memorialized by Denis Gaultier and Louis Couperin). A *tombeau* for Ferdinand IV, son of Ferdinand III, ends with a rising scale, accompanied in the imperial manuscript by a drawing of a sunburst with clouds to suggest Ferdinand's heavenly apotheosis.

Musical *tombeaux* were traditional in the French style, but in addition Froberger composed several autobiographical compositions, such as a lament after he was robbed by soldiers and a musical description of a ferry crossing of the Rhine River in which one of his companions fell overboard. The "Meditation" of Suite 20 lacks such specific extra-musical references, and its major mode might at first seem inappropriate to its subject. But its special character is evident in the striking gesture at the end of measure 1: a chromatic half step (c♯′–c♮′) followed by four rapid repeated notes, an imitation of the early-Baroque vocal ornament known as the *trillo*—one of several suggestions in this piece of the style of contemporary vocal monody. The sudden chromaticism early in the piece is echoed at the end of the first half, where e′ changes to e#′, leading to a cadence in the unexpected and, for the period, unusual key of F# minor. Such details were perhaps symbolic of life-and-death ruminations, although the sudden upward scale in measure 15 (a glance upward toward heaven?) and the serene conclusion, impossible in a minor key, are remote from conventional Baroque evocations of mortality; what, if anything, they represented for the composer must remain speculative.

Apart from its title, the "Meditation" is typical of keyboard allemandes in the French Baroque style. Like the following dance movements, it is in **binary form**, consisting of two halves, each repeated. Although the first half ends in an unusual key, a cadence at this point in a new key (usually the dominant or relative major) had become normal by the mid-seventeenth century. The second half returns to the tonic, as usual. Each of the following movements also employs the traditional rhythmic and other musical characteristics of its particular dance type. These characteristics recur in later Baroque instrumental music and, as we have already seen, in many vocal works. By identifying elements in a piece that correspond to a particular dance, it is possible to determine the piece's tempo and expressive character; this is true even in many works that are not explicitly identified as dances by their titles.[17]

The Allemande

The first dance movement of most Baroque keyboard suites is the **allemande**. As with many dances, the name is derived from that of a place or region in Europe, in this case the French word for Germany. But by the mid-seventeenth century the allemande had lost any direct association with its place of origin. Moreover, although the allemande had been a common dance from around 1550 to after 1600, the stylized allemandes of the French harpsichord and lute repertory have almost nothing in common with the actual dance. The allemande of the harpsichord or lute suite is a slow movement in common time $\left(\frac{4}{4}\right)$ employing a more or less improvisatory style. Many allemandes, including this one, lack regular themes or even melodies in the usual sense. Instead, like a French harpsichord or lute prelude, they tend to be composed largely of chords that are broken or arpeggiated in the manner typical of the *style brisé*. Thus the chord on the downbeat of measure 3 (in modern terms a dominant seventh) is arpeggiated by the right hand, and on beats 3 and 4 both hands participate in the breaking of a D-major chord, decorated by two instances of the nonchord tone b′.

As in the lute repertory, the intricate rhythmic notation of the *style brisé* can make the music look more complex than it actually is. Measure 3 of Froberger's "Meditation" is carefully notated in what appear to be four rhythmically independent voices, but in performance the texture sounds largely homophonic. Although relatively simple to notate in lute tablature, the development of ways

---

[17]The descriptions of the dances given below apply to the French Baroque versions of these dances; Italian composers used similar titles for sometimes very different types of music.

to write such textures in score was a significant achievement, marking the composer's specification of an element of performance—the expressive arpeggiation of chords—that had previously been left up to the player. Such precision was typical of the French style. It is curious, then, that Froberger rarely specified the ornaments that were an equally essential part of the French style. Later composers would mark them with great care.

The Gigue

The French **gigue** is a version of the dance referred to in England as the jig. The gigue of this suite, like Gaultier's example for lute, is in duple time, although Froberger also wrote gigues in compound duple time (6/4 or 6/8). French composers also wrote gigues that employ skipping rhythms (see Ex. 10.8a, mm. 2–5).[18] Froberger's gigues often employ fugal technique, a practice followed by many later Germans (including Bach). French composers did so as well, although their fugal gigues tend to be less strict than the present one (compare the free imitation in the gigue by Gaultier).

As in many fugal gigues, the binary form of the dance is reflected in the treatment of the subject, which is heard unaccompanied at the beginning of the first half. The second half employs an upside-down version of the subject, that is, its **inversion:** for each melodic interval in the subject, the inversion employs the same or a similar interval in the opposite direction. For example, the initial upward leap of a fifth (d′–a′ in m. 1) is converted into a downward leap involving the same notes (m. 12). Inversion is one of several compositional devices that were more commonly associated in the Baroque with the ricercars and other strict contrapuntal forms of the *stile antico*. Froberger's inclusion of such a device in a stylized dance represented the intrusion of learned style into a popular form. Such a mingling of styles appears to have been a special interest of German composers; Bach would use it particularly often (as in the gigues of his keyboard suites).

Toward the end of this gigue, the regular dotted rhythm is interrupted by a lyrical passage that returns briefly to the broken style of the allemande (mm. 18–19a). A few moments later, the tonality darkens to D minor, and a chromatic progression echoes one at the corresponding point in the allemande (compare m. 18 of the latter with mm. 20–21 of the gigue). Similar interrelationships between movements are common in Froberger's suites. The return to allemande style near the end of the gigue joins the two movements into a pair, justifying Froberger's unconventional ordering of the movements of the suite as a whole.

The Courante

In many suites, the allemande is followed immediately by one or more courantes. The **courante** resembles many gigues in being written primarily in compound

---

[18]The skipping rhythm was particularly characteristic of the type of gigue known in France as the *canarie*, after the Canary Islands, where it was supposed to have originated.

duple time $\left(\substack{6\\4} \text{ or } \substack{6\\8}\right)$. But its tempo is more moderate and the meter is elaborated by the presence of frequent **hemiola**: the substitution of one division of a triple measure by another. Thus in measure 11 the presence of three half notes in the bass marks a momentary shift to triple meter $\left(\substack{3\\2}\right)$. Hemiola is common in Baroque vocal and instrumental music in triple meter; its frequent presence in courantes made the latter the most complex and subtle of the French Baroque dances.[19]

The Sarabande

The **sarabande** is in triple time $\left(\substack{3\\2} \text{ or } \substack{3\\4}\right)$ and usually employs a moderate or, particularly in eighteenth-century examples, a slow tempo. In this case every two measures of triple time (3/4) are combined into a longer measure of 6/4. Often the second beat is strongly marked, as in measure 3 of our example, where the harmony changes and the melody leaps downward by a fifth on beat 2, and in measure 4, where the harmony heard on the downbeat is repeated and held at that point. The sarabande is usually simpler in rhythm, melody, and texture than the other dances, but the simpler texture does not preclude expressive effects, such as the chromatic bass line in measures 2–3 or the unexpected dissonant chord at the beginning of the second half. The weighty chords of many sarabandes, including this one, give them a grand or noble character, and the dance's position at the end of this suite emphasizes the grave, expressive character with which Froberger imbued the genre. Many later suites conclude with the livelier gigue or a simple minuet, reflecting fashions that favored a progression toward increasingly lighter, less serious music in the course of a suite or other multimovement work.

Jacquet de La Guerre

Among the numerous French keyboard players of the generations following Froberger was Elizabeth-Claude Jacquet (1665–1729), who became Jacquet de La Guerre after her marriage in 1684. She soon published her first book of harpsichord pieces (in 1687); another followed in 1707. A child prodigy, she enjoyed the patronage of King Louis XIV while still in her teens. She went on to become the first and only woman to compose a full-length opera produced by the French Royal Academy of Music (*Céphale et Procris*, 1694). Among her other vocal and instrumental works were some of the earliest published French cantatas and violin sonatas—excursions into Italian genres at a time when these were considered somewhat controversial in France.

Women in Baroque France enjoyed somewhat greater opportunities and freedoms than in most other European countries. They remained barred from the clergy and therefore from most important roles in the church (and in church music), but by the eighteenth century at least a few had gained appointments

---

[19]For examples of hemiola from Baroque vocal music, see Schütz, *Neige deine Himmel* (anthology, Selection 14), m. 55, and the opening passage of *Saul, was verfolgst du mich* (anthology, Selection 15), which alternates repeatedly between $\substack{3\\1}$ and $\substack{6\\2}$.

Figure 10.7 Portrait of Jacquet de la Guerre from Titon du Tillet, *Le Parnasse français* (n.p.: 1732). Library of Congress, Washington (CT1002.T6). On this page from a collection of imaginary memorial medallions, Jacquet is shown facing the opera composer André Campra (1660–1744). The motto on the reverse (shown below), where Jacquet is seen playing the harpsichord, reads: "I competed for the prize with the great musicians," implying that she was at least the equal of any of her male contemporaries. (The word *musicien* is grammatically masculine.)

as court musicians, and many others were active as composers and teachers. To be sure, most women musicians had the advantage of being born into musical families, as was Jacquet de La Guerre, or the aristocracy, but the same could be said of most male musicians as well. Jacquet de La Guerre never acquired a court title or indeed any professional position as a musician. But she appears to have directed the equivalent of a public concert series in her Paris home, gaining the reputation of one of the best harpsichordists in France (see Fig. 10.7).[20]

Jacquet de La Guerre's A Minor Suite

The third of the five suites in Jacquet de La Guerre's 1687 collection includes, in addition to the four dance movements found in Froberger's suites, a second courante, a chaconne, a gavotte, and a minuet (spelled *menuet* in French). There is also an opening prelude of the unmeasured type; considerably more fiery and virtuosic than most earlier French preludes for lute or harpsichord, it must reflect some of the characteristics that had won the king's admiration for Jacquet de La Geurre's playing.

The Prelude

The prelude to Jacquet de La Guerre's A minor suite (anthology, Selection 25), like all unmeasured preludes, captures on paper the spontaneous irregularity of an improvisation. Example 10.7 shows how the beginning of the prelude might be played; needless to say, this is only one of an infinite number of possible renditions. Still, the example shows that, like the keyboard allemande, the French unmeasured prelude is composed primarily of broken chords, arpeggiated in a constantly varied manner. The original notation, which in the earliest examples of the genre consists solely of whole notes, is clarified here by slurs and other lines, which indicate the holding of notes, as well as occasional smaller note values. Thus the first slur in the upper staff, over the notes a'–c''–d''–$f\sharp''$, indicates that each of these notes remains held after it has been struck, forming what we would call a D^7 chord. The two lines beneath this, in the lower staff,

Example 10.7 Jacquet de La Guerre, Suite in A minor, *prélude*, opening (possible performance)

<hr />

[20]Chambonnières had established a concert series as early as 1641, and musical gatherings at the homes of wealthy Parisian amateurs are known to have taken place throughout the century.

signify that the notes last struck by the left hand, (A/A') are also held, serving here as a pedal point.[21] Groups of smaller note values indicate lively passage-work, as in the sixteenths at the opening. Individual notes of small value, such as a' and e" at the end of the second system, are usually passing tones, inserted into the arpeggiation of certain chords but not held out with the other notes.

Despite the seemingly chaotic appearance of such music, it consists largely of the written-out embellishment of familiar chord progressions. Although the notation can make these progressions difficult to recognize, the bass notes are usually quite distinct. For example, after the initial pedal point on A and a flourish of descending figuration in sixteenth notes, the bass moves downward by step: F–E–D–C. Because each bass note tends to bear a distinct harmony, identifying these bass tones is the first step toward recognizing the chords that are arpeggiated in the upper voices. Jacquet de La Guerre, like earlier composers of unmeasured preludes, employs many of the same expressive devices found in Froberger's allemandes, which derive in turn from Frescobaldi's toccatas. But she reveals her independence in the occasional inclusion of lively figuration derived from more recent Italian music. An example of the latter is the rapid upward arpeggiation of a C-major chord by the right hand (notated in eighth notes), about two-thirds of the way through the present prelude.

Other Dances

Jacquet de La Guerre's A minor suite includes the four dances that were becoming standard by the late seventeenth century: allemande, courante, sarabande, and gigue—the last here in compound meter (see Ex. 10.8a). Following the gigue are three more dances that would appear with increasing frequency in later keyboard suites.

The **chaconne** is musically similar to the *passacaille* or passacaglia, with which it shares its triple meter and moderate tempo. The chaconne of the present suite (Ex. 10.8b) lacks the ostinato bass of most chaconnes. Instead it is in the form of the **rondeau,** a simple rondo form in which a single main theme (mm. 1–4) alternates with a series of contrasting phrases or couplets in the pattern ABACADA (etc.). This chaconne exploits the rich sonorities of the middle and low registers of the French harpsichord; the low tessitura of this movement has been explained as an imitation of chaconnes for the lute that intentionally avoid use of that instrument's highest string (called the *chanterelle*).

The **gavotte** is always in cut time $\left(\frac{2}{2}\right)$ and is usually notated so as to begin in the middle of the measure (Ex. 10.5c). The initial half-measure is an upbeat; if the first note is unduly accented in performance the barlines may seem to be drawn in the wrong place. This gavotte is typical of French examples in its moderate tempo and fairly delicate character; some German gavottes (including one

---

[21]A **pedal point** is a sustained note, usually in the bass, which is held against a series of changing harmonies in the other voices. It is so called because on the organ such a note might be played on the pedal keyboard.

Example 10.8 Jacquet de La Guerre, Suite in A minor, (a) gigue, mm. 1–6; (b) chaconne, mm. 1–7 (*rondeau* and opening of first *couplet*); (c) gavotte, mm. 1–4; (d) minuet, mm. 1–8

or two by Bach) are more energetic. A vocal example of this dance occurs in the air "Sur nos bords" from Rameau's *Les indes galantes* (anthology, Selection 19).

The **minuet** is musically the simplest of the common French Baroque dances, and our example is particularly light in character and texture (Ex. 10.5d). Minuets are always in triple time, often moving simply in quarters and eighths like the present one, with few hemiolas or other rhythmic complications. Most fall into regular four-measure phrases, although one type is composed of three-bar phrases (the *menuet de Poitou*). In the eighteenth century the first pieces learned by beginning keyboard players were frequently minuets, reflecting the fact that the minuet had become the most popular of the social dances and was the easiest to learn. For this reason, too, the minuet remained in use long after most of the other Baroque dances had been abandoned. It appears frequently as a movement in eighteenth-century sonatas and as the third movement of symphonies and string quartets composed during the second half of the eighteenth century and into the nineteenth. By then its musical character had changed, and the minuets of the Viennese

CHAPTER 11

MUSIC FOR SOLO INSTRUMENTS II
Fugues, and *Pièces*

The traditions described in Chapter 10 continued into the eighteenth century, albeit with modifications. During the seventeenth century, German musicians developed new genres that extended both the free and the contrapuntal idioms present in the Frescobaldian toccata. To the end of the Baroque, German as well as French composers also continued to cultivate the suite. This chapter focuses on music for keyboard instruments, but the lute, although declining in popularity, remained in use, and composers wrote music for other solo instruments as well.

LATER BAROQUE KEYBOARD MUSIC IN GERMANY

German composers continued, like Froberger, to create their own versions of idioms derived from existing Italian and French genres. The models provided by Frescobaldi and Froberger proved especially influential, continuing to be studied and copied into manuscripts well into the eighteenth century.

The North German Organ School

Northern Germany, that is, the area bordering on the North and Baltic seas, was linguistically, culturally, and politically a distinct region throughout our period. Dominated culturally by the port cities Hamburg and Lübeck, it was distinguished during the Baroque by a group of organist-composers now often identified as a North German "school." As in other instances (e.g., the "Netherlandish school" of the early Renaissance), the word *school* refers to a group of musicians sharing a general style and repertory, not to an actual educational institution. One common interest of North German musicians during the Baroque was the building of fine organs and the development of an idiomatic musical repertory for them. A number of these instruments survive or have been reconstructed; those by the builder Arp Schnitger (1648–1719) are particularly prized for their strong, clear tone and the rich registrational possibilities offered by their carefully designed sets of pipes.

Among the most prominent of the North German organist-composers were the Hamburg musicians Matthias Weckmann (1619–74), who had studied with Schütz, and the long-lived Jan Adamszoon Reincken (1643?–1722), whose teacher, Heinrich Scheidemann (1596–1663), also an important keyboard composer, had studied with Jan Pieterszoon Sweelinck (1562–1621). Sweelinck, the leading Dutch composer and organist of the late Renaissance, was, like English composer William Byrd, a writer of both sacred polyphony and a distinguished repertory of solo keyboard pieces. Through Sweelinck and his many students the North German tradition thus extended back to the sixteenth century; the tradition continued in the early works of J. S. Bach, who studied with (or at least visited) Buxtehude in 1705 and who also heard and later played for Reincken. The most characteristic products of the North German school are organ compositions in the *stylus fantasticus:* a "fantasy style" characterized by harmonic surprises, dramatic changes of texture, and virtuoso writing, often juxtaposed with passages of imitative counterpoint. This style, which could be traced to the toccatas of Frescobaldi and Froberger, is present above all in large organ *praeludia*, such as the one by Buxtehude discussed below.

Unfortunately, much of the music of these composers is lost. Hardly any was published during their lifetimes, their keyboard works being preserved in manuscripts written in German organ tablature, a form of notation that went out of use in the eighteenth century. Much of their music may have been improvised, never written down at all. The vocal works of these composers, which included sacred concertos and oratorios, are also scarce; many works are known to have been lost.

Buxtehude

The greatest of the North German Baroque composers was Dieterich Buxtehude (ca. 1637–1707), who served as organist at the church of St. Mary at Lübeck from 1668 until his death. The exact place and date of Buxtehude's birth are unknown; the family might have come from the North German city of Buxtehude, near Hamburg. Following local tradition, Buxtehude married his predecessor's daughter when he took the position at Lübeck. The reluctance of Handel and Bach, as well as other potential candidates, to continue the tradition apparently explains their failure to succeed Buxtehude. Both had been interested in the job, which was eventually taken by the opera composer Johann Christian Schieferdecker (1679–1732)—who did marry Anna Margreta, the oldest of Buxtehude's three daughters.

Buxtehude's works, like Bach's, have been listed in a modern *Werke-Verzeichnis* (catalogue of works). From this come the BuxWV numbers used to identify individual compositions. Buxtehude's organ works, like those of other North German musicians, were probably composed for use not only in church services but also in the public organ recitals that were a regular feature of musical life at the time in the major North German cities. At Lübeck, Buxtehude's predecessor Franz Tunder (1614–67) had regularly given recitals on Thursday afternoons. Buxtehude augmented this practice by including vocal works, and the concerts came to be known as *Abendmusiken* ("vespers concerts"), since the evening performances took place at the time of the liturgical office of vespers (which was still observed in Protestant countries, at least on certain days of the year).

Unfortunately, of the oratorios and other quasi-dramatic works that Buxtehude performed on these occasions, only some of the librettos survive. With one possible exception, the music appears to be completely lost. But over 100 sacred vocal works of a more strictly liturgical nature survive. These works, like those of his German contemporaries, represent a continuation of the older type of vocal concerto such as Schütz wrote. To this Buxtehude added more modern Italian elements, including various aria forms, as well as the distinctly German traditions associated with the Lutheran chorale.

Buxtehude's Organ Music

German organ music of the period falls into two main categories: compositions based on chorale melodies, and "free" works with no such preexisting element. Buxtehude's surviving chorale works number about fifty, ranging from brief preludes to longer fantasias; the free works include about thirty large *praeludia* and other compositions, all related to the Frescobaldian toccata, as well as a few separate fugues and other pieces. Both free and chorale works are written-out examples of the types of music that appear to have been routinely improvised by German organists. Throughout the Baroque, and indeed into recent times, prospective organists have undergone auditions requiring them to improvise at length in various styles, demonstrating both their technical proficiency at the keyboard and their mastery of harmony and counterpoint.

Chorale Works

Buxtehude's chorale pieces, like those of other German Baroque composers, continued to employ the older compositional techniques of cantus firmus and paraphrase, though with the inclusion of idiomatic keyboard figuration. The shorter chorale works are now referred to as **chorale preludes**: relatively brief settings of a hymn tune (chorale) that might have preceded congregational singing of the same chorale during a church service. In the chorale prelude *Nun bitten wir den heiligen Geist* (BuxWV 208; anthology, Selection 26), the traditional melody is played once through as a cantus firmus in the soprano, with three-part accompaniment below.

Buxtehude's setting focuses on his decoration of the cantus firmus. One might compare this organ setting with a four-part vocal setting of the same melody by Johann Hermann Schein (1586–1630), whose soprano part contains the same cantus firmus in simpler form (Ex. 11.1).[1] The melody would have been familiar to Buxtehude's listeners, who would have followed it within his decorated

---

[1]The melody, first published in 1524, is by Johann Walther (1496–1570). Schein was one of Bach's predecessors as cantor of the St. Thomas School in Leipzig.

Example 11.1 Johann Hermann Schein, Nun bitten wir den heiligen Geist, four-part chorale setting (complete) from *Cantional* (1627). Transposed up one step; note values halved. The irregular meter is typical of early chorale settings.

1 Nun bitten wir den heiligen Geist	Now pray we to the Holy Spirit
2 Um den rechten Glauben allermeist,	For true belief above all,
3 Dass er uns behüte an unserm Ende	That we should be protected until our end,
4 Wenn wir heimfahr'n aus diesen Elende.	When we come home from these miseries.
5 Kyrieleis.	Lord have mercy.

—Martin Luther

version, no doubt appreciating the expressive ornamentation and counterpoint of Buxtehude's setting. Buxtehude's decoration includes both florid embellishment reminiscent of the Italian style, written out in small note values, and ornaments typical of the French tradition, indicated by ornament signs.

The melody, in the soprano, is played by the right hand on an organ manual that would have been registered to sound a distinctive solo stop such as the *Cornet* (an imitation of the cornetto). The bass line is played by the feet on the pedals, the inner parts or voices by the left hand on a second, more quietly registered manual. The lower voices serve chiefly to accompany the melody in the soprano, but they also provide interludes and are composed throughout in contrapuntal, occasionally imitative, texture.

The interlude in measures 11b–12 employs an imitative subject that derives from the third phrase of the chorale melody; thus g'–g'–g'–$f\sharp'$–g' in the alto (mm. 11b–12) corresponds to b'–b'–b'–a'–b' in the soprano (mm. 13–15). The soprano states the motive in longer note values and in embellished form, but the motive is also imitated in plain eighth notes by the tenor (m. 12). This is an example of paraphrase technique, also used alongside a chorale cantus firmus in the opening chorus of Bach's Cantata 127 (anthology, Selection 20) and in other German Baroque vocal works. It is typical of this type of organ chorale prelude that the imitative subject first appears in the interlude *preceding* the entry of the corresponding phrase of the cantus firmus; for this reason the technique is sometimes referred to as **preimitation** (German *Vorimitation*).

German Baroque organists also wrote more extended chorale works for organ; these generally make more extensive use of paraphrase technique and are therefore usually described as **chorale fantasias**. Buxtehude and Bach wrote numerous examples of such works. A third category of chorale settings for organ comprises sets of variations on chorale melodies. Buxtehude and Bach wrote only a few of these, in which the individual variations may resemble either the prelude or fantasia types.

Free Works

Buxtehude's free keyboard compositions include suites and variations on secular tunes for clavichord or harpsichord, as well as a passacaglia and two chaconnes on ostinato basses, all for organ. Buxtehude's most important free works, however, are some two dozen *praeludia*. A *praeludium* of this type incorporates both improvisational and fugal sections descended from those of Frescobaldi's and Froberger's toccatas. Today such a piece is often described as a prelude and fugue, but with Buxtehude there may be multiple "prelude" and "fugue" sections, all connected, rather than forming self-contained movements.

The term *praeludium* is a Latin equivalent of English *prelude*, but it came to refer to a distinct genre of organ music in seventeenth-century Germany. A *praeludium* includes improvisatory opening and closing sections, similar in style to those in the toccatas of Frescobaldi and Froberger. But the main substance of the work usually lies in one or more fugal sections. Most of Buxtehude's *praeludia* include pedal parts and therefore achieve their full effect only on a large organ. Many contain virtuoso passages for the bass line, intended to demonstrate both the power of the North German organ's pedal division—those pipes reserved for the pedals—and the organist's mastery of pedal technique (see the *praeludium* in the anthology, Selection 27, mm. 3 and 115).

The organ *praeludia* of Buxtehude and other German composers nowadays are played frequently as preludes or postludes to church services. Many, however, were probably composed for recital performance, as may also have been the case with many chorale fantasias. The *praeludium* was the organist's equivalent of the sonatas that were being written at the same time for instrumental ensemble. Indeed, Buxtehude also wrote about twenty sonatas for instrumental ensemble that are comparable in form and style to his organ *praeludia*.

The *Praeludium* in A Minor, BuxWV 153

Like most of Buxtehude's organ music, this work (anthology, Selection 27) remained unpublished until after his death; the composer presumably wrote it for his own recital use at Lübeck. It comprises (1) an opening improvisatory or free section in common time: the "prelude" proper (mm. 1–21); (2) a four-part fugue also in common time (mm. 21–67); (3) a second fugue, also in four parts and using a variation of the subject of the first fugue, in compound time $\left(\frac{6}{4}\right)$ (mm. 67–104); and (4) a **coda** or closing section that returns to the free style of the prelude (mm. 105–25).

The opening and closing sections make much use of certain motives in small note values that are found throughout the North German repertory. These must have been formulas frequently heard in improvisations. The so-called "zigzag" motive played by both hands and feet in measures 1, 2, and 4 is one such formula; a related four-note motive, introduced by the tenor in measure 5, is developed imitatively through measure 14, after which the initial zigzag idea returns in inverted form (m. 15b). The latter occurs over a pedal point, another common device in seventeenth-century organ music. This dominant pedal point prepares the cadence that ends the opening section; the coda ends with another pedal point on the tonic (mm. 118–25). Such pedal points generate tension and are one of the chief sources of drama in works of this sort. Another source of drama is written-out arpeggiation, as in the last full measure of the prelude (m. 20). The notation here recalls the *style brisé* of French music for lute and harpsichord. But because the organ, unlike a plucked string instrument, is capable of sustaining notes indefinitely, the effect is that of a crescendo, as more and more notes are added to the sounding texture.

The presence of two fugues employing versions of the same subject in different meters derives from the contrapuntal works of Frescobaldi and Froberger—especially their capriccios and canzonas. The first fugue—which begins with the second note of the soprano in measure 21—is characterized by the numerous repeated notes in its subject, which exemplifies a so-called "repercussive" type favored by German Baroque organists. Unlike the imitative sections in the toccatas of Frescobaldi, the present fugue strictly maintains its four-voice texture—a practice typical of the contrapuntal works of Bach as well. Of course, the number of voices present at any given moment varies, just as in vocal polyphony. The full "ensemble," including the bass—played on the pedals—is employed only occasionally. By adding or subtracting voices from the texture, the composer could produce the effect of a crescendo or a diminuendo. Particularly dramatic results are achieved when, for example, the bass enters after a rest to complete the four-part texture (as in m. 28).

The first fugue ends with a short coda in free style (mm. 64–66). The passage includes a written-out trill in thirds (g♯–b) for the pedals, an example of the type of startling virtuosity typical of the *stylus fantasticus*. In the second fugue, some of the repeated notes of the original subject are replaced by a chromatic idea. Nevertheless, the shape of the subject remains recognizable, opening with an upward leap of a fourth or fifth and concluding with a larger upward leap to a syncopated or suspended note.

Analyzing Fugues

The analysis of fugues has interested musicians since the seventeenth century, when a number of musicians, among them Schütz's student Bernhard, wrote treatises on counterpoint and related topics. These were the ancestors of such eighteenth-century works as Fux's *Gradus ad Parnassum*. Such works were practical rather than theoretical in nature; their primary aim was to instruct composers in the writing of works that would be used in actual performance, especially church music.

The modern analysis of fugue employs terms and concepts that were developed largely from the study of Bach's fugues by nineteenth- and twentieth-century theorists. Their writings sometimes convey the misleading impression that fugue was a fixed form that can be understood by reference to a few frequently cited examples by Bach. There is, however, no one form or style for fugue. For Buxtehude, Bach, and other Baroque composers, fugue was simply one of several types of contrapuntal texture that might be employed in diverse ways within any vocal or instrumental work.

Box 11.1 summarizes some terms used in the present-day analysis of fugues, including the two fugal sections of the Buxtehude *praeludium*. Modern analysts do not always use the same terms in the same ways, however, and not all terms are relevant to all fugues. Some Baroque fugues are pedagogic pieces that were

---

Box 11.1

Fugue

A fugue is a contrapuntal composition (or a section or movement of a larger work) in which a theme, called a subject, is introduced in one voice and then imitated repeatedly at different pitch levels or in different keys by all of the parts. This box introduces a number of terms used in the modern analysis of fugue. Not all writers use these terms in the same way, nor do all these terms apply to all fugues.

Strict Fugue

In a **strict** fugue, the texture consists of a set number of voices or parts, often specified in the title (e.g., *Fuga a 3*, three-part fugue). All voices participate equally in the counterpoint, periodically stating the complete subject. In a keyboard fugue in strict style, these voices move within distinct ranges, just like real voices. They rarely cross, and the number of voices remains constant throughout the movement (although individual voices may rest from time to time). One purpose of a strict fugue is to demonstrate technical mastery using limited musical means. Hence, in a strict fugue most of the motivic material is derived from that of the subject (and any countersubjects; see below).

Subject

Most instrumental fugues begin with a monophonic statement of the **subject,** which is initially presented by a single voice; as each of the remaining voices enters in turn, the preceding one continues with new material. It is not always clear precisely where each entry of a subject begins or ends, nor is it necessarily important to determine exactly where this occurs. Fugues, unlike dances and other homophonic genres of the Baroque, comprise numerous overlapping phrases; as a result, fugues frequently lack the clear-cut articulations that mark off segments or sections in other types of music.

Exposition, Episode, and Bridge

A section of a fugue containing entries of the subject constitutes an **exposition**. A fugue is likely to contain several expositions, and in a strict fugue these will tend to contain a single entry of the subject in each voice. Some fugues consist of nothing but expositions; in such fugues, at any given point the subject is being stated by one voice or another. Usually, however, there are connecting passages and interludes from which the subject is absent (although motives extracted from the subject may be present). All such passages can be called **episodes**, although it is best to reserve this term for distinctly articulated sections—that is, interludes of significant length from which the subject is absent. Shorter passages that merely connect entries of the subject can be termed **bridges**. Within an exposition, there may be bridges connecting one entry of the subject to the next. But an episode is best regarded as a relatively lengthy passage that falls *between* two expositions.

Keys and Tonal Design

Fugal imitation differs from other types in that successive entries of the subject are usually in different keys. The first entry of a fugue is usually in the tonic, followed by one in the dominant, although other arrangements occur, particularly in seventeenth-century works (as in the first fugue of Buxtehude's *Praeludium* in A minor). Within the first exposition, entries alternate between tonic and (usually) dominant until all voices have entered. In subsequent expositions, the order of keys, like the order of voices, is likely to vary from that of the first exposition. Moreover, after the initial exposition the subject is likely to enter in a greater variety of keys, including the relative major or minor (this is especially true in eighteenth-century fugues).

To be more precise, the even-numbered entries of a typical first exposition are on the dominant, not *in* the dominant. "On" the dominant indicates that the modulation from tonic to dominant is only momentary, and indeed the music usually returns immediately to the tonic in the next entry. Subsequent modulations within a fugue may also be of a temporary nature. Fugues composed before the eighteenth century, including most of Buxtehude's, rarely contain lasting modulations, alternating between tonic and dominant and perhaps one or two other keys.

Stretto

An answering or imitating voice need not wait until the previous entry has been completed to make its own entrance. A fugue subject can be combined with itself through the technique of **stretto**. For example, in the second fugue of the Buxtehude *praeludium*, the bass entry in measure 100 is followed at a distance of only half a measure by an entry in the soprano. This is an isolated stretto entry, but it is possible to have an entire exposition composed through stretto. The word *stretto* literally means "acceleration"; it refers to the diminished time interval between entries. Stretto entries usually represent an intensification of the drama that is often present in a fugue, and they are likely to occur near the end of a movement, as is the case here.

Tonal Answer

Not every statement of the subject takes precisely the same melodic or rhythmic form. Sometimes it is necessary to alter certain melodic intervals in the subject, especially leaps, to ensure that an entry will remain in the desired key. In Buxtehude's A-minor *praeludium*, for example, the first statement of the subject (soprano, m. 21) opens with an ascending fifth (a′–e″). In the next entry, however (alto, m. 23), the initial leap turns into a fourth (e′–a′). This type of altered entry is called a **tonal answer**; the alteration affects the tonality of the entry and prevents it from modulating too far from the tonic. The next entry (tenor, m. 26) is termed a **real answer** because it reverts to the original form of the subject.

Inversion

Another type of alteration occurs in measure 30 of the same fugue, where the subject is **inverted**: every melodic interval is turned upside-down, moving upward where it originally moved downward (and vice versa). Indeed, measure 30 marks the beginning of an entire exposition using the inversion, as opposed to the original or **upright** form of the subject. (The Latin word *rectus* is also used for the original form of the subject.)

Thematic Variation and Motivic Development

Fugue subjects may also be varied and developed through the usual devices of thematic variation and motivic development. **Thematic variation** includes such procedures as melodic embellishment and rhythmic alteration. A subject that is varied retains its original length and basic shape. **Motivic development** involves detaching an isolated figure from the subject, such as an opening leap or a repeated note, and using it in a sequence or some other type of passage outside the subject itself. This is a commonly used technique in episodes, as in measures 94–99 in the second fugue of the Buxtehude *praeludium*. Sometimes a statement of a subject is simply truncated, its end left off. In such cases it may be hard to say (and unnecessary to decide) whether one is dealing with a shortened entry of the subject or merely a statement of its opening motive.

Countersubject

Many fugues contain more than one subject. For example, in the Buxtehude *praeludium* the soprano, having introduced the subject, continues (m. 23) with a second idea that is later combined with subsequent entries of the subject as well. A secondary subject that combines repeatedly with the main subject constitutes a **countersubject**. A fugue may have any number of countersubjects—or none at all. Countersubjects, like subjects, may undergo various types of alteration. It is rare, however, for the countersubject(s) to be treated as rigorously as the subject. In the Buxtehude fugue, the countersubject disappears after the first exposition, and even within the latter it undergoes greater variation than does the subject.

Second Subject

At some point after the first exposition, a fugue may contain another exposition employing an entirely new subject. Such a subject is termed a **second subject**. This differs from a countersubject, which serves chiefly to accompany the main subject, without receiving an exposition of its own. A second subject may even have its own countersubject(s).

Double Fugue

Usually, after a second subject has been thoroughly worked out in its own exposition, there is yet another exposition in which it is combined with the first subject. A fugue in which this occurs is termed a **double fugue**. It is also possible to have triple and quadruple fugues with corresponding numbers of subjects.*

Types of Fugues

Most fugues use only a selection of the devices described above. A few strict fugues by Bach and other composers intentionally incorporate many such devices in order to demonstrate the techniques of fugal counterpoint. But even in pedagogical works, such as Bach's *Well-Tempered Clavier*, the emphasis is usually not on fugue as a contrapuntal exercise but on fugue as a texture that permits expressive or dramatic music that is idiomatic for its chosen medium. Fugue was favored by Baroque composers not because of its rigidity or severity—characteristics that were attributed to it only after Baroque traditions of composition had died—but because of the freedom that it permitted. Fugues could even be improvised; indeed, the improvisation of fugues was one of the skills in which organists such as Bach were tested when they underwent auditions—a tradition that continues in some schools of organ playing today. Naturally, an improvised fugue would have been less strict than the rigorous examples in a work such as Bach's *Art of Fugue*. Both types, however, would have manifested the Baroque love of variety, technical virtuosity, and expressive intensity.

Symbols for the Analysis of Fugue

Tables 11.1 and 11.2 illustrate the use of certain symbols in the analysis of fugue. The meaning of the symbols is explained in the key that follows each chart. Different authors use in different symbols, and differences in the structure of various fugues require different analytical approaches.

*Some writers use the expression *double fugue* for any fugue that contains a regularly occurring countersubject. Here the term is confined to works in which a second subject receives its own separate exposition, as in the fugue in C♯ minor from Part 2 of Bach's *Well-Tempered Clavier*.

TABLE 11.1
Buxtehude: Praeludium in A minor, BuxWV 153, first fugue

	Expositions			
	1	2	3	4
Soprano	a 1 (1)	a* 2 e*	d—	a (a)*
Alto	d— 1	e* 2	a (1)	d—
Tenor	a	a*	d	(e*)—
Bass	d	e*—	a	(a*)
Measure	21b	30 31b	42b	54
Cadences		a	a	a

letters = tonalities of fugal entries (italics: tonal answers)
* = inverted entry
1, 2 = countersubjects
(symbols in parentheses) = incomplete or altered entry
— (dash) = bridge (free continuation of an entry)

intended to demonstrate to students the use of particular contrapuntal techniques. But many others are public works for concert or church use that employ
imitative counterpoint for its expressive and dramatic possibilities.

Table 11.1 provides an analysis of the first fugue in Buxtehude's A minor
praeludium. The table divides the fugue into four **expositions**: sections in which
the subject is present and treated in imitation. The first and third expositions
employ the subject in its upright or *rectus* form; its inversion forms the basis of
the second and fourth expositions, although in the last exposition all but one
of these entries is abbreviated, and the final entry is a tonal answer in upright
form. It is in the nature of fugue that the divisions between these sections are
somewhat blurred. For example, the table identifies measure 30 as the beginning of the second exposition, since this is where the soprans first states the
subject in inversion. Yet only a bit later, in the middle of measure 31, is there
a cadence to A minor that brings the first exposition to a conclusion. Thus the
first and second sections overlap, maintaining a fluid continuity typical of the
imitative counterpoint of both the Renaissance and the Baroque.

Also typical of fugue is the ambiguous character of the tonality in certain
statements of the subject, especially those described as tonal answers. Most
fugues place the first imitation at the dominant, and indeed the alto enters on
on e' in measure 23. But the alto changes the first melodic interval from a fifth
to a fourth, and it winds up on the subdominant (D minor) after the c#' on the
downbeat of measure 25. No lasting modulation takes place, however, and
within a few beats the tenor enters in the tonic. It is debatable whether true
modulations occur anywhere in this fugue, which, like most seventeenth-century
examples, has entries of the subject on only a limited number of scale degrees.
No strongly articulated full cadences occur in any key but the tonic. Buxtehude's
avoidance of the dominant key, in a piece centered on A, is a quasi-modal feature, reflecting reluctance to use the note D#, the leading tone of E (although

the note does occur in this piece). Later composers, including Bach, would continue to use archaic tonal designs like this one in old-fashioned fugues, as when they wished to invoke the *stile antico*. But Bach would also write numerous fugues with more up-to-date tonal designs that modulate more widely, as in the one discussed below.

J. S. BACH'S MUSIC FOR SOLO INSTRUMENTS

The composer who today is most closely identified with fugue is J. S. Bach. Fugue is actually only one of many contrapuntal textures employed by Bach, but he used fugue or fugal technique in nearly every genre in which he wrote. His keyboard fugues, in particular, have been closely studied by musicians ever since his students began making manuscript copies of them in the second decade of the eighteenth century.

Fugues constitute only a portion of Bach's solo instrumental music. The latter is mostly for keyboard instruments, but there are also several suites for lute as well as six suites for unaccompanied cello and six "solos" for unaccompanied violin. Baroque works for violin or cello normally include a basso continuo accompaniment, but Bach dispensed with continuo in these works, restricting the harmony to that which could be played as chords (multiple stops) or suggested through the use of melodies derived from arpeggiation. The six violin solos comprise three sonatas and three suites (called *partitas*); the second movement in each sonata is a fugue, demonstrating the possibility of writing imitative counterpoint for a solo bowed string instrument (see Ex. 12.6b).

Bach's Organ Music

Bach's organ works fall into essentially the same genres as Buxtehude's—chiefly the chorale prelude, the chorale fantasia, and the *praeludium* or prelude and fugue. Composed mainly during the period 1703–17, when Bach held a series of positions as organist at several central German towns (see Chapter 9), his chorale compositions include the *Orgelbüchlein* (Little organ book), a collection of forty-five chorale preludes assembled at Weimar around 1715, and a set of seventeen (later expanded to eighteen) larger chorale fantasias, gathered together and revised at Leipzig in the 1740s but mostly composed by 1717. He also published three volumes of organ music, including the third volume of his *Clavierübung* (Keyboard practice, 1739), which contained both free pieces and chorale settings, and the so-called Schübler chorales (ca. 1748), organ transcriptions of six of the chorale-fantasia movements from his church cantatas.[2]

Bach's free organ works consist primarily of about two dozen *praeludia* and related pieces. These too were mostly composed by 1717, although Bach

---

[2]The Schübler collection is named after its publisher, Johann Georg Schübler of Zella, in Germany.

subsequently revised existing works and wrote occasional new ones for the recitals that he continued to play for the remainder of his career. Many of these recitals took place in connection with the completion of a new instrument or the rebuilding of an old one. On such occasions, Bach and other leading musicians would be called upon to provide expert evaluations of the builders' work. Bach was famous for the rigorous testing of the instrument that took place when he sat down on such occasions to improvise or to play one of his larger compositions.

Most of Bach's *praeludia*, unlike Buxtehude's, consist of two distinct movements. No longer musically connected—indeed, they were often composed separately—the prelude and the fugue thus constitute independent, self-contained compositions. Among Bach's organ works of this type are several that have been given popular nicknames by later musicians. These include the Prelude and Fugue in E minor (BWV 548), known as the "Wedge" from the shape of its fugue subject, which expands through widening leaps in both directions from the tonic note; and the "Dorian" Toccata and Fugue in D minor (BWV 538), so called because it lacks the one-flat key signature now customary for works in this key.[3] Although the first movement of the latter work is called a toccata rather than a prelude, it has little in common with seventeenth-century toccatas. Another famous work of this type, the so-called Toccata and Fugue in D minor (BWV 565), is in some respects closer to the *stylus fantasticus*, but it is probably not by Bach. Seemingly anachronistic details suggest that it is the work of a younger eighteenth-century composer imitating somewhat earlier music.[4]

Bach's Harpsichord and "Clavier" Works

Few of Bach's keyboard works bear explicit instrumental designations, and most in theory could have been played on any keyboard instrument. But independent pedal parts in the works described above point to performance on the organ; in most works without pedal parts, the harpsichord would have been the instrument of choice, although in many cases organ or clavichord would have been possible alternatives.[5] Clearly for harpsichord are about two dozen suites modeled more or less closely on French harpsichord works; these include the collections known (somewhat misleadingly) as the English Suites, the French Suites, and the Partitas. Despite the varying titles, all combine the traditional French dance types with Italian and German stylistic elements. Also for harpsichord

---

[3]Many eighteenth-century works continued to be notated, as in the earlier Baroque, with fewer accidentals in the key signature than is now customary. This has no bearing on their tonality, however, since accidentals are supplied where needed in the score. Bach's "Dorian" prelude and fugue is as fully tonal as any of the composer's works.

[4]An ingenious hypothesis proposed by Peter Williams, according to which this was originally a work for unaccompanied violin, is not supported by any documentary evidence.

[5]Clavichords could even be fitted with pedalboards and used to play organ music, but there is no evidence that Bach wrote anything specifically for the clavichord, which was used primarily for teaching and private practice.

are several special works, including the *Concerto in the Italian Style* and the so-called Goldberg Variations, which comprise thirty virtuoso variations on an original "aria"; both compositions require the resources of a two-manual harpsichord.

In other works, Bach, probably intentionally, avoided calling for idiomatic features of the harpsichord. These compositions, for a generic keyboard instrument or "clavier," tend to focus on contrapuntal development, although this does not preclude their being deeply expressive or dazzlingly virtuoso as well. Among these "clavier" works are seven toccatas without pedal and several large preludes and fugues, including the famous one known as the Chromatic Fantasia and Fugue in D minor. These works, probably composed before Bach left Weimar in 1717, resemble his organ music of the same period and might have been written for performance during private palace concerts.

Many of Bach's other clavier pieces were composed for private study or for use in teaching. Among them are the fifteen two- and fifteen three-part **inventions**—short pieces in imitative texture that Bach first gathered together, alongside other pedagogic pieces, in the Little Keyboard Book for Wilhelm Friedemann Bach. This was a manuscript collection that he presented to his oldest son in 1720, a few months after the latter's ninth birthday.[6] Two years later Sebastian completed the first volume of a more advanced collection of pedagogic pieces, the *Well-Tempered Clavier*. A second volume was completed around 1740; by then Bach had begun his last major clavier work, the *Art of Fugue*. This consists of about twenty movements, all based on the same subject, that demonstrate various types of fugue and canon.

The *Well-Tempered Clavier*

Each volume of the *Well-Tempered Clavier* consists of twenty-four preludes and fugues, one in each of the twenty-four major and minor keys. The title refers to any of various systems of keyboard tuning, among them modern equal temperament, that made such a work possible. The word *clavier* refers to any musical keyboard; a **temperament** is any of various ways of tuning such an instrument to permit its playing in more than one key. Temperament involves the intentional mistuning of certain intervals—thirds and fifths—in order to produce pure octaves. For example, three pure thirds (C–E, E–G♯, G♯–B♯) do not add up to a pure octave; B♯ is slightly lower than C unless the thirds are tempered, that is, tuned slightly wider (the upper note sharper) than pure. Likewise, the circle of fifths—C–G, G–D, D–A, and so on to E♯–B♯—produces a true circle, with B♯ the same as C, only when some (or all) of the fifths are tuned a little narrower (the upper note lower) than pure. One can temper all twelve fifths by the same small amount, as in modern equal temperament, or one can leave some fifths pure and temper others more drastically, as in various historical systems.

Some temperaments allowed the pure tuning of certain major thirds, thereby creating very harmonious triads on such notes as C and F. But these temperaments left other intervals, such as the major thirds on B and A♭, audibly discordant.[7] Such temperaments favored the use of the most commonly employed keys but forced composers to avoid keys with more than two or three flats or sharps in the key signature. "Well-tempered" systems evened out these distinctions, making all keys usable; modern equal temperament is one such system, but others exist and it is uncertain which one or ones Bach used.

Older composers, notably the South German Johann Caspar Ferdinand Fischer (1656?–1746), had written collections similar in plan to Bach's *Well-Tempered Clavier*.[8] But most had stopped short of including all twenty-four keys, and none had produced a collection approaching Bach's in size or stylistic diversity. Moreover, with Bach, unlike some of his predecessors, the preludes are generally equal in length and musical significance to their accompanying fugues. Although not intended for public performance, many movements in the *Well-Tempered Clavier* provide opportunities for expressive playing as well as virtuoso display. At least some movements probably derive from earlier works that, like other surviving clavier pieces, Bach might have performed for friends or at the princely courts that he occasionally visited throughout his career.

Contradicting later impressions of Bach as a musical conservative obsessed with strict counterpoint, the first volume of the *Well-Tempered Clavier* is characterized above all by its unfailingly rich variety. Its preludes range from the improvisatory one in B♭ to the highly symmetrical binary form of the one in A minor. Its fugues include both the short, invention-like one in E minor and the massive five-part double fugue in C♯ minor. The second volume is similarly conceived. For this reason it is somewhat arbitrary to select any one prelude-and-fugue pair for study; every movement in both volumes repays careful attention.

The Prelude and Fugue in G from Part 1 of the *Well-Tempered Clavier*

This pair of movements (anthology, Selection 28) is of special interest for several reasons. Its prelude is one of several in the first volume that retains some tenuous connections to the improvised harpsichord preludes of the seventeenth-century tradition: its motivic material consists largely of broken chords, as is true of a number of other preludes in the volume as well. The fugue, in three voices, is one of the relatively small number by Bach that systematically illustrates a series of different fugal techniques.

The prelude opens over a tonic pedal point, articulated in the bass by a rhythmic motive characterized by leaping eighth notes (mm. 1–2). Over this the right hand plays four statements of an arpeggiated motivic idea, outlining a

---

[7]One such system, in widespread use during the sixteenth and seventeenth centuries, is known as **quarter-comma meantone temperament**; it can be heard in many modern performances of early keyboard music.

[8]Several fugues from Bach's *Well-Tempered Clavier* incorporate thematic material from Fischer's *Ariadne musica* (Augsburg [?], 1702), suggesting that Bach knew the latter work.

standard cadential progression (I–IV–V–I). The two ideas heard in the opening measures are then developed in a series of modulations to D major (the dominant, m. 5) and E minor (the relative minor, m. 9). A dominant pedal (mm. 11–13a) then prepares the final return to the tonic (m. 16). In the process, two new motives are introduced (right hand, mm. 4, 5), and the original ones become nearly unrecognizable, although the arpeggio idea returns in something close to its original form in measure 13 (left hand). Although short, the piece gains a dramatic profile through a gradual increase in its rate of motion. After the initial pedal point, the hands at first exchange motivic ideas in one-measure units (mm. 4–10). Measure 11 then marks the beginning of a sequential phrase in which each statement of an idea lasts half a measure. In the middle of measure 16 the pace quickens, with the harmony changing on every eighth note; this makes for a dramatic sweep into the final cadence.

The fugue, although organized as a demonstration of contrapuntal technique, is equally dramatic, but on a larger scale. Table 11.2 summarizes its formal design. The first exposition (mm. 1–14) presents the subject in upright form; the second exposition uses the inversion of the subject (mm. 20–30); the third exposition uses both forms of the subject (mm. 38–46). Later sections of the fugue (mm. 51ff.) employ both forms of the subject in stretto, eventually combining the upright and inverted forms of the opening motive in measure 79 as part of a grand coda. These contrapuntal devices are coordinated with a modulating tonal design: the third (combined) exposition and the strettos coincide with modulations to the relatively remote keys of E minor and B minor, respectively. The piece returns to the tonic after the "simple" entry of the inverted subject in measure 69. (For explanations of these terms, see Box 11.1.)

Despite its methodical use of these highly technical compositional devices, the fugue is anything but a dry, pedantic exercise. On the contrary, Bach chose a subject whose dancelike rhythm resembles that of a minuet. Yet the restrained character of the minuet is contradicted by a bridge passage within the first exposition (mm. 9–10), which introduces a lively motive in sixteenth notes reminiscent of the type of solo violin figuration found in Italian concertos of the time. This motive, like the subject, is developed through inversion (already in m. 10) and embellishment (thirty-second notes, starting in m. 47). Another motive, the little descending figure heard twice at the end of the subject (m. 4), is eventually extended into brilliant scales that span more than an octave and a half, both descending (m. 34) and ascending (m. 36). For the most part this fugue avoids Bach's characteristic chromaticism and expressive use of dissonance. But near the end the two hands leap in opposite directions to a startling diminished-seventh chord (m. 81); this signals the preparation for the final cadence.[9] In short, contrapuntal and motivic development combine with tonal planning and effective harmony to yield a virtuoso display piece whose intensity gradually increases, reaching a dramatic climax in the final moments.

---

[9]The diminished chord, on the second half of measure 81, is a secondary dominant; measure 82 contains the dominant-seventh chord that resolves to the tonic on the downbeat of measure 83 (followed by a tonic pedal point). The diminished chord momentarily suggests the minor mode, an expressive device placed near the end in many of Bach's works in major keys.

TABLE 11.2
J. S. Bach: *Well-Tempered Clavier*, Part 1, Fugue in G

	Rectus (R) Exposition	Episode	Inversus (I) Exposition	Episode	Exposition Using R and I	Episode
Soprano	G 1		D* (1*)		e— (1*)	
Tenor	D— (1)		G* 1*		(1) (C/e*)	
Bass	G		G*			
Measure	1	15	20	31	38	47

	Stretto (R)	Episode	Stretto (R)	Episode	Exposition (I)	Episode	Stretto (R + I)	Coda
Soprano	(b)		(D)		(1*)		(b/G)	
Tenor			(D)		G*		(G*)	
Bass	(b)						(G)	
Measure	51	56	60b	65	69b	73	76	83

letters = tonalities of fugal entries (slash between letters: entry *on* the first pitch level indicated, but *in* the second one)

* = inverted entry

1 = countersubject

(symbols in parentheses) = incomplete or altered entry

— (dash) = bridge (free continuation of an entry)

R = *rectus* (upright) form of subject

I = *inversus* (inverted) form of subject

EIGHTEENTH-CENTURY KEYBOARD MUSIC IN FRANCE

At the same time that Bach and other German musicians were exploring the possibilities of contrapuntal elaboration and new tonalities, French composers were extending traditions established during the seventeenth century. Although their music continued to employ the *style brisé* and precisely notated ornamentation, many French composers also admitted virtuoso elements of Italian style, as Jacquet de La Guerre was already doing in the late seventeenth century. And while continuing to employ the traditional dance rhythms, French composers also wrote growing numbers of pieces whose titles signified not a dance but a person, place, or expressive characteristic that its music was supposed to represent. Such a work, which is intended to depict or describe something or someone, is often referred to as a **character piece.**

Character pieces are examples of **programmatic** works—instrumental compositions that represent an extramusical idea or a narrative. Such works were composed throughout the Baroque, in some cases with the subject of the music clearly spelled out in titles or a detailed preface.[10] In the French *pièce de clavecin*, however, the relationship between subject and music is usually more ambiguous, perhaps intentionally so. It is clear from Baroque vocal music that composers had at their disposal a large vocabulary of meaningful musical symbols and expressive devices. When combined with a suggestive title, these allowed the listener to draw associations between the musical events of a given piece and various ideas: images, emotions, or personal characteristics.

François Couperin

The most important French composers of harpsichord music from around 1700 and later are Rameau, whose vocal works were discussed in Chapter 8, and François Couperin (1668–1733). Couperin was a member of a musical family; his uncle Louis (ca. 1626–1661) was one of the earliest French Baroque keyboard composers whose works have survived, noted particularly for his unmeasured preludes. François succeeded to his uncle's organist position in Paris in 1685, and he soon became organist and later harpsichordist as well at the royal court. In that capacity he composed and performed chamber works for various wind and string instruments with continuo accompaniment. Among these are some of the earliest sonatas for instrumental ensemble composed in France as well as two collections of suites in which Couperin made a point of combining the French and Italian styles. His title *Les goûts réunis* (The reunited styles) for the second set, published at Paris in 1724, reflects the lively interest during Couperin's lifetime in the differences and relative merits of the two styles. Couperin and his French contemporaries must have been highly conscious of the Italian elements in these

---

[10]Programmatic compositions depicting battles were written by Frescobaldi and Biber (see Chapter 12), among others. Johann Kuhnau (1660–1722), Bach's predecessor as cantor at Leipzig, published a set of six Biblical Sonatas for keyboard instrument (Leipzig, 1700) on subjects such as the battle of David and Goliath and Jacob's marriage; each work is accompanied by a detailed prose account of the underlying story.

pieces, such as the use of simple "singing" melodies in some slow movements. Yet French style remains predominant, notably the reliance on dance genres and the careful notation of every detail of ornamentation and rhythm.[11]

Couperin also wrote works for organ as well as sacred and secular vocal music. But he is best known for his four books of harpsichord music, which contain 220 distinct pieces. His two daughters continued the family tradition; both were musicians, the younger one (Marguerite-Antoinette) succeeding him as royal chamber musician.

Couperin bears the same relationship to the harpsichord that Frédéric Chopin (1810–49) does to the piano. No one has written harpsichord music that is more idiomatically conceived for the instrument, that uses it so imaginatively, or that is so meticulously composed and so precisely notated to take advantage of its particular capabilities. Many works of both composers are often erroneously regarded as miniatures. But although many pieces are short in duration, they are so well crafted and contain such original musical ideas that they hardly are trifles. This is true even when, as is often the case with Couperin, the pieces bear witty titles. Like most of his contemporaries in France, Couperin avoided strict counterpoint of the type found in Bach's keyboard works. But there is an underlying contrapuntal component in most of his music, as well as a sophistication of harmony and modulation that goes far beyond what is found in the so-called rococo or *galant* pieces of his younger contemporaries.

Couperin carefully oversaw the production of his four volumes of harpsichord music, insuring that, among other things, the ornament signs were precisely drawn and placed (see Fig. 11.1). Moreover, like Caccini and Frescobaldi a century earlier, he provided a guide for the performance of his music. This took the form of a short treatise, *L'art de toucher le clavecin* (The art of playing the harpsichord, Paris, 1716), which proved widely influential. Couperin's keyboard music was influential as well, furnishing models for character pieces by the next two generations of composers, including Bach's son Carl Philipp Emanuel and other Germans. J. S. Bach, who had eagerly collected works by Couperin's French predecessors, knew at least some of his music; one piece appears in the second Little Keyboard Book for Anna Magdalena Bach, which served as a collection of study material for the Bach children.[12]

Ornaments in French Harpsichord Music

For modern performers, one of the most distinctive elements of French Baroque keyboard notation is the presence of numerous ornament signs. **Ornaments** are

---

[11] Although Couperin's collection *Les goûts réunis* contains some movements in Italian style, he had made his closest approach to the pure Italian style in several sonatas for instrumental ensemble composed in the 1690s; three of these were included in his later publication *Les nations* (Paris, 1726) alongside a fourth, more recently composed, sonata.

[12] In addition to the Little Keyboard Book for his son Wilhelm Friedemann Bach, J. S. Bach presented his second wife, Anna Magdalena, with two manuscript books of keyboard music, dated 1722 and 1725; both contain suites and individual dances, including many by Bach's contemporaries in the 1725 book.

Figure 11.1 Couperin, *La reine des cœurs*, from *Quatrième livre de pièces de clavecin par Monsieur Couperin* (Paris, 1730). The process of engraving, used for printing this and most other Baroque keyboard music, permitted precise duplication of the composer's signs for ornaments and slurs; the latter take the form of both straight lines (m. 1) and brackets (mm. 3, 4). Note the changing clefs, used to avoid leger lines.

small, stereotyped melodic figures consisting of short notes that decorate a longer one. Such figures can be distinguished from *embellishments*, which involve greater numbers of small note values; embellishments cannot be expressed by simple signs and must therefore be written out. The presence of numerous ornaments and their notation through distinctive signs were defining features of French Baroque style, and composers used a growing number of symbols to indicate precisely which ornaments were to be played. This was especially true for keyboard music, but similar developments occurred in French music for other instruments (such as the viola da gamba) as well. Clearly, French composers had precise intentions about the melodic content of their works, and they expected players to follow them scrupulously.

Despite the proliferation of ornament signs, the basic ornaments were few in number and, probably, quite standard in execution. But the signs and even the names for them varied from one composer to another. For this reason, many French publications included tables explaining what each ornament sign meant. These tables cannot serve as guides to the precise interpretation of the signs, since the exact rhythm of an ornament cannot be precisely notated; that is why symbols were used in the first place! Performers who specialize in this music base their interpretations of the ornament signs on published ornament tables together with information from treatises and other documents, as well as their analysis of the music and their experience performing it.

The anthology (Selection 29) includes extracts from the ornament tables of three important French keyboard composers of the later Baroque: Jean Henry d'Anglebert (1689), François Couperin (1716), and Jean-Philippe Rameau (1724). Rameau apparently based his system on d'Anglebert's, and therefore their ornament signs occupy the first two columns of the table. There are three basic ornaments: the appoggiatura or *port de voix*; the mordent or *pincé*; and the trill or *tremblement*. Most of the remaining entries in the tables represent combinations or variations of these basic ornaments. In addition, there are various types of arpeggiation, some involving the insertion of nonchord tones (acciaccaturas). Couperin used a number of further signs not shown here, including a sort of comma used to mark the ends of certain phrases (as in m. 16 of *La reine des cœurs*).

La reine des cœurs and *La Couperin*

Couperin published his *pièces de clavecin* in numbered suites, of which there are twenty-seven in all. He used the term *ordre* instead of *suite*. But as in the works of other French composers, there is little to unify the movements of each suite, apart from the use of the same key and perhaps a general commonality of style or tone. It is unlikely that players always performed all movements of each suite in their entirety.

The five suites of Couperin's first volume (published 1713) include the traditional dances—allemandes, courantes, sarabandes, and gigues, alongside others—in what had become by 1700 the traditional order. There are numerous character pieces as well, with such titles as "The Bees," "The Sentiments," and "Fanfare for the Followers of Diana"—this last referring to the Roman goddess, and probably also to an actual woman who may or may not have been named Diane. Most of the pieces, dances as well as others, are in binary form; others are *rondeaux*, like the chaconne from Jacquet de La Guerre's A-minor suite (see Chapter 10). By the fourth book (1730), few untitled dances remain, and the suites are shorter. We shall consider two of the five pieces from the *Vingt-unième ordre* (Twenty-first suite; anthology, Selection 30).

The first piece, *La reine des cœurs* (The queen of hearts), is in $\frac{3}{8}$. It is in binary form and has, for the most part, the regular eight-bar phrasing of a minuet. Yet it does not exactly fit any dance type. This point is emphasized by Couperin's tempo indication, which, characteristically for him, is very precise: *Lentement, et très tendrement* (Slowly and very tenderly). The piece's title is the name of a playing card. But it might also have referred to a particular woman—perhaps one whose personality is represented by the piece's musical character (or at least by its tempo mark!).

The same playful use of titles is evident in the third piece from the suite, *La Couperin*, whose title seems to refer to the composer himself.[13] There was a tradition of musician portraits by French composers; Antoine Forqueray

---

[13] The fact that the title uses the feminine form of the French definite article, *la*, is irrelevant, since the word *pièce* is feminine; *all* such titles for Baroque pieces, even those referring to men, are grammatically feminine.

(1672–1745), who played viola da gamba in the royal chamber concerts alongside Couperin, wrote musical portraits not only of Rameau and the violinist Leclair but of himself (these pieces were published posthumously in 1747). Couperin's musical self-portrait bears the modest tempo marking *d'une vivacité modéré* (with moderate vivacity). But to what degree this is or was meant to be a true characterization of Couperin is impossible to say. The piece somewhat resembles an allemande, although its unusual upbeat—a measure containing $2^3/_4$ beats—is not characteristic of that dance or any other. It is, however, in the expected binary form. As in many such pieces, each half begins and ends with similar melodic gestures but is otherwise freely composed.

If one is seeking clues to Couperin's personality, one might note the chromatic bass line at the beginning of the piece (mm. 1–4), with suspensions in the upper voices. This suggests a grieving or at least a deeply emotional character. Yet, the next phrase contains a forceful sequence, the left hand striking octaves in measures 5 and 6. This is more in keeping with the vivacious character implied by the tempo mark, as are the ascending sequences in the piece's second half (mm. 13–14, 18–19). It would be reasonable to conclude that Couperin was a changeable character—or that he has been teasing us by inviting us to see him in this difficult-to-characterize piece.

Both pieces illustrate Couperin's ability to make full use of the idiomatic capabilities of the eighteenth-century French harpsichord. For example, in the second half of measure 2 of *La Couperin*, the upper note in each pair of two sixteenths is held out as an eighth note. This not only brings out the melodic line ($d\sharp''$–e''–$f\sharp''$–g''); it also creates a warmer sonority, contrasting with drier passages such as measures 7–8, where no notes are held out; instead some are marked with staccato signs to ensure crisp performance.

OTHER EIGHTEENTH-CENTURY KEYBOARD COMPOSERS

The eighteenth century saw a tremendous increase in the composition and publication of instrumental music, including keyboard works. By 1760 or so this had turned into a flood as composers and publishers catered to a growing amateur market. The later development of this trend lies beyond our scope, for the music in question is increasingly closer to what we call the Classical and even the Romantic styles than to what we recognize as Baroque.

Stylistically, much of this music, even French examples from the first half of the century, reflects the ongoing transition from Baroque to Classical style, which included a diminishing focus on counterpoint and the adoption of textures and formal plans derived from the sonata for instrumental ensemble—an Italian genre. Nevertheless, the distinctions between French and Italian style that had been clear since the mid-seventeenth century remain discernible well into the latter part of the eighteenth century, the time of Haydn amd Mozart—both of whom were essentially Italianate in their adherence to a style characterized by virtuosity and "singing" melody, as opposed to French "speaking" types of melody and dance rhythm.

Two composers whose works represented the opposing styles as the middle of the century approached are Rameau, whose vocal music we saw in Chapter 8, and Domenico Scarlatti (1685–1757). The son of Alessandro Scarlatti (see Chapter 5), Domenico began his career writing operas and sacred vocal music at Rome. In 1720 he took a position in Lisbon as harpsichord teacher of Maria Barbara, princess of Portugal, following her to Seville and later Madrid after she married crown prince Ferdinand of Spain. Scarlatti's keyboard music consists of over 500 one-movement sonatas, whereas Rameau's comprises several suites of pieces, most of them, like Couperin's, bearing descriptive titles. These are as distinctly French in style as Couperin's pieces, treating the instrument sensitively in music that shows considerable eloquence and expressive use of harmony (as in *L'Enharmonique*, characterized by enharmonic progressions). Yet even in his keyboard dances, Rameau adopts elements of Italian style shared with Domenico Scarlatti.

One such element is the use of virtuosity to create dramatic gestures, displayed most spectacularly in **hand crossing,** where one hand flies over the other to play notes at the extreme upper or lower end of the keyboard. Even Bach employed this device in a few pieces, notably the Goldberg Variations (where the crossing hands usually play on separate keyboards). Rameau made a special point of using the technique in a piece called *Les trois mains* (The three hands, Ex. 11.2a). Another piece using the same device is *L'Egyptienne*, whose title refers not, as one might think, to an Egyptian girl, but rather to a gypsy, or Roma, woman (reflecting the same interest in ethnicity seen in Rameau's *Indes galantes*). *L'Egyptienne* also includes other virtuoso devices,

Example 11.2 Rameau, (a) *Les trois mains*, mm. 1–6; (b) *L'Egyptienne,* mm. 1–4 and 11–14. Asterisks indicate points where hands cross; "l.h." = left hand. For the meaning of the ornament signs, see anthology, Selection 29.

Example 11.3 Domenico Scarlatti, (a) hand crossings and leaps from Sonata in A, K. 182, mm. 35–41; (b) acciaccaturas from Sonata in A, K. 181, mm. 57–60 and 96–100. Double asterisks signify the presence of acciaccaturas.

including rapid alternations of two hands on the same note, which Rameau called *batteries* (mm. 12 and 14 in Ex. 11.2b). Both pieces, like most of Rameau's, are substantial works, much longer than the typical binary-form dance of the seventeenth century.

The same is true of Scarlatti's one-movement sonatas. These go beyond Rameau in their demands on the player, incorporating not only hand crossings but wild leaps and other technical challenges. They also incorporate sometimes startling harmonic progressions and dissonant nonharmonic tones (acciaccaturas). Example 11.3 shows relatively modest examples from a pair of sonatas in A major, K. 181–82; far more extreme instances occur in other works.[14] Yet despite their remarkable technical and harmonic innovations, virtually all of Scarlatti's sonatas fall into the same binary form used for the majority of pieces by Rameau and other French composers. Scarlatti treats this form with extraordinary inventiveness, often ignoring norms followed by Rameau and other contemporaries, such as the use of similar motivic material at the beginning of each half. Together, the two composers demonstrate the very different sorts of music that could emerge within the type of rational, symmetrical design favored by eighteenth-century musicians generally.

---

[14]Scarlatti's sonatas bear numbers assigned (in roughly chronological order) by the American harpsichordist Ralph Kirkpatrick. Many of these works are preserved as pairs of sonatas in a common key; probably the most extreme examples of both hand crossing and dissonant acciaccaturas occur in the pair K. 119–20 in D.

CHAPTER 12

MUSIC FOR INSTRUMENTAL ENSEMBLE I
The Sonata

The sonatas, concertos, and other instrumental genres of the seventeenth and eighteenth centuries are among the most familiar parts of the Baroque repertory. A number of them, mostly works from the first half of the eighteenth century, such as J. S. Bach's flute sonatas and the Vivaldi violin concertos known as *The Four Seasons*, have long been in the modern concert repertory and are among the first examples of "early music" encountered by many musicians and listeners. This chapter focuses on the sonata, which by 1650 or so had become the chief genre in the Italian style of instrumental music for smaller ensembles (two to five or six instuments). Chapter 13 focuses on the concerto, also an Italian genre, which emerged later and involved newer types of virtuoso writing and scoring.

Isolated examples of polyphonic music for instrumental ensemble are preserved from the fourteenth century and perhaps earlier. But a vigorous tradition of composing such music, as opposed to various unwritten traditions, dates from only the sixteenth century. Even then, the repertory, consisting chiefly of dances and contrapuntal pieces such as fantasias, was usually written for unspecified instruments. Composers did not concern themselves with the actual instrumental sonorities, and any idiomatic instrumental effects or melodic decoration would have been added improvisatorily by the players. Around the turn of the seventeenth century, composers such as Giovanni Gabrieli began not only to specify the instrumental participants in their ensemble music but also to use idiomatic devices particular to one instrument or another. Some composers, including Gabrieli and Frescobaldi, did so only occasionally; most of their ensemble canzonas and sonatas remain for unspecified instruments. Others, however, explored the possibility of writing music that exploited the capabilities of particular instruments.

For the first time, it became necessary for composers to be familiar with instruments—their ranges, techniques, and the types of figuration that each can and cannot play conveniently. Nowadays it is taken for granted that learning such things is part of the training of a composer, but that view emerged only gradually in the course of the seventeenth century, as the number of instruments routinely employed in serious music making increased. Although preceding chapters have included remarks about instruments, it will be useful to summarize some of the main features of the instruments most frequently used in seventeenth- and eighteenth-century music for instrumental ensemble before proceeding to the works themselves.

THE CHIEF ENSEMBLE INSTRUMENTS OF THE BAROQUE

String Instruments

The **violin** family, already in widespread use for dance music during the sixteenth century, had become the main instrumental component of French and Italian ensemble music by the mid-seventeenth century. Music for the quieter lute and viola da gamba continued to be composed well into the eighteenth century, but these instruments could not compete in volume with the violin, which therefore dominated the ensemble genres of sonata, concerto, and overture. The viol and the violin represent distinct families of bowed string instruments that both emerged around the late fifteenth century; the viol was not a predecessor of the violin. The Renaissance and Baroque members of the violin family were distinct from their modern counterparts, with different construction and different performance techniques (Fig. 12.1). Technique and construction varied with time and place; for instance, distinct types of bows and performance practice were associated with the French and the Italian styles, respectively, of the seventeenth century.

The French style, which centered on the playing of overtures and dances in Lullian opera and ballet, emphasized tightly controlled ornaments, precise articulation, and rhythmic exactness. Ensembles such as the Twenty-Four Violins of the French king were renowned for their rhythmic precision and unanimity of ensemble. These characteristics of the French style were reinforced by performance conventions that all members of the ensemble had to master. For instance, the so-called rule of downbow required players to use downward bow strokes on downbeats. This led to frequent retaking of the bow, which was facilitated by the relatively short bows used in French violin playing. Italian playing, on the other hand, emphasized fluent passagework in quick movements and sustained melodic lines in slow movements; the latter was encouraged by the somewhat longer bow favored by Italian players. Both traditions differed from present-day playing in the more restricted use of vibrato and the more frequent use of open strings—which were of gut, not metal—and of low left-hand positions generally. It would be wrong, however, to conclude that Baroque violin playing involved a lesser degree of virtuosity than that of later periods. Italian-style works from throughout the Baroque include difficult passagework in high positions, sometimes involving exotic bow strokes. Even in the French style, the required precision of ornamentation and rhythm makes considerable technical demands.

The Baroque **viola**, which furnished as many as three inner parts in some ensembles (including the Twenty-Four Violins), tended to be somewhat larger than later examples although normally tuned the same way, a fifth below the violin.

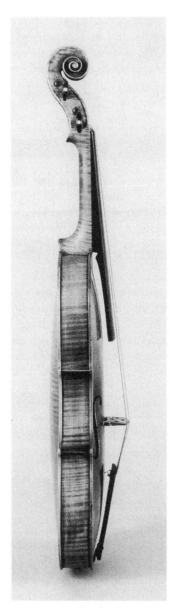

Figure 12.1 Violin by Jacob Stainer, Absam bei Innsbruck (Austria), 1668. National Music Museum, Vermillion, South Dakota, Board of Trustees in memory of Arne B. and Jeanne F. Larson, 1989 (no. 4548). The violinist-composer Heinrich Biber owned a violin by this maker, from whom he also ordered instruments for his employers at Kroměříž and Salzburg. Note the relatively short neck, which forms a straight line with the body of the instrument. On modern violins the neck is longer and angled back, and most surviving instruments from the Baroque, unlike this one, have been altered accordingly. See Figure 1.4 for a typically short Baroque bow.

(The four strings of the violin are tuned g, d′, a′, and e″; of the viola, c, g, d′, and a′.) The **cello** was a late addition to the violin family; it was made possible by new technologies in string making that allowed a relatively small instrument to play in the bass register (the cello's four strings are tuned C, G, d, and a). The cello gradually replaced the **bass violin**, a larger instrument that originally descended only to G or F but by the seventeenth century often went down to B♭′. The two instruments might have coexisted in some ensembles during the later seventeenth century, with the cello—sometimes equipped with a fifth string (d″ or e″) and sometimes held on the shoulder, like a violin—functioning as a soloist.

Double-bass instruments, used to play bass lines an octave lower than written, were rare in Baroque ensembles before the eighteenth century. The word *violone*, found in many Baroque scores, literally means "big string instrument" and can refer to the bass violin, cello, or bass viola da gamba, not necessarily a true double bass.[1] Sometimes, as in Schütz's music and perhaps even some of Bach's earlier works, the word may indicate an extra-large bass viola da gamba descending down to G′. By the eighteenth century, however, true double-bass instruments going down to D′ or even C′ were being used in larger ensembles. Their precise construction and technique varied, but the instrument usually retained characteristics of the viol family, such as tuning in fourths rather than fifths (as is true of the modern double bass, normally tuned E′, A′, D, G).

Modern players and instrument builders have reconstructed the various techniques and types of instrument and bow used in the Baroque. As with keyboards, they have relied heavily on surviving instruments and on documentary sources. Notable among the latter are the prefaces to several collections of suites and sonatas for instrumental ensemble by the organist-composer Georg Muffat (1653–1704). Muffat knew both Lully and Corelli before taking up positions at Salzburg and later Passau in southern Germany. Thus he was able to provide instructions for playing in both the French and Italian styles of the late seventeenth century. A treatise by a later Salzburg composer, Mozart's father Leopold (1719–87), is of great value to understanding violin playing in the first half of the eighteenth century although published as late as 1756.[2]

The predominance of the violin in Baroque instrumental music gave it a vast repertory of sonatas, concertos, and other works, and violinist-composers were among the most important writers of instrumental music, especially in Italy. Sonatas and other works with solo cello parts also were written, beginning in the late seventeenth century (see Chapter 13), and there is a small eighteenth-century repertory with parts for solo viola, mainly by German composers. Other string instruments continued to be cultivated alongside members of the violin family. In the early seventeenth century, composers in France, England, and Italy continued to write polyphonic fantasias and other works for combinations of one or more viols with lute, organ, or harp. Solos and duos for viola da gamba (with and without continuo) continued to appear in France and Germany well into the eighteenth century.

Woodwinds

Renaissance woodwinds included both flutes and double reeds. Most types were built in bass to soprano and even sopranino (piccolo) sizes, so that complete

---

[1]The word *violoncello*, which we usually abbreviate to *cello*, actually means "small big string instrument"—that is, a small version of the violone.

[2]See bibliography under "Instruments and Instrumental Practice" for editions and translations of Muffat's and Mozart's writings.

ensembles or **consorts** could be assembled from various sizes of a single type of instrument, as was also done in the case of the violin and viol. This became less true during the Baroque, when the higher members of the woodwind families came to be used as solo instruments while the lower ones, with the exception of the bassoon, were abandoned or limited to occasional use. Like their Renaissance counterparts, Baroque woodwinds were built almost entirely of wood, metal being used only for a few keys on certain types or sizes of instrument.

In the seventeenth century, woodwinds were employed mainly to add color or contrast in works for string-based ensembles, or as optional alternates to members of the violin family in sonatas and other pieces. It is likely that woodwind consorts were also used, as in previous centuries, for impromptu transcriptions of music originally scored for voices or other instruments and in unwritten dance music. Sonatas, concertos, and other works with idiomatic solo woodwind parts

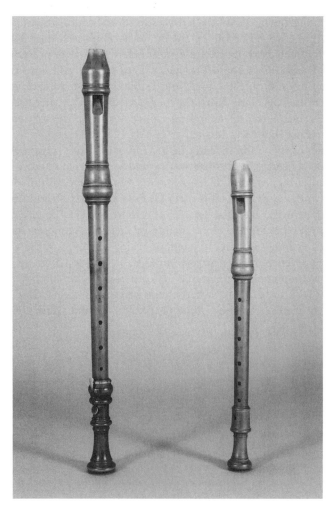

Figure 12.2 Alto and tenor recorders by Jacob Denner, Imperial City of Nürnberg (Nuremberg, Germany), ca. 1715. Ex coll.: Albrecht Kleinschmidt, Neu Ulm, Germany. National Music Museum, Vermillion, South Dakota. Purchase funds gift of Cindy and Tom Lillibridge, Bonesteel, South Dakota, and Linda and John Lillibridge, Burke, South Dakota, 1997 (nos. 6043–4). A single key on the larger (tenor) instrument allows the player to reach the lowest of the seven tone holes (an eighth hole for the thumb is on the back of the instrument).

were first composed in significant numbers only in the early eighteenth century, using forms and styles similar to those found in music for strings.

Eighteenth-century woodwind players normally mastered more than one type of instrument and were often expected to double on two or more (e.g., oboe and recorder), sometimes switching between instruments within a single multimovement work. As in string playing, great emphasis was placed on the precise articulation of notes and the controlled performance of ornaments. The eighteenth century saw the publication of numerous instructional manuals for woodwind instruments, especially the recorder and flute, reflecting the popularity of the latter among amateurs. Among these are the flute treatises of the French composer Jacques Hotteterre (1674–1763) and the German flutist, composer, and flute maker Johann Joachim Quantz (1697–1773).

Flutes included both **recorders,** held downward (Fig. 12.2), and **transverse flutes,** held sideways like the modern flute (Fig. 12.3). Both types date back

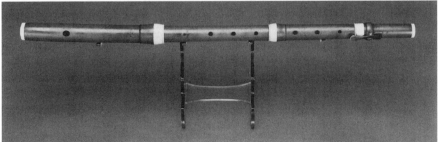

Figure 12.3 Transverse flute by Philip Borkens, Amsterdam, ca. 1725–50, its three pieces shown disassembled (above) and mounted on a display stand (below). National Music Museum, Vermillion, South Dakota. Board of Trustees, 1994 (no. 5795). The single key, absent on older seventeenth-century instruments, is for E♭.

at least to the early Renaissance. Older transverse flutes have a sweet or mellow, usually very quiet, sound, and a relatively limited range, which made them less practical for combination with louder instruments than the more brilliant and versatile recorder. But the eighteenth century saw the introduction of more powerful flutes that were, in addition, equal in virtuoso capability to the violin and other instruments. During the first third of the eighteenth century, composers employed both recorders and flutes in a large and varied repertory, in both solo and ensemble capacities. In addition to many sonatas and concertos, early-eighteenth-century composers wrote large numbers of arias in operas and cantatas that contain flute and recorder parts. After 1740 or so the latter instrument virtually disappeared, but until then the word *flute* most often referred to the recorder. Thus the *flûtes* or *flauti* called for in scores from Lully to J. S. Bach are usually recorders, not flutes, although both composers also used the transverse instrument, specifying it by *flûte d'Allemagne, flauto traverso*, or an equivalent expression.[3] Present-day players often substitute the nineteenth-century silver flute in both recorder and flute parts.

Both types of flute were already undergoing substantial changes in the late seventeenth century, gaining expanded ranges and somewhat greater volume as well. Keys, at first entirely absent, were gradually added to the transverse flute over the course of the eighteenth period. But until well after 1750, most transverse flutes had but a single key (those built by Quantz have two), and both types of flute, like all Baroque winds, were easy to play in only a limited number of tonalities. The transverse flute was most often used in tonalities that employ sharps in their key signatures, whereas the recorder was more commonly used in "flat" keys. Such patterns should not be understood as limitations; the association of an instrument with particular keys was as much a part of each instrument as its range and tone color. Composers made good use of these instrumental characteristics, occasionally writing for instruments in "bad" keys in order to create special timbral effects or to give virtuosos a chance to display their mastery of difficult keys. In his *St. John Passion* Bach included flutes in an aria in F minor ("Zerfließe, mein Herze"), using the instruments' dark, somewhat muted color when played in that key to deepen the mournful effect of the aria.

The chief double reed of the Renaissance, the **shawm**, had been a somewhat raucous instrument employed mainly in loud dance music. Like the flutes, it was built in several sizes, and seventeenth-century shawm bands sometimes served a military function, reflected in the use of double reeds for marches and similar music in theatrical works (cf. Fig. 12. 4). But Lully and later composers required a more refined instrument for use in opera and ballet: the result was the **oboe**, believed to have been developed from the shawm by seventeenth-century Dutch instrument makers (Fig. 12.5 and 12.6). By 1700 the oboe had become the chief woodwind instrument, often doubling the violins in larger ensembles and possessing a growing chamber music repertory as well.

---

[3]An exception occurs in works of the early eighteenth-century Dresden composers Johann David Heinichen, Johann Adolph Hasse, and others, for whom *flute* usually means the transverse flute.

Figure 12.4 Banquet for the coronation of Louis XIV with a double-reed ensemble, 7 June 1654, engraving from Antoine Lepautre, *Le sacre et couronnement de Louis XIV* (Paris, 1717). A band of oboes and bassoons or other double-reed instruments, used for military and ceremonial functions, was employed at the French court throughout the Baroque. The repertory probably consisted largely of dances from ballets and operas.

Like flutes and recorders, oboes were built in various sizes, each playing at a different pitch and favoring particular keys. The regular oboe of the later Baroque had middle C as its lowest note and was, like the recorder, especially favored in "flat" keys. A tenor form, known by the French word *taille* (which could in fact refer to any tenor part), was pitched a fifth lower; a version of the same instrument with a flaring metal bell was known as the **oboe da caccia.** German composers, including Bach, also used an alto instrument based on the note a and used primarily in "sharp" keys; this is called the **oboe d'amore.**

The **bassoon,** another double-reed instrument employed since the later Baroque as the bass of the oboe family, has a distinct history, being derived from the seventeenth-century curtal and dulcian. Bach and his contemporaries in Germany knew both the *Fagott*, usually as part of the continuo group, and the *basson*; the words, used in modern German and French, respectively, for the bassoon, were apparently applied to two different instruments. The *basson*, the more modern one, joins the oboes as the bass of Bach's double-reed group, a practice derived from that of Lully. A double-bass instrument corresponding to the modern contrabassoon was occasionally used to double the bass line in works for

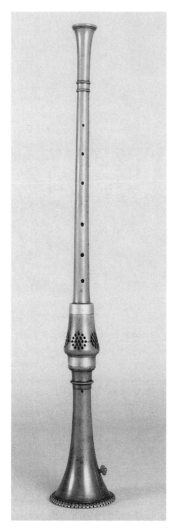

Figure 12.5 Deutsche schalmei by Richard Haka, Amsterdam, ca. 1690. National Music Museum, Vermillion, South Dakota. Board of Trustees, 1988 (no. 4545). Still close in many respects to the sixteenth-century shawm, instruments similar to this one (shown without its double reed) would have furnished the upper line in the ensemble depicted in Figure 12.4 or in Lully's early ballets. Differing only in details, the Baroque oboe was already in use in France when this instrument was made by one of the leading Dutch woodwind makers of his time.

very large ensemble. Early-Baroque sonatas sometimes include solo parts for bassoon-like double-reed instruments, but during the later Baroque such instruments are largely confined to bass lines. Vivaldi, however, wrote many bassoon concertos, and during the later eighteenth century bassoons, often employed in pairs, came to have independent parts in symphonies and other orchestral works.

The **clarinet**, a single-reed instrument, originated in the early eighteenth century as a refined version of the *chalumeau*. The eighteenth-century clarinet retained much of the older instrument's strident, trumpetlike character—hence the name, derived from the Italian word for a high trumpet (*clarino*). Clarinet parts occur occasionally in sonatas, concertos, and opera arias from the first half of the eighteenth century, including works by Vivaldi and Handel, who used it as a sort of substitute for the trumpet in keys unsuitable for that instrument.

Figure 12.6 Oboe by Jan Steenbergen, Amsterdam, ca. 1725. National Music Museum, Vermillion, South Dakota, purchase funds gift of Julie and Chris Bauer, Yankton, South Dakota, 1997 (no. 6089). A direct descendent of the instrument shown in Figure 12.5, this type of oboe (shown here without its reed) was used during the first half of the eighteenth century.

But the clarinet did not become a regular member of most orchestral ensembles until the late eighteenth century.

Brass Instruments

Baroque Brass instruments included trumpets, horns, and trombones; each had distinct uses. Because of their role as military signal instruments, trumpets (along with timpani) were generally played by members of special ensembles that were distinct from any other musical ensembles maintained by a given court or city (Fig.12.7). The horn originally resembled a coiled trumpet; it was used for signaling during the court hunts that were an important part of aristocratic life in the Baroque, and for this reason the instrument was often referred to as the *corno da caccia* (hunting horn).

Baroque **trumpets** and **horns** were both **natural** instruments: they lacked keys or valves and thus were confined largely to playing the harmonic overtones of a single **fundamental** pitch. As a result, each example of these instruments could play essentially only in one major key, and even then the complete scale of the key was available only at the very top of the range; in lower registers the instrument was restricted to notes of the tonic triad (see Ex. 9.2). Individual members of the traditional trumpet ensemble specialized in playing in the high,

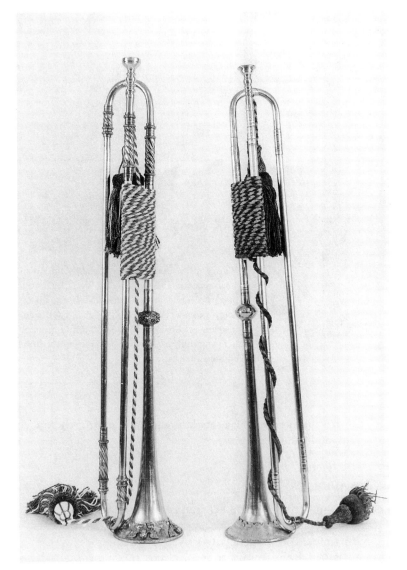

Figure 12.7 Two trumpets by Johann Wilhelm Haas, Nuremberg, ca. 1690–1710 (right) and ca. 1710–20 (left). National Music Museum, Vermillion, South Dakota, Board of Trustees, 1985 (nos. 3600–1). Note the absence of valves, typical of brass instruments before the nineteenth century. The Baroque trumpet was also made in a coiled shape.

middle, or low portion of the range; eighteenth-century orchestral parts tended to use the trumpet only in the highest part of its range, where the instrument was designated the *clarino*. As with woodwinds, the technical features of the natural instruments should not be considered limitations. Baroque trumpeters developed a sophisticated technique that permitted them to produce notes of exceptional purity throughout their range and to play complex passagework in the top register. Composers took advantage of this, occasionally using nonharmonic tones for special effect (as we have seen in Bach's Cantata 127).

Composers nevertheless tended to use trumpets only for grand or ceremonial music in major keys, especially C and D. Works with independent trumpet parts are rare until the late seventeenth century, which saw the development of a substantial repertory of works for one or two trumpets with strings, mostly from Italy but with examples from Germany and England as well. Like woodwinds, trumpets were often used in pairs, but Bach and some other eighteenth-century German composers frequently wrote for them in three parts, joined by timpani. The virtuoso *clarino* technique developed by Baroque trumpeters in Italy and Germany appears to have been largely lost after 1750; the trumpet parts in Classical works are relatively simple and in some cases even optional. By the end of the eighteenth century, instrument builders were experimenting with the use of keys and later of valves, which eventually led to the fully chromatic trumpet of the nineteenth-century orchestra. Modern players sometimes use so-called Bach trumpets for eighteenth-century *clarino* parts, but these small valved trumpets lack the rich sonority and pure intonation that the natural instrument possesses when properly played.

The horn underwent a development parallel to that of the trumpet, although it was rarely used in serious music before the early eighteenth century. After 1700 natural horns quickly became common members of orchestral ensembles. At first they tended to be restricted, like the trumpet, to particular keys—especially F—and to special types of piece, such as marches and arias sung by hunting characters. But through various techniques, such as the use of "stopped" tones (produced by inserting the hand into the bell of the instrument), horn players could attain a nearly complete chromatic scale. In addition, by substituting metal tubes of varying lengths (called *crooks*) for a portion of the instrument's length they could alter the pitch of the instrument, enabling it to play in any key. By 1750 the combination of two horns and two oboes had become the standard wind complement of the string orchestra, a practice that continued into the Classical style. Valved horns were invented early in the nineteenth century, but many composers continued to specify the natural instrument, and like the natural trumpet it has been revived today for use in eighteenth-century music.

The Baroque **trombone** remained close to its Renaissance version, the **sackbut.** Like the latter, the trombone continued to be built in several sizes that could constitute a complete choir, like the early woodwinds. The soprano part of the trombone ensemble, however, was usually supplied by the **cornetto,** a woodwind instrument fitted with a brass-style cupped mouthpiece. Despite their very different ways of producing sound, the two instruments blend well together, and each is fully chromatic over a wide range. Thus Bach employed cornetto and three trombones to double the four vocal parts in several highly chromatic choral movements in his cantatas.

In the early Baroque, especially in Italy, the cornetto was an important solo instrument, with a repertory of sonatas and other works rivaling that of the violin. It became rare in the eighteenth century, although for a time Bach and other German composers continued to use it. Much the same holds for the trombone, which appears in numerous seventeenth-century sonatas but rarely in chamber or orchestral music of the later Baroque. Cornetto-and-trombone ensembles nevertheless had a special use throughout the Baroque in many cities of Italy and Germany, furnishing ceremonial music for civic events and playing for the public at specified times from watchtowers or other public sites. For this reason there exists a seventeenth-century repertory of dances and march-like pieces for these instruments. They were also used in opera and ballet, although the trombone ensemble tended to be associated with scenes in which a solemn effect was desired, as in the underworld scenes in Monteverdi's *Orfeo*. Trombones and cornettos were also frequently used in sacred choral music, as in the works of Gabrieli (see Chapter 7); later composers, such as Bach, used them, particularly in old-fashioned works in the *stile antico*.

A number of German composers, including Bach, occasionally used a type of **slide trumpet**. Such an instrument, a hybrid between the trumpet and the trombone, could play a complete scale even in its lower register. But it lacked agility and was therefore usually restricted to playing slow-moving cantus firmus lines, as in the opening movements of Bach's chorale cantatas.

Percussion Instruments

Percussion parts were rarely written out until the early eighteenth century, and then chiefly for the **timpani** or kettledrums, which had traditionally served as the bass instrument of the trumpet ensemble. Earlier works that include trumpets—certain sacred works for large ensembles and theatrical marches and battle scenes—might have included improvised timpani parts. Other percussion instruments must have been employed in dances and marches and for special effects in theatrical works, but their use was rarely specified by composers.

The Scoring of Instrumental Works

The types of orchestral ensemble heard in Baroque opera, cantata, and other large-scale vocal works were also used in purely instrumental compositions. But permanent large orchestral ensembles were rare, especially before 1700, and even in the eighteenth century were largely restricted to opera houses and court chapels in the major capitals, such as Paris, Vienna, and Dresden. Such ensembles, dominated by strings, were characterized by multiple violinists, usually divided into two parts, as well as a large group of continuo instruments. By the eighteenth century the continuo group in such an ensemble might have included several cellos and other bass string instruments as well as several keyboard and lute-type instruments. Naturally, the size of the continuo group varied in proportion to the size of the ensemble as a whole. Within a movement, the continuo group might be reduced for lightly scored passages; Bach, for example, often limited the violone (string double bass) to the ritornellos of his arias, retaining only the cello and keyboard in the continuo part in passages where the voice sings.

Winds, initially rare, were already used for color in Lully's operas and were gradually added to ensembles elsewhere, beginning with pairs of oboes, bassoons, and horns. Nevertheless, much Baroque instrumental music, even eighteenth-century works played by large ensembles, consists essentially of just one or two violin parts with continuo, winds and violas either doubling one of those lines or adding simple "filler" parts. This was particularly true in the Italian style; French composers retained the traditional five-part string scoring of the Twenty-Four Violins of the King into the eighteenth century, and German composers, such as Bach, favored complex counterpoint in which even the viola has a melodically independent role. When composers did write for larger numbers of independent parts—as in certain types of sonata and concerto—they often employed the polychoral scoring found in the canzonas and sonatas of Gabrieli. In effect, the strings served as the main choir, to which brass or woodwind choirs might be added. For example, in the last two of Bach's orchestral suites the four-part string group is joined by a double-reed group (two or three oboes and bassoon) and a brass group (three trumpets and timpani).

Woodwind and brass players usually doubled on several different instruments. For this reason, even large ensembles rarely included more than a few wind players; as in a modern jazz ensemble, wind players were expected to switch from one instrument to another as needed. Thus the same piece rarely calls simultaneously for trumpets and horns, or for flutes, recorders, and oboes. Moreover, each of these instruments tends to be used only in certain keys; thus trumpets, for example, rarely occur outside pieces in C or D major, and neither trumpets nor horns are often used in slow movements or works in minor keys. Smaller instrumental works used a considerable variety of scorings, some of them discussed below. Like works for larger ensembles, these usually included a continuo part, which in the eighteenth century was most often played by a bowed string (cello) or bassoon alongside a keyboard or lute-type instrument. In some repertories the upper parts might also be doubled as well, turning what we would call chamber works, for a single player on each part, into orchestral pieces. Nevertheless, most Baroque instrumental works, including the concertos and sinfonias examined in Chapter 13, remained playable by a single performer on each part. Undoubled performance may even have been preferred in most such works, which were typically played in relatively small spaces, including private homes, as opposed to theaters or large churches.

TYPES OF BAROQUE MUSIC FOR INSTRUMENTAL ENSEMBLE

We have already encountered several types of instrumental music cultivated during the Baroque. The sinfonia that opens the Scarlatti cantata (Chapter 5) is essentially a small sonata for two violins and continuo; the operas by Lully and Handel both include French overtures, and Lully's operas contain numerous dances as well.

Apart from the overture and the sinfonia, dances and sonatas were the most important genres of seventeenth-century music for instrumental ensemble, joined at the very end of the century by the concerto. The earliest sonatas were published in collections that also contained dances or sacred vocal music, implying that sonatas were heard in church as well as at court and in private homes. Early examples were probably intended for performance by professionals, but by the end of the Baroque easy sonatas were being published in large numbers for amateur use.

The idea of sacred instrumental music may seem a contradiction in terms. But in Roman Catholic countries, sections of the mass or office could be replaced by pieces for organ or for instrumental ensemble. Italian composers from Gabrieli onward wrote innumerable sonatas and other works for this purpose, and by the eighteenth century sonatas for the church were sometimes distinguished by the Italian words **da chiesa,** as in the expression *sonata da chiesa* (church sonata). Church concertos (*concerti da chiesa*) were also written. Musically, there is little that is distinctly sacred or religious in character about such pieces, although a sonata or concerto *da chiesa* might be more likely to include fugal movements, whose contrapuntal texture recalled the quasi-Renaissance *stile antico*, used in sacred vocal music throughout the seventeenth and eighteenth centuries.

In Italy, music *da chiesa* was regarded as contrasting with music **da camera:** literally, music "for the chamber," which today may suggest private domestic or home use but at the time probably also pointed to performance in concerts sponsored by learned academies and similar gatherings. (The term is the source of the modern expression *chamber music.*) Instrumental works originally composed for the church could also be performed at home, and thus there was frequent blurring of the theoretical distinction between sacred and secular instrumental music. Much music was published with titles indicating that it was appropriate for both uses, although works for the "chamber" were often distinguished by the presence of dances and other movements that had originated in opera, ballet, and other theatrical genres.

The Sonata

The **sonata** originated in Italy around 1600 and at first could be almost any sort of work for instrumental ensemble; the Italian word *sonata*, literally meaning "played," contrasted with *toccata* ("touched"), referring to pieces for keyboard or lute, and *cantata* ("sung"), used for vocal chamber music. After 1650 or so the sonata could be defined as a work for a relatively small number of instruments, usually serious in nature and comprising several sections in contrasting tempos or meters. As such it displaced earlier types of Italian instrumental chamber music, especially the *canzona* and *fantasia.* By the end of the seventeenth century the short sections of the earliest sonatas had become self-contained movements that could stand on their own, although they might be connected by short transitional passages (usually slow in tempo). A century later, in what we call the Classical period, the instrumental sonata had become typically a three-movement work, with movements in the order fast-slow-fast. But only after 1720 or so did any such standardization begin to emerge. Works entitled sonata could contain anywhere from one to a dozen or more sections or movements falling in any conceivable order, ranging in length from a few measures to five minutes or more.

Baroque sonatas could be for any number of instruments, although after 1650 the greatest number are for one or two high instruments—most often violins—with continuo. Today sonatas for a single instrument plus continuo are often described as **solo sonatas;** those for two melody instruments and continuo are called **trio sonatas,** since they consist of three distinct lines of music—even though the continuo part might involve two or more players. These expressions are useful for eighteenth-century works, but they obscure the distinctions made earlier in the Baroque between solos, duos, trios, and other types of scoring. In common to all these types was the assumption that a single instrument normally plays each part, with a single continuo instrument—a keyboard or plucked string instrument—accompanying. This reflects the fact that these types of sonatas originated in northern Italy as the instrumental equivalents to the vocal solos, duos, and trios with continuo that also emerged there during the early seventeenth century.

String instruments dominate these early sonatas, but parts are also found for cornetto, trombone, and dulcian or curtal. A century later, the genre had spread across Europe and many of its original conventions had changed. Dance pieces, originally a separate genre, were often incorporated as movements into sonatas, and sonatas were being composed for flute, oboe, and other woodwinds. Nevertheless, for the first century of its existence, the sonata was largely an Italian phenomenon, cultivated in Italy and by imitators of Italian music in England and the German-speaking parts of Europe. Only shortly before 1700 did French composers such as Couperin adopt the genre, and others such as Rameau continued to avoid it completely. But within a few decades French publishers were issuing sonatas for flute, violin, and other instruments in numbers as great as anywhere.

The Concerto

In addition to sonatas, Italian composers wrote sinfonias, which could serve as overtures for cantatas and operas and also as independent instrumental pieces (see Chapter 13). Toward the end of the seventeenth century the inclusion of solo brass or string parts within some sinfonias led to the emergence of a new genre, the instrumental **concerto.** Previously the term *concerto* had been used for music that combined voices and instruments; in the nineteenth century, the same word would refer to a work featuring a soloist who plays alongside a full symphony orchestra. Eighteenth-century concertos, however, are usually for smaller ensembles, in which one or more soloists are joined by additional players in certain passages.

Not all Baroque concertos contain distinct solo parts. Some early concertos are simply sonatas with amplified instrumentation, recalling the vocal concertos of the seventeenth century, which may include optional *capella* parts that double or accompany the soloists. But by 1720 or so the word *concerto* had acquired the modern meaning of a multimovement work for one or more soloists and a larger ensemble. Most often there are three movements in the order fast-slow-fast, which remained the norm through the nineteenth century. The individual movements of such works most often employed a version of ritornello form, similar to that used in the arias of Italian opera and cantata, thus accommodating the display of a virtuoso soloist or soloists.[4]

The earliest concertos are for string ensembles with continuo, and in the first half of the eighteenth century concertos for solo violin and string ensemble are by far the most common type. But by 1720 concertos were being composed for all manner of solo instruments, both singly and in various combinations. Like the sonata, the concerto was regarded as an Italian genre, but whereas French composers such as Couperin and Jacquet de La Guerre were composing sonatas by the end of the seventeenth century, they were slower to adopt the forthright virtuosity of the Italian concerto. The violinist Jean-Marie Leclair (1697–1764), apparently trained in Italy, wrote some remarkable concertos and sonatas for flute as well as his own instrument, but Couperin and Rameau avoided the concerto entirely.[5]

Dance, Overture and Suite

The sixteenth century had seen a flourishing tradition of dance music both for solo instruments (lute and keyboard) and for four- or five-part instrumental ensemble. This tradition continued in the Baroque; we have seen in Chapters 6 and 10 how dances such as the courante and chaconne were incorporated into French opera and adapted for lute and keyboard. During the early Baroque, the same Italian publications that included "solo" and "trio" sonatas often included dances as well, and collections of dances for larger ensembles continued to be published. Sometimes these ensemble dances were grouped into suites, as in the *Banchetto musicale* (Musical banquet) for five-part instrumental ensemble, published in 1617 by the German composer Johann Hermann Schein (1586–1630).

The overtures and dances from Lully's operas and ballets proved enormously popular. Such works were often performed as independent instrumental pieces not only in France but in Germany, where the term *Ouverture* came to refer not only to the overture itself but to a complete suite in the French style. Among the composers of such music were Muffat, Handel, and J. S. Bach, whose works for larger ensembles, such as the four *ouvertures* of Bach, are often referred to today as **orchestral suites**.[6]

---

[4]An important category of Baroque concerto that lacks solo parts is scored for four-part string ensemble and continuo; these are sometimes termed **ripieno concertos** or *concerti a quattro*. Occasionally, works for smaller ensembles or even for a single instrument were designated concertos (as in Bach's *Italian Concerto* for solo harpsichord).

[5]Rameau's *concerts* are actually *pièces de clavecin* with optional parts for violin or flute and viola da gamba.

[6]Handel's orchestral suite *The Water Music* is so called because portions of it are thought to have been performed for King George I by musicians seated in a barge on the River Thames during a so-called water party in 1713.

During the later Baroque, works for smaller ensembles, including sonatas, often took the form of suites as well, incorporating movements in the style of overtures and dances. This is particularly true of French chamber music, which includes a large repertory of pieces for viola da gamba and continuo. Marin Marais (1656–1728), the leading gamba player of his generation, published five books containing suites for his instrument with basso continuo. Like Couperin's *ordres* for harpsichord, these comprise dance movements alongside named character pieces, including a moving *tombeau* for Lully.[7]

The Baroque Sonata

The earliest works to bear the title *sonata* may be some of the pieces for large polychoral ensemble published by Giovanni Gabrieli in Venice just before the turn of the seventeenth century. Similar to his canzonas (see Ex. 7.2), these are somewhat different from the sonatas for smaller ensembles that came to be typical of the genre. Although Venetian musicians continued to be prominent as both players and composers of such works, several other cities in northern Italy—Milan, Mantua, and Bologna—also were important early centers for the sonata. This is not surprising, since the same region was also home to the best early makers and players of the violin, the instrument for which the greatest number of Baroque sonatas would be written. As early as the 1620s, violinist-composers from northern Italy were traveling to politically allied cities such as Vienna and Salzburg, where German-speaking composers soon took up the genre; it would later spread to England, France, and Scandinavia. In the process, not only did the sonata evolve as a compositional genre; virtuoso violinist-composers extended the technique of their instrument to dazzling heights, with corresponding extensions of the expressive and dramatic possibilities of the genre. The most important of these composers, such as Marini and Biber, were not only master players and composers of violin music but significant writers of vocal music as well.

Early seventeenth-century sonatas tend to belong to two quite different types. Most are through-composed, often alternating, like contemporary keyboard toccatas, between improvisatory and contrapuntal passages. Another type consists of variations on popular tunes and ostinato basses. Sonatas of both types appear together in a number of early published collections, which often contain individual dance pieces as well. Eventually, during the latter part of the seventeenth century, dances and variations would become incorporated as individual movements of many sonatas.

From the beginning, variety was an important feature of the Baroque sonata. Early sonata collections include works using diverse types of scoring; only later in the seventeenth century did it become customary to publish homogeneous sets of, say, twelve sonatas for violin and continuo, as Corelli would do. At first,

---

[7]On the French memorial *tombeau*, see Chapter 10. Marais is depicted holding a viola da gamba on the dust jacket of this book.

solo sonatas—that is, *sonate a uno* (sonatas for one part, plus continuo)—were relatively rare. More common were duo sonatas *(sonate a due)*, that is, sonatas for two instruments plus continuo. These might be for two soprano instruments, as in Example 12.1a; we can designate such a work an "SS" sonata. Another possibility, involving one soprano and one bass instrument, as in Example 12.1b, constitutes an "SB" sonata. Both examples are typical in opening with imitation between the two upper parts. Example 12.2 shows a passage from another

Example 12.1 Castello: (a) *Sonata terza a 2*, opening, from *Sonate concertate*, book 2 (Venice, 1629) (b) *Sonata ottava a 2*, opening, from *Sonate concertate*, book 1 (Venice, 1621)

Example 12.2 Salomone Rossi, *Sonata in dialogo La Viena*, mm. 22–36

SS sonata, but here the two upper parts engage in a sort of dialog evidently modeled on contemporary duets for two vocal parts and continuo.

In each of these early types of duo sonata, the continuo—always shown on the bottom staff in modern scores—may double the lower of the two upper parts. But the continuo rarely presents motivic material on its own. Rarely is the instrumentation precisely specified, although the possibilities—violin or cornetto for the upper parts, trombone, "violone," or bassoon-like woodwind for lower ones—would have been clear from the ranges of the individual parts. Theorbo, organ, or harpsichord would have usually furnished the continuo.

Sonatas with three melodic parts might be scored for three high instruments, as in Gabrieli's *Sonata con tre violini* (Ex. 7.3)—an "SSS" work. But more frequently one of the parts is for a bass instrument, as in Example 12.3. An "SSB" sonata of the latter type superficially resembles a duo sonata of the SS type, and in modern terminology both are called "trio sonatas." Yet only in an SSB sonata is there a bass instrument that participates in the counterpoint as an equal partner. In Example 12.3 the bass part introduces a subject which is then imitated by the two upper parts. The bass part may also have solos and other lines independent of the continuo (as in mm. 91ff. of the work shown in anthology, Selection 32).

Other types of scoring also occur in early-Baroque sonatas, which include works for four or more parts as well as echo sonatas in the style of Gabrieli's polychoral *canzoni*. Despite the presence of cornetto, trombone, and bassoon-like instruments in the earliest sonatas, such wind parts become rare in later Italian Baroque sonatas. On the other hand, sonatas and similar types of work with solo trumpet parts emerge in the later seventeenth century, and after 1700 composers of sonatas increasingly took advantage of the new types of woodwinds recently developed in France. Even French composers contributed to what had

Example 12.3 Castello, *Sonata decima a 3*, mm. 16–22, from *Sonate concertate*, book 2 (Venice, 1629)

originally been an Italian genre, as in the sonatas for two flutes and continuo published in 1707 by Michel de La Barre (ca. 1675–1745; see Ex. 12.4).[8]

Eighteenth-century composers in France, England, and Germany would eventually compose hundreds of solo and trio sonatas for most of the commonly used instruments. Sonatas for solo keyboard and lute also appear, especially after 1720 or so. Many of these sonatas extended the technical and expressive range of their instruments. Typical in this regard are the flute sonatas of Quantz, which use keys and modulations rare in earlier flute works (Ex. 12.5a) as well as virtuoso passagework modeled on that written for string instruments (Ex. 12.5b). These last two examples also illustrate two further types of sonata scoring used especially in the early eighteenth century: a type of trio sonata in which one of the upper parts is played by the right hand of the keyboard player; and a quartet sonata (*sonata a quattro*) for three upper parts and continuo.[9]

In expanding the vocabulary of the flute sonata, Quantz was explicitly imitating earlier violinist-composers. Seventeenth-century composers had extended the normal upward range of the violin from b″ or c‴ up to g‴ (as at the beginning of the sonata by Biber in the anthology, Selection 34). Probably as early as 1626, Marini had published a solo violin sonata played "with two strings" (*con due corde*) that includes polyphonic passages in double stops (Ex. 12.6a). This technique, perhaps inspired by polyphonic lute music, would lead to the highly contrapuntal violin writing in the solo sonatas of Biber and Corelli (see below). The practice culminates in Bach's sonatas and partitas for unaccompanied violin, which even include three-part fugues without continuo (Ex. 12.6b). Other

---

[8]The painting on the dust jacket of this book depicts La Barre, standing, presenting a copy of this work to a patron, who is seated on the right holding a valuable ivory flute.

[9]Like many other *obbligato*-keyboard works, the sonata shown in Example 12.5a originated as an ordinary trio sonata for flute, violin, and continuo. Bach wrote six such sonatas for violin and harpsichord and at least two for flute and harpsichord. For a somewhat different sort of quartet sonata, see anthology, Selection 41.

Example 12.4 Michel de La Barre, *Première Sonate*, opening, from *Troisième livre des trio* (Paris, 1707). The *dessus* (soprano) parts are intended for flute, although the suites published in the same volume are for two violins, recorders, or oboes and continuo.

Example 12.5a Quantz, Sonata in G minor for flute and keyboard, QV 2:35, second movement, mm. 13–20, modulating from E♭ to F minor

Example 12.5b Quantz, Quartet in E minor for flute, violin, viola, and continuo, QV 4: 9, first movement, mm. 36–39; the flute imitates the figuration played in the preceding measures by the viola and violin, respectively.

Example 12.6 (a) Marini, *Sonata IV per sonar con due corde per violino solo*, mm. 36b–41, from *Sonate*, op. 8 (Venice, 1629); (b) J. S. Bach, Sonata 2 in A minor for unaccompanied violin, BWV 1003, second movement, opening

special types of writing in Baroque violin sonatas include *scordatura*, especially favored by German violinists. Here one or more strings were retuned to permit the playing of chords that would otherwise be impossible (see Exx. 12.8 and 12.9). Another special device involves the technique known as **bow vibrato**, signified by repeated notes under a slur. This occurs in quiet, harmonically inspired passages in some early sonatas (Ex. 12.7).[10]

The remainder of this chapter surveys the history of the sonata during the seventeenth century. Chapter 13 examines two other genres that grew out of the sonata; Chapter 14 turns to two late-Baroque varieties of the sonata, which would remain a central form of instrumental music through the Classical and Romantic periods.

---

[10] Also called *slurred tremolo*, the technique involves articulating the repeated eighths or sixteenths through pressure on the bow, resulting in a shimmering sound. For a later example in a work by Bach, see anthology, Selection 40, first movement, measures 50ff. (continuo and solo violin parts).

Example 12.7 Marco Uccellini, Sonata 18 *a doi violini*, from *Sonate* (Modena, 1645), mm. 102–6, passage using bow vibrato or slurred tremolo (called *tremolo* in the original); note the 7–6 suspensions and the absence of a tuneful melody, signs of a harmonically inspired texture

Salamone Rossi

Although probably not the first to write sonatas with violin parts, the Mantuan composer Salamone Rossi (?1570–ca. 1630) was the first to publish a significant number of such works, mostly for two violins and continuo. These appeared alongside dances and other pieces in four collections issued from 1607 to 1622. Mantua was Monteverdi's home for more than twenty years, and it saw the first performance of his opera *Orfeo* in 1607. As one of the leading violinists in town, Rossi probably participated in that performance, perhaps playing one of the "small French violins" used in Act 2 (see anthology, Selection 6a). Mantua had a significant Jewish community, of which Rossi was a member; although by no means equal in status to their fellow citizens, the Jews of Mantua enjoyed an unusual degree of protection from the ruling dukes, who engaged a number of them as musicians. Besides Rossi himself, these included his sister, a singer known as Madama Europa, who also performed at court. In addition to his instrumental music, Rossi published eight books of madrigals and other Italian vocal works as well as a volume containing polyphonic settings of Hebrew texts—apparently the first, though not the only, example of sacred Jewish polyphony from the Baroque, probably intended for the Venetian Jewish community.

Rossi appears to have been the first in a line of violinist-composers active at Mantua or in nearby cities who continued to publish instrumental works similar to his into the second half of the century. Chief among these were Giovanni Battista Buonamente (d. 1642), who presumably brought the style to Vienna while working for the Austrian emperor during the 1620s; and Marco Uccellini (ca. 1603–1680), whose publications include the first volume devoted to solo sonatas and other works for one violin and continuo (1649).

Rossi's *Sonata sopra La Bergamasca*

Rossi's sonatas include numerous examples of the type consisting of variations on a popular tune or an ostinato bass. Many, such as his two sonatas on the

Romanesca, use the same ostinato or ground basses found in variation works by Frescobaldi and other contemporaries (compare Ex. 10.5). The sonata on "La Bergamasca" (anthology, Selection 31) is based on a popular tune whose simple bass line is little more than a repeated cadential formula (I–IV–V–I).[11] The sonata is from Rossi's fourth and final instrumental collection, which appeared in 1622. Although Rossi did not specify the instrumentation of the upper parts, their range and style leave little doubt that they were meant for violins. The continuo part was explicitly intended for theorbo (chitarrone).

The tune, heard in more or less its original form at the opening, is less important as a basis of variation than the underlying harmonic progression. The latter is occasionally varied by the substitution of F♮ for one of the traditional bass notes (as in m. 18). The note is a reminder of the tune's modal character, and the F-major chords heard above it provide just enough variety to prevent the tune's traditional harmonization from growing stale. Like Rossi's other variation sonatas, the piece contains no formal subdivisions. Instead it is shaped by the trend of the variations toward increasing motion in small note values. The climax occurs in the final variation, where the upper parts play in sixteenths that are virtually uninterrupted, save for the concluding *groppi* (trills). Several slower-moving variations (nos. 6, 10, 12) provide relief, however, and the general level of virtuosity remains modest.

The upper parts engage in occasional imitation (as in mm. 20–21, 24–25), and their frequent voice crossing creates a kaleidoscopic interweaving of the sounds of the two violins (see especially the playful variation 10). A peculiarity of the conterpoint, as in other seventeenth-century music, is the tolerance for what would later be considered hidden parallel fifths. For instance, in measures 18–19 the upper part and the bass outline in succession the vertical intervals g/d'', f/c'', and e/b'. Another oddity is the absence of even a single full measure of rest for any of the parts. All these features might reflect unwritten traditions for ostinato variations established during the late Renaissance, when pieces of this sort might have been frequently improvised. Duo sonatas of this type ceased to be written in large numbers after the middle of the seventeenth century. But more virtuosic types of variation piece for solo instruments as well as grand chaconnes and passacaglias in the French style would take their place, as in the sonata by Biber discussed below.

Dario Castello

Whereas Rossi presumably headed a band of violinists at a small north Italian court, Dario Castello was "head of the wind instruments" (*capo di istromenti da fiato*) at St. Mark's Basilica in Venice. As such he must have played cornetto or trombone. Virtually nothing is known of him beyond his title, even though he published two sets of sonatas that were reprinted several times, implying widespread admiration and potential influence. These first appeared in in 1621

---

[11]The tune takes its name from the north Italian city of Bergamo; Uccellini wrote a variation sonata on the same tune.

and 1629, respectively. The title of each volume describes the contents as *concertato* sonatas in "modern style" (*stil moderno*). Exactly what these terms meant is uncertain. But they appear to have pointed to the works' diverse scoring and virtuoso style, which distinguished them from more conservative sonatas and canzonas still being composed at the time.

The twelfth work from Castello's second book (anthology, Selection 32) is a *sonata a tre* for two soprano instruments and one bass instrument, with continuo. Like most of Castello's sonatas, it consists of several connected sections that alternate between imitative and free styles. These can be summarized as follows:

Section	Measures	Features
1	1–34	allegro, imitative texture
2	35–51	adagio alternating with allegro
3	52–90	allegro; imitative texture, triple meter
4	91–129	solo passages alternating with presto for the whole ensemble
5	130–52	shortened reprise of opening section (mm. 12–33)
6	152–62	coda

The opening section is a fugue whose subject begins with a series of repeated notes, an idea that goes back to the sixteenth-century canzona. So too does the idea of concluding after a repetition of the opening section, which can be found in Giovanni Gabrieli's ensemble canzonas; Castello must have performed these frequently at St. Mark's. Also traditional was the inclusion of a second imitative section in triple meter, a common element in early-Baroque canzonas for solo keyboard as well as for instrumental ensemble. But sections 2 and 4 consist of diverse improvisatory phrases more reminiscent of the "free" sections in Frescobaldi's toccatas. The solo passages in section 4 achieve extraordinary virtuosity, probably inspired by solo singing that Castello would have accompanied at St. Mark's. Such writing returns in the coda, which consists essentially of a single plagal cadence (IV–I): the first harmony is extended into a long pedal point, prolonged through extraordinary figuration for the two upper parts. The figuration incorporates echoes that are signified by Castello's original dynamic markings: *forte* for the first part, *piano* for the second.[12]

Biagio Marini

In the same year that saw the publication of Castello's sonata, the violinist Biagio Marini (1594–1663) published a large collection of sonatas and other works for

---

[12]Gabrieli had introduced dynamic markings in his *Sonata pian'e forte* (see Chapter 7). It was once thought, incorrectly, that sudden contrasts of *forte* and *piano* were the only type of dynamics used in Baroque music; they are sometimes called *terraced dynamics*.

one to six parts with continuo. The works of the two composers are very different, illustrating the diversity of possibilities within the new genre. Unlike Castello, who apparently spent his entire life in Venice, Marini traveled widely from his native Brescia in northern Italy. He served in Venice and other Italian cities as well as Vienna, Brussels, and other northern European capitals. Although he worked at times as a church musician (in 1615 at St. Mark's, Venice), he also served as music director for at least one German court and for an *accademia* in Brescia. Institutions of the latter sort were being founded in most Italian cities (recall that Barbara Strozzi performed frequently at her father's academy in Venice). It is possible that many of Marini's instrumental works were first performed at such gatherings, which were among the forerunners of the modern concert series.

Already in 1617 Marini had issued in his Opus 1 some of the earliest solo and duo sonatas specifically for two violins. His Opus 8, apparently first published in 1626 and reprinted in 1629, contained sixty-eight sonatas, dances, and other pieces, including five extraordinary works for one violin and continuo—making him the first important composer of such music. He continued to publish violin music until at least 1655, when his Opus 22 came out, containing a similar assortment of twenty-five pieces. Marini also wrote significant examples of sacred and secular vocal music in the new monodic style. Echoes of the latter might be detected in the singing quality that alternates with virtuoso violin writing in his instrumental music, including the work discussed below. Marini's music must have made a deep impression on subsequent generations of violinists, including northerners such as Biber who would have encountered it in the courts of the Austrian empire.

Marini's *Sonata variata*

Our work (anthology, Selection 33) is the third of the solo sonatas in Marini's Opus 8. Each has a descriptive title pointing to some important musical or technical feature. This sonata is described as *variata*, perhaps reflecting its constantly changing musical style as well as its use of diverse performance techniques. The latter include double stops (chords), rapid repeated notes, and passagework that leaps from string to string. Like the best later virtuoso violinist-composers, Marini used such technical devices for artistic purposes rather than mere show. In our work, the flashy virtuoso passages are framed between slower-moving sections that open and close the work in a contemplative style.

As in the contemporary sonatas of Castello—or the keyboard toccatas of Frescobaldi—the individual sections are too brief to be considered separate movements:

Section	Measures	Signature	Meter	Cadences	Features
1a	1–15	none	C	d	lyrical, then quick passagework
1b	16–38	one flat	C	g, G, C	mostly = section 1a a fifth lower
2	39–50	one flat	triple	g	imitative (double stops)

Section	Measures	Signature	Meter	Cadences	Features
3	51–58	one flat	C		
4	59–68	one flat	triple	d	triplets (except at final cadence)
5	69–87	one flat	C, triple	C	leaps (especially sixths)
6	88–101	none	C		accelerating passagework
7	101–120	none	C	a, d	scales
8	121–46	none	C	a, g, C, a	imitative (violin, bass)

Changes of meter and "key" signature delineate sections, but some passages extend over a change of time signature. For instance, section 4, characterized by triplets in the violin part, is best viewed as continuing until the cadence in measure 68. Section 5 is unified by leaping sixths in the violin part, despite switching to triple meter for several measures. The work reaches a climax in section 6, where the figuration gradually accelerates, reaching its liveliest motion with the violin's thirty-second notes (mm. 94ff.).

The contrasts between the sections are so great that at first the sonata may seem chaotic. But the overall symmetry is readily apparent: the first and last sections (mm. 1–15 and 121–46) share a generally quiet, restrained style. Moreover, the closing section returns to a motive played by the continuo in measure 1, developing it in imitation (beginning with the second note of the violin in m. 122). Another motivic echo occurs at the beginning of section 6, where the slow rising scale introduced by the violin (mm. 101–4) recalls the descending scale in measures 31ff.

Section 1b repeats the first fifteen measures transposed downward by a fifth—a device rare prior to 1600, but symptomatic of the emerging tonal thinking of the Baroque (compare the use of transposition in Monteverdi's *Luci serene*, Selection 4 in the anthology). The transposition is signaled at measure 16 by the new signature of one flat, which remains in effect through section 5. The cadences in these sections do not clearly define a tonal plan of the sort familiar from later music, and the avoidance of modulations to the dominant is characteristic of modal compositions with final on D or A. Nevertheless the sonata returns to its opening "tonality" in the last two sections.

Heinrich Biber

The improvisatory combination of virtuosity and expressivity seen in Marini's solo sonatas reaches a culmination in the works of Biber composed later in the century. Heinrich Ignaz Franz Biber (1644–1704) was born in Wartenberg, Bohemia (now Stráž pod Ralskem), near Liberec in what is now the northern Czech Republic. By 1668 he was working for the bishop of Liechtenstein-Kastelkorn at Kroměříž in Moravia, 150 miles to the southeast. Two years later he entered the service of the archbishop of Salzburg in western Austria, eventually becoming kapellmeister (1684) and lord high steward (1692). Bohemia would continue to provide talented composers to the German-speaking courts

of the Holy Roman Empire through the eighteenth century, among them Jan
Dismas Zelenka (1679–1745), whose distinctive sacred vocal works would be
admired by Bach.

Biber composed three operas and important church works, including a magnificent Requiem (funeral mass) in F minor. He also was probably the composer
of an immense polychoral mass for no fewer than fifty instrumental and vocal
parts.[13] His instrumental music is of great significance and originality, consisting mainly of sonatas: some twenty-five for violin and continuo and another
thirty or so for larger ensembles.

Biber is best known for his music for solo violin, which includes fifteen early
works known as the "Mystery" or "Rosary" Sonatas. The manuscript preserving
them attaches to each sonata a printed visual emblem that depicts a religious
"mystery," that is, an event in the lives of Jesus and the Virgin Mary.[14] Hence
these works, like some of Froberger's keyboard pieces (see Chapter 10), were
imbued with programmatic significance, in this case of a sacred nature. A
remarkable feature of the "Mystery" sonatas is their systematic exploration of
scordatura: the retuning of the strings of the violin to allow the playing of otherwise unobtainable figuration and chords. Thus, in Sonata no. 10, which depicts
the Crucifixion, the top string is lowered, giving the violin two D strings an
octave apart (g–d'–a'–d''). Biber notated the violin part as it would be fingered,
not as it actually sounds; thus the middle staff of Example 12.8 shows the original notation, the top staff the sounding notes. Sonata no. 11, representing the
Resurrection, contains the most radical retuning of all: the two inner strings
must be switched to produce the remarkable tuning g–g'–d'–d''. The latter
makes possible a passage in triple octaves for violin and continuo (Ex. 12.9): a
symbolic representation of the Holy Trinity central to Christian belief.[15]

Biber's Sonata 5 of 1681

Whereas the "Mystery" sonatas were evidently intended for church performance,
a set of eight sonatas that Biber published in 1681 seems purely secular in
nature, though both were dedicated to the archbishop of Salzburg, Biber's
employer. The 1681 sonatas largely avoid scordatura, but they nevertheless take
violin technique to new heights, both literally and figuratively. This is evident
from the very opening of Sonata 5 (anthology, Selection 34), where the violin
begins an octave above its highest string. It then ascends above that, then
plunges downward in rapid figuration—the first of many dramatic shifts of
pacing and register in this rhapsodic opening section. Chords are plentiful here

---

[13]This so-called *Missa salisburgensis* is preserved anonymously; it appears in a modern edition by
Guido Adler in *Denkmäler der Tonkunst in Österreich*, vol. 20, with an improbable attribution to
the Roman composer Orazio Benevoli (1605–72). The figure of fifty parts does not include the
continuo or two oboes that may have been later additions.

[14]A sixteenth work in the manuscript comprises a passacaglia for unaccompanied violin, a type
of piece previously composed by Marini and later by Bach.

[15]Note the apparent parallel fifths on the middle staff of Ex. 12.9. At this point violin and continuo play the melody of the Gregorian hymn *Surrexit Christus hodie* (Christ is risen today).

Example 12.8 Biber, "Mystery" Sonata 10, first movement, mm. 1–5. The middle staff shows the original notation for *scordatura* violin, the upper staff the actual pitches.

Example 12.9 Biber, "Mystery" Sonata 11, mm. 127–33

and in the following sections. A number of them involve the open string e″, which in measures 29 and 31 is played simultaneously with a trill on d#″. The startling dissonance is an example of the *bizzarria,* or extravagance, cultivated especially in the earlier Baroque; it is also a way of announcing the unusual intensity of the variations that follow (the note E can be explained here as a sort of tonic pedal point).

Each sonata in Biber's 1681 collection alternates between variations and other types of section; although played without a break, the four sections of Sonata 5 are long enough to be considered separate movements:

Section	Measures	Description
1	1–27	free, alternating between adagio passages and lively figuration
2	28–82	sixteen variations on an ostinato (plus short adagio transition to the next section)
3	83–117	presto (12/8), imitative
4	118–57	"aria" with four variations

The initial section, broadly comparable to the free opening section of a toccata or *praeludium* for keyboard instrument, contains hints of recitative or arioso, as in the speechlike rhythm of the final adagio phrase (mm. 22–7). Both variation sections are composed over unchanging ostinato bass lines. But whereas the violin part in section 2 consists of harmonically inspired passagework over its four-measure bass line, much of the violin writing in section 4 can be considered embellishment of the melody in measures 118–25. Between the two variation sections is a contrapuntal presto in gigue rhythm. Here the violin plays in two, three, even four parts; the bass also participates in the counterpoint (as in its initial entrance in mm. 85–7, imitating the top voice of the violin).

The ostinato that serves as the basis of the second section seems to have been chosen to be as simple as possible. Little more than an alternation between tonic and dominant, it nevertheless leads to passagework of stunning virtuosity, as in the flying scales and leaps of variations 7 and 8. The emergence of such dazzling music from a seemingly simplistic ostinato was only one of the dramatic surprises that Biber built into this sonata. Clearly this virtuoso music was meant to have a stunning impact on the listener, yet, like Marini, Biber chooses to end thought-fully. The climax occurs toward the end of the first variation movement, and the third of the four variations in the final section is a quiet adagio. The concluding variation therefore seems anticlimactic, its thirty-seconds looking back to those of the second section rather than constituting a climax in themselves.

Giovanni Legrenzi

Biber's sonatas represent the final, extreme development of the free, impro-visatory writing that had characterized Baroque instrumental music since its beginnings around 1600. By the time these works were being written, a rather different approach was being cultivated in Italy, where Baroque style had begun. This new approach produced works that are relatively restrained in style and make fewer technical demands on the player. Hence this repertory may seem less exciting, and it has attracted less attention from modern players and audi-ences. Yet it was from this tradition that the most important Italian violinist-composer of the later Baroque, Corelli, would emerge a generation or two later.

Representative of this style are the more than sixty sonatas of Giovanni Legrenzi (1626–90), which appeared in four collections published in Venice from 1655 to 1673. Legrenzi was a priest, as were the earlier violinist-composers Buonamente and Uccellini. Like them he worked in a number of north Italian cities, including his native Bergamo. But by 1670 he had moved to Venice, still the musical capital of Italy if not of all Europe. There he worked at St. Mark's Basilica as assistant music director (vice–*maestro di capella*) from 1681 until his death. He wrote operas and much sacred music, but he is now best known for his duo and trio sonatas, which he probably composed for perfor-mance at concerts given at private academies and in his own house in Venice. Among the younger composers in the city who must have known his music was Vivaldi (see Chapter 13); Bach wrote an organ fugue based on a theme from an unidentified work of Legrenzi's.

Our example of Legrenzi's work (anthology, Selection 35) is from his first collection of sonatas, published as Opus 2 in 1655. It therefore falls chronologically between Castello's and Marini's publications of 1629 and the works of Corelli discussed below. Stylistically it is closer to the latter in its clear division into more or less self-contained movements and its rational, orderly musical construction. Our sonata is the fourth of eighteen in the collection (one sonata is by Legrenzi's father). As in some other collections of the period, the individual pieces are named for Venetian noble families, whose members might have commissioned the works or otherwise supported the composer. Our work is entitled *La Strasolda;* it is a duo sonata of the SS type for two violins and continuo.

There are two main sections or movements, with a short transitional Adagio connecting the first two and a brief coda at the end:

Section	Measures	Meter	Features
1	1–45	C	marked *presto;* imitative
2	46–54	C	marked *adagio;* harmonically inspired
3	55–87	triple	imitative
4	88–98	C	contrapuntal

Except for the Adagio, all sections are quick in tempo and contrapuntal in texture. The concluding section returns to the style of the first one, although without restating any of the latter's thematic material. (Some of the other sonatas in Legrenzi's Opus 2 return to the opening material at this point, as in the Castello sonata.)

The use of two imitative sections, one in duple or quadruple time, one in triple, is again a reflection of the older canzona, as is the seemingly conservative style throughout the quick sections. Yet Legrenzi cultivates a more systematic or integrated approach to motivic work and tonality that would prove attractive to future generations of Baroque musicians. As customary in a duo sonata, at the outset the first violin introduces a subject which is then imitated by the second violin but never the bass. The first imitation takes place at the original pitch level, in C major; hence by later standards the first movement would not be considered a fugue. Yet the movement has an elegantly contrapuntal texture, and it follows a rational formal design based on principles of tonality that were gradually replacing older modal principles. Thus in the opening and closing sections the subject enters only in the tonic or the dominant. These sections frame a series of inner phrases (mm. 10–35a) that modulate to relatively remote keys, including A minor (m. 13), E minor (m. 16), and D minor (m. 25). Although the subject as a whole is heard only once in the inner section, the latter develops motivic ideas taken from the subject. For instance, the end of the subject (violin 1 at m. 4) becomes the basis of the modulating sequence in measures 17–21; then measures 22–28 develop a broken-chord motive derived from notes 3–5 of the subject. The subject in its complete form returns at the beginning of the final section (m. 35b, violin 1).

This type of highly rational, if unassuming, design must have appealed to the cultivated intellectuals who gathered in the north Italian academies. Equally attractive were certain recurring patterns that made the music predictable without becoming monotonous. Among these was the **chain of suspensions** first heard in measures 29–31. There the second violin plays a series of suspensions and resolutions, while the first violin adds counterpoint that includes an ascending scale. The chain of suspensions recurs in measures 32–34, where the two violins exchange parts. Another example occurs at the beginning of the adagio.

In measures 29–31, the descending scalar motion of the bass line, together with its recurring 7–6 figuration, shows that the chain of suspensions is an elaboration of simple sequential voice leading. Sequences, especially ones based on chains of suspensions, would become increasingly common in sonatas and other Italian-style pieces of the later Baroque. This trend reflected a growing preference for regular patterning, as opposed to the irregular, improvisatory writing favored previously. In place of the constant invention characteristic of earlier sonatas, Legrenzi reveals an interest in integration, that is, in creating extended movements that cohere through restriction to a limited number of related motives and through frequent use of sequences, voice exchange, and other types of systematic repetition. This approach to composition suggests serious thought about the possibilities inherent in abstract musical form, similar to what Bach would later do in his keyboard fugues.

Arcangelo Corelli

The composer who integrated the various strands of the seventeenth-century sonata into a type whose cultivation would continue through much of the eighteenth century was Arcangelo Corelli (1653–1713; Fig. 12.8). Perhaps the greatest violinist-composer of the Baroque, he was arguably its second most influential Italian composer after Monteverdi. Apart from several lost or doubtful trumpet works, he appears to have composed nothing but string music. He was born in the north Italian town of Fusignano, near Bologna, which in the later seventeenth century saw a flourishing cultivation of instrumental music. Corelli adopted much of the Bolognese style (further discussed in Chapter 13), but by 1675 he was working as a violinist in Rome, where he spent the rest of his career. His patrons included some of the city's most important royal and aristocratic supporters of the arts, among them the exiled Queen Christina of Sweden and Cardinal Pietro Ottoboni. The latter headed the so-called Arcadian Academy, founded in 1690, whose periodic gatherings, like those of other academies, included sometimes lavish musical performances. Beginning in 1706, the membership included three musicians: initially Corelli, Alessandro Scarlatti, and the Roman harpsichordist-composer Bernardo Pasquini (1637–1707). Corelli was also regularly engaged elsewhere in Rome to direct performances of operas, oratorios, and other major works, including those of Pasquini and Handel.

Corelli's chief works are his forty-eight trio sonatas, twelve solo sonatas, and twelve concerti grossi. These were published in six numbered collections of twelve works each, beginning with four sets of trio sonatas. The second set

ARCANGELUS CORELLIUS de FUSIGNANO dictus BONONIENSIS.

Liquisse Infernas Jam Credimus Orphea Sedes | Divinus patet Ipse Orpheus. dum numine digna,
Et terras habitare, hujus sub imagine formæ. | Arte modos fingit, vel chordas mulcet utramque
—————————————————————— | Agnoscit Laudem, meritosque BRITANNUS honores

Figure 12.8 Arcangelo Corelli, engraving by William Sherwin after a portrait by Hugh Howard
(ca. 1698), published as the frontispiece to Walsh's edition of Opus 5 (London, ca. 1711). Marcellene and
Walter Mayhall Collection. As in many Baroque portraits, the composer holds a page of music as a symbol of his occupation and learning. The lines of Latin poetry beneath the portrait liken Corelli to Orpheus.

(Opus 2, 1685), bearing the title *Sonate da camera* (Chamber sonatas), contains
mostly dance movements, as does the fourth set (Opus 4, 1694). Hence it has
become customary to regard Corelli's two other sets of trio sonatas—Opus 1
of 1681 and Opus 3 of 1689—as *sonate da chiesa* (church sonatas), although
Corelli never designated them as such. The two subsequent collections of solo
sonatas (Opus 5, 1700) and concertos (Opus 6, published posthumously in
1714) are each divided between works of the so-called church and chamber
types as well.

Each of Corelli's publications was reissued throughout the eighteenth century in numerous editions. Bach imitated Corelli's *sonate de chiesa* (church sonatas) in both his trio sonatas and his sonatas for unaccompanied violin. Handel wrote a set of twelve concerti grossi (also designated Opus 6, 1739) in tribute to Corelli. Countless other Italian, German, and even French composers also wrote works modeled on Corelli's. Some even arranged Corelli's works for keyboard, recorder, and other settings.

Part of the appeal of Corelli's music must have lain in its regularity and restraint. Compared to earlier violin writing, such as Marini's or Biber's, it seems predictable. Even more than with Legrenzi, everything is in its proper place, each gesture in one direction exquisitely balanced by one in another. This aspect of the works is evident even in superficial aspects, such as their publication in regular sets of twelve. With few exceptions, the works in each volume are constructed out of a few standard types of movement.

In fact, Corelli's works do contain harmonic surprises, and his own playing was reported to be extremely impassioned and full of fire. But this impression may have been due chiefly to improvised embellishment, for, except in some of the solo sonatas, the music as written requires relatively little outright virtuosity. For this reason, string teachers ever since have tended to use Corelli's works as pedagogic pieces. Yet the music is not really easy to play. Like all well-composed works, Corelli's sonatas are more demanding than they may first appear to be, requiring sensitive and controlled phrasing, articulation, and embellishment.

Corelli's first four volumes all comprise *sonate a tre* of the SSB type. Yet except in Opus 1 the bass part is nearly always the same as the continuo, and the modern expression *trio sonata* can be applied to these works without danger of misleading. The sonatas of Opus 2 and Opus 4, consisting largely of dances, are in effect suites, but Italian composers never used this term. Most of these sonatas open with a short nondance movement, designated *preludio.* The dances themselves, although similar to those used by French composers, are distinctly Italian in style.

For instance, the last movement from the first sonata in Opus 2, shown in its entirety in Example 12.10, is a gavotte. We have previously seen this dance in its French form (see Ex. 10.8c, as well as Rameau's air "Sur les bords," anthology, Selection 19). But unlike a French gavotte, this one starts on the downbeat, and its allegro character is more forthright than that of the gentler French dance. Hence the titles of the dance movements in these sonatas are given in their Italian forms (*allemanda, corrente, giga,* etc.). As in the French style, however, most of these dances are in binary form. Thus the *gavotta* in Example 12.10 is divided by a double bar, and, although unusually short, it includes features of many longer binary sonata movements: the first half ends with a cadence in the dominant, and the second half begins with material derived from the opening of the first half.

The Sonata in C, op. 5, no. 3

Corelli's twelve solo sonatas, published in 1700, consist of six *sonate da chiesa* and six *sonate da camera.* Most of the latter resemble Corelli's trio sonatas *da camera* in consisting of a *preludio* followed by dances. Only the last sonata differs; it comprises a single movement, a set of variations on *La Folia,* a traditional

Example 12.10 Corelli, Sonata in D, op. 2, no. 1, fourth movement (complete)

ostinato bass.[16]Although the violin part predominates, these sonatas contain vestiges of the old SB duo scoring, inasmuch as the continuo frequently contains essential melodic material, especially in the fugues of the six "church" sonatas.

These first six sonatas resemble the trio sonatas *da chiesa* in that they lack designated dance movements. Nevertheless, many movements in these works contain readily identifiable dance characteristics. A more significant element of these sonatas is the presence of fugues, usually as the second movement and sometimes as the last movement as well. Music history texts often describe the church sonata as comprising a four-movement sequence, slow-fast-slow-fast. The first six sonatas of Opus 5, however, each contain five movements. These are arranged in varying orders, but the sonatas always open with a slow prelude followed by a fugue and conclude with a quick movement. The prelude as well as one of the subsequent movements is usually marked *adagio*, signifying that by now a slow movement could be a self-contained section and not merely an improvisatory transition between quick movements.

In one of the many eighteenth-century reprints of Opus 5 (Amsterdam, 1710), the publisher, Étienne Roger, added an embellished version of the violin part. This, according to him, contained "the ornaments for the adagios . . . composed by Corelli as he plays them." A London publisher quickly pirated Roger's edition (Fig. 12.9). Although it remains uncertain whether Roger had truly obtained

---

[16]Corelli's Opus 2 had similarly concluded with a sonata consisting solely of a *ciacona*, a chaconne in the form of variations on an ostinato bass line.

Figure 12.9 Corelli, opening of the Sonata in C, op. 5, no. 3, as printed about 1711 by the London publisher John Walsh. Marcellene and Walter Mayhall Collection. The lower two staves of each system show Corelli's original score as previously published in Rome and elsewhere; the top staff gives embellishments that were claimed to be also by Corelli. Unlike the typeset music shown in Figure 5.1, this page was printed from an engraved plate and thus presents a more elegant appearance, with unbroken staff lines, beams, and slurs.

Corelli's embellished versions of these movements, his edition illustrates the type of embellishments that a virtuoso of the time might have improvised in the slow movements of the "church" sonatas. Modern editions of Opus 5 often reproduce these embellishments on a separate staff above the original violin part.

The opening adagio of the Sonata in C, op. 5, no. 3 (anthology, Selection 36) serves as prelude to the second movement, the fugue. Here, as in fugal violin works by Biber and Bach, the violin's double-stopping capabilities permit it to provide both soprano and alto parts. There are three- and even four-part chords as well, but the extra notes provide additional sonority rather than real contrapuntal voices.

Although this movement is a genuine three-voice fugue, it is not a *strict* fugue. After the initial two entries of the subject, the latter never appears in its complete form again, and there are no subsequent entries at all in the alto. There is a countersubject, but it consists of nothing more distinctive than a short chain of suspensions; it is more a motive than a subject. Much of the movement is taken up not by fugal expositions but by two long episodes. The first of these (mm. 9–14a) initially employs a motive from the subject but soon moves on to unrelated material. The second episode (mm. 21b–30) is composed entirely of virtuoso figuration of the type that would soon become especially characteristic of the solo concerto.

This free sort of construction illustrates how Baroque composers used fugal texture to open a movement that then moves to different types of writing. After beginning fugally, the movement reaches its climax in the virtuoso figuration of the middle. It then returns to fugal texture (mm. 31–41), only to conclude with a coda that is again composed of virtuoso figuration (mm. 42–50). Similar fugues occur in the other "church" sonatas of Corelli's Opus 5. They provided models for the dazzling virtuoso fugues in Bach's three sonatas for unaccompanied violin, as well as some of his fugues for organ, harpsichord, and lute.

Corelli did not write out the figuration for the final five measures. Instead, the word *arpeggio* indicates that the player is to invent a way of arpeggiating the chords in some idiomatic pattern. Similar markings appear occasionally in keyboard and lute music as well.

The second adagio is in a contrasting key, the relative minor, a practice adopted in the slow movements of many sonatas and concertos of the later Baroque. Its true ending is on the downbeat of measure 50. This is followed, however, by a short passage ending with a so-called Phrygian cadence to the dominant chord (E major). The passage serves as a bridge to the next movement; in this respect Corelli maintains the old tradition of the sonata as comprising connected sections rather than separate movements. Although the adagio ends on an E-major chord, the following movement is again in the tonic, C, not the expected A minor. Many Baroque works contain bridges of this sort, which depend on the close relationship between a major key (C) and its relative, minor (a).

The fourth movement, an allegro, is virtually an étude (study piece or exercise) consisting almost entirely of virtuoso figuration for the violin. All the church sonatas of Corelli's Opus 5 contain such movements, but they are rare in sonatas by other composers. As in the episodes of the fugue, the figuration consists of arpeggiation such as would soon become typical of the solo sections of a concerto. Although such figuration may appear mechanical on the page, the precise pattern of the arpeggiation changes constantly, and it falls into phrases of varying lengths. A good performer can bring out this variety through subtle inflections of tempo, dynamics, and articulation.

The closing movement is a *giga* (jig) although not marked as such, in keeping with the conventions of the church sonata. Although longer than the named dances of Corelli's Opus 2, it retains their binary form. It ends, surprisingly with a phrase in the minor mode, which is repeated *piano*. The echo effect exaggerates the surprise created by ending in the minor mode; it is impossible to know whether the composer infended this to be witty, expressive, or both.

CHAPTER 13

MUSIC FOR INSTRUMENTAL ENSEMBLE II
Sinfonia and Concerto

The instrumental concertos of the late Baroque by Bach, Handel, and Vivaldi are probably the best-known compositions of the entire period and among the few that are familiar to most mainstream musicians and audiences today. The term *concerto*, like *cantata* and *sonata*, has meant different things at different times. In the early Baroque it referred to works combining voices and instruments, sometimes in relatively large numbers (see Chapter 7). In music from around 1700 and later it describes works that usually involve one or more instrumental soloists who play alongside or in alternation with a larger group. Such works emerged during the 1690s, although similar compositions were being composed somewhat earlier under the titles *sonata* and *sinfonia*.

THE BOLOGNESE TRUMPET SINFONIA

Among the seventeenth-century genres resembling the concerto was a type of work, usually called a *sonata* or *sinfonia*, that included parts for one or two trumpets together with three or four string parts and continuo. In these works the trumpets often serve as a sort of solo choir that sometimes alternates and sometimes combines with the strings. Such works, whose composers included Biber and Purcell, were composed for court as well as for church; some served as opera overtures as well. A distinctive repertory of such compositions is associated with the church of San Petronio (St. Petronius) in the north Italian city of Bologna, which had become a major musical center by the 1660s. One of the chief composers of such works was also among the first to write concertos in the modern sense.

Giuseppe Torelli

Born in Verona, Giuseppe Torelli (1658–1709) came to Bologna by 1684, where in 1686 he became a regular member of the orchestra of San Petronio. He apparently served there as a violist, although he also performed in nearby cities as a violinist. Prominent musicians who preceded him in Bologna included

Adriano Banchieri (1568–1634), a composer of madrigal comedies and author of several informative treatises, and Maurizio Cazzati (1616–78), one of the first to publish sonatas for trumpet and strings. Corelli too had spent a few years there and owed something of his style to earlier Bolognese composers. Financial difficulties led to the temporary disbanding of the musical establishment of San Petronio in 1696; Torelli then worked for several years in German-speaking Europe, serving in particular as a court musician in Ansbach, where he taught the German violinist-composer Johann Georg Pisendel (1687–1755). He returned to Bologna in 1701 when the ensemble at San Petronio was reestablished.

Ruled by the pope, Bologna attracted musicians not only through employment at the large church of San Petronio but by the presence of the Accademia Filarmonica. The latter, unlike most such institutions, had a membership comprising mostly professional musicians rather than noble amateurs. The academy—which still exists—gave regular concerts and also sponsored learned debates concerning music. Famous members, in addition to Torelli and Corelli, would include the castrato Farinelli, Mozart, and Rossini.

Torelli's works include some of the earliest published concertos as well as sinfonias for one or two trumpets and strings. Not all of the works entitled "concerto" correspond to the modern idea of such a piece. They include traditional trio sonatas for two violins and continuo, and a set of "concertini" published in 1688 consists of duos for violin and cello (apparently without continuo). But Torelli's later published collections include several examples of what we call the solo concerto for violin and strings as well as concerti grossi of the type also composed by Corelli (see below). These works tend to avoid the outright virtuosity of later concertos, but, like the music of Legrenzi and Corelli (see Chapter 12), they are elegantly composed, each movement being constructed from a relatively small number of related motives. Torelli's music was highly valued by his contemporaries; Bach made an arrangement for solo harpsichord of a violin concerto probably by Torelli.

A "Sinfonia with Trumpet" by Torelli

This *Sinfonia con tromba* (anthology, Selection 37), listed as number 8 in the modern catalogue of Torelli's works, is one of about thirty sinfonias by the composer for one or two trumpets and strings. Most, like similar works by other Bolognese composers, were probably composed for performance during mass on special occasions in the church of San Petronio. Unlike the other instrumental works discussed in this chapter, the manuscripts preserving these sinfonias include multiple copies of each string part—implying orchestral performance in the modern sense.[1] Although dates of composition are uncertain, some of these works are thought to have been composed for the trumpeter Giovanni Pellegrino Brandi, known to have performed on special occasions at San Petronio from 1679 to 1699. As in most such works, the present trumpet part includes traditional trumpet motives, such as the quick repeated notes heard at the very end.

---

[1]Torelli's pupil Pisendel would likewise direct performances of orchestral music at Dresden, in southeastern Germany.

Our work comprises three main movements, each marked *allegro*, plus an adagio that, as in the Legrenzi sonata, connects the first two movements. The opening and closing allegro movements alternate between passages for strings on the one hand and passages for trumpet on the other (all accompanied by continuo). As we shall see, instrumental concertos would involve similar alternation between full ensemble and soloist. In movement 1, the alternation resembles that between ritornello and soloist in an aria. Thus the soloist enters briefly in measures 5–6, as in the so-called *Devise*, or motto entrance, of an Italian aria (compare the example in the cantata by Alessandro Scarlatti, anthology, Selection 10a). A longer solo entry, beginning in measure 9, leads to a cadence in the dominant and a new ritornello in that key (mm. 13–17). On the other hand, the movement ends with trumpet joining the strings rather than with a restatement of the ritornello as in an aria. Prior to that, the trumpet is joined by two solo violins in a passage that illustrates the flexibility of scoring that was possible with the orchestral forces available at San Petronio (mm. 34–38).

Although requiring considerable virtuosity in the high register of the instrument, the trumpet part never has the type of passagework that would become typical of solo writing in eighteenth-century concertos. In addition, the natural trumpet was restricted to the tonic and related keys (cf. Ex. 9.2); therefore it is silent in the central portion of the movement, which modulates momentarily to the relative minor (mm. 20–21). For the same reason, the trumpet is silent in the adagio, which opens in what was at the time the rare key of F♯ minor. A harmonically inspired bridge rather than a full-fledged movement, the adagio then modulates to the dominant, preparing a type of movement unique to the Bolognese repertory: a short duet for trumpet and solo cello. The latter, which was still a relatively new instrument (see Chapter 12), here detaches itself from the continuo, as it would also do in some of the concertos that would be composed during the next few decades. The final movement resembles the first allegro, but it is in the compound meter ($\frac{6}{8}$)associated with the gigue.

The Baroque Concerto

Among the works published as concertos during the 1690s are several in which a single violinist alternates with the full ensemble, much as the trumpet does with the strings in the sinfonia described above. Torelli included two concertos of this type in his Opus 6 (1698). In other works from the same set, two violinists serve as soloists. Such scoring might have derived from a Roman practice of opposing a solo choir of two or three instruments against a larger group. An example occurs within the string parts of the Torelli sinfonia: at one point, two of the violins play as soloists while the remaining violins rest (movement 1, mm. 34–37).

The larger group of violinists, who usually double one of the two solo parts, constitute the **ripieno**. There is also a ripieno bass part, possibly intended for a double-bass instrument, that plays with the continuo group but rests during solo passages. The word *ripieno* literally means "filling out"; originally it referred to extra parts that double or accompany other parts but are not strictly necessary for its performance. The term has come to be used for the parts of a concerto other than those of the soloists.

The use of ripieno parts might have originated in Rome or Bologna as impromptu additions to conventionally scored sonatas and sinfonias. But by 1700 the idea of alternating between soloists and ripieno was being composed into the scores of these works. Simultaneously, the term *concerto* came to have a more definite meaning as the name of the new genre. Hundreds of concertos would be composed during the first few decades of the eighteenth century. As with the sonata, the first generation or two of concerto composers were mostly Italians, but the genre was soon taken up in Germany, England, and even France. Woodwind, brass, and eventually keyboard instruments joined violin and cello as common soloists. Apart from Torelli, important composers included Corelli and the Venetians Tomaso Albinoni (1671–1750) and Antonio Vivaldi (1678–1741). Albinoni is known in particular for his oboe concertos—works for one and for two oboes, with strings and continuo—some of the first significant solo works for that instrument. Vivaldi was a particularly prolific and influential concerto composer; his works were widely published and imitated in Germany, France, and England, as well as in Italy. Among the German composers influenced by Vivaldi were Georg Philipp Telemann (1681–1767) and J. S. Bach, as well as the latter's sons, whose numerous concertos for keyboard instruments transformed the genre, providing models for the Classical piano concerto of Haydn, Mozart, and Beethoven.

Modern writers often distinguish between a concerto in which a single solo part is pitted against a larger ensemble, described as a "solo" concerto, and a work involving multiple soloists, referred to as a concerto grosso (plural: concerti grossi). But eighteenth-century musicians did not always use the terms in this way. An early eighteenth-century concerto might have multiple solo parts in one movement and only one soloist, or none at all, in another. Although patterns of scoring and structure were becoming standardized by the 1720s, earlier works show a wide variety of formal designs and instrumentation. Emblematic of this variety are the twelve concertos of Vivaldi's *L'estro armonico* (published in 1711) or Bach's six Brandenburg Concertos, all composed by 1721, which lack the predictable patterns of scoring and structure typical of the next generation. For example, in the Fourth Brandenburg Concerto a solo violin and two recorders are joined by four additional string parts and continuo. It is fruitless to agonize over whether this work is a solo violin concerto or a concerto grosso in which the recorders are also soloists; Bach, clearly, was satisfied with the designation *concerto* alone.

Arcangelo Corelli and the Concerto Grosso

The twelve works of Corelli's Opus 6, published in 1714, a year after his death, were indeed designated concerti grossi, but this was an indication that they are actually not concertos at all in the sense that the word was acquiring. For these are essentially trio sonatas with optional ripieno parts, scored for a basic texture of two violins and continuo. To this a ripieno of two violins, viola, and a second continuo part is added. An early account of Corelli's performance practice, by the German composer Georg Muffat, showed how a work in trio sonata scoring could be augmented by the addition of ripieno players.[2] In later concertos, the ripieno is not usually optional; indeed, its presence is an essential element in the solo concerto. Even Corelli's concerti grossi, although playable without the ripieno parts, contain four-part fugues and other textures distinct from those of his trio sonatas and must have been conceived primarily for orchestral performance.

Corelli's Concerto Grosso in G Minor, op. 6, no. 8

This work (anthology, Selection 38) is a so-called church concerto (*concerto da chiesa*, described in the original edition as having been composed for performance on Christmas Eve. Such indications were rare, but Torelli had included a similar work in his Opus 8 (Bologna, 1709). Both works are therefore known as "Christmas" concertos, but they were not necessarily composed specifically for church performance. Our work might, however, have been heard in private Christmas Eve concerts known to have taken place at the palace of Corelli's patron Cardinal Ottoboni in Rome.

In modern scores of Corelli's concerti grossi, the basic trio sonata group is notated on the three upper staves and is designated the *concertino* (literally, the "small ensemble"). The ripieno appears on the lower four staves, which are labeled, somewhat confusingly, as the *concerto grosso* (the "big ensemble"). The concertino plays throughout; the two ripieno violins and the ripieno continuo part enter now and then to double the concertino in select passages. The viola has an independent part, but on the rare occasions where it presents thematic material it doubles one of the concertino parts.

The work opens with a brief introductory passage followed by a slow (*grave*) movement in imitative texture. The latter alludes to vocal polyphony of the sixteenth century through its use of *stile antico*, as is shown by its archaic notation in whole and half notes. In addition, Corelli specifies a departure from normal practice by adding, after the tempo mark: "Use sustained bows and [play] as is." An unusual indication, this is evidently a request that the players not add embellishments, such as they would normally have done in a slow movement. The reason, presumably, is to create an effect of heightened solemnity and mystery appropriate to the pre-Christmas season during which this music might have been performed.

The remaining movements consist largely of dances, although most are not labeled as such, in keeping with the tradition of the "church" concerto. The first Allegro is close in style to the *allemanda*, the Italian version of the French allemande, such as Corelli included in the trio sonatas of his Opus 2 and Opus 4. The Vivace (mvt. 4) and the second Allegro (mvt. 5) constitute a *menuetto* (minuet) and a *gavotta*, respectively. Only the third movement lacks a dance character; it is a free da capo form, with an *adagio* A section and an *allegro* B section.

The final movement is designated a *pastorale ad libitum*. A **pastorale** is a slow version of the *giga*, using the same compound meter $\left(\frac{12}{8}\right)$ and skipping rhythm (quarter–eighth). The dance was associated with shepherds, as its name implies

---

[2]For Muffat's account, published in 1701, see the translations listed in the bibliography under "Collections of Readings."

(Latin *pastor* = "shepherd"). Its use here is a reference to the shepherds mentioned in the New Testament as tending their flocks on the night of Jesus' birth. The movement contains a programmatic detail unique in Corelli's works, although it is encountered in other "pastoral" music of the period, including Torelli's Christmas concerto: much of the movement is built over pedal points, such as the repeated G's of the solo cello in measures 1–2. These pedal points represent the *zampogne*, a type of bagpipe played by Italian peasants. The **bagpipe,** a traditional wind instrument, is characterized by a **drone,** an unchanging bass note that is held out underneath the melody. This drone was imitated in works by later composers, including Bach in the musette movement of his Third English Suite and Handel in the *pifa* movement of his *Messiah*.[3]

The Solo Concerto

A number of composers, notably Handel, published imitations of Corelli's concerti grossi. By the time of the latter's publication in 1714, however, the solo concerto was becoming more fashionable. Such works provided greater opportunities for soloistic expression and display, paralleling developments in Italian opera, where the aria had long been established as the principal element. As Bolognese composers had already demonstrated in their trumpet sinfonias, the solo instrumentalist could play a role analogous to that of the virtuoso singer in opera. Accordingly, the individual movements of many solo concertos follow a version of ritornello form.

As employed in the concerto, ritornello form involved an alternation between passages scored for the entire ensemble, called the **tutti** (Italian for "all"), and more lightly scored passages involving one or more soloists accompanied by continuo. Like an aria, a concerto movement of this type opens with a ritornello, followed by what we will refer to as the first of several **solo episodes** (or simply solos). These alternate with restatements of the ritornello, usually in altered or abbreviated forms; the movement usually concludes with another restatement of the ritornello, in whole or part.

Ritornello form involves more than just an alternation between tutti and soloist. Equally crucial is the presence of modulations, so that successive ritornellos are usually in different keys, the first and last normally being in the tonic. Most of the modulations take place during the solos, so that the opening of each ritornello serves as a point of arrival. In other words, the ritornellos are the main guideposts of the movement, each one confirming any modulation that has taken place during the preceding solo episode.

This type of ritornello form differs in several crucial ways from that typically found in contemporary opera arias. First, the number and length of the ritornellos are generally greater than in an aria, with a correspondingly greater number of solo episodes, although the number of ritornellos and episodes tended to diminish in the course of the eighteenth century as the individual sections grew longer. In addition, unlike the singer in an aria, the soloist or soloists in a Baroque concerto normally play as part of the tutti. Thus the soloists are present in the ritornellos as

---

[3]The **musette** is a French type of bagpipe; the *pifa* is a Mediterranean folk instrument.

well as the solo passages. Moreover, many concerto movements blur the distinction between ritornello and solo sections by including passages for the tutti or for individual ripieno parts within an episode. Composers such as Vivaldi and J. S. Bach (and their audiences) were apparently less interested in the regular alternation of rigidly defined sections than in the free, fluid development of motivic material within a type of movement characterized by continually varied scoring. Particularly with Bach, a movement may open with well-defined ritornello and solo passages, but as the music progresses the two types of passage may exchange motivic material or otherwise become assimilated to each another, to the point that it is arbitrary to define one passage as a ritornello and another as a solo.

Vivaldi

Antonio Vivaldi (1678–1741) was born in Venice. He probably learned music from his father, a violinist (possibly also a composer) who held a position at St. Mark's Basilica. By Vivaldi's time, Venice's economic and political importance had declined in relation to that of France, Austria, and other European states. Nevertheless, it remained one of the busiest and most influential artistic centers on the continent. Its thriving musical institutions included not only opera theaters and churches but four *ospedali*, charitable organizations resembling a cross between an orphanage and a convent. Some of the women residing in these institutions received advanced musical training, and to raise money the *ospedali* gave public concerts that were famous throughout Europe. The women who performed in these concerts included distinguished musicians, yet most never left the *ospedale*. During concerts they were hidden from the audience, who heard but could not see them; it would have been considered scandalous for these unmarried women to be seen performing publicly.

In 1703 Vivaldi became violin teacher at one of these institutions, the Pio Ospedale della Pietà. He continued to work there (with interruptions) for most of his life, and many of his concertos were composed for performance at the Pietà. At various times he also worked for noble patrons as well as for several opera theaters, and he undertook journeys to Rome, Mantua, Amsterdam, and elsewhere in connection with performances of his operas and in search of further patronage. He died in Vienna while on one of these trips. Although ordained a priest in 1703, this did not prevent him from maintaining a long association with the contralto Anna Giraud, an opera singer at Venice and elsewhere from 1724 to 1747.

In addition to his students at the Pietà, Vivaldi taught, or at least was visited by and deeply influenced, such German composers as Johann David Heinichen (1683–1729), Pisendel (who had also studied with Torelli), and the flutist Johann Joachim Quantz (1697–1773). All three were based at the Saxon court in Dresden, although Quantz later worked for the Prussian king Frederick the Great in Berlin. From Dresden they helped disseminate Vivaldi's works and style throughout northern Europe, not only through copies of his music that they brought back with them but through their own instrumental works closely modeled on his. Vivaldi found imitators in France as well, where Leclair (mentioned in Chapter 12) made a particularly original adaptation of the Vivaldi style in his solo and trio sonatas and concertos.

Vivaldi's music includes some fifty operas and other theatrical works, forty or so cantatas, and over fifty sacred vocal works. He is best known for his enormous output of sonatas and concertos: some ninety solo and trio sonatas, and about five hundred concertos, including over two hundred solo violin concertos. Only a portion of his output was published during his lifetime, but among this were some of his most important and influential instrumental works. Of special significance were three publications, each comprising twelve concertos. Opus 3, entitled *L'estro armonico*, appeared in 1711; it is discussed below. Opus 4, entitled *La stravaganza* (1716), was a set of solo violin concertos; Opus 8, *Il cimento dell'armonia e dell'inventione* (The contest of harmony and invention, 1725), includes the four solo violin concertos known as "The Four Seasons." The latter are descriptive or programmatic works, like the last movement of Corelli's "Christmas" Concerto and a number of other Baroque concertos. "The Four Seasons" goes beyond other such works in the richness and ingenuity of its musical depictions, which represent seasonal images described in four accompanying poems.

Like several other highly prolific Baroque composers, Vivaldi is often disparaged; one may hear, for example, that "he wrote the same concerto five hundred times." Yet Vivaldi's best works are characterized by inventive writing for individual instruments as well as clever and varied use of the ensemble as a whole. Many works contain harmonic and rhythmic surprises that may be both witty and dramatic at the same time. The frequent repetitions and sequences in the music can make it seem simple, yet, as with Corelli, the impression of simplicity is actually an indication of its sophistication. From Vivaldi's music, Bach and other composers learned how to produce vivid, dramatic effects without indulging in the complex counterpoint or chromatic harmony of earlier Baroque composers. In this the music of Vivaldi and his contemporaries represents an important change in style—the beginning of the development toward the *galant* and Classical styles of the mid- and late eighteenth century, respectively.

Several catalogues or lists of Vivaldi's works exist, each referred to by a letter abbreviation. The most complete and up-to-date is that of the Danish scholar Peter Ryom. His "R" (or "RV") numbers are now the preferred ones, used alongside opus numbers for Vivaldi's published works.

Vivaldi's Concerto in E, op. 3, no. 12, R. 265

The title of Vivaldi's Opus 3 means something like "Harmonic inspiration"; it might have referred to the twelve concertos' brilliantly varied scoring. As is true of most of the sonatas and concertos we have been examining, a purchaser acquiring a copy of the work—whether printed or in manuscript—would have gotten not a score but a set of separate parts. Opus 3 was published in eight partbooks: one each for four violins, two violas, cello, and continuo. The continuo part might have been shared by the keyboard player with either a second cellist or perhaps a double-bass player. The other parts would most likely have been used by single players, who would have quickly discovered that their roles varied from one work to another within the set.

Four of the concertos are examples of what today are called double concertos, since two of the violins have solo roles. In four other concertos all four violinists function as soloists, at least in certain movements. In both of these groups of concertos the first cello has occasional solo roles as well. In the four remaining concertos, however, only the first of the violin parts takes a solo role. These concertos therefore constitute solo concertos; among them is the one in E major, the last in the set (anthology, Selection 39).

It is primarily from Vivaldi's solo concertos that the modern understanding of Baroque ritornello form has been derived. Like the great majority of solo concertos by Vivaldi and later composers, our work is in three movements, in the order fast-slow-fast. The outer movements, both marked *allegro*, employ ritornello form; the design of the third movement, the simpler of the two, is summarized in Table 13.1. As the chart shows, this movement has a nicely symmetrical form in which five ritornellos alternate with four solo passages. The most remote key, the relative minor, is reached at the end of the third ritornello, close to the exact center of the movement (m. 64). Similar designs can be found in many of Vivaldi's concerto movements.

Yet this symmetrical picture is not entirely accurate. For one thing, no two ritornellos are exactly the same. The opening ritornello of the third movement is never restated in full, and only a portion of it returns at the end. Whereas the opening and closing ritornellos remain in the tonic, the central ritornello (mm. 42–64) reaches the relative minor only after modulating from the dominant. Two short tutti passages in the later stages of the movement (at mm. 81 and 99) repeat motivic material from the opening ritornello but use it in new ways.[4]

Each solo section in the third movement is constructed in a logical way out of a relatively small number of motives. No material is ever literally restated, but subtle motivic relationships insure the integration of the movement as a whole. For example, the first solo section (mm. 22–41) opens with lively figuration in sixteenths, built out of two motives: a turning motive on beat 1 (with a slur on notes 1–3) and a repeated leaping figure on beats 2–3. These motives are repeated in sequence (mm. 22–26), then replaced by a further series of motives in sixteenths (mm. 28–35); one of these subsequent motives is similar to the original turning figure (compare beat 1 in m. 22 and m. 30). The second

TABLE 13.1
Antonio Vivaldi: Concerto in E, op. 3, no. 12 (R. 265), third movement

Section	R	S	R	S	r	S	r	S	R
Key	E	E →	B →	c♯ →	E:V	E	E	E	E
Measure	1	22	42	64	81	85	99	103	112

R = ritornello
S = solo section
lowercase letters = shorter sections

---

[4]The first of these abbreviated ritornellos, at m. 81, appears to be in the dominant, B major. But this key is only weakly tonicized, and there is an immediate modulation back to E; for this reason Table 13.1 shows the passage as being "on" the dominant, symbolized as E:V.

solo section (mm. 64–80) seems unrelated; the solo violin part is notated in three-part chords, which probably were meant to be broken as rapid arpeggios. Accompanying this, however, the ripieno violins play a motive consisting of a chord broken in eighth notes. The same motive appears in the ripieno violin parts when they accompany the first solo (mm. 22–35). The motive, whose use connects the two solo episodes, ultimately derives from the ritornello (cf. m. 1, violins 1–2, last three notes).

The first movement is somewhat longer and more complex than the third, with a greater number of distinct ritornellos and solos. Moreover, it is unusual for the tonal instability of its ritornellos; even the opening one (mm. 1–8) modulates from tonic to dominant. Nevertheless, the fundamental design of this movement is similar to that of the last, with a move to the relative minor (m. 31) and a lengthy modulating ritornello (mm. 32–45) occurring in the inner sections.

Some of Vivaldi's concertos lack an independent slow movement, using the adagio or other such section as a transition between self-sufficient quick movements. Such examples continue the seventeenth-century practice of composing instrumental pieces as continuous wholes, played without a break. Here, however, the Largo is a full-fledged movement, simpler in form and in its technical demands on the players, although the soloist was presumably expected to supply improvised melodic embellishment. This Largo differs from the slow movements of many eighteenth-century concertos in being in the tonic; in later concertos an inner slow movement is usually in a contrasting key, most often the relative minor or major. Also notable here is the four-part fugal texture of the ritornello; even the violas enter with a statement of the short four-note subject (m. 2). This is unexpected although by no means unheard-of in eighteenth-century Italian instrumental music, which is predominantly homophonic.

J. S. Bach and the Concerto

In a sense, J. S. Bach was one of Vivaldi's best students. Though he never traveled to Italy or met Vivaldi, Bach studied works from the latter's Opus 3 and Opus 4, arranging a number of concertos from each set as solos for harpsichord or organ around 1713.[5] At the time, Vivaldi's music represented an exciting avant-garde, and Bach, like other German composers, must have eagerly acquired copies of it for study, performance, and imitation. A number of Bach's harpsichord and organ works—the preludes of the English Suites and several *praeludia* whose first movements resemble ritornello forms—might have been among his first original compositions based on Vivaldi's models. Real ensemble concertos for violin and other instruments followed, most of them probably composed during his last years at Weimar (1714–17) and at Cöthen (1717–23).

---

[5]Bach's arrangement of Vivaldi's Concerto op. 3, no. 12, is the fifth in the series of such transcriptions for harpsichord (BWV 976). Bach later arranged one of the works from Opus 3 with four solo violin parts (Concerto no. 10 in B minor, R. 580) as a concerto in A minor for four harpsichords and strings, BWV 1065.

The Brandenburg Concertos

Bach's most famous concertos are the set of six works that he copied out in 1721 into a manuscript dedicated to Christian Ludwig, the margrave of Brandenburg-Schwedt. Eighteenth-century works were often referred to by the name of their dedicatee—hence the nickname Brandenburg Concertos. Christian Ludwig had no actual power; Brandenburg was ruled by his nephew, King Frederick William I of Prussia, in whose capital city of Berlin Bach had played several years earlier for the margrave. The king's mother, Sophie Charlotte, had been a significant patron of music; Corelli's Opus 5 had been dedicated to her, as was Torelli's Opus 6. But Frederick William had little interest in music; not until 1740, when his son Frederick became king, would Prussia again have a great patron of the arts on its throne.

Hence Bach's six concertos may not have been heard in Berlin during his lifetime. Bach, however, must have directed performance of all six concertos by the Weimar or Cöthen court ensembles, and at Leipzig he arranged several movements for use in his cantatas. Reflecting Bach's study of Vivaldi's ingenious and varied instrumentation, the set is remarkable for its diversity. No two of the works have the same scoring or form. As Table 13.2 shows, the set includes such novelties as a solo piccolo violin—a violin tuned a third above normal—and a work for three violins, three violas, and three cellos with continuo. There is also a work with a solo harpsichord part (Concerto no. 5), in which Bach himself must have served as soloist. Modern impressions of the Brandenburg Concertos have been distorted by performances in which parts intended for single players

TABLE 13.2
Johann Sebastian Bach: The Brandenburg Concertos

No.	Key	Instrumentation	Movements
1	F	2 horns, 3 oboes, bassoon, violino piccolo, 2 violins, viola, cello, b.c.	F–S–F–[rondeau]*
2	F	trumpet, recorder, oboe, violin, *2 violins, viola, violone,* b.c.	F–S–F
3	G	3 violins, 3 violas, 3 cellos, b.c.	F–F**
4	G	2 recorders, violin, *2 violins, viola,* cello, violone, b.c.	F–S–F
5	D	flute, violin, harpsichord, *violin, viola,* cello, violone	F–S–F
6	B♭	2 violas, 2 violas da gamba, cello, b.c.	F–S–F

italics = instruments designated by Bach as ripieni

b.c. = basso continuo (i.e., harpsichord); includes violone in nos. 1, 3, and 6; includes cello in no. 2

F = fast

S = slow

*minuet alternating with (1) trio and (2) polonaise (polacca)

**connected by two chords marked adagio

have been given to entire orchestral sections. In fact, like many Baroque concertos, these were composed as chamber works in the modern sense, for a single player on each part (both solo and ripieno).

Brandenburg Concerto no. 2 in F, BWV 1047

As with all six concertos, the date of composition for Concerto no. 2 (anthology, Selection 40) is unknown, although it was complete by 1721. It contains solo parts for trumpet, recorder, oboe, and violin, as well as a continuo part for cello and harpsichord and ripieno parts for two violins, viola, and "violone."[6] The trumpet part is for a natural (valveless) instrument in F, apparently higher than the usual trumpet in C or D and thus presenting particular difficulties to players of modern instruments.[7] Like the concerto grosso by Corelli, this work is performable by soloists and continuo alone, that is, without the four ripieno string parts. Bach may have originally written it in this form, although no such version survives. Nevertheless, the first movement is in ritornello form, never used by Corelli. In addition, its three movements fall in what would soon become the standard fast-slow-fast sequence.

The first movement, although opening with the usual passage for the tutti (mm. 1–8), soon begins to blur the lines between ritornello and solo sections. Passages for soloists and for the tutti alternate in rapid succession, and the ritornello never returns in its original form. For this reason, no analysis along the lines of a simple alternation of ritornello and solo sections is entirely satisfactory. Table 13.3 employs a number of special symbols intended to reflect the unique elements of this movement.

The texture throughout is highly contrapuntal, as one might expect of Bach. As in Cantata 127, the opening ritornello combines three distinct motivic ideas in invertible counterpoint (played by trumpet, the other soloists, and continuo, respectively). The first few solo passages then introduce a contrasting theme, played by each of the soloists in a series of imitative entries (mm. 9, 13, 17, 21), beginning with the violin.

One later passage in the movement, labeled "BACH" in Table 13.3, is of special interest. In the first appearance of the passage, in measures 50–55, the bass line begins with the notes e♭–d–f–e♮. This may seem unremarkable, but when the passage is restated later in the movement the notes are transposed to spell out B♭–A–c–B♮ (mm. 109–11). In German, the note B♭ is designated simply B, whereas B♮ is called H; thus the bass line spells out Bach's name (B–A–c–H). This was no accident, as is clear from the recurrence of this BACH motive in other works by Bach and his sons.[8]

---

[6]The *violone di ripieno* called for in Bach's score of this work was perhaps not a double-bass instrument but a French bass violin or a large viola da gamba playing at written pitch.

[7]Bach's performances probably used the normal D trumpet; the apparent high pitch is due to the fact that the other instruments would have been tuned in what is known as *tief Kammerton*, the lowest of several different pitch standards used in Bach's day.

[8]The most famous instance of the BACH motive is in the incomplete *Fuga con 3 soggetti* from Bach's *Art of Fugue*.

TABLE 13.3
J. S. Bach: Brandenburg Concerto no. 2 in F (BWV 1047), first movement

Section	R	S*	r	s	R*	seq	BACH	r	S*	R*	seq	R*	r	BACH	r
Key	F	F→	C	→	d	d→	→	B♭	B♭→	g	g→	a	F	→	F
Measure	1	9	23	29	31	40	50	56	60	75	84	94	103	107	115

S* = begins as a solo, but includes tutti passages

R* = a tutti passage combining portions of R with a new sequential phrase

seq = a long sequence derived from mm. 1–2 of the ritornello

BACH = a sequence with the "BACH" motive in the bass line

The restatement of this passage points to an important aspect of Bach's compositional process. Unlike Vivaldi, who composed in a seemingly improvisatory manner, rarely repeating anything exactly, Bach often restates substantial portions of a movement, frequently in transposed or otherwise varied form. This procedure helps establish the "architectural" quality for which his music is sometimes noted—that is, the impression that each movement resembles a monumental, solidly constructed edifice. The recurrence of the BACH passage is particularly striking, for it stands out against the surrounding music by virtue of its relatively homophonic texture, its *piano* dynamic marking, and its somewhat surprising harmonies. Clearly, Bach gave the passage in which he "signed" his name a crucial role in the movement's formal design.

The trumpet and the ripieno instruments drop out in the second movement, an Andante in D minor. The natural trumpet could have played only a very limited part here, and its military assocations would have been inappropriate to the quiet tone of the movement. Similarly reduced scoring characterizes the slow movements of most of the other works in the set and is common throughout the eighteenth-century concerto repertory. Here, the three remaining soloists and continuo are enough to provide complex four-part counterpoint. The texture stays constant throughout the movement: sustained lines for the three upper parts are written in imitative counterpoint, while the continuo moves in steady eighth notes, except at cadences.

The use of a single, unvarying texture is typical of many late Baroque works; we have seen an earlier example in the fourth movement of Corelli's Sonata in C, op. 5, no. 3, with its steady arpeggiation in sixteenths for the violin. Some contrast arises out of the modulations through a series of different keys, and the imitative technique used in the three upper voices produces a kaleidoscopic effect as the main theme passes from one part to another, creating a constant variation of sonority.

Two aspects of the movement are particularly characteristic of Bach. First, it is extremely dissonant. The chord on the downbeat of measure 6, for example, is a IV^7, with the dissonant seventh (f ″) appearing in the oboe. When the oboe resolves the dissonance, moving downward by step (to e″), it creates another dissonance, forming a tritone with the bass and the recorder. (The sonority as a whole is a diminished seventh chord). Similar progressions occur in almost every measure of the piece, giving it an anguished character shared with many of Bach's works.

The same passage illustrates a second aspect of the movement, its high frequency of so-called **sigh motives**. A sigh motive is a two-note slurred figure consisting of a dissonant appoggiatura (accented passing tone) and its resolution, such as the oboe's two-note motive on the downbeat of measure 6. The slur implies a decrescendo from the accented appoggiatura to its unaccented resolution, producing an expressive effect. Sigh motives are particularly prominent in the passage beginning at measure 16 (recorder: c‴–b♭″, b♭″–a″, etc.).

Sigh figures are extremely common in sonatas, concertos, and arias written in the so-called *galant* style of Bach's younger Italian and German contemporaries (see Chapter 14). His use of such a figure here and in other works is one

TABLE 13.4
J. S. Bach: Brandenburg Concerto no. 2 in F (BWV 1047), third movement

	1st Exposition	Episode	2nd Exposition	Episode	3rd Exposition	Episode & Coda
Trumpet	F 1 2 C	i	1	iv ⋯ iii	(2) 1 1	ii ⋯ (F)
Recorder	C—1	ii	(2) 1 2	i ⋯ v	F 2	iii
Oboe	C—1 2 3	iii	d	v ⋯ i	B♭ 2	iv
Violin	F 1 2	iv	C—2	ii ⋯ ii		i
Basso Continuo	(2 2 3 3)	v	(1) 3 A/d—	iii ⋯ iv	(1) C/F—	v (1)
Cadence	C		C d:V	g	B♭ F:V	F
Measure	1	41	57 72	80 85 97	107 119	126 136

letters = keys of fugal entries
X/Y (slash between letters) = entry on note X but in key Y
— (dash) = bridge (free continuation of an entry)
numbers = countersubjects
roman numerals = lines of quintuple invertible counterpoint in episode
(symbol in parentheses) = incomplete or highly altered entry
The "cadence" line lists major arrivals, not all cadences.

of many signs that he was happy to incorporate up-to-date, fashionable gestures into his music. But few of his contemporaries would have used such motives within such a densely contrapuntal texture, preferring a simpler and more direct style. Movements like this one eventually gave Bach the not entirely undeserved reputation of a composer of complex, difficult music—which might explain why margrave Christian Ludwig apparently ignored him.

Bach's penchant for complexity comes to the fore in the last movement, a five-voice fugue. The trumpet returns, stating the subject at the opening. It is joined by the other soloists, entering in turn with the subject. After the completion of the first exposition, the ripieno instruments return as well in a special sort of episode (mm. 47–57; see Table 13.4).

Like many episodes in other Bach fugues, this one is restated several times in different keys, varied each time through invertible counterpoint (at mm. 79, 97, and 126). An essential element in strict fugues and other contrapuntal genres, invertible counterpoint always involves the exchange of two or more melodic lines between different parts. In **double counterpoint,** two parts exchange two melodic lines; **triple counterpoint** involves three lines and three parts. This episode, exceptionally, employs **quintuple counterpoint**—invertible counterpoint in which no fewer than five distinct melodic ideas are shuffled between the four soloists and continuo, as shown by the lowercase roman numerals in Table 13.4.

Most listeners will not consciously recognize such a device. Nor need they do so in order to enjoy this movement, which, despite its fugal complexity, is as energetic and accessible as any work of Vivaldi's. This might have been Bach's point: the same music could satisfy both a learned composer such as himself and a prince who was, at best, a musical amateur. The composition of such music was an intellectual and creative feat of the highest magnitude. It was the type of achievement toward which most Baroque musicians probably aspired, even if few approached or even attempted it.

CHAPTER 14

A MID-EIGHTEENTH-CENTURY EPILOGUE
The *Galant* Style

As noted at the outset of this exploration of Baroque music, the periods into which we divide music history are in many respects arbitrary. It has become customary to draw a dividing line at the mid-eighteenth century, partly because 1750 is a conveniently round figure, partly because a number of important composers, especially Bach and Handel, died in or about that year. Nevertheless, as in the period around 1600, few people at the time would have guessed that they were living through what would later be regarded as a transition period. The most prestigious and influential genre of the eighteenth century, opera seria, continued to develop in an unbroken tradition right through the century. So too did the sonata and the concerto, with composers such as the Italians Giuseppe Tartini (1692–1770) and Pietro Antonio Locatelli (1695–1764) continuing to write music that at first was very much in the tradition of Vivaldi and other members of the previous generation. In this they were followed by composers such as the French Leclair, the Germans Pisendel and Quantz, and the English Thomas Augustine Arne (1710–78).

Nevertheless, by 1750 the Baroque style exemplified for us by the fugues of Bach and the oratorios of Handel was becoming a thing of the past. Rameau and Handel were still alive and composing, but many younger composers now regarded as Classical (or pre-Classical), including Gluck, the sons of Bach, and even Haydn, had already begun their careers. An old-fashioned work such as J. S. Bach's *Art of Fugue* had yet to be published. But Bach's son Carl Philipp Emanuel was writing keyboard sonatas and concertos that have many points in common with those of Haydn and even Beethoven. Opera composers such as Hasse and Jommelli were creating a style that in some respects anticipated the so-called reform operas of Gluck and those of Mozart. And G. B. Sammartini, Monn, and Wagenseil were writing symphonies and chamber music that are at times virtually indistinguishable from early works of Haydn. Although we think of 1750 as the end of the Baroque, by that date Monn and some other short-lived pre-Classical composers, notably Giovanni Battista Pergolesi (1710–36), had already passed away.

THE *GALANT* STYLE

During the eighteenth century, the French adjective *galant* was used to describe fashionable styles of poetry, music, even food and manners. Music historians have adopted the expression **style galant** to describe music of post-Baroque and pre-Classical styles, especially that of German composers active in the decades before and after 1750.[1] The term is sometimes translated literally as "gallant style," but the English adjective *gallant* hardly conveys an accurate idea of what the expression signifies in music history. A *galant* musical work was, essentially, one that avoided strict counterpoint and chromatic harmony or modulation, which were increasingly seen as archaic. Instead such a work employed simple homophonic textures, with diatonic harmony and singable melodies. By this standard, most late-Baroque Italian opera arias and French dances were already *galant*. So too were solo sonatas and concertos, at least as long as they avoided fugues. Today the term is used more specifically to refer to mid-eighteenth century works whose melody, harmony, and texture represent a further simplification of those of the Baroque.

The term *galant* is particularly appropriate for various types of Italian vocal and instrumental music that have been viewed as direct predecessors of the Viennese Classical style. Among these are the operatic works of Pergolesi, including his famous comic intermezzo *La serva padrona* (Naples, 1733). In such works, even fully scored orchestral passages tend to consist of simple textures in which a single melodic line—often played by first and second violins in unison—is accompanied by a simple continuo part (doubled by the viola, whose part may not even be written out). If two upper lines are present, they often move in parallel thirds or sixths (Ex. 14.1). One rarely finds independent inner voices, and harmony in four or more real parts is rare. This trend was already evident in Italian instrumental and vocal music of the late seventeenth century. But in the *galant* style it extends to a point where even the bass line loses much of its former melodic and rhythmic independence, often being reduced to repeated notes (so-called **drum basses**), as in measures 2 and 9 of Example 14.1. Also typical of the style are the so-called Lombardic rhythm seen in measure 1 of the example, the appoggiaturas (written as small notes) in measures 2 and 9, and the slow **harmonic rhythm** or rate of harmonic change. In the example, the harmony rarely changes more than twice in each measure, and is moreover restricted to little more than an alternation of tonic and dominant. An earlier Baroque composer would have been embarrassed to write such music, but the aim here was a directness and simple elegance that could not be achieved in the older style.

This style proved popular throughout Europe, particularly in its operatic manifestation, although a distinct style descended from that of Lully remained recognizable in French music through the time of Mozart. In Germany, Italian opera dominated theaters at Dresden, Berlin (after 1741), and other capitals and courts, where the *galant* style served as a vehicle for such virtuoso singers as the castrati Farinelli and Senesino and the (female) sopranos Faustina Bordoni and

---

[1] Another term is *rococo*, used particularly with respect to French music and art of the period.

Example 14.1 Pergolesi, duet "Per te ho nel core," originally from the opera *Flaminio* (1735), used posthumously as a replacement for the final duet of *La serva padrona* (violins and viola omitted)

Serpina, Uberto
E vero il sento già,
Ma questo ch'esser può,
Io nol so, nol so io.
Caro sposo/cara sposa! Oh Dio!
Ben te lo puoi pensar.

Serpina, Uberto
It's true, I hear it [heartbeats],
But what it might be
I don't know.
Dear spouse—Oh, God!—
You may well think yourself such.

Francesca Cuzzoni. Germans such as Handel were among the leading composers of eighteenth-century Italian opera; among them were Johann Adolph Hasse (1699–1783), who became the chief opera composer at Dresden (and who married Bordoni), and Carl Heinrich Graun (1704–57), his counterpart at Berlin. Their works exerted considerable influence on instrumental as well as vocal music by their contemporaries. Solo and trio sonatas adopted the styles of melody and accompaniment employed in operatic arias and duets, and concertos increasingly took on the dramatic style and ritornello form of the aria.

One result of the spread of *galant* writing was a weakening of the sharp division between French and Italian styles that had marked seventeenth- and early eighteenth-century music. Another was the abandonment of what were seen—rightly or wrongly—as overly complicated, inexpressive or incomprehensible types of outmoded music, including the contrapuntal choral and instrumental works of J. S. Bach, whose style was seen by at least one commentator as "dark" and "unnatural" by the middle of the century.[2]

Older traditions were not entirely abandoned. In England, composers such as William Boyce (1711–79) retained elements of Handel's style into the last decades of the century. In Italy and Austria, many composers continued to cultivate the contrapuntal *stile antico* in church music; Haydn and Mozart still used it in some of their masses and other choral works. In Germany, the wide circle of musicians who had studied with J. S. Bach (or with his students) preserved the legacy of contrapuntal keyboard music. It is often thought that Bach's music was forgotten after his death, only to be revived in the nineteenth century, but this applies chiefly to his vocal music and works for instrumental ensemble. His keyboard works enjoyed ever widening circulation and were eagerly studied by such musicians as Mozart and Beethoven.

Modern writers have sometimes found *galant* music to be stylistically impoverished by comparison to the more complex music of J. S. Bach, Handel, and others. But eighteenth-century musicians and their audiences, including Bach and Handel, clearly found positive values in it. The relatively simple textures and harmony of *galant* music focused attention squarely on what was viewed as expressive and "natural" melody. Moreover, the changes in bass-line writing and instrumentation made possible new types of orchestral scoring, paving the way for the wide variety of orchestral textures used in later Classical and Romantic music. Solo keyboard music was equally transformed as the new focus on melody led to the invention of new types of idiomatic accompaniment. Among the latter was the so-called **Alberti bass,** a type of accompaniment consisting chiefly of broken chords. Named for one of its early users, the Venetian composer Domenico Alberti (ca. 1710–1740), it found widespread use as a keyboard equivalent for some of the new types of orchestral accompaniment. The broken chords of the left hand (lower staff) in Example 14.2 were an idiomatic keyboard

Example 14.2 Domenico Alberti, Sonata in E♭, second movement, mm. 1–4

[2]The most famous document for this view is the attack on Bach's vocal music published in 1737 by Johann Adolph Scheibe, a critic and composer who favored the *galant* style; see *The New Bach Reader*, 337–38.

adaptation of such orchestral textures as the repeated notes of the strings in Example 14.3, from *Cleofide*, a famous example of opera seria by Hasse. Bach is thought to have attended the Dresden premiere of the latter work in 1731, and he evidently encouraged his sons and students to imitate such music.

To be sure, the *galant* style does seem to have made it possible for mediocre composers to produce vast quantities of bland, forgettable vocal and instrumental music, much of it for the amateur market. Such music uses major keys almost exclusively and avoids surprises and intensely expressive or dramatic effects. Yet even Bach admired and imitated the *galant* works of some of his contemporaries, such as Telemann and Hasse, and his students were among the most important proponents of the style. The musical developments of the later eighteenth century, including the emergence of the Viennese Classical style, cannot be fully understood without considering the *galant* music that preceded it.

Example 14.3 Johann Adolph Hasse, *Cleofide* (1731), Act 3, aria "Dov'è? si affretti," mm. 1–3

GEORG PHILIPP TELEMANN

Although we tend to focus on Bach and Handel when considering music history in the first half of the eighteenth century, at the time the most respected and possibly the most influential composer in the German-speaking parts of Europe was Georg Philipp Telemann (1681–1767). He was capable of writing both contrapuntal church music in the manner of Bach and expressive oratorio arias and choruses such as Handel's. But unlike those composers, Telemann was not a virtuoso performer, and much of his enormous output consists of relatively undemanding, accessible music. Born in Magdeburg, in eastern Germany, in 1701 he began university studies in nearby Leipzig. By the following year had founded the Leipzig Collegium Musicum—later directed by Bach—and was also directing the Leipzig Opera.[3] After holding a series of musical positions in Poland and Germany—including that of kapellmeister in Bach's hometown of Eisenach—Telemann was appointed cantor and music director at Hamburg in 1723, a prestigious position that he held until his death. Telemann knew both Handel, with whom he carried

---

[3]The Leipzig Opera had ceased operation by the time Bach came to town in 1723.

on a lifelong correspondence, and J. S. Bach, whose son Carl Philipp Emanuel was his godson and succeeded him in his Hamburg position.

Like Vivaldi, Telemann's reputation has suffered because of the enormous quantity of his works. In the case of Telemann the judgment is particularly unfair because many of his major works remain unpublished. His instrumental music, which includes hundreds of sonatas, concertos, and suites for every imaginable combination of instruments, has become fairly well known. Yet his vocal works, which are even more numerous and substantial, remain relatively obscure; they include over a thousand church cantatas and close to fifty passions, as well as several oratorios composed late in life that are remarkable for their original, highly expressive responses to their texts.[4]

Telemann's "Paris" Quartets

In 1737 Telemann visited Paris. There, as he proclaimed in his autobiography of 1739, a number of his quartets were played with great success by an ensemble comprising several of the most famous French musicians of the day. Among them were the flutist Michel Blavet (1700–1768), composer of flute sonatas and other works, and the viola da gambist Jean-Baptiste Antoine Forqueray (1699–1782), son of the composer Antoine Forqueray.[5] The works in question were no doubt the six *Nouveaux quatuors* (New quartets) that Telemann published in Paris in 1738 during his stay here (Fig 14.1). This set was a continuation of six similarly scored works that had been first published in 1730. Both sets are now referred to as Telemann's "Paris" Quartets; among the subscribers whose names appear printed in the 1738 volume was "Bach of Leipzig."

A "quartet" in the early eighteenth century was a sonata for three melody instruments and continuo—that is, one more instrument than in a trio sonata; the present works are for the unusual combination of violin, flute, and viola da gamba. By including an independent part for the viol, Telemann continued the long tradition of chamber music for that instrument in France (there were also still a few famous viol players in Germany). Nevertheless, to facilitate performance for ensembles without a gambist, Telemann included an alternate part for cello. A harpsichord furnishes the continuo, to which might be joined a second cello, although this option is not made explicit.

Nouveau quatuor no. 6 in E Minor, TWV 43:e4

The "new" quartets can be described as suites. Particularly impressive is the concluding work in E minor (anthology, Selection 41), which consists of a French overture followed by five dancelike movements designated *Gay, Vite, Gracieusement,*

---

[4]A multivolume thematic catalogue of Telemann's works is being published gradually; it assigns a TWV number to each work.

[5]The younger Forqueray published an edition of his father's gamba pieces; it is unclear to what degree these are actually arrangements or revisions of the latter's music. A separately published version of the same pieces for harpsichord, in a style reminiscent of Rameau, might have been the work of the younger Forqueray's wife, the harpsichordist Marie-Rose Dubois.

Figure 14.1 Telemann, *Nouveau quatuor* no. 6 in E minor, TWV 43:e4, opening page of the flute part, from its first edition (Paris, 1738). Note the clean lines of the stems and beams and the precise placement of slurs and ornament signs (in the form of crosses or plus signs), typical of French music engraving in the eighteenth century.

Distrait, and *Modéré*. The presence of an overture and dances signifies that the style is French, yet the music throughout contains substantial elements of the Italian style, as in the frequent use of arpeggiated figuration. To be sure, by this date Italian style had thoroughly permeated French music, as in the operas of Rameau.

The opening movement reveals some of the ways in which the old ceremonial genre of the Lullian overture could be transformed in the hands of an inventive *galant* composer such as Telemann. In the opening section the dotted rhythms are maintained less consistently than in the pure Lully style; indeed, they are interrupted by some Italianate arpeggiation for the violin (mm. 9–11). The tempo marking *à discrétion* (with freedom) probably applies in particular to this violin solo, which might therefore be played rhapsodically, like an improvisation—a far cry from the rhythmic precision of the Lullian opera orchestra.

The following section, marked *très vite* (very lively), opens without the fugal exposition frequently encountered at this point in the traditional French overture. Moreover, the main theme contains some catchy hemiolas, a witty surprise in such a movement (mm. 15–16, 17–18, etc.). All three upper parts, especially the violin, have virtuoso passagework also characteristic not of the traditional French style but of Vivaldi and other Italians. Yet the texture remains predominantly contrapuntal, including some passages in invertible counterpoint, and the movement closes with the conventional recapitulation of the opening section.

Of the four short movements that follow, two are clearly dances: the second movement, marked *Gay*, is a gavotte, as is evident from its half-measure upbeat, whereas the fourth, designated *Gracieusement* (gracefully—not in the anthology), is probably a *loure*, a type of slow French gigue resembling the Italian pastorale (Ex. 14.4). The fifth movement, headed *Distrait*, does not belong to any of the traditional categories; rather, it is a sort of character piece, although it is hard to say how the music reflects its title, which means "absent-minded" (literally "distracted"). As in many French Baroque keyboard pieces, the connection between title and music is elusive, but it must have something to do with the syncopated rhythmic motive heard in the flute and violin in the A section (mm. 1–24) and in the gamba at the beginning of the B section (mm. 25–56). The form of this movement is the same used in the paired dances that constituted the Baroque antecedent of the Classical minuet and trio. Couperin, Bach,

Example 14.4 Telemann, *Nouveau quatuor* no. 6, fourth movement, mm. 1–5

Telemann, and other contemporaries frequently grouped two short binary-form movements together, repeating the second one at the end to produce an ABA design.[6] The *Gay* movement has the same form; as in many such movements, the second section (B) is in a contrasting mode (major) and uses altered instrumentation—exceptionally, without continuo.

The last movement is a chaconne over a six-bar ostinato bass. The same unusual bass line occurs in a passacaglia for solo harpsichord by Johann Philipp Krieger (1649–1725), an important predecessor of Telemann and Bach as a composer of German sacred cantatas. Possibly Telemann borrowed the bass line

---

[6]It is uncertain whether both halves of the A section were repeated the second time around, as has been argued for the Classical minuet and trio.

as well as several melodic ideas from the older composer, whose work might also have suggested the present movement's languishing, elegiac character, very different from the rhythmic energy typical of the traditional Lullian or Ramellian version of the dance. The sustained notes of the bass line, together with such details as the drooping motive of the flute and violin at the opening and the slurred chromatic lines of measures 13–15, creates a profoundly moving effect in performance, belying the notion that Telemann's music lacks depth or seriousness.

CARL PHILIPP EMANUEL BACH

C. P. E. Bach extended to the *galant* style the expressive harmony and rhythmic complexity found in the music of his father. Emanuel Bach's lifespan almost exactly straddled the middle of the century, overlapping what we consider the late Baroque and early Classical periods. We can recognize elements of both styles in his music, but his works are best understood as an intensely personal development of the same *galant* style seen in the works of Telemann, Hasse, and other older contemporaries.

The Bach Sons

Five sons of J. S. Bach (1685–1750) became professional musicians; four were also composers, and of these three were of considerable importance. All tended to avoid the contrapuntal aspects of their father's music in favor of the *galant* style. This may well have been at J. S. Bach's insistence, for only by adopting the more fashionable and up-to-date style could they hope for successful careers of their own. Both Wilhelm Friedemann (1710–84) and Carl Philipp Emanuel (1714–88) were keyboard virtuosos whose instrumental works, especially keyboard sonatas and concertos, are of special significance. On the other hand, Johann Christian (1735–87), the youngest son, became a composer of Italian opera and Italianate symphonies and chamber music. He settled in London, where his music was a major influence on the young Mozart, whose early works closely resemble Christian Bach's.

In the music of Friedemann and Emanuel Bach, the conventional *galant* style is deepened by chromatic harmony and expressive, often improvisatory, melodic fragmentation and surprise. Their style and that of a few contemporaries in northern Germany is often described today as the *empfindsamer Stil* ("sensitive" or "expressive style"). This is a reference to its frequent use of pathetic or dramatic expressive effects, although the music of both composers is also marked by touches of witty humor, like that of Telemann.

Emanuel Bach was the most prolific of the Bach sons. He was widely admired for his keyboard playing as well as his compositions, which, like those of his father, include all the major genres of the time except for opera. He was born at Weimar and grew up in Cöthen and Leipzig, where, according to his autobiography of 1773, his sole teacher was his father. In 1740 he became court keyboard player to the Prussian king Frederick II (the Great) at Berlin. There he regularly accompanied the flute-playing king in private concerts alongside a few other distinguished musicians.[7] In 1768, after the death of Telemann, Bach left Berlin to take over his godfather's position as cantor and church music director at Hamburg, where he spent his remaining twenty years.

Emanuel's career roughly paralleled his father's, culminating in a position as music director in a major city after a period as a court musician. Like his father, he wrote numerous cantatas and other sacred vocal works. But his most important compositions are his 150 keyboard sonatas and 52 keyboard concertos.[8] In addition to old-fashioned solo and trio sonatas (mostly before 1750), he also composed German songs (lieder), keyboard trios (for piano, harpsichord, or clavichord with violin and cello), and a number of fantasias, rondos, and other keyboard pieces. Like his Berlin colleague Quantz, he also wrote an influential performance treatise: *Essay on The True Manner of Playing Keyboard Instruments*, which provides valuable information on keyboard playing in the *galant* and earlier styles. The book was published in two volumes; volume 1 (Berlin, 1753) is a treatise on keyboard playing in general, with special focus on the clavichord, whereas volume 2 (Berlin, 1762) is concerned with figured bass realization and improvisation. Much in the book, particularly in the second volume, probably derives from the teaching of J. S. Bach. But its immediate concern is the performance of *galant* music, naturally including Emanuel's own.

The Keyboard Sonatas

Emanuel Bach's keyboard sonatas constitute the earliest important repertory of multimovement sonatas for solo keyboard instruments. Written throughout his career, they reveal the composer's stylistic evolution from a post-Baroque manner, containing occasional echoes of Sebastian Bach's inventions and suites, to a style that is often described as Classical or even pre-Romantic. The keyboard sonata hardly existed as a genre when Emanuel began writing such works, in the early 1730s, while still a student at Leipzig. Since his father wrote no keyboard sonatas of this type, Emanuel must have modeled them on solo sonatas for flute or violin and continuo by such *galant* composers as Telemann and Hasse. But even Emanuel's earliest sonatas reveal an original, idiomatic adaptation of the genre to the keyboard.

During his first few years at Berlin, Emanuel Bach published two influential sets of six sonatas each, the "Prussian" Sonatas of 1742 and the "Württemberg" Sonatas of 1744. Further sets appeared after 1750, including a famous series of six volumes published at Hamburg under the subtitle *für Kenner und Liebhaber* ("for connoisseurs and amateurs," 1779–87); the first volume comprised six sonatas, whereas the next five included distinctive types of rondos and fantasias as well. Following eighteenth-century tradition, Emanuel did not usually specify the medium of his keyboard works, and they can be played on the harpsichord

---

[7] The concerts were led by violinist-composer Franz Benda (1709–86). Quantz, the king's teacher, attended the concerts but probably did not usually perform in them.

[8] A few of the concertos also exist in versions for flute or cello. Much of Emanuel Bach's sacred music, formely believed to have been lost during World War II, was rediscovered in the 1990s.

as well as the fortepiano. In his own playing, however, he favored the clavichord. Eighteenth-century German instrument makers expanded the clavichord's keyboard compass and dynamic capabilities, and contemporary accounts of Emanuel's playing, such as that published in 1773 by the English writer Charles Burney (1726–1814), describe his brilliant performances and impassioned improvisations on such instruments.

"Württemberg" Sonata no. 1 in A minor, W. 49/1

This work (anthology, Selection 42) was the first in the set of six keyboard sonatas published as Emanuel Bach's Opus 2 in Berlin in 1744; it had been composed in Berlin two years earlier. The collection received its popular name from its dedicatee, the young duke Carl Eugen of Württemberg, who presumably studied with the composer during an extended visit to Berlin. Emanuel Bach's first publication, the "Prussian" sonatas, also consisting of six sonatas, had been dedicated to the newly crowned King Frederick of Prussia.[9]

By the time these works appeared, Emanuel was a master composer, and the three movements of the present sonata exemplify his approach to the idiom. As in most ensemble sonatas of the period, these form the sequence fast-slow-fast.[10] Although the imitative counterpoint of J. S. Bach is absent from this sonata, echoes of the simple three-part polyphony of the late-Baroque trio sonata can be heard in many passages, especially in the slow movement. There the upper parts tend to move in parallel thirds or sixths, but elsewhere the texture is often reduced to two parts, filled out by occasional chords that, on the harpsichord, would have served as accents (as in the opening chord of the first movement, echoed at m. 9). Often the bass line is quite simple, as in the last movement, where it provides a drum bass as in orchestral music of the period.

As in the arias and sinfonias of *galant* opera, such textures focused attention on the melody, which is full of ornate details notated in small note values. Some of the quick notes constitute arpeggiated passagework or figuration of the sort that was also heard in the solo episodes of Emanuel's keyboard concertos (e.g., last movement, mm. 55–62). Elsewhere, as at the opening of the first movement, the melodic figuration is less regular, broken up by rests and shifting rhythmically between sixteenths, thirty-seconds, and triplets. Sigh figures, as in the recurring two-note slurs of the third movement (mm. 2, 3, 5, and 6), add an expressive, languishing element that counters the forward energy of the drum basses and the virtuoso passagework. Such contrasts are an important element of Bach's so-called *empfindsamer* style, of which this work is an early

---

[9]Several numbering systems exist for the works of C. P. E. Bach. The "W" numbers used here are those assigned by Alfred Wotquenne in the early twentieth century. A more recent work list prepared by E. Eugene Helm was, confusingly, issued in two versions, leading to two somewhat different series of "H" numbers, and remains in need of further revision.

[10]Emanuel Bach's flute sonatas, like those of Quantz written for the king, use instead the order slow-fast-fast; this Berlin custom continued as late as 1795, when Beethoven used it in two cello sonatas dedicated to one of Frederick's successors.

example. Similar writing occurs in the music of Quantz, Graun, and other contemporaries, but rarely with Bach's dramatic use of harmonic tension. Characteristic of the latter is the delay of a cadence that we are led to expect in the first movement during the first half of measure 16. The bass drops out on the third beat, and the following measure pauses on a dissonance, which is sustained by a fermata. The resolution of the latter—an extended sigh motive on e″–d♯″— yields another dissonance, in modern terms a diminished-seventh chord. The anticipated full cadence to E minor arrives only in measure 20, concluding the first section of the sonata.

Early Sonata Form

Through such devices as those described above, Bach transferred the drama of Italian opera to the keyboard sonata. Yet just as opera seria contained its drama within a highly schematic form, the quick outer movements of Bach's sonata encompass their *empfindsamer* details within a regular design. This design was the same one used in countless contemporary instrumental sonatas by Quantz and other, older composers. Descended from the binary form of seventeenth-century French and Italian dances, it would become the basis of thousands of individual movements in eighteenth- and, ultimately, nineteenth- and twentieth-century works.

This design today is known as **sonata-allegro** (or just **sonata**) form. Somewhat confusingly, this modern expression describes the form of a single movement, not of a complete sonata. Versions of the same design occur in movements from concertos, symphonies, and other genres as well as in works called sonatas. Modern accounts of sonata form tend to be based on works from the Classical period, using terminology developed in the nineteenth century. Works by Emanuel Bach and his contemporaries employ a distinct, in some respects simpler, version of sonata form.

As realized in the outer movements of this work, sonata form is an expansion of a three-part form—in eighteenth-century terms, three-*period* form—as shown in Table 14.1. Although there are three main sections, the form is actually binary, in the sense that there are only two repeated units, signified by the double bar after the first section. This first section opens with the statement of a principal theme; it then modulates from the tonic to either the dominant (as in the first movement) or the relative major (as in the last movement). Each of the two main sections that follow the double bar is in a sense a varied restatement of the first section. Both of these sections open with a restatement of the principal theme; section 2 then modulates to a new key, using motivic material similar to that of the first section. Because section 3 opens in the original key, it remains in that tonality to the end.[11]

---

[11]In the nineteenth century these three sections of sonata form came to be described as exposition, development, and recapitulation, respectively. These three expressions are not entirely appropriate to early sonata form, however, since there the sections lack the functional distinctions implied by the later terminology.

TABLE 14.1

Sonata Form in C. P. E Bach: "Württemberg Sonata no. 1 in A minor (W. 49/1)

First movement						
Section	1		2	retransition	3	
Key	a →	e :‖:	C→	F→	a→	a :‖
Measure	1	20	21	39	42	55b

Third movement						
Section	1		2	retransition	3	
Key	a→	C :‖:	d:V→	e→	a→	a :‖
Measure	1	70	71	104	128	176

Seemingly cut and dry on paper, sonata form was in fact a way of dramatizing the abstract processes of modulation and thematic development. In particular, the beginning of section 3—the so-called **return** (or **double return**), where the opening theme returns in the opening key–can become the focus of great drama. This is especially so when, as in both outer movements of the present work, the return is prepared by an extra modulating passage. This passage, known as the **retransition**, connects the end of the second main section and the beginning of the third, that is, the return. The retransition is particularly exciting in the third movement (mm. 104–27), where it contains an exceptionally long and virtuosic development of the passagework first heard at measure 37.

It is possible to analyze both movements further. For instance, section 1 of the first movement is subdivided by a restatement of the opening theme in the dominant at measure 9b (the bass continues the restatement of the theme at m. 10b). This sort of subdivision would become a normal element in nineteenth-century sonata form, where a new theme might be introduced at this point. But eighteenth-century composers were far from consistent in subdividing the sections of a sonata-form movement in this way, and sections 2 and 3 of the present movement lack any corresponding subdivision. For Emanuel Bach, as for his contemporaries, what we call sonata form was a set of basic procedures that could be elaborated creatively in every new composition. Composers might omit the double bar or the retransition, or they might even reduce the number of main sections from three to two, leaving a two-period form, as was especially common in slow movements.

In the slow movement of this particular sonata, Bach takes a somewhat different approach. As had become customary, this movement is in a contrasting key, A major. But here, as in several other works of the 1740s, Bach departs from convention and writes a sort of free rondo form, based on recurrences of the opening theme. The latter returns twice, first in the tonic (m. 21) and then in the relative minor (m. 33). Just before the end, the music pauses on a fermata, which is set over what we would call a I_4^6 chord. Fermatas in Baroque music were often an invitation for a soloist to improvise, and this is a particular example of that tradition: a **cadenza**. The word, Italian for "cadence," points to the fact that this was an improvised elaboration of a cadence such as could occur at the end of any major formal division. Today we expect to find cadenzas in the quick movements of a concerto, and indeed that would become the most common place for them by the end of the eighteenth century. But earlier in the century they occur in arias and sonatas as well as concertos. In Berlin they were typically placed at the end of a slow movement, a tradition that Bach follows here. What performers actually did at these moments is indicated in treatises and in written-out examples of cadenzas left by Emanuel Bach and other contemporaries (see anthology).

Emanuel Bach's Concertos

During his Berlin years, in addition to writing numerous keyboard concertos, Emanuel Bach perfected a type of concerto for keyboard instrument (harpsichord or fortepiano) and strings. By the 1730s, his father had created similar works, but these are thought to have been arranged from lost earlier works in which the solo instrument was violin or, in one or two cases, oboe. Thus the two concertos for harpsichord and strings that Emanuel composed at Leipzig in the early 1730s are among the earliest original works of this type. The solo concertos of both composers broadly resemble those of Vivaldi in their use of ritornello form as the basis of each movement (see Chapter 13). But with C. P. E. Bach the individual sections are fewer in number, though longer; three main solo episodes in each movement correspond to the three sections of a contemporary sonata form, with ritornellos inserted before and after each of these sections. In addition, many of Emanuel's concertos adopt a heightened version of his *empfindsamer* style, resulting in an unprecedented level of drama for a purely instrumental work.

During the 1740s Emanuel devoted particularly intensive efforts to the keyboard concerto, composing twenty such works as well as one concerto for two harpsichords, all with string accompaniment. These were probably performed at private or semipublic gatherings, including regular Saturday concerts given at the home of Johann Friedrich Agricola (1720–74), a student of J. S. Bach and C. H. Graun's eventual successor as royal opera composer.[12] Emanuel continued to write harpsichord concertos into his Hamburg years, when he probably played many of them at public concerts under his direction. His last concerto, written in 1788, is a double concerto for harpsichord, fortepiano, and orchestra.

Perhaps the most intense expression of the *empfindsamer* style occurs in Emanuel's D-minor concerto (W. 23) of 1748, composed six years after his First "Württemberg" Sonata and a year after his father's famous visit to Berlin. The ritornello of the first movement opens with a slashing theme characterized by leaps over double octaves, sudden dynamic contrasts, and a dramatic pause preceded by a long, particularly dissonant appoggiatura (Ex. 14.5). The latter derives special intensity from the combination of startling chromaticism ($d\sharp''$) with the *pianissimo* dynamic

---

[12]Agricola, like Quantz and C. P. E. Bach, was an important writer on music; he was responsible for the German translation of Tosi's singing treatise as well as an annotated version of an encyclopedic work on organs and other keyboard instruments by Jacob Adlung, *Musica mechanica organoedi* (Berlin, 1768), which provides valuable information about the performance of J. S. Bach's music.

Example 14.5 C. P. E. Bach, Concerto in D minor, W. 23, first mvt., mm. 1–10

marking. The solo part later enters with a variation of this theme, transformed into the type of virtuoso passagework that dominates the rest of the solo episode (Ex. 14.6). This first episode, as well as the last one in the movement, ends with a fermata—a signal for a cadenza, originally left to the performer but later written out by the composer. Cadenzas for the soloist would become common fixtures in later keyboard concertos, but at this date they were usually restricted to slow movements, as in the A-minor "Württemberg" Sonata.

Another extraordinary gesture occurs at the opening of the second movement: the latter is in the contrasting key of F major, yet its ritornello opens with a dissonance, establishing the new tonic only after a series of startling modulations (Ex. 14.7). Similar writing in some of his later works for solo keyboard has given C. P. E. Bach the reputation today of a composer whose concern with intense expression went beyond the emerging Classical style to foreshadow that of the Romantics. Although the Classical composers Haydn, Mozart, and Beethoven knew some of C. P. E. Bach's vocal works and solo keyboard compositions and might have been influenced or inspired by them, they probably had no access to this concerto.

By the mid-eighteenth century, the threefold design described above had become a feature of most sonata and concerto movements, at least in Germany. That Emanuel Bach should have adopted this formal convention reveals a paradox fundamental to his so-called *empfindsamer* style. Despite the highly individualized, irregular thematic material and the many dramatic harmonic and rhythmic gestures, most instrumental movements follow essentially the

Example 14.6 C. P. E. Bach, Concerto in D minor, W. 23, first mvt., mm. 48–53 (lower strings omitted)

Example 14.7 C. P. E. Bach, Concerto in D minor, W. 23, second mvt., mm. 1–8

same formal pattern, one also used by his contemporaries. Hence, for all their expressive detail, most of C. P. E. Bach's works are more regular and predictable in their formal designs than are the works of Vivaldi or J. S. Bach. Exceptions occur chiefly in his fantasias and other improvisatory works for solo keyboard.

Some such regular patterning was typical of music at midcentury. It was probably necessary in order to produce movements of the length and complexity found in Emanuel Bach's sonatas and concertos. An intense musical drama lasting over eight minutes, as in the first movement of his D-minor concerto, could not have been achieved with the more irregular or episodic forms employed in most Baroque works. Paradoxically, some standardization of musical form was necessary in order to make individual musical compositions more dramatic. This idea would be central to the symphonies, sonatas, and string quartets of the Classical and Romantic styles.

BIBLIOGRAPHY

This is less a comprehensive bibliography of Baroque music than a guide to further reading. It is restricted largely to recent books in English; a few journal articles, dissertations, and foreign-language works are included for subjects not covered in recent monographs. It includes scholarly collected editions for individual composers discussed in the text and, in some cases, facsimiles and other special resources, but editions of specific compositions must be sought in library and thematic catalogues.

The ever-growing number of internet sites includes several worthy of inclusion, but the ephemeral nature and derivative character of many pages devoted to "classical" music militates against their being listed. Online databases such as RILM (*Répertoire international de la littérature musicale*) are useful for those who know what they are looking for, but the bibliographies at the ends of entries in *Grove Music Online* may prove more helpful for focused searching (where these have been kept up to date). It is worth remembering, too, that *Grove* offers the most recent and most comprehensive English-language discussions of many topics, large and small. Even for major composers, such as Gabrieli and Schütz, there are no recent books on the life and works equal in coverage or reliability to the *Grove* entries.

Not listed here are older bibliographic guides in print format. The "Bibliographical Notes" at the ends of chapters in the textbook by John Walter Hill (see *Baroque Music* below) provide useful introductions to the basic literature on many special topics.

Items are listed by type and subject under the following categories: (1) reference works, collections of readings, and other general works; (2) regional and cultural contexts, genres and repertories, and music theory; (3) performance practice and organology (instruments); and (4) writings about specific composers and their music (including information about musical editions). A number of frequently cited university presses are abbreviated as follows:

CUP   Cambridge, U.K.: Cambridge University Press

HUP   Cambridge, Mass.: Harvard University Press

IUP   Bloomington and Indianapolis: Indiana University Press

OUP   London, New York, and/or Oxford: Oxford University Press (including its Clarendon Press imprint)

PUP   Princeton, N.J.: Princeton University Press

UCP   Berkeley and Los Angeles: University of California Press

REFERENCE WORKS, COLLECTIONS OF READINGS, AND OTHER GENERAL WORKS

Background: General European History

Recent historical writing has tended to focus on cultural, sociological, and economic approaches, which can be useful for understanding the contexts in which artistic production has taken place. But such writings are frustrating if one seeks information about specific rulers, historical events, or political structures as they affected individual composers, compositions, and musical performance. Moreover, important musicians, such as J. S. Bach, often worked in regions of Europe that were relatively unimportant politically and consequently have been neglected in current English-language historiography.

For general historical background, one may turn to such works as Helmut Georg Koenigsberger, *Early Modern Europe, 1500–1789* (London: Longman, 1987), and John M. Merriman, *A History of Modern Europe: From the Renaissance to the Present* (New York: Norton, 1996). For information about specific events, rulers, and places, particularly in more "peripheral" regions such as Italy and Saxony during our period, one may need to turn to older reference works such as *The New Cambridge Modern History*, vols. 4–6 (CUP, 1970, 1961, 1970); vol. 14 includes a good historical atlas.

Reference Books on Music

Music dictionaries and encyclopedias. The standard English-language music reference is *The New Grove Dictionary of Music and Musicians*, 2d ed., edited by Stanley Sadie and John Tyrell (London: Macmillan, 2001), online as *Grove Music Online* (http://www.grovemusic.com). Particularly valuable are the detailed work lists and bibliographies attached to the articles on major composers. Expanded articles on musical instruments from the first edition of this work appear in a separate publication: *The New Grove Dictionary of Musical Instruments*, edited by Stanley Sadie, 3 vols. (London: Macmillan, 1984).

Good one-volume music dictionaries include *The Harvard Dictionary of Music*, 4th ed., edited by Don Michael Randel (HUP, 2003), and *The Oxford Dictionary of Music*, 2d ed., edited by Michael Kennedy (OUP, 2006), each of which exists in a smaller "concise" version as well.

Special-topic reference works. Of special relevance to our topic is the dictionary-style *Companion to Baroque Music*, edited by Julie Anne Sadie (UCP, 1998). Valuable for understanding Baroque librettos and ballet scenarios is *The Oxford Guide to Classical Mythology in the Arts 1300–1990*, edited by Jane Davidson Reid with the assistance of Chris Rohmann (OUP, 1993).

Historical music dictionaries. Encyclopedic works produced during the Baroque remain valuable today. Among these are Michael Praetorius, *Syntagma musicum*, 3 vols. (Wolfenbüttel, 1613–20; mod. ed., Kassel: Bärenreiter, 2001), portions translated by David Z. Crookes as *Syntagma Musicum II: De organographia: Parts I and II* (OUP, 1986), and by Jeffrey Kite-Powell as *Syntagma musicum III* (OUP, 2004); Marin Mersenne, *Harmonie universelle* (Paris, 1636; facs., Paris: Centre National de la Recherche Scientifique [CNRS], 1963), portions translated by Roger E. Chapman as *Harmonie universelle: The Books on Instruments* (The Hague: Nijhoff, 1957); and Athanasius Kircher, *Musurgia universalis* (Rome, 1650; facs., Hildesheim: Olms, 2004).

Usable for both French and Italian terminology around 1700 is Sébastien de Brossard, *Dictionnaire de musique* (Paris, 1703), translated by Albion Gruber (Henryville, Pa.: Institute of Mediaeval Music, 1982); for an eighteenth-century English adaptation, see James Grassineau, *A Musical Dictionary* (London, 1740; facs., New York: Broude, 1966). From the circle of J. S. Bach comes Johann Gottfried Walther, *Musicalisches Lexicon* (Leipzig, 1732; mod. ed., Kassel: Bärenreiter, 2001).

Music Bibliography and Writing about Music

Online databases have superseded many traditional research tools, but for locating and identifying older materials the following may still be useful. For general bibliography, see John H. Baron, *Baroque Music: A Research and Information Guide* (New York: Garland, 1993). A guide to scholarly editions of music, which are especially numerous for our subject, is George R. Hill and Norris L. Stephens, *Collected Editions, Historical Series and Sets, and Monuments of Music: A Bibliography* (Berkeley, Calif.: Fallen Leaf Press, 1997).

For proper style and formatting in writing about music, the standard guide is Kate L. Turabian, *A Manual for Writers of Term Papers, Theses, and Dissertations*, 7th ed., revised by Wayne C. Booth et al. (Chicago: University of Chicago Press, 2007).

Collections of Readings

A widely used anthology of readings is *Source Readings in Music History*, ed. Oliver Strunk, rev. ed., edited by Leo Treitler (New York: Norton, 1998). More specialized collections appear below under specific headings.

Surveys and Collections of Essays

An older textbook valuable for its keen critical insights is Manfred F. Bukofzer, *Music in the Baroque Era from Monteverdi to Bach* (New York: Norton, 1947). A more recent, comprehensive survey (with a companion anthology of scores) is John Walter Hill, *Baroque Music: Music in Western Europe, 1580–1750* (New York: Norton, 2005). For essays of a general nature surveying much of the Baroque, with a companion audio CD, see *The World of Baroque Music: New Perspectives*, edited by George B. Stauffer (IUP, 2006). In-depth essays on seventeenth-century repertories as well as issues in aesthetics and cultural studies appear in *The Cambridge History of Seventeenth-Century Music*, edited by Tim Carter and John Butt (CUP, 2005). Overlapping with the latter is *European Music, 1520–1640*, edited by James Haar (Rochester; N.Y.: Boydell Press, 2006). Somewhat older but still useful on historical and cultural context (with valuable illustrations) is the series *Music and Society*, which includes two relevant volumes: *The Early Baroque Era: From the Late 16th Century to the 1660s*, edited by Curtis Price, and *The Late Baroque Era: From the 1680s to 1740*, edited by George J. Buelow (both Englewood Cliffs, N.J.: Prentice Hall, 1994).

MUSIC IN REGIONAL AND CULTURAL CONTEXTS, GENRES AND REPERTORIES, AND MUSIC THEORY

Music in Regional and Cultural Contexts

On music in specific places and regions of Europe, see the *Music and Society* series (just above) as well as James R. Anthony, *French Baroque Music From Beaujoyeulx to Rameau*, rev. ed. (Portland, Ore.: Amadeus Press, 1997); Caroline Wood and Graham Sadler, *French Baroque Opera: A Reader* (Aldershot, U.K.: Ashgate, 2000); Eleanor Selfridge-Field, *Venetian Instrumental Music*, 3d ed. (New York: Dover, 1994); Michael Talbot, *Venetian Music in the Age of Vivaldi* (Aldershot; U.K.: Ashgate, 1999); Stephen Bonta, *Studies in Italian Sacred and Instrumental Music in the 17th Century* (Aldershot, U.K.: Ashgate, 2003); and *Church, Stage, and Studio: Music and Its Contexts in Seventeenth-Century Germany*, edited by Paul Walker (Ann Arbor; Mich.: UMI Research Press, 1989). A fascinating study on the relationship between music and military aspects of life is Kate van Orden, *Music, Discipline, and Arms in Early Modern France* (Chicago: University of Chicago Press, 2005).

Women in music. Still fundamental is Jane Bowers and Judith Tick, *Women Making Music: The Western Art Tradition, 1150–1950* (Urbana: University of Illinois Press, 1986). For the biography of a fascinating figure, see Claire Fontijn, *Desperate Measures: The Life and Music of Antonia Padoani Bembo* (OUP, 2006). Three localized studies of women religious musicians are Craig Monson, *Disembodied Voices: Music and Culture in an Early Modern Italian Convent* (UCP, 1995), primarily on music in Bologna; Robert L. Kendrick, *Celestial Sirens: Nuns and Their Music in Early Modern Milan* (OUP, 1996); and Colleen Reardon, *Holy Concord Within Sacred Walls: Nuns and Music in Siena, 1575–1700* (OUP, 2002). Representative of recent feminist scholarship are the essays in *Musical Voices of Early Modern Women: Many-Headed Melodies*, edited by Thomasin LaMay (Aldershot; U.K.: Ashgate, 2005). See also the work by Heller below under "Opera, cantata, and oratorio."

Genres and Repertories

These are listed below in the order in which they occur in the chapters of the main text. See also the further sections on "Performance Practice and Organology" and on individual composers.

The madrigal. A general survey: Jerome Roche, *The Madrigal*, 2d ed. (OUP, 1990). A detailed study of an important pre-Baroque repertory, with a volume of musical examples: Anthony Newcomb, *The Madrigal at Ferrara, 1579–1597*, 2 vols. (PUP, 1980).

Opera, cantata, and oratorio. An older survey strong on Baroque opera is Donald J. Grout, *A Short History of Opera*, 2d ed. (New York: Columbia University Press, 1965). A more recent study of early opera in one of its first major centers, with many substantial examples from otherwise unavailable works, is Ellen Rosand, *Opera in Seventeenth-Century Venice: The Creation of a Genre* (UCP, 1991). A more specialized study of early Venetian opera is Wendy Heller, *Emblems of Eloquence: Opera and Women's Voices in Seventeenth-century Venice* (UCP, 2003). On later opera see Reinhard Strohm, *Dramma per musica: Italian Opera Seria of the Eighteenth Century* (New Haven, Conn.: Yale University Press, 1997). Also focusing on opera seria is Daniel Heartz, *Music in European Capitals: The Galant Style, 1720–1780* (New York: Norton, 2003).
    On the vast Italian cantata repertory one must consult works on individual composers (see below) or specific repertories, such as John Walter Hill, *Roman Monody, Cantata, and Opera from the Circles around Cardinal Montalto* (OUP, 1997). For France there is David Tunley, *The Eighteenth-Century French Cantata*, 2d ed. (OUP, 1997).

Sacred music. On polychoral music, with copious musical examples, see Anthony F. Carver, *Cori spezzati: The Development of Sacred Polychoral Music to the Time of Schütz*, 2 vols. (CUP, 1988). Oratorios are surveyed in Howard E. Smither, *A History of the Oratorio*, vol. 2, *The Oratorio in the Baroque Era: Protestant Germany and England* (Chapel Hill: University of North Carolina Press, 1977). Much can be learned about sacred music in seventeenth-century Germany from Mary E. Frandsen, *Crossing Confessional Boundaries: The Patronage of Italian Sacred Music in Seventeenth-Century Dresden* (OUP, 2006).

Keyboard music. A useful reference work, although increasingly dated, is Willi Apel, *The History of Keyboard Music to 1700*, translated by Hans Tischler (IUP, 1972). More up-to-date essays can be found in *Keyboard Music Before 1700*, 2d ed., edited by Alexander Silbiger (New York: Routledge, 2004), and *Eighteenth-Century Keyboard Music*, 2d ed., edited by Robert L. Marshall (New York: Routledge, 2003). Special aspects of French music are subjects of David Ledbetter, *Harpsichord and Lute Music in 17th-Century France* (IUP, 1988); and *The Art of the Unmeasured Prelude for Harpsichord, France, 1660–1720*, 3 vols., edited by Colin Tilney (London: Schott, 1991). Specialized essays ranging from Frescobaldi to J. S. and C. P. E. Bach are in *The Keyboard in Baroque Europe*, edited by Christopher Hogwood (CUP, 2003).

Sonata and concerto. Although somewhat dated, useful information can still be found in William S. Newman, *The Sonata in the Baroque Era*, 4th ed. (New York: Norton, 1983), and

Arthur Hutchings, *The Baroque Concerto*, rev. ed. (New York: Scribner's, 1979). For early Baroque string music generally, see Willi Apel, *Italian Violin Music of the Seventeenth Century*, edited by Thomas Binkley (IUP, 1990). More specialized is Peter Allsop, *The Italian "Trio" Sonata from Its Origins until Corelli* (OUP, 1992). See also Selfridge-Field, *Venetian Instrumental Music* (above under "Music in Regional and Cultural Contexts").

Music Theory and Compositional Practice

History of theory and composition. On sixteenth-century modality, see Bernhard Meier, *The Modes of Classical Vocal Polyphony: Described According to the Sources*, translated by Ellen S. Beebe (New York: Broude, 1988). A classic study of the emergence of tonality is Carl Dahlhaus, *Studies On the Origin of Harmonic Tonality*, translated by Robert O. Gjerdingen (PUP, 1990). Also valuable on this topic is Stein, "Between Key and Mode" (see below, "Composers and Their Works," under Carissimi).

On later theory, centering on the role of Rameau, see Joel Lester, *Compositional Theory in the Eighteenth Century* (HUP, 1992); Thomas Street Christensen, *Rameau and Musical Thought in the Enlightenment* (CUP, 1993); and Chapters 1 and 3 in David Kopp, *Chromatic Transformations in Nineteenth-Century Music* (CUP, 2002). For Rameau's own writings, see under his name in "Composers and Their Music," below.

For case studies of compositional teaching and practice, see Alfred Mann, *The Great Composer As Teacher and Student: Theory and Practice of Composition: Bach, Handel, Haydn, Mozart, Beethoven, Schubert* (New York: Dover, 1994), as well as individual items on Bach and Handel under "Composers and Their Music," below.

Fugue. The theory and practice of fugue have a large modern literature, centering on the works of J. S. Bach. Three representative works are Alfred Mann, *The Study of Fugue* (New Brunswick, N.J.: Rutgers University Press, 1958); William Renwick, *Analyzing Fugue: A Schenkerian Approach* (Stuyvesant, N.Y.: Pendragon Press, 1995); and Paul Mark Walker, *Theories of Fugue from the Age of Josquin to the Age of Bach* (Rochester, N.Y.: University of Rochester Press, 2000).

Expression, meaning, and aesthetics. The large literature on the philosophy of music can be divided between historical writings and those presenting contemporary views. Among historical treatments, Edward Lippman, *A History of Western Musical Aesthetics* (Lincoln: University of Nebraska Press, 1992) includes two chapters on our period. Relevant writings from the period can be found in works by Mattheson (see below) and by C. P. E. Bach and Quantz (under "Voices and Instruments," below) and in extracts in Strunk, *Source Readings* (under "Collections of Readings," above).

A modern work that draws particularly on the Baroque writer Johann Mattheson is Peter Kivy, *Sound Sentiment: An Essay on the Musical Emotions, Including the Complete Text of "The Corded Shell"* (Philadelphia: Temple University Press, 1989). Useful ideas on Baroque music can be gleaned from Raymond Monelle, *The Musical Topic: Hunt, Military and Pastoral* (IUP, 2006). An older classic article is Manfred Bukofzer, "Allegory in Baroque Music," *Journal of the Warburg and Courtauld Institutes* 3 (1939–40): 1–21. On musical rhetoric, a useful handbook is Dietrich Bartel, *Musica poetica: Musical-Rhetorical Figures in German Baroque Music* (Lincoln: University of Nebraska Press, 1997), but see the cautionary article by Peter Williams, "The Snares and Delusions of Musical Rhetoric: Some Examples from Recent Writings on J. S. Bach," in *Alte Musik: Praxis und Reflexion*, edited by Peter Reidmeister and Veronika Gutmann (Winterthur, Switzerland: Amadeus, 1983), 230–40.

Baroque theoretical treatises. Numerous works from the period, ranging from elementary pedagogic manuals to sophisticated technical treatises, appear in modern facsimiles and editions. For translations of three manuscript treatises on performance practice and composition by a student of Heinrich Schütz, see Walter Hilse, "The Treatises of Christoph Bernhard," *Music Forum* 3 (1973): 31–79. The classic eighteenth-century work on counterpoint is Johann Joseph Fux, *Gradus ad Parnassum* (Vienna, 1725; facs., New York: Broude, 1966); portions appear in English in Alfred Mann, *The Study of Counterpoint from Johann Joseph Fux's Gradus ad Parnassum*, rev. ed. (New York: Norton, 1965).

See also the writings listed in "Composers and Their Works," below, by C. P. E. Bach, Rameau, and Schütz.

PERFORMANCE PRACTICE AND ORGANOLOGY

Reference, Bibliography, and Readings

Useful for performance practice in general (as well as organology) are the articles on the major instruments in *New Grove*. See also the historical music dictionaries listed under "Reference Books on Music," above, especially the translations from works by Praetorius and Mersenne, as well as Roland Jackson, *Performance Practice: A Dictionary-Guide for Musicians* (New York: Routledge, 2005). Two journals, *Early Music* and *Performance Practice Review*, contain numerous articles on the subject; the latter has been succeeded by an online version at http://ccdl.libraries.claremont.edu/col/ppr/. Also online is the *Journal of Seventeenth-Century Music* (http://sscm-jscm.press.uiuc.edu/jscm/), which has published a number of articles on performance issues (including audio and video clips).

Some useful extracts from Baroque treatises appear in Strunk, *Source Readings* (above, under "Collections of Readings"); see also the Donington work under the next heading. An encyclopedic work valuable for its documentation of contemporary practice is Johann Mattheson, *Der vollkommene Capellmeister* (Hamburg, 1739), modern edition by Friederike Ramm (Kassel: Bärenreiter, 1999); portions relevant to performance practice appear in Ernest C. Harriss, *Johann Mattheson's Der vollkommene Capellmeister: A Revised Translation with Critical Commentary* (Ann Arbor, Mich.: UMI Research Press, 1981).

General Works on Historical Performance

On the history of the discipline, which has focused to a considerable degree on Baroque music, see Harry Haskell, *The Early Music Revival: A History* (Mineola, N.Y.: Dover, 1996). Philosophical issues have been the subject of a number of books, not always accompanied by sympathetic understanding of the subject; one recent, well-informed study is Peter Walls, *History, Imagination, and the Performance of Music* (Rochester, N.Y.: Boydell Press, 2003).

An influential if increasingly dated introduction to the topic, still valuable for its numerous extracts from historical treatises, is Robert Donington, *The Interpretation of Early Music*, new rev. ed. (New York: Norton, 1989). Essays on special topics appear in Stewart Carter, *A Performer's Guide to Seventeenth-Century Music* (New York: Schirmer Books, 1997). For in-depth examinations of specific performance issues in works by Bach, Corelli, Couperin, and Handel, see Peter Le Huray, *Authenticity in Performance: Eighteenth-Century Case Studies* (CUP, 1990).

Special Topics

Useful as a comprehensive reference on ornaments, despite the author's tendentious interpretations, is Frederick Neumann, *Ornamentation in Baroque and Post-Baroque Music: With Special Emphasis on J. S. Bach* (PUP, 1978).

Figured bass realization and continuo playing have been subjects of numerous works. Still useful for its extracts from historical treatises, with commentary, is Frank T. Arnold, *The Art of Accompaniment from a Thorough-Bass*, 2 vols. (OUP, 1932; reprint, New York: Dover, 1965). Harder to find but equally valuable is Peter Williams, *Figured Bass*

Accompaniment, 2 vols. (Edinburgh: Edinburgh University Press, 1970). Available in translation are *Accompaniment on Theorbo and Harpsichord: Denis Delair's Treatise of 1690*, translated by Charlotte Mattax (IUP, 1991), and the relevant chapters of the works by C. P. E. Bach (listed in the following section) and Rameau (under his name in "Composers and Their Works," below). A valuable recent study is Guilia Nuti, *The Performance of italian Basso Continuo: Style in Keyboard Accompaniment in the Seventeenth and Eighteenth Centuries* (Aldershot, U.K.: Ashgate, 2007).

For a survey of rhythmic conventions, see Stephen E. Hefling, *Rhythmic Alteration in Seventeenth- and Eighteenth-Century Music: Notes Inégales and Overdotting* (New York: Schirmer Books, 1993). On the French prelude, see Tilney, *Art of the Unmeasured Prelude*, above under "Genres and Repertories."

Of the many studies of historical tuning, the most useful may be Thomas Donahue, *A Guide to Musical Temperament* (Lanham, Md.: Scarecrow Press, 2005). But for sheer accessibility to a difficult topic, it would be hard to beat Ross W. Duffin's *How Equal Temperament Ruined Harmony (and Why You Should Care)* (New York: Norton, 2007). Pitch is the topic of Bruce Haynes, *A History of Performing Pitch: The Story of "A"* (Lanham, Md.: Scarecrow Press, 2002).

Voices and Instruments

Baroque vocal technique. Unfortunately there exist no books in English that can serve as general guides to Baroque vocal performance. On the castratos, see Angus Heriot, *The Castrati in Opera* (London: Secker and Warburg, 1956). Early recordings of actual castrato singers from the early twentieth century are collected in *Moreschi: The Last Castrato* (Sparrows Green, U.K.: Pavilion Records [Opal CD 9823], 1987). For examples of period embellishment, see Franz Häbock, *Die Gesangskunst der Kastraten* (Vienna: Universal, 1923), and Dean, *Three Ornamented Arias* (under Handel in "Composers and Their Works," below).

Two important treatises that present the mature French and Italian Baroque styles, respectively, are available in translation: Bénigne de Bacilly, *Remarques curieuses sur l'art de bien chanter* (Paris, 1668), translated by Austin B. Caswell as *A Commontary Upon the Art of Proper Singing* (Brooklyn, N.Y.: Institute of Mediaeval Music, 1968); and Pier Francesco Tosi, *Opinioni de' cantori antichi e moderni* (Bologna, 1723), translated by Julianne C. Baird from the German version of Johann Friedrich Agricola (*Anleitung zur Singkunst*, Berlin, 1757) as *Introduction to the Art of Singing* (CUP, 1995). For earlier Italian vocal practice, see under Caccini in "Composers and Their Works," below.

Instruments and instrumental practice. These topics are often discussed together in the encyclopedic works listed above, many of which contain entries on individual instruments. Cambridge University Press has been issuing a *Practical Guide* series comprising general introductions to particular types of historical instruments and their performance practices; keyboards, violin and viola, flutes, clarinets, and horns are among the instruments covered thus far. A similar *Musical Instrument Series* from Yale University Press includes volumes on the flute, oboe, trombone, and timpani and percussion. On transitions in instrument making during the Baroque, see *From Renaissance to Baroque: Change in Instruments and Instrumental Music in the Seventeenth Century*, edited by Jonathan Wainwright and Peter Holman (Aldershot, U.K.: Ashgate, 2005).

On bowed string instruments, see David Dodge Boyden, *The History of Violin Playing from Its Origins to 1761 and Its Relationship to the Violin and Violin Music* (OUP, 1990). Among the most important Baroque sources are Georg Muffat's prefaces to his published music, edited in their original German, Latin, French, and Italian in *Denkmäler deutscher Tonkunst*, vols. 1/2 (Vienna, 1894), 2/2 (Vienna, 1895), and 11/2 (Vienna, 1904); for English translation with commentary see *Georg Muffat on Performance Practice*, edited and translated by

David K. Wilson (IUP, 2000). A later treatise on string playing, relevant for early-eighteenth-century practice in the Italian style, is Leopold Mozart, *A Treatise on the Fundamental Principles of Violin Playing*, translated by Editha Knocker, 2d ed. (OUP, 1985). For the viola da gamba, there is no English-language monograph, but the *Journal of the Viola da Gamba Society of America* contains numerous useful articles.

On woodwinds, the two major Baroque treatises are Jacques Hotteterre, *Principles of the Flute, Recorder, and Oboe*, translated by Paul Marshall Douglas (New York: Dover, 1983); and Johann Joachim Quantz, *Versuch einer Anweisung die Flöte traversiere zu spielen* (Berlin, 1752), translated by Edward R. Reilly as *On Playing the Flute*, 2d ed., reissued with additional material (Boston: Northeastern University Press, 2001). For a study of the latter work in relation to compositions and surviving instruments by Quantz, see Mary Oleskiewicz, "The Flutes of Quantz: Their Construction and Performing Practice," *Galpin Society Journal* 52 (2000): 201–20. The latter draws on a larger study by the same author, "Quantz and the Flute at Dresden: His Instruments, His Repertory, and Their Significance for the *Versuch* and the Bach Circle" (Ph. D. diss., Duke University, Durham, N.C., 1998).

Brass: Anthony Baines, *Brass Instruments: Their History and Development* (New York: Scribner, 1978); Don L. Smithers, *The Music and History of the Baroque Trumpet Before 1721*, 2d ed. (Carbondale: Southern Illinois University Press, 1988).

Keyboard instruments have a large literature. An overview of keyboard organology can be obtained from John Koster, *Keyboard Musical Instruments in the Museum of Fine Arts, Boston* (Boston: Museum of Fine Arts, 1994). Focusing on the harpsichord, with samples of historical instruments on audio CD, is Edward L. Kottick, *A History of the Harpsichord* (IUP, 2003). The best concise guide to the organ remains Peter Williams, *A New History of the Organ from the Greeks to the Present Day* (London: Faber, 1980).

On performance, two major eighteenth-century performance treatises are Carl Philipp Emanuel Bach, *Versuch über die wahre Art das Clavier zu spielen* (Berlin, 1753–62), translated by William J. Mitchell as *The True Art of Playing Keyboard Instruments* (New York: Norton, 1949); and François Couperin, *L'Art de toucher le clavecin/The Art of Playing the Harpsichord*, bilingual edition with English translation by Mevanwy Roberts (Leipzig: Breitkopf und Härtel, 1933). Modern treatments include Howard Schott, *Playing the Harpsichord* (New York: Dover, 2002), and Ann Bond, *A Guide to the Harpsichord* (Portland, Ore.: Amadeus, 1997). Relevant especially to the organ but useful for all keyboard players are Quentin Faulkner, *J. S. Bach's Keyboard Technique: A Historical Introduction* (St. Louis, Mo.: Concordia, 1984), and George Ritchie and George Stauffer, *Organ Technique: Modern and Early* (Englewood Cliffs, N.J.: Prentice Hall, 1992).

On plucked strings see *Performance on Lute, Guitar, and Vihuela: Historical Practice and Modern Interpretation*, edited by Victor Anand Coelho (CUP, 1997). Fundamental for accompaniment is Nigel North, *Continuo Playing on the Lute, Archlute, and Theorbo* (IUP, 1987).

Two often-overlooked Baroque instruments are the subjects of Albert R. Rice, *The Baroque Clarinet* (OUP, 1992), and James Tyler, *The Early Guitar: A History and Handbook* (OUP, 1980); see also James Tyler and Paul Sparks, *The Guitar and Its Music from the Renaissance to the Classical Era* (OUP, 2002).

Dance

Bibliography: Judith L. Schwartz and Christena L. Schlundt, *French Court Dance and Dance Music: A Guide to Primary Source Writings, 1643–1789* (Stuyvesant, N.Y.: Pendragon Press, 1987). For a catalogue of dances preserved in Baroque choreographies: Meredith Little, *La danse noble: An Inventory of Dances and Sources* (Williamstown, Mass.: Broude, 1992). Two useful videos, both produced by Paige Whitely-Bauguess, are *Introduction to Baroque Dance: Dance Types* and *Dance of the French Baroque Theatre* (New Bern, N.C.: BaroqueDance, 1999 and 2005).

The classic survey of French Baroque dance, *Dance of Court and Theater: The French Noble Style, 1690–1725*, is included in *Dance and Music of Court and Theater: Selected Writings of Wendy Hilton* (Stuyvesant, N.Y.: Pendragon Press, 1997). A unique study and edition of a seventeenth-century French ballet is Rebecca Harris-Warrick and Carol G. Marsh, *Musical Theatre at the Court of Louis XIV: Le mariage de la Grosse Cathos* (CUP, 1994).

COMPOSERS AND THEIR WORKS

J. S. Bach

Bach's complete works were issued in the nineteenth century by the German Bach-Gesellschaft (Bach Society) as *J. S. Bach's Werke* (Leipzig, 1851–99). Known as the "BG" (for *Bachgesamtausgabe*), this edition has been the source of many subsequent reprints, including cantatas, keyboard music, and concertos issued by Kalmus and Dover. Usually more accurate and complete is the so-called NBA (*Neue Bach-Ausgabe*), published as the *Neue Ausgabe sämtlicher Werke* (Kassel, Germany: Bärenreiter, 1954–). Several volumes in this series have been superseded, however, notably that of the *B-Minor Mass*; for the latter, see the recent editions by Joshua Rifkin (Wiesbaden, Germany: Breitkopf und Härtel, 2006) and Christoph Wolff (Frankfurt, Germany: C. F. Peters, 1997). For an excellent edition of the *Well-Tempered Clavier*, see that of Richard Jones in two volumes, incorporating the famous commentaries by Donald Francis Tovey (London: Associated Board of the Royal Schools of Music, 1994). Numerous facsimiles of Bach's manuscripts and original editions are also available in several series.

Editions of individual works within the BG or NBA are most quickly located through the work lists in the *New Grove Dictionary* or *Bach* Composer Companion (see below). More complete bibliographic information is available in the thematic catalogue by Wolfgang Schmieder, *Thematisch-Systematisches Verzeichnis der musikalischen Werke von Johann Sebastian Bach: Bach-Werke-Verzeichnis (BWV)*, 2d ed. (Wiesbaden, Germany: Breitkopf und Härtel, 1990). For even more detailed listings, see Hans-Joachim Schulze and Christoph Wolff, *Bach Compendium: Analytisch-Bibliographisches Repertorium der Werke Johann Sebastian Bachs (BC)* (Frankfurt, Germany: C.F. Peters, 1986–).

A good point from which to begin a survey of the vast literature on Bach and his music is Daniel R. Melamed and Michael Marissen, *An Introduction to Bach Studies* (OUP, 1998). There is also a searchable website, Yo Tomita's *Bach Bibliography*, at http://www.music.qub.ac.uk/tomita/bachbib/, mirrored at http://www.npj.com/bach/.

Available in the Oxford Composer Companions series is *Bach*, edited by Malcolm Boyd (OUP, 1999), a dictionary-style reference book that includes entries for most of Bach's individual works, including each cantata. Essays on more general topics are found in *The Cambridge Companion to Bach*, edited by John Butt (CUP, 1997).

A German annual containing scholarly articles and reviews is the *Bach-Jahrbuch* (Berlin: Evangelische Verlagsanstalt, 1904–). Two American serials featuring writings in English are *Bach Perspectives* (currently published by Illinois University Press) and *BACH: The Quarterly Journal of the Riemenschneider Institute*.

The New Bach Reader: A Life of Johann Sebastian Bach in Letters and Documents, edited by Hans T. David and Arthur Mendel, revised by Christoph Wolff (New York: Norton, 1998), includes translations of numerous documents, among them the complete text, in translation, of the first biography of Bach, by Johann Nicolaus Forkel (1802).

Recent biographies of Bach include Peter Williams, *J. S. Bach: A Life in Music* (CUP, 2007); Christoph Wolff, *Johann Sebastian Bach: The Learned Musician* (New York: Norton, 2000); and Malcolm Boyd, *Bach*, 3d ed. (New York: OUP, 2000). For the first volume in a projected two-volume survey of Bach's complete output, see Richard D. P. Jones, *The Creative Development of Johann Sebastian Bach,* vol. I, *1695–1717: Music to Delight the Spirit* (OUP, 2007).

On the vocal works, in addition to the Oxford Bach Companion (above), see Alfred Dürr, *The Cantatas of J. S. Bach: With Their Librettos in German-English Parallel Text*, revised and translated by Richard Jones (OUP, 2005), and Daniel Melamed, *Hearing Bach's Passions* (OUP, 2005). A valuable study of one of Bach's greatest vocal works is George B. Stauffer, *Bach: The Mass in B Minor* (New York: Schirmer Books, 1997). On the vocal forces used in Bach's sacred works, see Andrew Parrott, *The Essential Bach Choir* (Woodbridge, U.K: Boydell & Brewer, 2000).

On individual instrumental works, see Malcolm Boyd, *Bach: The Brandenburg Concertos* (CUP, 1993); Michael Marissen, *The Social and Religious Designs of J. S. Bach's Brandenburg Concertos* (PUP, 1995); David Schulenberg, *The Keyboard Music of J. S. Bach*, 2d ed. (New York: Routledge, 2006); Peter F. Williams, *The Organ Music of J. S. Bach*, 2d ed. (CUP, 2003); and Joel Lester, *Bach's Works for Solo Violin: Style, Structure, Performance* (OUP, 1999).

C. P. E. Bach

A modern edition of C. P. E. Bach's collected works is under way (Los Altos, Calif.: Packard Humanities Institute). For older editions of individual works one can consult the Helm catalog (below). Particularly useful is a facsimile edition of the solo keyboard works by Darrell Berg (New York: Garland, 1985), who has also edited selected keyboard sonatas in 3 vols. (Munich, Germany: Henle, 1986–89).

In addition to the old thematic catalogue by Alfred Wotquenne (Leipzig: Breitkopf und Härtel, 1905) there is E. Eugene Helm, *Thematic Catalogue of the Works of Carl Philipp Emanuel Bach* (New Haven, Conn.: Yale University Press, 1989). The most recent biography is Hans-Günter Ottenberg, *C. P. E. Bach*, translated by Philip J. Whitmore (OUP, 1987). On individual works, see David Schulenberg, *The Instrumental Music of Carl Philipp Emanuel Bach* (Ann Arbor, Mich.: UMI Research Press, 1984). Collections of essays, both entitled *C. P. E. Bach Studies*, have been edited by Stephen L. Clark (OUP, 1988) and Annette Richards (CUP, 2006).

Bach's indispensible *Essay* on keyboard performance is listed above under "Voices and Instruments."

Biber

Most of Biber's music has now appeared in modern edition in various volumes of the *Denkmäler der Tonkunst in Österreich*. The only English-language monograph is Eric Thomas Chafe, *The Church Music of Heinrich Biber* (Ann Arbor, Mich.: UMI Research Press, 1987), which discusses many instrumental as well as vocal works.

Buxtehude

An unfinished collected edition, *Dietrich Buxtehudes Werke* (Klecken, Germany: Ugrino, 1925–37), has been revived (New York: Broude Trust, 1977–) and thus far includes vocal works and works for instrumental ensemble. There are several editions of the keyboard works, most recently that of Christoph Albrecht (Kassel, Germany: Bärenreiter, 1994–).

Thematic catalogue: Georg Karstädt, *Thematisch-Systematisches Verzeichnis der musikalischen Werke von Dietrich Buxtehude: Buxtehude-Werke-Verzeichnis (BuxWV)*, 2d ed. (Wiesbaden, Germany: Breitkopf und Härtel, 1985).

The exemplary biography is Kerala J. Snyder, *Dieterich Buxtehude, Organist in Lübeck*, rev.ed. (Rochester, N.Y.: University of Rochester Press, 2007). On context, see Geoffrey Webber, *North German Church Music in the Age of Buxtehude* (OUP, 1996).

Giulio Caccini and Francesca Caccini

Giulio Caccini's *Le nuove musiche* (Florence, 1601) is available in facsimile (New York: Broude, 1973) and in a modern edition by H. Wiley Hitchcock (Madison, Wis.: A-R, 1970), which includes a translation of Caccini's important preface.

The vocal chamber music of Francesca Caccini is available in facsimile in *Florence, Italian Secular Song 1606–1636*, vol. 1, edited by Gary Tomlinson (New York: Garland, 1986).

Carissimi

For "Urtext" editions of Carissimi's oratorios one must turn to the rare edition (using "old" clefs) by Friedrich Chrysander, *Oratorien*, vol. 2 of *Denkmäler der Tonkunst* (Bergedorf, Germany: Weissenborn, 1861). Most of the more recent editions add stylistically inappropriate "expression" markings or basso continuo realizations; an exception is *Jephte*, edited by Gottfried Wolters (Wolfenbüttel, Möseler, 1969).

On Carissimi and his works, see Graham Dixon, *Carissimi* (OUP, 1986); Andrew V. Jones, *The Motets of Carissimi* (Ann Arbor, Mich.: UMI Research Press, 1982); and Beverly Ann Stein, "Between Key and Mode: Tonal Practice in the Music of Giacomo Carissimi" (Ph.D. diss., Brandeis University, Waltham, Mass.,1994).

Castello

His known printed works are edited in Dario Castello, *Sonate concertate in stil moderno*, 2 vols., edited by Rudolf Hofstötter and Ingomar Rainer, *Wiener Edition alter Musik*, vols. 2–3 (Vienna: Doblinger, 1998). The most substantial English-language discussion is in Andrea (Andrew) Dell'Antonio, *Syntax, Form and Genre in Sonatas and Canzonas 1621–1635* (Lucca, Italy: Libreria Musicale Italiana, 1997).

Cavalieri

The music by Cavalieri and others for the intermedi to *La Pellegrina* appears in *Les fêtes du mariage de Ferdinand de Médicis et de Christine de Lorraine, Florence, 1589* (Paris: CNRS, 1963). For a biography, see Warren Kirkendale, *Emilio de' Cavalieri, "Gentiluomo romano": His Life and Letters, His Role as Superintendent of All the Arts at the Medici Court, and His Musical Compositions* (Florence: Olschi, 2001).

Cavalli

The prologue and act 1 of *Giasone* appear in *Publikationen älterer praktischer und theoretischer Musikwerke*, edited by Robert Eitner, vol. 12 (Leipzig: Breitkopf und Härtel, 1883; reprint, New York: Broude, 1966). Further selections appear in Rosand, *Opera in Seventeenth-Century Venice* (see "Genres and Repertories," above).

For biography, see Jane Glover, *Cavalli* (London: Batsford, 1978).

Corelli

Corelli's works are edited by Hans Oesch in *Historisch-kritische Gesamtausgabe der musikalischen Werke* (Cologne, Germany: Arno Volk, 1976–). Numerous "practical" editions of the solo violin sonatas and concerti grossi contain anachronistic slurs, dynamics, and continuo realizations.

The only recent biography in English is Peter Allsop, *Arcangelo Corelli: New Orpheus of Our Times* (OUP, 1998).

Couperin

A collected edition, *Œuvres complètes* (Paris: éditions de l'Oiseau Lyre, 1932–3), is in process of revision. The four books of harpsichord pieces have been issued in facsimile (New York: Broude, 1973) and in a good modern edition by Kenneth Gilbert, *Pièces de clavecin*, 4 vols. (Paris: Heugel, 1969–72).

For biography see David Tunley, *François Couperin and "The Perfection of Music"* (Aldershot, U.K.: Ashgate, 2004), and Wilfrid Howard Mellers, *François Couperin and the French Classical Tradition*, new rev. ed. (London: Faber, 1987).

Frescobaldi

A collected edition is in progress: *Opere complete* (Milan: Suvini Zerboni, 1976–). Some recently identified keyboard works appear in facsimile in vols. 1, 2, and 15/1–3 of the series *17th-Century Keyboard Music: Sources Central to the Keyboard Art of the Baroque*, with valuable prefaces by Alexander Silbiger (New York: Garland, 1987–9).

The sole life and works in English remains Frederick Hammond, *Girolamo Frescobaldi* (HUP, 1983); see also *Frescobaldi Studies*, edited by Alexander Silbiger (Durham; N.C.: Duke University Press, 1987).

Froberger

"Complete" editions of the keyboard works by Howard Schott (Paris: Heugel, 1979–92) and Siegbert Rampe (Kassel, Germany: Bärenreiter, 1993–) stand in need of revision in the light of recent discoveries, such as the manuscript copy reproduced in *Toccaten, Suiten, Lamenti: Die Handschrift SA 4450 der Sing-Akademie zu Berlin*, 2d ed., edited by Peter Wollny (Kassel, Germany: Bärenreiter, 2006). Facsimiles of three autograph manuscripts, with informative prefaces by Robert Hill, appear in volumes 3/1–3 of *17th Century Keyboard Music: Sources Central to the Keyboard Art of the Baroque* (New York: Garland, 1988).

There are no English-language books devoted to Froberger; useful essays (some in English) appear in *J. J. Froberger, musicien européen: Colloque organisé par la ville et l'Ecole Nationale de Musique de Montbéliard, 2–4 novembre 1990* (N.p.: Klincksieck, 1998).

Giovanni Gabrieli

A modern edition of Gabrieli's ensemble works (vocal and instrumental), *Opera omnia*, vols. 12/1–11 in *Corpus mensurabilis musicae* (American Institute of Musicology, 1956–), is now complete; several older volumes in the series have already appeared in revised versions. The popular works for instrumental ensemble are in vols. 10–11. What little survives of Gabrieli's keyboard music is in *Composizioni per organo*, edited by Sandro Della Libera (Milan: Ricordi, 1957–59).

Thematic catalog: Richard Charteris, *Giovanni Gabrieli (ca. 1555–1612): A Thematic Catalogue of His Music with a Guide to the Source Materials and Translations of His Vocal Texts* (Stuyvesant, N.Y.: Pendragon Press, 1996).

Gaultier

The lute works are edited in Ennemond Gaultier, *Œuvres du vieux Gautier*, 2d ed., edited by André Souris (Paris: CNRS, 1980), which also contains a historical introduction (in French) by Monique Rollin.

Gesualdo

Gesualdo's madrigals appear in his *Sämtliche Werke*, edited by Wilhelm Weisman and Glenn E. Watkins (Hamburg: Ugrino, 1957–67). The standard biography, with a foreword by Igor Stravinsky, is Glenn Watkins, *Gesualdo: The Man and His Music*, 2d ed. (OUP, 1991).

Handel

Handel's music was edited in the nineteenth century by Friedrich Chrysander in *Werke* (Leipzig; Germany: Breitkopf und Härtel, 1858–1903). Numerous volumes have been issued in unaltered reprints. A modern successor in progress is the *Hallische Händel-Ausgabe* (Kassel, Germany: Bärenreiter, 1955–); it includes the *Händel-Handbuch*, a four-volume thematic catalogue (Kassel, Germany: Bärenreiter, 1978–).

Two German periodicals, both containing occasional English-language articles, are the *Händel-Jahrbuch* (Leipzig, 1928–33 and 1955–) and *Göttinger Händel-Beiträge* (Kassel; Germany: Bärenreiter, 1984–).

The most up-to-date biography in English remains Donald Burrows, *Handel* (New York: Schirmer Books, 1994). Useful for chronicling Handel's life and times is Christopher Hogwood, *Handel* (New York: Thames and Hudson, 1985). A more specialized revisionist work, including text translations for the composer's early Italian cantatas, is Ellen T. Harris, *Handel as Orpheus: Voice and Desire in the Chamber Cantatas* (HUP, 2001).

On the theatrical works, see Winton Dean and John Merrill Knapp, *Handel's Operas, 1704–1726* (OUP, 1987), and Winton Dean, *Handel's Operas, 1726–1741* (Rochester, N.Y.: Boydell Press, 2006), as well as the latter's *Handel's Dramatic Oratorios and Masques* (OUP, 1959). A more recent book on the same subject is David Ross Hurley, *Handel's Muse: Patterns of Creation in His Oratorios and Musical Dramas, 1743–1751* (OUP, 2001). For Handel's most famous vocal work, see Donald Burrows, *Handel: Messiah* (CUP, 1991); two of his most famous instrumental works are the subjects of Christopher Hogwood, *Handel: Water Music and Music for the Royal Fireworks* (CUP, 2005). Essays on special topics are in *The Cambridge Companion to Handel*, edited by Donald Burrows (CUP, 1997).

Handel's written-out vocal embellishment for the opera *Ottone* is in *Three Ornamented Arias*, edited by Winton Dean (OUP, 1976). His teaching of composition and figured bass is the subject of David Ledbetter, *Continuo Playing According to Handel* (Oxford and New York: OUP, 1990); see also Mann, *The Great Composer*, under "Music Theory and Compositional Practice," above.

Jacquet de La Guerre

The keyboard works have been edited by Carol Henry Bates (Paris: Heugel, 1986). The only monographic biography is Catherine Cessac, *Elisabeth Jacquet de La Guerre: Une femme compositeur sous le régne de Louis XIV* (Paris: Actes Sud, 1995).

Lalande

There is no collected edition, although many of the *grands motets* have appeared separately; Lionel Sawkins has prepared a reliable edition of *De profundis* (London: Faber Music, 2001). The chief English-language resource is Lionel Sawkins, *A Thematic Catalogue of the Works of Michel-Richard de Lalande (1657–1726)* (OUP, 2005).

Lassus

An old collected edition remains the sole modern source for many of the madrigals and other works: *Sämmtliche Werke* (Leipzig, Breitkopf und Härtel, 1894–27). This work is being replaced by an ongoing project to publish Lassus's motets, by Peter Bergquist, in *Recent Researches in Music of the Renaissance*, various vol. nos. starting with 102 (Madison, Wis.: A-R, 1995–). There is also a new complete edition: *Sämtliche Werke, neue Reihe* (Kassel, Germany: Bärenreiter, 1956–).

The only English-language biography (apart from the major article by James Haar in *New Grove*) remains Jerome Roche, *Lassus* (OUP, 1982).

Legrenzi

There is no collected edition, but Stephen Bonta has edited the sonatas of Opus 2 and Opus 10 (HUP, 1984, 1992); for selected cantatas, see Bonta's facsimile edition in *The Italian Cantata in the Seventeenth Century*, vol. 6 (New York: Garland, 1986). Bonta's *New Grove* article remains the only significant English-language writing.

Lully

A collected modern edition of Lully's works so far has issued only a few volumes (Hildesheim, Germany: Olms, 2001–); fortunately, among the first volumes to appear was Lois Rosow's edition of *Armide* (2003). Ten volumes, including several several operas and ballets, appeared in an older collected edition, also incomplete, by Henri Prunières (Paris, 1930–9).

Thematic catalogue: Herbert Schneider, *Chronologisch-Thematisches Verzeichnis sämtlicher Werke von Jean-Baptiste Lully (LWV)* (Tutzing, Germany: Schneider, 1981).

There is no recent, reliable biography in English. For essays on special topics, many in English, see *Lully Studies*, edited by John Hajdu Heyer (CUP, 2000), and *Jean-Baptiste Lully: Actes du colloque Saint-Germain-en-Laye, Heidelberg 1987*, edited by Jérôme de La Gorce and Herbert Schneider (Laaber, Germany: Laaber, 1990). See also Caroline Wood, *Music and Drama in the Tragédie en Musique, 1673–1715* (New York: Garland, 1996).

Luzzaschi

The solo madrigals for the *concerto delle donne* appear in *Madrigali*, edited by Adriano Cavicchi (Brescia, Italy: L'Organo; and Kassel, Germany: Bärenreiter, 1965); Anthony Newcomb is editing the "unaccompanied" madrigals (Middleton, Wis.: A-R Editions, 2003–). For biographical matter, see the latter's *The Madrigal at Ferrara* (under "Genres and Repertories," above).

Marini

The three main surviving collections of instrumental music, *Opere* 1, 8, and 22, have been edited as vols. 15, 23, and 19 of the series *Monumenti musicali italiani* (Milan: Suvini Zerboni, 1990, 2004, 1997). The sole English-language studies remain two Yale University dissertations on the vocal music (Willene B. Clark, 1966) and the instrumental works (Thomas D. Dunn, 1970).

Monteverdi

A new collected edition, still in progress, is the *Opera omnia* (Cremona: Athenaeum Cremonense, 1970–). Unreliable but reasonably complete is *Tutte le opere*, edited by G. F. Malipiero (Asolo, Italy: Malipiero, 1926–42; reprint, with minor revisions, Vienna: Universal, 1968). The fourth, fifth, and eighth books of madrigals from this edition have been reprinted with translations of texts by Stanley Appelbaum (New York: Dover, 1986–91). Useful editions of *Orfeo* and *Poppea* are those of Clifford Bartlett (Huntingdon, U.K.: King's Music, 1993) and Alan Curtis (London: Novello, 1989), respectively.

Biographical works: Paolo Fabbri, *Monteverdi*, translated by Tim Carter (CUP, 1994); Silke Leopold, *Monteverdi: Music in Transition*, translated by Anne Smith (OUP, 1991); Denis Arnold, *Monteverdi*, 3d ed., rev. Tim Carter (London: Dent, 1990). See also *The Letters of Claudio Monteverdi*, translated by Denis Stevens, rev. ed. (OUP, 1995).

Of great value on the operas is Tim Carter, *Monteverdi's Musical Theatre* (New Haven, Conn.: Yale University Press, 2002). For individual operas see *Claudio Monteverdi: Orfeo*, edited by John Whenham (CUP, 1986); and Ellen Rosand, *Monteverdi's Last Operas: A Venetian Trilogy* (UCP, 2007). Massimo Ossi discusses the *seconda prattica* and relationships between text and music in the madrigals in *Divining the Oracle: Monteverdi's Seconda prattica* (Chicago: University of Chicago Press, 2003). On Monteverdi's most famous sacred work, see Jeffrey Kurtzman, *The Monteverdi Mass and Vespers of 1610: Music, Context, Performance* (OUP, 1999).

Palestrina

The more recent of the two collected editions of Palestrina's works is that of Raffaeli Casimiri (Rome: Fratelli Scalera, 1939–65), most of which was reprinted in a different format by Kalmus. A useful (and necessary) concordance is Alison Hall, *An Index to the Casimir, Kalmus, and Haberl Editions* (Philadelphia: Music Library Association, 1980).

The only English-language biography (apart from the *New Grove* article by Lewis Lockwood et al.) remains Jerome Roche, *Palestrina* (OUP, 1971).

Purcell

A much improved version of the undependable collected edition organized by The Purcell Society (London: Novello, 1878–) has been under way since 1957. For Purcell's songs, the best sources are often the original printings in his *Orpheus britannicus* (reprint, New York: Broude, 1965).

The Purcell tercentenary year, 1995, elicited a number of works, including *The Purcell Companion*, edited by Michael Burden (Portland, Ore.: Amadeus Press, 1995). Biographies include that of the conductor Robert King, *Henry Purcell* (New York: Thames and Hudson, 1994), as well as Jonathan Keates, *Purcell: A Biography* (Boston: Northeastern University Press, 1996), and Peter Holman, *Henry Purcell* (OUP, 1994). Essays on performance are in *Performing the Music of Henry Purcell*, edited by Michael Burden (OUP, 1996). Useful for understanding the original dramatic contexts of the songs and other vocal works is Curtis Alexander Price, *Henry Purcell and the London Stage* (CUP, 1984). For a study of Purcell's most famous work, including a complete score, see Ellen T. Harris, *Henry Purcell's "Dido and Aeneas"* (OUP, 1987).

Quantz

A recent thematic catalogue by Horst Augsbach, *Johann Joachim Quantz: Thematisch-Systematisches Werkverzeichnis (QV)* (Stuttgart, Germany: Carus, 1997), already stands in need of revision; see the review by Mary Oleskiewicz in *Notes* 56 (1999–2000): 694–97. For Quantz's important essay on flute playing as well as a study thereof, see under "Voices and Instruments," above.

Rameau

A new thematic catalogue is in progress: Sylvie Bouissou, *Jean-Philippe Rameau: Catalogue thématique des œuvres musicales* (Paris: CNRS, 2003–). A new collected edition, *Opera omnia*

(Paris: Billaudot, 1996–), has so far issued only a few volumes, replacing the old *Œuvres complétes* (Paris: Durand, 1895–1924), which in fact was never completed. Many volumes in the latter series are rendered useless by inaccuracies and the addition of fabricated wind and string parts. For many works one must still consult vocal scores in the nineteenth-century series *Les chefs d'œuvres classiques de l'opéra français* (reprint, New York: Broude, 1972). The two sets of keyboard suites originally published in the 1720s are available in facsimile (New York: Broude, 1967) and in the complete modern edition of the keyboard works by Kenneth Gilbert (Paris: Heugel, 1979).

The only English-language biography (apart from the *New Grove* article by Graham Sadler) remains Cuthbert Morton Girdlestone, *Jean-Philippe Rameau: His Life and Work* (New York: Dover, 1969). On his stage works, see Charles William Dill, *Monstrous Opera: Rameau and the Tragic Tradition* (PUP, 1998).

Rameau's first and most important treatise, the *Traité de l'harmonie* (Paris, 1722), is available in facsimile (New York: Broude, 1965) and as part of *The Complete Theoretical Writings of Jean-Philippe Rameau*, edited by Erwin R. Jacobi (N.p.: American Institute of Musicology, 1967–72); it is translated by Philip Gossett as *Treatise on Harmony* (New York: Dover, 1971). See also Christensen, *Rameau and Musical Thought*, under "Music Theory and Compositional Practice."

Salomone Rossi

A collected edition of Rossi's works by Don Harràn (including the Hebrew settings *Hashirim ashir liSh'lomo*) comprises Part 100 of the *Corpus mensurabilis musicae* (Stuttgart, Germany: Hänssler, 1995–). Biography: Don Harràn, *Salamone Rossi, Jewish Musician in Late Renaissance Mantua* (OUP, 1998).

Alessandro Scarlatti and Domenico Scarlatti

There is no collected edition of the works of either composer. Several of Alessandro's operas appear in *The Operas of Alessandro Scarlatti* (HUP, 1974–83), but few of his cantatas are available in dependable modern editions; one must consult instead the selections given in facsimile in his *Cantatas*, edited by Malcolm Boyd (New York: Garland, 1986). Domenico's keyboard sonatas have been published in facsimile, edited by Ralph Kirkpatrick (New York: Johnson Reprint, 1972), and in a good modern edition by Kenneth Gilbert (Paris: Heugel, 1971–). The old edition by Alessandro Longo (Milan: Ricordi, 1906–8), although available in cheap reprints, is inaccurate and groups the sonatas arbitrarily into suites.

There is an idiosyncratic double biography of both composers: Robert Pagano, *Alessandro and Domenico Scarlatti: Two Lives in One*, translated by Frederick Hammond (Hillsdale, N.Y.: Pendragon Press, 2006). On Alessandro's operas one can consult Donald Jay Grout, *Alessandro Scarlatti: An Introduction to His Operas* (UCP, 1979), and Strohm, *Essays on Handel and Italian Opera* (see above under Handel).

An older, still-usable biography of Domenico is Ralph Kirkpatrick, *Domenico Scarlatti* (PUP, 1983); the German translation, under the same title (Munich: Ellermann, 1972), includes a thematic catalogue. On Domenico's keyboard sonatas, see W. Dean Sutcliffe, *The Keyboard Sonatas of Domenico Scarlatti and Eighteenth-Century Musical Style* (CUP, 2003).

Schütz

Two collected editions of Schütz's works exist: the *Sämmtliche Werke*, edited by Philipp Spitta and Arnold Schering (Leipzig, Germany: Breitkopf und Härtel, 1885–1927), and the *Neue Ausgabe sämtlicher Werke* (Kassel, Germany: Bärenreiter, 1955–). In some cases the latter transposes the music, making the earlier edition preferable, despite its "old" clefs.

The best English-language treatment, with a comprehensive list of works (including SWV numbers), is the *New Grove* biography by Joshua Rifkin. Schütz's own writings are edited in Gina Spagnoli, *Letters and Documents of Heinrich Schütz, 1656–1672: An Annotated Translation* (Ann Arbor, Mich.: UMI Research Press, 1990). An annual publication of scholarly articles (occasionally in English) is the *Schütz-Jahrbuch* (Kassel, Germany: Bärenreiter, 1979–).

Strozzi

Despite a continuing proliferation of recordings, little of Strozzi's music has appeared in reliable modern editions, although facsimiles of most of her original publications are available. For a selection, including an informative introduction, see her *Cantatas*, edited by Ellen Rosand (New York: Garland, 1986). Although superseded on biographical matters by the author's *New Grove* article, Ellen Rosand, "The Voice of Barbara Strozzi," in Bowers and Tick, *Women Making Music* (see above under "Music in Regional and Cultural Contexts"), remains valuable for its survey of the music.

Telemann

Selections from Telemann's vast output have been appearing in his *Musikalische Werke* (Kassel, Germany: Bärenreiter, 1950–). The vocal works are catalogued by Werner Menke, *Thematisches Verzeichnis der Vokalwerke* (Frankfurt: Klostermann, 1982–), instrumental ones by Martin Ruhnke, *Georg Philipp Telemann: Thematisch-Systematisches Verzeichnis seiner Werke: Telemann-Werkverzeichnis (TWV)* (Kassel; Germany: Bärenreiter, 1984–).

The *New Grove* article by Steven Zohn is currently the chief resource in English; forthcoming from the same author is *Music for a Mixed Taste: Style, Genre, and Meaning in Telemann's Instrumental Works* (OUP). Also in preparation is Jeanne Swack, *Composition and Performance in the Music of Georg Philipp Telemann* (CUP).

Torelli

There exist only scattered editions of individual works. The chief English-language writings are the *New Grove* article and the chapter on Bologna in the early-Baroque volume of the series *Music and Society* (see under "Surveys and Collections of Essays," above).

Vivaldi

Virtually all of Vivaldi's instrumental works are available in the edition of Gian Francesco Malipiero (Milan: Ricordi, 1948–72), which, unfortunately, often adds inappropriate expression markings and distorts the original scoring of many works. The quickest way to locate works in this edition is to search for "M" numbers in the work list in the *New Grove*, which correspond to volumes in this series. Vivaldi's vocal works are in process of publication in the new *Edizione critica* (Milan: Ricordi, 1982–).

There exist several catalogues and numbering systems for the instrumental works; the one now in use is Peter Ryom, *Répertoire des œuvres d'Antonio Vivaldi* (Copenhagen: Engstrom & Søndering, 1986).

The most authoritative biography is Michael Talbot, *Vivaldi* (OUP, 2000); the same author more recently has published *The Chamber Cantatas of Antonio Vivaldi* (Woodbridge, U.K.: Boydell Press, 2006). See also Karl Heller, *Antonio Vivaldi: The Red Priest of Venice*, translated by David Marinelli (Portland, Ore.: Amadeus Press, 1997). On the operas, see Strohm, *Essays on Handel and Italian Opera* (listed above under Handel).

INDEX

This index includes all terms defined in the text, most musical compositions, and proper names of composers, artists, and others relevant to the history of music or to specific works. Page numbers in **boldface** indicate a term's definition or principal discussion (for a few terms this occurs more than once); *italics* indicate that the term is illustrated in a figure or example. Asterisks designate works whose scores are included in the anthology.

Abendmusik, 249–50
Absolutism, royal, 3–5
Académie Royale de la Musique. *See* Royal Academy of Music (Paris)
Academies (*Accademie*), 35, 91, 298, 302, 304
Academy, Arcadian, 304
Accademia degli Incogniti, 91
Accademia degli Invaghiti, 67
Accademia Filarmonica, 311
Acciaccatura, 268
Accidentals, 23n
Accompanied recitative (*Accompagnato*). *See under* Recitative
Adlung, Jacob, 339n
Affect, 20, 28, 161
Agricola, Johann Friedrich, 58n, 339
Air, 110; *à boire,* 113; *de cour,* 113, 114; *sérieux,* 113
Alberti, Domenico: Sonata in E-flat, *329*
Alberti bass, *329–30*
Aleotti, Raffaella, 52
Aleotti, Vittoria, 37n, 52
Albinoni, Tomaso, 313
Alfabeto, 218n
Alfonso II, Duke of Ferrara, 51
Allegory, 134
Allemanda, 306, 314
Allemande, 99, 119, 224, 241–42
Altus, 20
Anglebert, Jean Henry d', 132–34, 237; *ornament table, 268; Passacaille from Armide, 237
Answer: real, 256; tonal, 256
Anthem, 107, 171
Antico. See Stile antico

Antiphony, 20
Appoggiatura, 75n, 103, 201, 268
Arcadelt, Jacopo, 34
Arcadian Academy, 304
Archilei, Vittoria, 54
Archlute, *49,* 216n, *220*
Arco, Livia d', 51n
Aria, **69,** 70–71, 85–87, 160–61; bipartite, 206; da capo (ternary), 71, 74, 104–5, 162, 167, 174–75; "rage," 173; strophic, 58, 69, 71; strophic variation, 74, 81, 92; text of, 70–71, 100. *See also* Air, Ritornello, Song
Ariette, 182
Arioso, 70–71
Ariosto, Lodovico: *Orlando furioso,* 171–73
Arne, Thomas Augustine, 326
Arpeggio (Arpeggiation), **46,** 224, 241, 268, 309
Artusi, Giovanni Maria, 38–39
Austria, 3

Bach, Anna Magdalena, Little Keyboard Book for, 266
Bach, Carl Philipp Emanuel, 178, 197, 225, 331, **334–36;** concertos, 206n, 335, 339–42; keyboard works, 266, 335–36; sonatas, 335; Concerto in D minor for Harpsichord and Strings, W. 23, *339–40; Essay on the True Manner of Playing Keyboard Instruments,* 335; *"Württemberg" Sonata no. 1 in A minor,* **336–39**
Bach, Johann Christian, 164, 170, 186, 334
Bach, Johann Christoph, 191
Bach, Johann Sebastian, 6, 10, 18, 147, 148, 178, 186, *187–95,* 228, 249, 300, 330;

arrangements, 319n; cantatas (sacred), 187, 194, 195–96, 283–84; cantatas (secular), 192–93; concertos, 206n, 319, 339; fugues, 260, 261, 263, 309, 325; inventions, 192, 261; keyboard ("clavier") music, 192, 226, **260–61**; oratorios, 204; organ music, 192, 252, **259–60**, 302, 319; passions, 194, 204; sonatas (*obbligato*-keyboard), 292n; sonatas and partitas (violin), 192, 259, *292–94*, 306, 309; students, 329; suites (cello), 192, 259; suites (keyboard), 192, 239n, 242, 260, 319; suites (orchestral), 285, 288; toccatas, 261; trio sonatas, 292n, 306; *Art of Fugue*, 195, 261, 321n; B Minor Mass, 10, 18, 195; Brandenburg Concertos, 47, 192, 313, **320–21**; *Brandenburg Concerto no. 2 in F, **321–25**; Brandenburg Concerto no. 4 in G, 313; Brandenburg Concerto no. 5 in D, 206n; *Canon triplex*, *188*; Cantata no. 7, *198*; Cantata no. 9, *197*; Cantata no. 71, 190; Cantata no. 78, 134; *Cantata no. 127, 32n, *196–203*; Cantata no. 198, 194n; *Capriccio on the Departure of a Most Beloved Brother*, 89; *Clavierübung*, 194, 259; Chromatic Fantasia and Fugue, 261; Coffee Cantata (Cantata no. 211), 194; English Suite no. 3 in G minor, 315; Goldberg Variations, 194, 261; *Italian Concerto*, 261, 288n; Little Keyboard Books, 261, 266; *Musical Offering*, 195; *Orgelbüchlein*, 259; Peasant Cantata, 195; Prelude and Fugue in D minor (organ), "Dorian," 76, 260; Prelude and Fugue in E minor (organ), "Wedge," 260; *Prelude and Fugue in G (Well-Tempered Clavier, part 1), **262–64**; *St. John Passion*, 278; *St. Mark Passion*, 194n; Toccata and Fugue in D minor (organ), 260; *Well-Tempered Clavier*, 192, 257, **261–62**

Bach, Wilhelm Friedemann, 334; Little Keyboard Book for, 261
Bacilly, Bénigne de, 58n
Bagpipe, 315
Ballet, 61, 113, 179–80. See also *Divertissement*
Balletto, 99
Balzac, Honoré de: *Sarrasine*, 165n
Banchieri, Adriano, 311
Baragagli, Girolamo: *La pellegrina*, 53, 54, 56
Barberini, Cardinal Francesco, 67
Bardi, Giovanni, Count, 51, 54
Barlines, 21n, 22
Baroque, defined, 1; distinguished from Renaissance, 42–45
Bass, Alberti, *329–30*
Bass, drum, 327

Bass, fundamental, **178**
Bass (stringed instrument). *See* Bass violin; Violone
Basse-taille, 156
Basso continuo, 45–46, 229
Basson, 279
Bassoon, 125, *279–80*
Bassus, 21n
Bass violin, 73, 275
Batterie, 271
Bavaria, 28
Beethoven, Ludwig van, 46, 186, 247, 329, 336n
Bellotto, Bernardo, 6
Benda, Franz, 335n
Benevoli, Orazio, 300n
Berlin, 320; opera at, 161, 327
Bernardi, Francesco (Senesino), 171, 327
Bernhard, Christoph, *147*, 253
Biber, Heinrich Ignaz Franz, 134, 265n, 274, **299–300**; trumpet sonatas, 310; *Sonata 5 (1681), **300–302**; *Missa salisburgensis*, 300; "Mystery" ("Rosary") Sonatas, *300*; Passacaglia, 300n; Requiem, 300
Binary form, 159, **241**
Binchois, Gilles, 15
Birnbaum, Johann Abraham, 189n
Blancrocher (Charles Fleury), Sieur de, 224, 240
Blavet, Michel, 331
Blow, John, 108
Boësset, Antoine, 113
Bohemia, 6
Böhm, Georg, 190
Bologna, 289, 304, 310, 311
Bordoni, Faustina, 327
Borkens, Philip, *277*
Bourrée, 110–11
Bow, stringed instrument, *10, 11*, 48, 273, *274*
Bow vibrato, *294*
Boyce, William, 329
Brahms, Johannes, 46, 186
Brandenburg, 320
Brandi, Giovanni Pellegrino, 311
Brass instruments, 281–84; natural, 203, 282. *See also* Horn, Trombone, Trumpet
Bridge, in fugue, 255
Brisé. See Style brisé
Brockes, Barthold Heinrich, 204n
Broschi, Carlo. *See* Farinelli
Buffoons, Debate of the, 177
Buonamente, Giovanni Battista, 295, 302
Burmeister, Joachim, 16
Burney, Charles, 336
Busenello, Gian Francesco, 82

Buxtehude, Dieterich, 147, 168, 186, **249–50**; chorale settings, 250–52; oratorios, 250; *praeludia*, 252; sonatas, 252; suites and variations, 252; **Nun bitten wir den heiligen Geist*, 250–51; **Praeludium in A minor, 252–59*
BuxWV numbers, 249
BWV numbers, 191
Byrd, William, 107, 136, 249; fantasias, 232

Caccini, Giulio, 51, **54–57**; *Le nuove musiche*, 57–58; **Sfogava con le stelle*, **58–60**
Caccini, Francesca, 60
Cadence, **23**, 149n, 167n; Phrygian, **95**; in Renaissance polyphony, *23–24, 25*
Cadenza, 338–39
Cambert, Robert: *Pomone*, 116
Camera, sonata (concerto) da. See under Sonata
Camerata, Florentine, 51, 58
Campra, André, 180, *244*
Canarie, 242n
Canon, **21n**, *213*
Cantata, 10, **90–91**, 95–97; sacred, 96, 186. *See also* Chorale cantata
Cantus, **20**
Cantus firmus, **200**
Canzona, **142–43**, 230
Canzonetta, 34, 58, 69
Capeci, Carlo Sigismondo, 171n
Capella, **141**, 150
Cappella Sistina, 166
Capriccio, 230
Carissimi, Giacomo, 91, **152–53**; **Jephte*, 153–54
Castello, Dario, 236, **296–97**; sonatas, *290, 292*; **Sonata 12 (book 2), 297*
Castrato, 83, *164–66*
Casulana, Maddalena, 52
Catalog, thematic, **148**
Catholic Church. *See under* Church
Cavalieri, Emilio de', 54, 152; *Godi turba mortal, 54–56*; *Rappresentatione di anima et di corpo,* 54n, 152
Cavalli, Francesco, 67, 82, 87; *Ercole amante,* 112; **Giasone*, **87–89**, 94; *Serse,* 112
Cazzati, Maurizio, 311
Cello, 48, **274–75**, 312
Cervantes, Miguel de: *Don Quixote*, 110
Cesti, Marc'Antonio, 67, 91
Chaconne, **130–31**, 184, *246*, 333
Chain of suspensions, 304
Chalumeau, 280
Chamber music, 286
Chambonnières, Jacques Champion de, 237, 245n
Chant, Gregorian, 18, 26, 152, 200n

Chanterelle, 246
Chapel Royal, 107, 108
Character piece, **265**
Charpentier, Marc-Antoine, 113, 116, 154; *Le malade imaginaire*, 117; *Médée*, 116; *Orphée descendant aux enfers*, 65n
Chiesa, sonata (concerto) da. See under Sonata
Chitarrone, **48**
Choir. *See* Chorus
Chopin, Frédéric, 266
Chorale, 194, **196–97**
Chorale cantata, 196, 197, 199
Chorale fantasia, 200, **252**
Chorale prelude, **250**
Chorale variation, 252
Chord, broken, 46, 241
Choreinbau, 201n
Chorus, 71, **72–73**, 123, 137n, 196. *See also* Polychoral works
Christian Ludwig, Margrave of Brandenburg-Schwedt, 47, 320
Christina, Queen of Sweden, 304
Chromaticism, **32**, 33, 36, 75, 141
Church: Anglican, 5; Roman Catholic, 5
Ciacona, 131, 307n
Cicognini, Giacinto Andrea, 87
Cittern, *10*, 217
Civil War (England), 5, 107
Clarinet, 280–81
Clarino, 283
Classical, 1; pre-Classical, 327
Clavichord, **50**, 225, 260n, 336
Clavier, 261
Coda, 252
Collegium Musicum (Leipzig), 194, 330
Collier, Edward, *240*
Colonna, Giovanni Ambrosio, *221*
Concert, public, *11*, 152, *155*, 245, 339
Concertato, 136
Concertino, 314
Concerto (instrumental), 164, 286, **287–88**, 310, 311, **312–14**, 326; piano, 313; solo, 313, 315–16
Concerto (vocal), **135**
Concerto a quattro, **288n**
Concerto delle donne. See Ferrara
Concerto grosso, 313–14
Concert Spirituel, 155
Concitato. See Stile concitato
Confraternity, 138
Consonances, 23n
Consort, 48, 276
Continuo. *See* Basso continuo
Continuo madrigal, **76**
Corbetta, Francesco, 217, *220*
Corbiau, Gérard: *Farinelli*, 165n

Corelli, Arcangelo, *304–6*, 311; concerti grossi, op. 6, 305, 313–14; solo sonatas, op. 5, 305, 306, 320; trio sonatas, 304–5, 306; *Concerto Grosso in G minor, op. 6, no. 8, "Christmas," 314–15; *Sonata in C, op. 5, no. 3, *306–9*; Sonata in D Minor, op. 5, no. 12, *La Folia*, 306; Trio Sonata in D, op. 2, no. 1, *306*

Cornet: modern brass instrument, 139; organ stop, 251

Cornetto (Cornett), *30*, *139–40*, 283–84, 291

Corno da caccia, 281

Corrente, 223, 306

Corsi, Jacopo, 57n

Cöthen, 192

Counterpoint, 20; double, **325**; imitative, 16, 19, 21; invertible, **201**, 325; quintuple, **325**; triple, **325**. *See also* Inversion

Counter-Reformation, 7–8, 18, 77

Countersubject, **256**

Couperin, François, 113, 177, **265–66**; *ordres*, 268, 289; *ornament table, 268; *pièces de clavecin*, 266, 268; sonatas, 265, 288; *L'art de toucher le clavecin*, 266; *La Couperin*, **268–69**; *Les goûts réunis*, 265–66; *La reine des coeurs*, 267, **268**

Couperin, Louis, 237, 265

Couperin, Marguerite-Antoinette, 266

Courante, 119, *223–24*, *242–43*

Course (on lute), **48**, 216

Court, 5, 7; court opera, 67. *See also Air de cour, Ballet de cour*

Cremona, 61n

Cristofori, Bartolomeo, 227

Crook, 283

Cross relation, *31–32*

Crusades, 77

Curtal, 279, 287

Cuzzoni, Francesca, 328

Cyclic mass, 17

Da capo (aria). *See under* Aria

Dance, *12, 118–19*, 222, 287, 288. *See also* Ballet; Stylized Dance; *and specific dances*

Declamation, musical, 22, 33

Denner, Jacob, 276

Deutsche schalmei, *280*

Development; motivic, **256**: section (in sonata form), 337n

Devise (Devisenarie), 105n

Dialogus, 153

Discrétion, 332–33

Dissonances, 23n; treatment of, *25*, *39–40*; unprepared, 75

Divertissement, 123, *128–34*, 184

Double bass, see Violone

Double counterpoint, **325**

Double dotting, *120*

Double fugue, **257**

Double return, **338**

Double stop, 308

Doubling, 141, 285

Dowland, John, 60, 107, 217

Dowland, Robert: *A Musical Banquet*, 60

Dramma per musica, 96. *See also* Opera seria

Dresden, 6, 8, 146, 161, 327

Drone, **315**

Drum. *See* Percussion

Drum bass, 327

Dryden, John, 110

Duet, 72

Dufay, Guillaume, 15

Dulcian, 279, 287

Du Mont, Henri, 155

Dynamics, 81, 151, 297

Eber, Paul, 199

Echo, 309

Edlinger, Thomas, *218*

Einbau, 201

Embellishment, 52, **122**, 251, 267; in arias, 167; in sonatas, *307–8*

Emblem, 89n, 239–40

Empfindsamer Stil, 334, 336

Empire (Austrian or Holy Roman), 5, 6

England, 3, 5, 107

English oratorio, 170, **204–5**

Engraving. *See* Printing and publishing of music

Enharmonic progression, *182–83*, 270

Enjambment, **38**

Enlightenment, 177–78

Ensemble (in opera), 72

Entr'acte, 127

Entrée, 128, 180; *entrée grave*, 127

Episode: in concerto (solo), 315–16: in fugue, 255

Esclamazione, 58

Ethos, modal, 28

Étude, 309

Euripides: *Alcestis*, 50, 51

Exposition: in fugue, 255, 258; in sonata form, 337n

Expression. *See* Affect, Ethos, Rhetoric, Text painting

Fagott, 279

Falconieri, Andrea, *221*

Fantasia, 108n, 230, *232–33*, 275. *See also* Chorale fantasia

Farinelli (Carlo Broschi), 165, 167, 327

Ferdinando I de' Medici, Grand Duke of Tuscany, 54

Fermata, 338

Ferrara, 35, 41, 231; Three Ladies of, 51–52

Feuillet, Raoul Auger, *117*

Figure, rhetorical, 16

Figured bass, 45. *See also* Basso Continuo

Final (modal), 26

First practice, **39**

Fischer, Johann Caspar Ferdinand, 262; *Ariadne musica*, 262n

Florence, 41; *intermedi* of 1589, 53–54, 47. *See also* Camerata, Florentine

Flute, *11, 30, 277–78*; terminology for, 13, 278

Follia (Folia), 233n, 306–7

Form, musical, 21–22, 33, 159; sonata-allegro, 337–38; through-composed, 22, 34. *See also* Aria; Binary form; Recapitulation; Ritornello; Tonality

Forqueray, Antoine, 268–69

Forqueray, Jean-Baptiste Antoine, 331

Fortepiano, **227–28**

France, 3, 5, 106, 112

Frederick II, "the Great," King of Prussia, 8, 195, 320, 334–35, 336

French horn. *See* Horn

French overture, *122, 127,* 173, 202, 288, 332

Frescobaldi, Girolamo, *231–32,* 238, 265n; *capricci,* 233; *canzoni,* 233, 272; fantasias, 232–33; ricercars, 233; toccatas and partitas, 233–34; vocal music, 233; *Fiori musicali,* 233; *Partite sopra l'Aria della Romanesca, 233; Toccata 9 (book 1), 235; *Toccata 7 (book 2), **234–36**

Fret, *45, 49*

Froberger, Johann Jacob, 154, **237–38**; allemandes, 246; toccatas, 238; suites, 238–39; *tombeaux,* 240; *Suite 20, **239–43***

Fugue, 209–10, **253–59,** 263, 308, 325; double, **257**; strict, 254

Fundamental, **282**

Fundamental bass, *178*

Fux, Johann Joseph: *Gradus ad Parnassum,* 185–86, 195, 253

Fuzelier, Louis, 180

Gabrieli, Andrea, 136, 139, 142, 147; toccatas, 230

Gabrieli, Giovanni, 29, 64, **136–37,** 272; canzonas, 297; sonatas, 289; toccatas, 230; *Canzon septimi toni, 143; Ego sum qui sum, 137; *In ecclesiis, **140–42**; Intonazione del secondo tono, 231; Sonata con tre violini, 143–44; Sonata pian'e forte, 151, 297n; Timor et tremor, 29*

Galant (style), 158, **327–30**

Galilei, Galileo, 51n

Galilei, Vincenzo, 51

Galliard, 119

Gamba. *See* Viola da gamba

Gaultier, Denis, 222, 224, 237

Gaultier, Ennemond, 222; *L'immortelle, 223–24; *Tombeau de Mesangeau, 220, 224; *La poste,* **224**

Gavotta, 306, 314

Gavotte, 182, *246,* 333

Genre, 2, 90

Germain, Jacques, *226*

German College (Rome), 152

Germany, 3, 5, 191

Gesualdo, Don Carlo, da Venosa, 35; *Beltà poi, che t'assenti, 35–36; Luci serene, 37; T'amo mia vita, 37n*

Giga, 306, 309

Gigue, *118,* 119, 224, 239n, **242,** *246*

Giraud, Anna, 316

Giustini, Ludovico, 228

Gluck, Christoph Willibald, 65n, 326

Goldberg, Johann Gottlieb, 194

Grande Bande, 115, 156

Grand motet, **155**

Graun, Carl Heinrich, 328

Great Britain. *See* England

Greece, ancient, drama and poetry, 72, 113, 134, 162; music, 50–51; music theory, 24, 28, 182

Gregorian chant. *See* Chant, Gregorian

Grimaldi, Nicolò (Nicolini), *165*

Groppo, 58, 236

Ground (bass), *132; see also* Ostinato

Gualfreducci, Onofrio, 54

Guarini, Anna, 51n

Guarini, Giambattista, 51n; *Il pastor fido,* 52–53

Guarracino, Onofrio, *31*

Guédron, Pierre, 113; *Vous que le bonheur rappelle, 114*

Guitar, 48, *217–22*

Haas, Johann Wilhelm, *282*

Habermann, Franz, *213*

Haka, Richard, *280*

Hamburg, 3, 7, 248; opera at, 67, 168

Hand crossing, *270–71*

Handel, George Frideric, 10, 127, **167–70,** 204–5, 249, 280, 304; arias, 163; borrowings, 154, *210–13*; cantatas, 96, 97, 170; concerti grossi, 171, 306; keyboard works, 171, 173n; oratorios, 204–5; organ concertos, 206; *Brockes-Passion,* 204n; *Esther,* 206; *Giulio Cesare* (Julius Caesar), 171; *Israel in Egypt,* 205; *Jephtha, 205, **206–13**; Lotario, 212–13; Messiah, 170, 204–5, 315; Music for the Royal Fireworks, 171; *Orlando, 163–64, **171–74**; Poro, 161; La resurrezione, 204; Rinaldo, 125, 165, 170, 171; Rodelinda, 171; Samson, 154, 212; Tamer-*

lano, 171; *The Triumph of Time and Truth*, 205; *Water Music*, 171, 288n
Harmonic rhythm, **327**
Harmonic series, *203*
Harmony, theory of, 178
Harp, 48, 230, 275
Harpsichord, 50, **225–27**. *See also* Keyboard music, Virginal
Hasse, Johann Adolph, 164, 186, 278n, 326, 328; *Cleofide*, *310*
Haussmann, Elias Gottlob, *188*
Haute-contre, 124
Haydn, Franz Josef, 65n, 164, 170, 186, 227, 247, 329
Heinichen, Johann David, 278n, 316
Hemiola, **128**, **243**
Historia, 204
Historicus, 153
Holland. *See* Netherlands
Homophony, **20**
Hooch, Pieter de, *10*
Horn (French horn), 173n, 281, **283**
Hotteterre, Jacques, 277
Howard, Hugh, *305*
Huguenots, 112

Idiomatic music, **215**
Imitation, contrapuntal, **21**; paraphrase and parody, 18n; preimitation, **251**
Improvisation, 43, 220, 229; of fugues, 257. *See also* Embellishment, Ornamentation
Incipit, 93
India, Sigismondo d', 60
Indians (American), 180
Inequality, rhythmic. *See Notes inégales*
Ingegneri, Marc'Antonio, 62
Instrumentation (scoring), 73, 124–25, 139–40, 155–56, 166, 174, 182, 284–85, 317–18, 320. *See also* Basso continuo
Instruments, musical, 43, 46–47, 139–40, 214–16; pitch of, **283**. *See also specific instruments*
Intonazione: keyboard piece, *230–31*; ornament, 54, 58
Intermedio, **54**
Invention, **261**
Inversion, **242**; in fugue, 256. *See also* Counterpoint
Italy, 3, 5

Jacquet de La Guerre, Elizabeth-Claude, *243–45*; cantatas, 96, 243; harpsichord pieces, 237, 243; sonatas, 243, 288; *Céphale et Procris*, 243; *Suite in A minor*, *245–47*
Jewish musicians, 295
Jig. *See* Gigue

Jommelli, Niccolò, 326
Josquin des Prez, 15, 147

Kammerton, tief, 321n
Kapsperger (Kapsberger), Giovanni Girolamo, 217, *220–21*, 223
Karp, Gregor, 47
Keiser, Reinhard, 168; passions, 204
Kettledrum. *See* Timpani
Key, **26**; on instruments, 278; key signature, 94, 260n. *See also* Tonality
Keyboard instruments. *See* Clavichord; Fortepiano; Harpsichord; Organ
Keyboard music, 50, 229–30, 269–71; in France, 236–37, 265–69; in Germany, 236, 248–64; in Italy, 230–36
Kircher, Athanasius, 152, 154, 238
Kirkpatrick, Ralph, 271n
Köchel, Ludwig von, 148
Köthen. *See* Cöthen
Krieger, Johann Philipp, 186, 333
Krügner, Johann Gottfried, *193*
Kuhnau, Johann: *Biblical Sonatas*, 265

La Barre, Michel de, 292
La Guerre, Elizabeth-Claude Jacquet de. *See* Jacquet de La Guerre, Elizabeth-Claude
Lalande, Michel-Richard de, **154–55**; *De profundis*, **155–57**
Lambert, Michel, 113, 115
Lament, 76, 89; in *Arianna*, 65; in *Dido and Aeneas*, *109–10*; in *Giasone*, 87–89; in *Orfeo*, 75
Lancret, Nicolas, *11*
Landi, Stefano: *Il Sant'Alessio*, 67
Largo, 100n
Lassus, Orlande de (Orlando di Lasso), **28**, **34**, 136, 138, 147; *Missa Io son ferito*, 29; *Patrocinium musices*, *30*; *Sibylline Prophecies*, 29; *Timor et tremor*, **29–34**
Lautenklavier, 227
Lawes, Henry, 107
Lawes, William, 107
Leclair, Jean-Marie, 288, 316, 326
Legrenzi, Giovanni, **302**; *Sonata La Strasolda*, 303–4
Leipzig, *193*
Le Jeune, Claude, 113; *Le printemps*, 113n
Libretto, **65**, 68n, 84–85; of opera seria, 160–62
Lira da braccio, 57
Lirone, 57n
Locatelli, Pietro Antonio, 326
Lombardic rhythm, 327
London, 5, 7, 8: opera at, 7, 67, 161; oratorio, 170
Loredano, Giovanni Francesco, 93

Lotti, Antonio: *Alessandro Severo*, 161
Louis XIII, King of France, 117
Louis XIV, King of France, 114, 115, 117, 125n, 134, 155
Loure, *333*
Lübeck, 192, 248, 249
Lully, Jean-Baptiste, 113, 114–18, 177; ballets, *116–17*; compared to Rameau, 180–84; *Alceste*, 123; **Armide, 120–22, 124, 125–34*, 184; *Atys*, 123; *Ballet de la nuit*, 115; *Le bourgeois gentilhomme*, 115; *Cadmus et Hermione*, 115; *Roland, 117*; *Te Deum*, 115
Lute, 30, 48, *216–22*, 230, 275. *See also* Archlute; Theorbo
Luther, Martin, 5, 196
Luzzaschi, Luzzasco, 51–53; keyboard music, 231; *O Primavera, 52–53*; *T'amo mia vita*, 37n

Madrigal, 34–35, 76; English, 107
Madrigal comedy, 76, 311
Maio, Giuseppe de: *Il sogno d'Olimpia, 162*
Mantua, 41, 61n, 289, 295
Manual, 228, 251
Marais, Marin, 289
Marcello, Alessandro, 8
Marcello, Benedetto, 8, 163
Marcellus II, Pope, 18
Marchand, Louis, 190
Marenzio, Luca, 35, 39
Margherita, Duchess of Ferrara, 51n
Marini, Biagio, 297–98; Passacaglia, 300n; *Sonata con due corde*, 292, 294; **Sonata variata, 298–99*
Marini, Giambattista, 37n
Mark (St.), Basilica of, 61, 138, 139, 296
Masque, 107
Mass, 17, 186; cyclic, 17–18
Mattheson, Johann, 168
Meantone (temperament), 262n
Meissner, Christoph Gottlob, 198
Melisma, 22, 33
Menuetto, 314
Merulo, Claudio, 235
Mesangeau, René, 222
Mesomedes, 51
Metastasio, Pietro, 161
Mielich, Hans, 29
Milan, 289
Minuet, 119, *247*
Mizler, Lorenz, 186
Modality, 24, 28, 43, 200. *See also* Mode
Mode, 24, 26–27; authentic, 26; plagal, 26; transposed, 27, 76. *See also* Modality
Modulation. *See* Tonality

Molière, Jean-Baptiste, 115; *Le malade imaginaire, 117*
Molza, Tarquinia, 51n
Monica, 233n
Monn, Georg, 326
Monody, 50–51, 69
Monteverdi, Cesare, 39
Monteverdi, Claudio, 18, 36–37, *61–63*, 91, 135, 147; madrigals, 37, 63, 64; sacred works, 136; *Arianna*, 65, 73n; *Armato il cor*, 149n; **Combattimento di Tancredi e Clorinda*, 76–82; *L'incoronazione di Poppea*, 64, 72, *82–84*, 94; *Lamento della ninfa*, 76, 89; **Luci serene*, 37–40; *Ohimè, dov'è il mio ben? (aria di Romanesca)*, 233n; **Orfeo*, 9, 22n, 64, *65–76*, 295; *Il ritorno d'Ulisse in patria*, 64; *Selva morale*, 64; *Sfogava con le stelle*, 59n; *T'amo mia vita*, 37n; *Vespers (1610)*, 64, 135; *Zefiro torna e di soavi accenti*, 149n
Mordent, 268
Morell, Thomas, 206
Moresca, 69n
Moreschi, Alessandro, 166n
Motet, 15, 17, 186. *See also* Grand motet
Motive, development of, 256
Motto (aria), 105
Moulinié, Etienne, 113
Mozart, Leopold, 275
Mozart, Wolfgang Amadeus, 164, 170, 186, 227, 247, 311, 329, 334
Muffat, Georg, 116, 119, 275, 288, 313–14
Munich, 28, 29
Musette, 315n
Musica ficta, 23n
Musique mesurée, 113

Naldi, Antonio, 54
Naples, 161, *162*
Natural (brass), 203, 282
Nero, 82
Netherlands, 5, 15
Neumeister, Erdmann, 186
Nicolini (Nicolò Grimaldi), *165*
Notation, 12–13, 23n; *alfabeto*, 218n; "Dorian," 76; of ornaments, 167n, 266–68; rhythmic, 120, 224; *scordatura*, 294, *300–301*; tablature, *218–20*
Notes inégales, 119, *120–22*

Obbligato keyboard, 292n
Oboe, 174, *278–81*
Oboe da caccia, 279
Oboe d'amore, 279
Ockeghem, Johannes, 15, 147
Ode, 108

Opera, 7, 61, **65–68**, 84–85; French, 123, 179–80; Italian, 164; staging of, *128. See also* Opera buffa; Opera seria
Opera buffa, 160, 164n
Opera of the Nobility, 171
Opera seria, 160–64, 326
Opus numbers, 147–48
Oratorio, 151–52, 186, 204, 206. *See also* English oratorio
Oratorio passion, **204**
Oratory, 152
Orchestra, 124, 166, 284; orchestral music, 311
Ordinary (of the mass), 17
Organ, 48–49, 215, **228–29.** *See also* Keyboard music
Ornamentation, 43, 58, **122–23,** *332;* in keyboard music, *266–68. See also* Embellishment; Trill; Turn
Orpheus, 65, *305*
Ortiz, Diego: *Tratado de glosas,* 50, 222
Ospedali, 316
Ostinato, **88,** *130–32, 220–22,* 233
Ottoboni, Cardinal Pietro, 304
Ouverture, 288n
Overdotting, *119–120*
Overture, 71. *See also* French overture

Palestrina, Giovanni Pierluigi da, 15–16, 18–19, 138, 147, 185; **Dum complerentur,* *19–23; Io son ferito,* 28; *Missa Dum complerentur,* 19n; *Pope Marcellus* Mass, 18
Paraphrase, 18n, **201,** 251
Paris, 5, 8, *12,* 68; opera at, 68, 115
Parody, **18n,** 65, 149, 193, 195
Partita: keyboard, 233, 260; violin, 259
Pasacalles, 131n
Pasquini, Bernardo, 204, 304
Pasquini, Ercole, 231
Passacaglia, **130–31,** 300n
Passacaille, 130
Passagework, **93**
Passion, 194, 204
Passion oratorio, **204n**
Pastorale, **314–15**
Paul (St.), 150
Pavane, 119
Pedalboard, **228,** 260n
Pedal point, **246,** 253
Pedersøn, Mogens, 37n
Percussion, 284
Performance practice (performing practices), 12–14, 44, 47; of cantatas, 195–96; in opera, 166–67; of oratorio, 206. *See also* Basso Continuo, Instruments, *Notes inégales,* Ornamentation, Overdotting, Recitative, Tempo

Pergolesi, Giovanni Battista, 326; *La serva padrona,* *327; Flaminio,* 328
Peri, Jacopo, 51, 54, 57; *Dafne,* 51, 57
Petite chœur, 156
Petit motet, 155
Peverara, Laura, 51n
Phrygian cadence, **95**
Piano. *See* Fortepiano
Picardy third, 76n, **150**
Piece (keyboard), 236; character piece, **265.** *See also Pièce*
Pièce: de clavecin, 236, 265; *d'orgue,* 236
Pietism, **186–87**
Pifa, 315
Pincé, 268
Pipe (organ), 49
Pisendel, Johann Georg, 311, 316, 326
Pitch, 321n; pitch references, xiv
Pizzicato, **79,** 202
Plato, 57, 79, 134
Plectrum: on harpsichord, 50; on lute, 216
Poland, 5, 6
Polychoral works, *137–40,* 147, 150, 285
Polyphony, vocal, **16**
Pope, Alexander, 206
Port de voix, 268
Portugal, 8, 270
Praeludium (Prelude and Fugue), 252, 259
Praetorius, Michael, 139
Pre-Classical, 327
Preimitation, 251
Prelude. *See* Chorale prelude; *Praeludium;* Unmeasured Prelude
Prez, Josquin des, 15, 147
Prima pratica, **39**
Printing and publishing (music), 6, 68, *92,* 229–30, *267, 308, 332*
Programmatic music, **265,** 300, 315
Proper (of the mass), 17
Protestant Reformation, 5
Psalms, numbering of, 155n
Publishing (music). *See* Printing and publishing (music)
Punteado, 217
Purcell, Henry, 87, **108–10,** 134, 226; anthems, 171n; fantasias, 108; trumpet sonatas, 310; *Dido and Aeneas,* 89, *108,* 109–110; *Don Quixote,* 110;*From Rosy Bowers,* 110–11, 159; *King Arthur,* 110

Quantz, Johann Joachim, 277, 278, 316, 326, 335n, 337; flute quartets, *292;* flute sonatas, *292,* 336n
Quartet, 292, 331
Querelle des Bouffons, 177
Quinault, Philippe, 115, 117, 125

Quintus, 21

Railich, Pieter, *49*
Rameau, Jean-Philippe, 87, **175–76**, 265; *concerts*, 288n; keyboard music (*pièces de clavecin*), 177, *270–71*; operas, 332; *ornament table, 268; theory of harmony, *178–79*; *L'Egiptienne*, *270–71*; *Hippolyte et Aricie*, 176, *182–83*; *Les Indes galantes*, **179–80**; *Laboravi clamans*, 178; *Les sauvages*, 180, 184n; *Les trois mains*, 270; theoretical writings: *Génération harmonique*, 182n; *Traité de l'harmonie*, 177, *179*
Rank (organ), **228**
Rasgueado, 217
Realization, of figured bass, **45–46**; written-out, 103n
Recapitulation, 337n
Récit, 156
Recital, public, 249. *See also* Concert, public
Recitative, 59, 69; accompanied (*accompagnato*), 70, 81, 100, *102*, 166; French, 123–24; performance of, *103–4*, 123–24; simple (*semplice, secco*), 70, 100n, 166; text of, 100
Recorder, *10*, 13, 125, *276–78*
Rectus, 256
Reformation, Protestant, 5
Refrain, 22n, 75, 141
Register, **226**
Registration, 226, 228
Reincken, Jan Adamszoon, 249
Renaissance, 1, 15–16; distinguished from Baroque, 42–45
"Repercussive" subject, 253
Resolution (of dissonance), 25, *39–40*
Restoration (England), 107
Retransition, **338**
Return (double return), **338**
Rhetoric, musical, **16–17**, 32–34, 93
Rhythm: harmonic, **327**; Lombardic, 327. *See also* Notation; Performance practice
Ribatutta, 236
Ricci, Marco, *165*
Ricercar, 230, **233**, 242
Rinuccini, Ottavio, *54–56*, 59; *Euridice*, 57
Ripieno, **312–13**; ripieno concerto, **288n**
Ritornello, 72, **73**, 87, 104; ritornello form, 163, **174–75**, 288, 315–16, 318; ritornello theme, **105–6**
Robusti, Domenico: *Tancred Baptizing Clorinda*, 78
Roche (Rocco), Saint, Academy of, 138
Rococo, 327n
Roger, Étienne, 307
Romanesca, *233*, 296

Rome, 5, 8, 11–12, 91, 106; opera at, 67, 151; oratorio, 153
Rondeau, 184n, **246**
Rore, Cipriano de, 34, 35, 39
Rosenmüller, Johann, 147
Rossi, Luigi, 67, 91; cantatas, 95n; *Orfeo*, 65n, 112
Rossi, Salamone, 295; *Sfogava con le stelle*, 59n; Sonata *La Viena*, *291*; *Sonata sopra La Bergamasca*, **295–96**
Rossini, Gioacchino, 163, 311
Rousseau, Jean-Jacques, 176
Royal Academy of Music (London), 169
Royal Academy of Music (Paris), 112, 115, 176, 243
Ruggiero, 233n
Ryom, Peter, 317

Sackbut, **139**, 283
Saint-Lambert, Michel de, 122n
Sammartini, Giovanni Battista, 326
Sanz, Gaspar, 217
Sarabande, 119, *128*, 184, **243**
Saxony, 6
Scarlatti, Alessandro, **95–97**, 163, 185, 304; *Correa nel seno amato*, *97–106*
Scarlatti, Domenico, 97, 171n, **270–71**; sonatas, *271*
Schalmei, Deutsche, *280*
Scheibe, Johann Adolph, 189n, 329n
Scheidemann, Heinrich, 249
Schein, Johann Hermann, 250; *Banchetto musicale*, 288; *Nun bitten wir den heiligen Geist*, *250–51*
Schenker, Heinrich, 178
Schieferdecker, Johann Christian, 249
Schmieder, Wolfgang, 191
Schnitger, Arp, 248
Schübler, Johann Georg, 259n
Schütz, Heinrich, 18, 136, 139, **144–46**, 170, 275; madrigals, 147; *Es steh Gott auf*, 149; *Herr, neige deine Himmel*, *149–50*, 243n; *Saul, Saul, was verfolgst du mich?*, **150–51**, 243n; *Symphoniae sacrae*, 148–49
Scordatura, 294, *300–301*
Scoring. *See* Instrumentation
Secco. See under Recitative
Seconda pratica, **39**, 63
Second practice, **39**
Sellas, Matteo, *49*
Seneca, 82
Senesino (Francesco Bernardi), 171, 327
Serenata, 96
Sextus, 21n
Shawm, **240**, 278
Sherwin, William, *305*

Sigh motive, 182, **201**, 323–24
Simpson, Christopher, 222
Sinfonia, 72, **73**, 99; with trumpet, 310
Sistine Chapel, 166
Slide trumpet, **284**
Solo (episode or passage), **315**, 316
Soloeinbau, 201n
Sonata, 142, *143–44*, 272, **286–87**, *289–95*,
    326; duo sonata (*sonata a due*), *290–91*,
    303; for keyboard, 271, 335; quartet
    sonata (*sonata a quattro*), *292*, 331; solo
    sonata (*sonata a uno*), 287, 290, 295; *sonata
    da camera* (chamber sonata), **286**; *sonata da
    chiesa* (church sonata), **286**, 307; variation
    sonata, 289, *295–96*. *See also* Form; Trio
    sonata
Sonata-allegro form. *See under* Form
Song, 107, 108–9; *see also* Aria
Soprano. *See* Voices
Spain, 3, 8, 270
Spinet, 227
Stainer, Jacob, *274*
Steenbergen, Jan, *281*
Steffani, Agostino, 96
Stile antico, 44, 97, 135, 147, 185, 230, 314,
    329
Stile concitato, 79, 81, 130, *208–9*
Stile moderno, 44–45, 297
Stil, empfindsamer, 334, 336
Stop: on harpsichord, organ, **49, 228**; double
    stop, *292*, 298, 308
Stradella, Alessandro, 96
Stradivari, Antonio, 61n, 215, *219*
Stravinsky, Igor, 36
Stretto, **255**
Striggio, Alessandro, 65
Strophic aria. *See under* Aria
Strophic variation. *See under* Aria
Strozzi, Barbara, **91**; **Ardo in tacito foco, 92–95*
Strozzi, Giulio, 91
Style, 2; French and Italian, contrasted, 158–59,
    177
Style brisé, **224**, 237, 241–42, 265
Style galant. See Galant
Stylized dance, **217**, 236–37
Stylus fantasticus, 249, 253
Subject, 21, 209–10, **254**; countersubject, **256**;
    inverted, **256**; "repercussive," 253; second,
    257; upright (*rectus*), **256**
Suite, **237**; orchestral, 288
Suspension, 25; chain of suspensions, 304
Sweelinck, Jan Pieterszoon, 249
Switzerland, 5
Sibylla, Duchess of Württemberg-Montbéliard,
    238, 239
Syllabic setting, 22

Symphonie, 156
Symphony, 73

Tablature, *218–20*
Taille, **279**
Tangent (on clavichord), **50**
Tartini, Giuseppe, 326
Tasso, Torquato, 77; *Gerusalemme liberata*,
    77–79, 125, 171
Telemann, Georg Philipp Telemann, 3, 187,
    313, **330–31**; vocal works, 331; **Nouveau
    quatuor* no. 6 in E minor, *331–34*; "Paris"
    Quartets, 331
Temperament, 192, **261–62**
Tempo, 100, 119, 149, 151n
Tenore, **20**
Ternary form. *See under* Aria
Terraced dynamics, 297n
Tetrachord, **88–89**
Text painting, 32. *See also* Rhetoric, musical
Texture, 17, **20–21**; antiphonal, 21; contrapun-
    tal, 20; homophonic, 21
Theile, Johann, 147
Thematic variation, **256**
Theme. *See* Ritornello; Subject
Theorbo, 48, 54, 216n
Thirty Years' War, 5, 6, 146
Thoroughbass, 45
Three Ladies of Ferrara, 51–52
Through-composed form, 22
Timpani, 140, **284**
Tintoretto, 77
Titon du Tillet: *Le Parnasse français*, *244*
Toccata, **230–31**; in opera, 74n
Tombeau, 224, 239, 289
Tonality, 24, 43, 75, 94, 158–60; in fugue,
    255, 258–59
Torelli, Giuseppe, **310–11**; concertos, 312, 320;
    trio sonatas, 311; Christmas Concerto, 314,
    315; *Concertini*, 311; **Sinfonia con tromba*,
    311–12
Tosi, Pier Francesco, 58n, 163, 339n
Tragédie en musique, 117, 179
Tremblement, 268
Tremolo, 79
Trill, **52**, 167n, 236, 268; in thirds, 253
Trillo, 58, 240
Trio sonata, 99, **287**, 291
Trombone, 139, **283–84**, 291
Trumpet, 140, 203, *282–83*, 321, 323; slide
    trumpet, **284**; trumpet sinfonias and
    sonatas, 310–12
Tunder, Franz, 249
Tuning, of stringed instruments, 217, 274,
    275; re-entrant, **216n**, 217n. *See also* Pitch;
    Temperament

Turn, 52
Tutti, 315
Twenty-Four Violins of the King, 112, 119, 273

Uccellini, Marco, *295*, 302
Unequal notes. *See* Notes inégales
Unisoni, Accademia degli, 91
United States, 180
Unmeasured prelude, 217, **237**, *245–46*, 265
Upright (subject), **256**
Urfey, Thomas D', 110

Variation, *233*; chorale, 252; in sonatas, 289; thematic, 256
Variation, strophic. *See under* Aria
Vecchi, Orazio: *L'Amfiparnasso*, 76
Venice, 3, 5, 8, 91, 106, 289, 302, 316; opera, 7, 64, 67, 82, 160; sacred music, 136–37. *See also* Mark (St.), Basilica of
Versailles, 112, 115
Vers mesuré, 113–14
Vibrato, bow, *294*
Vienna, 5, 8, 161, 289
Vihuela, **217**
Villanesca, 34
Vinci, Leonardo, 161
Vingt-quatre Violons du Roy. See Twenty-Four Violins of the King
Viol. *See* Viola da gamba
Viola, 48, **273**, 314
Viola da braccio, 48, 73
Viola da gamba, *10*, *30*, *47–48*, 273, 275, 331
Violin, *10*, 48, 73, *273*
Violoncello. *See* Cello

Violone, 149, 150, **275**, 321
Virginal, *30*, *31*, 227
Visée, Robert de, 217
Vivaldi, Antonio, 280, 302, **316–17**; concertos, 313, 317; motets, 186; *Concerto in E, op. 3, no. 12, **317–19**; *L'estro armonico*, 313, 317; *The Four Seasons*, 317
Voices, 13; in cantatas, 195–96; in French music, 124; in Italian opera, 164–65
Vokaleinbau, 201n

Wagenseil, Georg Christoph, 326
Walsh, John, *305*, *308*
Walther, Johann, 250n
Weckmann, Matthias, 147, 249
Weimar, 192
Weiss, Silvius Leopold, 216
Welcome song, 108
Wert, Giaches de, 35, 38n
Westminster, 108
Woodwinds, 275–81. *See also specific instruments*
Word painting. *See* Text painting
Work, musical, 147–48
Women in music, 11–12, 16n, 51–52, 91, 165, 195, 237, 243–44, 266, 295, 316. *See also* Ferrara, Three Ladies of; *and names of individual musicians*
Wotquenne, Alfred, 336n

Zachow, Friedrich Wilhelm, 168
Zampogne, 315
Zarlino, Gioseffo, 23, 28
Zelenka, Jan Dismas, 300
Zeno, Agostino, 161
Zink. *See* Cornetto